IN THE

CAUSE OF

TRUE

EDUCATION

IN THE

CAUSE OF

TRUE

EDUCATION

Henry Barnard &

Edith Nye MacMullen

Nineteenth-Century

Yale University Press

School Reform

New Haven & London

Designed by Sonia L. Scanlon
Set in Galliard type by Marathon Typography Service, Inc., Durham, North Carolina.

Printed in the United States of America by BookCrafters, Inc., Chelsea, Michigan.

Library of Congress Cataloging-in-Publication Data
MacMullen, Edith Nye, 1929–
  In the cause of true education : Henry Barnard and nineteenth-century
  school reform / Edith Nye MacMullen.
      p. cm.
  Includes bibliographical references.
  ISBN 0-300-04809-2 (alk. paper)
    1. Barnard, Henry, 1811–1900. 2. Educators — United States
  — Biography. I. Title.
  LA2317.B18M33 1990
  370′.92 — dc20
  [B]   90-36417
              CIP

The paper in this book meets the guidelines for permanence and durability of the Committee on Production Guidelines for Book Longevity of the Council on Library Resources.

10 9 8 7 6 5 4 3 2 1

To Sandy, Polly, Willy, and Lukey
Who serve in the Cause

CONTENTS

ILLUSTRATIONS

PREFACE AND

ACKNOWLEDGMENTS

During his lifetime Henry Barnard was considered second only to Horace Mann as the leader of the common school reform movement. At his death he was hailed as the Nestor of American Education; today he is memorialized only by a number of red brick schools in various Connecticut towns. While the statue of his Massachusetts contemporary stands guard in front of the State House in Boston, Yale University has renamed the former Barnard Hall with a street number. The intent of this study is to attempt to answer two related questions: was the high repute which Barnard enjoyed during his lifetime deserved, and is his relative obscurity today equally deserved? If the answer to the first question is yes, how then can the answer to the second also be yes?

Henry Barnard was born in Connecticut and lived most of his life there; the setting, therefore, is that small, conservative New England state, the "land of steady habits," and its capital, Hartford. The date of his birth was 1811, and he died in 1900. Thus he lived through an era of staggering social and economic change and saw his native state evolve from a homogeneous, agrarian community into a polyglot, mercantile, economic power. His formative and most productive years were the antebellum ones, and many of his mentors were leaders in the ambitious and optimistic reform movements of the period; they were also affiliated with the Whig party and supported its agenda of active governmental intervention for economic purposes. These three elements combined in the education of Henry Barnard—the stability came from Connecticut, the challenge from the alterations in society, and the potential solutions from his contemporary social and political activists.

Barnard was born into comfort and benefited from the advantages that came with his class—he was well educated and, for his time, well traveled. His career was varied—he was a legislator, an appointed state school administrator, a college president, the first national commissioner of education, and above all, an editor and historian. For his entire adult life he had ample leisure and could afford to do precisely what he wanted. He had masses of friends and corresponded, constantly and at length, with many of the leading reformers of his day; he read voraciously, in the classics and in the major reform periodicals of the period. He was, in the true sense of the word, an amateur, a man who loved what he did and was thoroughly engaged in it. In this he represented a particular antebellum type, a species whose days were numbered. Economic necessity and the increasing sophistication within social and intellectual movements were soon to make such gentlemen obsolete.

Henry Barnard was held in high esteem by his contemporaries; in the world of the schoolmen, his name was on every list. When the promoters of school reform in any state sought to galvanize the citizenry, Henry Barnard was brought in to lecture; when the governor of Rhode Island wanted a man to energize the school movement in his state, he turned to Barnard; when the trustees of a midwestern university needed a man to implement their ambitious schemes, they consulted Barnard—and on more than one occasion. There were others, it is true, and to some extent Henry Barnard may have exaggerated his own reputation, but only to a degree. He was *primus inter pares* in his particular world for thirty years or more.

It may appear contradictory to assert that Barnard's world was a some-what isolated one; how could a man dedicated to social reform and a member of numerous national organizations be isolated? Many of Barnard's friends among the humanitarian activists of the period were caught in the swirl of contemporary life, concerned with the degradation and misery brought on by urbanization, and especially with the horrors of slavery and the national agony which culminated in the Civil War. The schoolmen, however much they might fulminate against the discomfort and the inconvenience of schoolhouses, the inadequacy of the struggling teachers, or even the wickedness and vice of city life, remained dispassionate, their rhetoric notwithstanding, and their single-mindedness made it conveniently easy to turn away from comparable crushing evils. Henry Barnard was comfortable within the safety of the righteousness of school reform if not with its battles; he never liked to dirty his hands except in his own garden.

An examination of the life of Henry Barnard is instructive for the light it sheds on the common school reform movement; that movement emerges as an evolution rather than the revolution its leaders called it. His life also tells us something about the succession of leadership within that movement; he and his allies had a particular role to play, and once their act had finished, they exited, he without a curtain call. Oddly, his life fails to tell us very much about him. Despite his prominence, despite his wide acquaintance with the great and near-great, despite his massive publications, he remains a benign and shadowy figure, a type more than an individual.

The form of the problem dictated the nature of my research. Henry Barnard, himself, was of course the principal source. His masses of publications tell the story of education, as seen through his lens, and, more subtly, they tell his story, again through his perspective. The box upon box of letters to him which remain, those from him which can be found in scattered archives, and the tantalizingly few journals, from his younger days, balance the published record. What one discovers is the extent to which balance is needed. Barnard's limitations were those of his class, his party, and his region; when he recorded the deeds of eminent men and their domination of the school movement, he wrote of his colleagues, their goals and their achievements, and in so doing he wrote of himself. That he perpetuated their story was his great achievement, and their story was his story. As he emphasized the contributions of the eastern New England schoolmen, he underlined his place among them.

Barnard's career divides rather neatly into distinct chronological periods; each is the focus of a chapter. Henry Barnard the Whig reformer, the school administrator, the educator of teachers, the college president, the national commissioner, and the editor are considered, and for each topic secondary materials provide the context. What emerges from an examination of the context is that Barnard ignored many of the predecessors of the innovations he hailed; school reform did not spring fully clad from the brow of James Carter much less Horace Mann. Nor did educational publishing.

Henry Barnard chose to focus on education, first the provision of schooling, then the administration of schools, then the training of teachers; school texts, school buildings, school apparatus, school teachers, all came under his supervisory and editorial eye. Each of these was the concern of the broad coalition of antebellum schoolmen reformers, but Barnard, for a number of years, was their voice. He contributed, in addition, to the reform agenda by his selection of what to stress. One was the actions of individuals, another was the institutions they founded. But education had always meant more than common schools or academies or even colleges to Barnard, and included community-wide agencies such as the Young Mens' Institute, one of his first endeavors, and libraries, which he never failed to promote. In the end, through the means of his *American Journal of Education*, he saw himself as the educator of all those concerned with the guidance of the rising generation, particularily of the teachers that nurtured them. That he did not speak to the generation which followed him is one of the reasons for his obscurity.

The two major archives of Barnard materials are in the Watkinson Library of Trinity College and the Fales Library of New York University.

(It was because of the raiding of the former by Will S. Monroe that the latter acquired its collection.) My heartfelt thanks are due to Margaret Saxe of the Watkinson and Frank Walker of the Fales; the latter, especially, has welcomed me early and allowed me to stay late time and again and was constantly helpful and encouraging. The guidance of Lawrence Cremin through the entire project has been a sensitive balance of support and pressure, and I am grateful. Elizabeth Sader, Meg Marshall, and especially Jon Kauffman gave me timely, and cheerful, help when I was desperate, and they know that I thank them. Judith Calvert provided prompt, professional, extremely friendly, and much appreciated editorial support throughout the publication process. Above all, I must tip my hat to my husband, who supported, bolstered, even prodded me, and always provided insightful criticism. More important, it has been he, over the years, who has exemplified to me how history should be written.

ABBREVIATIONS

AII	*American Institute of Instruction*
AJE	*American Journal of Education* (Hartford, 1855–80)
AmJEd	*American Journal of Education* (Boston, 1826–30)
CC	*Connecticut Courant*
CCSJ	*Connecticut Common School Journal*
CHS	Barnard Papers, Connecticut Historical Society, Hartford, Connecticut
HDC	*Hartford Daily Courant*
JHU	Daniel Coit Gilman Papers, MS 1, Special Collections, Milton S. Eisenhower Library, The Johns Hopkins University, Baltimore, Maryland
JRIII	*Journal of the Rhode Island Institute of Instruction*
MHS	Horace Mann Papers, Massachusetts Historical Society, Boston, Massachusetts
NE	Henry Barnard, *National Education: Systems, Institutions & Statistics of Public Instruction in Different Countries* (1854; 1872)
NEA	*Proceedings of the National Teachers' Association*
NS	Henry Barnard, *Normal Schools and other Institutions, Agencies, and Means designed for the Professional Education of Teachers* (1851)
NYU	Henry Barnard Papers, Fales Library, Elmer Holmes Bobst Library, New York University, New York, New York
OHGS	Henry Barnard, *The Old Hartford Grammar School* (1878)
RI	Henry Barnard, *Preventive, Correctional and Reformatory Institutes and Agencies in Different Countries* (1857)
RIC	Letters of Henry Barnard, Special Collections, James P. Adams

Library, "Small Collection #1," Rhode Island College, Providence, Rhode Island

RIHS   Manuscript Collection, Rhode Island Historical Society, Providence, Rhode Island

SA   Henry Barnard, *School-house Architecture* (1842)

TC   Henry Barnard Manuscript Collection, Trinity College and Watkinson Library, Hartford, Connecticut

WHS   Lyman Draper Collection, The State Historical Society of Wisconsin, Madison, Wisconsin

WJE   *Wisconsin Journal of Education*

YU   Henry Barnard Papers and Elias Loomis Papers, Beinecke Rare Book and Manuscript Library, Yale University, New Haven, Connecticut

IN THE

CAUSE OF

TRUE

EDUCATION

Henry Barnard, circa 1836

I

THE

FORMATIVE

YEARS

*All that goes to form the man, to develop or
to modify his original character, to work any
change whatsoever in the natural, innate
disposition and force of his faculties and
temper make a part of his education.* (Connecticut Common School Journal *II, 12
[July 1840]: 187)*

Henry Barnard was born into a stable world. Connecticut, at
the time of his birth in 1811, was small, homogeneous, agrarian, and conservative, the "land of steady habits," ruled by a Standing Order of Ministers of the Gospel and Yale College graduates. At the time of his death the
state was still geographically small, becoming more densely populated,
with large ethnic minorities; it was a premier manufacturing state and the
national home of the insurance industry. Barnard had lived out his life in
a changing world.

In 1800 Connecticut had a population of only about 250,000. Its citizens lived in 114 towns and five "cities"—New Haven and Hartford, the
co-capitals, and Middletown, Norwich, and Saybrook; Hartford, the largest and Barnard's hometown, had only 6,003 citizens in 1810.[1] Farmers,
tilling the rocky soil, predominated; they lived with their families in small
towns where the Congregational church remained the visual symbol of

1. Charles W. Burpee, *The Story of Connecticut*, II (New York: S. J. Clarke Publishing
Co., 1939). See also Jarvis Means Morse, *A Neglected Period in Connecticut's History,
1818–1850*, (New Haven: Yale University Press, 1933, repr., 1978), 7. The population of
Hartford is from the *Hartford Directory, 1810*.

1

the culture and the unity of the state and its people. It was a Protestant state and a conservative one, the inheritor of the colony founded by those who had, for a variety of reasons, originally fled from Massachusetts. Unlike other states, Connecticut had kept its eighteenth-century royal charter after the revolution. "The Puritan might hate king and bishops, but in Connecticut he allowed the rule of the educated, wellborn, and respectably wealthy."[2] All of the towns had equal representation in the annual legislature, a fact that would hinder effective reform throughout the nineteenth century. Governors served long terms, and three had come from one family, the Trumbulls. The Congregational church was not established until 1818, and Yale influence prevented the chartering of any competing college until after disestablishment. (There was no Catholic church or parish priest until the late twenties.) Elementary schools, until a law of 1798, had been essentially parochial, and even when the supervision of the schools had been transferred to the local school societies, those bodies remained coterminous with the congregations, and ministers dominated the school society committees. Down in New Haven Pope Dwight ruled Yale, and from Yale came the ministers and lawyers who ruled the state, the Standing Order.

Although the constitution of 1818 brought religious toleration, some measure of governmental reform, a revised code of law, and the Republican party to power (for a time), the character and background of the men who ruled the state remained essentially the same. The state was governed by men "who worshipped the same ideals as those revered by former generations" and there were "no important changes beyond those embodied in the constitution."[3] Connecticut citizens were suspicious of change throughout the antebellum period, protective of the established rule of law, and anxious to save money. Some more liberal measures were enacted in the twenties, a law exempting women for imprisonment for debt, one removing discriminatory legislation against aliens, some tax reform, but little fundamental changed. "But in the early constitutional period, Connecticut had a government not of laws, or of men, but of traditions."[4]

Tradition, too, ruled the economy. Despite poor soil, except in the Connecticut River valley, agriculture dominated, and for the most part the small subsistence farmer toiled away as had his forefathers. Forward-looking men such as David Humphrey labored to introduce new meth-

2. Richard J. Purchell, *Connecticut in Transition, 1775–1818* (1918, repr. Middletown: Wesleyan University Press, 1936), 137.

3. Morse, *A Neglected Period*, 84ff.

4. Jarvis Means Morse, *Under the Constitution of 1818: The First Decade* (New Haven: Yale University Press, 1933), 19.

ods through agricultural societies and expositions and new stock (Humphrey imported a hundred merino sheep and created something of a momentary craze for the breed) to little avail. One new crop, silk, did sweep the state for a time; advertisements for mulberry trees figure in every edition of the newspapers of the thirties, and it was estimated that three-quarters of the families in the town of Mansfield were involved in silk production during that decade. Of more lasting significance was the introduction of large-scale tobacco farming into the fertile river valley, beginning in a modest way about 1810; eventually production of high quality leaves for cigar wrappers would become an international cash crop. As late as 1850, however, the annual value of the hay crop in the state exceeded that of the tobacco crop and was a million dollars more than that of the total textile production of the state—and textiles were the state's leading industry.[5] Nature, as well as geology, conspired to make life miserable for the farmers. The severity of the year 1816—when there was frost in every month—may well have helped to stimulate the flow of emigration to the West where the lands of the Western Reserve promised a life more rewarding if not easier.[6]

Next in importance to farming, and closely related to it, was trade. The location of the five small cities offers proof that Connecticut lived partially by shipping; each is either on Long Island Sound or on that long inland highway, the Connecticut River. Trade was coastal and with the West Indies, and increasingly directed to the interior of the new nation, up the river to northern New England or after trans-shipment onto wagons, west along the turnpike from Hartford toward upstate New York. The leading citizens of the state were the first to invest in trade, and their politics followed their mercantile interests. Instinctively they were Federalists, and the Jeffersonian Embargo and Non-Inter-course Acts nearly ruined the West Indian trade; the British blockade of the Sound during the War of 1812 was costly. Economic self-interest and cultural loyalty did as much to motivate the men of the Hartford Convention as did state's rights.[7] A contemporary rationalized it:

5. Purchell, *Transition*, 105–06; the statistic is from Morse, *A Neglected Period*, 293. Josiah Holbrook, the father of the American lyceum began as an agricultural reformer; in 1824–25 he conducted an Agricultural Seminary to introduce new methods of farming and "to combine manual labor with education"; see *American Journal of Education* (henceforth *AJE*), VII, xx (March 1860).

6. Samuel Goodrich, *Recollections of a Lifetime* (New York: Miller, Orton & Mulligan, 1857), II, 78ff.; Purchell, *Transition*, 91; see also Albert E. Van Dusen, *Connecticut* (New York: Random House, 1961), 200.

7. The first marine insurance policy was issued in 1794, and the first incorporation was that of the Mutual Assurance Company of Norwich.

Common sense as well as Christianity . . . should demand that hos-
tilities be at least suspended between two Protestant nations, united
by language, mutual interests, and blood.[8]

Hartford, the city in which Barnard was born and where, eighty-nine
years later, and in the same house, he died, depended on the river. A
rather critical contemporary, who had moved happily to Boston, described
the town:

> It was then a small commercial town, of four thousand inhabitants,
> dealing in lumber, and smelling of molasses and Old Jamaica. . . .
> Though the semi-capital of the State . . . it was strongly impressed
> with a plodding, mercantile and mechanical character. There was a
> high tone of intelligence and social responsibility about the place,
> but . . . not a single institution, a single monument, that marked it
> as even a provincial metropolis of taste in letters, art, or refinement.
> The leading men were thrifty mechanics, with a few merchants, and
> many shopkeepers. . . . There were lawyers, judges, and public
> functionaries—men of mark—but their spirit did not govern the
> town. There were a few dainty patricians who held themselves aloof,
> secure of that amiable worship which all ages have rendered to the
> rank.[9]

Dr. Joel Hawes was equally unimpressed when he was called to a Hartford pulpit from Boston. He found a coldness, a negativity, but he had
also to admit that his congregation was "intelligent, dignified, and
devout." After years in the city, and when he stood among the leading
citizens, he was more flattering. His compatriots

> were intelligent, cautious, enterprising; not easy of acquaintance
> nor forward to make professions of friendship; but steady in their
> attachments, and in acts of public and private charity not surpassed
> by any place of equal population in the country.[10]

Such were Barnard's neighbors in his boyhood years.

The citizens of Hartford numbered in 1810 just about 6,000; by 1880

8. Theodore Dwight, *History of Connecticut* (Hartford, 1844), 417ff., quotation 435.
Dwight credits, or blames, the West Indian trade for the founding of the Temperance
Society because of the "moral evil"—rum, 440.

9. Goodrich, *Recollections*, I, 435–36; Goodrich had moved to Boston, so the harsh-
ness of his judgments stems as much from his nouveau cultural superiority as from his
Federalism. James H. Trumbull, *A Memorial History of Hartford County Connecticut,
1633–1884* (Boston: E. L.Osgood, 1886), II, 602–04, quotes this description.

10. Trumbull, *Memorial History*, 604; Joel Hawes, *An Address* (Hartford: Belknap &
Hamersley, November 1835).

there were 42,550. For the most part they were of modest means. In this very Puritan town there were six churches and twelve schools, but the upright could quench their thirst in twenty-one taverns and eighteen alehouses! There were over fifty small shops and "factories." A factory could employ as many as thirty-six (making hats) or as few as four (a button maker). For every fifty families there was one merchant, and by 1820 these merchants had begun to specialize. And along with this specialization and expansion came the growth of banking and of insurance, especially stimulated by the desire to reduce the risks incurred by the War of 1812.[11]

Hartford was situated at the head of the navigable waters of the river; its location made the city a very active port, both for shipping and transshipment. On a single day in the summer of 1838 eight schooners and nine sloops docked; six packet boats and two steamship lines advertized runs to New York and Boston. A ferry had plied back and forth across the river until a bridge was built in 1808; and after 1825 the ferry ceased operations. Warehouses lined the banks of the river where boats, sometimes three or four deep, waited to unload at one of the more than twenty wharfs. Packing houses stood beside the warehouses, for beef and pork were major exports, and there were even a few shipbuilders. The slow up-river flatboats went north, the lumbering wagon trains west along the Albany Turnpike, taking with them settlers and news. For a brief time canals and ultimately the railroads dramatically changed the character of Hartford's economy. Manufacturing, banking, and insurance would largely replace commerce by 1850, but during Barnard's boyhood his home was a port town. Small wonder that at the age of twelve he thought of running away to sea.[12]

Barnard's letters and reminiscences do not give us much of a detailed picture of his hometown or neighborhood, for they deal mostly with his schooling and were edited in old age, when he was little interested in autobiographical detail unconnected with his professional image. A few specifics emerge: memories of a political torchlight procession, of skating on the river, of games on the Green. From Gurdon Russell's charming memoir, however, we can picture vividly the early republican Hartford of

11. Trumbull, *Memorial History*, 208; Gurdon W. Russell, *"Up Neck" in 1828* (Hartford, 1890), 41. According to Russell there were only 28 gold watches in the city at the time of Barnard's birth; such a statistic serves to illustrate a 19th century change, for watch and clock making were to become a major Connecticut industry.

12. See *Connecticut Courant*, August 30, 1838, for shipping news. The story of Barnard's running away to sea is told by all the early biographers and repeated in Vincent P. Lannie, *Henry Barnard: American Educator* (New York: Teachers College Press, 1974), 2. The Albany road was famous for its twenty taverns in the first tweenty miles—so much for temperance!

Barnard's youth. Using Russell's map we can mentally walk through a certain section of the town. On one side of the street, heading north, was a dwelling, then a storehouse, then a joiner's shop (with four workers it was a factory), next a farmer's house, then one of a rope-maker (his rope-walk would be nearer to the river, as the farmer's fields would be outside the town), another farmhouse, this one with a barn, next the "brick house of the dame teacher," and, finally, the town arsenal—dwellings and places of work, of craftsmen and farmers, all intermingled. It was a comfortable and homogeneous community; not until the middle of the century would an Irish ghetto be located in the low-lying land along the river.

Society was not entirely static. An enterprising Yankee could, and did, get ahead, and did so by ingenuity. Between 1801 and 1848 nearly 16,000 patents were granted to Nutmeggers, or one for every 285 inhabitants. Allyn Goodrich first made silver spoons in his house; then he had a shop where he produced cloth-covered buttons. Across the road from him lived Thomas Belden who began as a pump-maker, then ran a store for the West Indian trade; he prospered and was soon the owner of a woolen factory and a distillery in nearby Simsbury. Like his friends and neighbors, the Terry brothers, he became a pillar of the community, active in his church and the founder of a bank. The Terrys each had a store and ample warehouses; customers came from as far away as Bellows Falls, Vermont. Eliphalet Terry became the first president of the Hartford Insurance Company, and his brother Robert of the Exchange Bank—one of the three banks on Main Street, where Barnard lived. Eliphalet was also instrumental in raising money for the new theological school in East Windsor, in an effort to preserve the ideological and theological purity of the city from the subversive new ideas emanating from Yale College to the south. It was he, too, who in 1834 personally collected his company's and his own assets and drove by sleigh, on a frigid morning, to New York where on the day after the disastrous fire, he was able to meet all of the claims of the insured victims, thereby saving his, and his company's name, and insuring the future of the insurance industry.[13]

Although David Humphrey insisted, despite his own literary interests, that "success was first and literature second," Hartford was not quite the cultural wasteland Mr. Goodrich had depicted. The "sweet singer of Hartford," Mrs. Lydia Huntley Sigourney, set the tone, both literary and social in her drawing room and in verse:

---

13. Russell, *"Up Neck,"* 34–35, 62–63, 69, 77; Emerson Davis, *The Half-Century* (Boston: Tappan & Whittemore, 1851), 270–71; Trumbull, *Memorial History*, 211, notes the apple crop and the cider-brandy distilleries; in 1840 there were 114 in Hartford County alone. The present day suburb of Hartford, Warehouse Point, recalls the river trade.

Mingling in the gayeties of our social gatherings, she led us all toward intellectual pursuits and amusements. The ripples thus begun extended over the whole surface of our society, producing a lasting and refining effect.[14]

Hartford, as a literary center, was between the Wits, who were dead or scattered, and Twain, and *"belles lettres* were overshadowed by theology and by the uninspiring course of partisan politics."[15] Readers did not seek frivolous reading, and publications were, for the most part, didactic.

The press thrived. Sermons and theological works, such as those of Horace Bushnell, rolled off the many presses. There were at least twenty papers in the state, most of them weeklies, and most of them staunchly, even stridently, partisan. The papers carried local news, reports of catastrophes, travel accounts, gleanings from more cosmopolitan papers, and, apparently, whatever the editor found interesting or would fill space. A serious journal, the *North American Review* had its offices in the city —until they were destroyed by fire, and the *Review* moved to Boston. Of particular relevance to this study were the textbook publishing houses —there were more than 30 firms producing texts between 1820 and 1830.[16] In this period, too, came the start of literary clubs and of small libraries, always private, and nearly always devoted to self-improvement. What leisure there was had to be spent earnestly. Russell recalled going with his brother to see a play staged in the rear of the Hartford Hotel; they were doomed to disappointment, for the actors "were driven off to jail for violating some ordinance for the public good."[17] This was still a Puritan town where the Bible, Webster's spelling book, and the conservative *Connecticut Courant* were the bastions of local culture.[18]

The Reverend Thomas Gallaudet, who was to serve as Barnard's mentor, serves as a representative of the Standing Order. Educated at Yale, he dabbled in law, studied for the ministry, and ultimately devoted his life to the education of the deaf mutes. He was a member of various reform groups, such as the Colonization Society and the Tract Society, of which he was Connecticut's president; he was a leader in the lyceum, chaplain at

14. Goodrich, *Recollections*, II, 125. Mrs. Sigourney first came to Hartford as a teacher in a school for girls; her place in society was secured when she married one of the city's leading lights.

15. Stanley Thomas Williams, *The Literature of Connecticut* (New Haven: Yale University Press, 1936), 7, 17.

16. Christopher B. Bickford, *The Connecticut Historical Society, 1825–1975* (Hartford: Connecticut Historical Society, 1975), 12–13. Barnard's enormous collection of textbooks is now housed in the Watkinson Library of Trinity College.

17. Russell, *"Up Neck"*, I, 37.

18. Goodrich, *Recollections*, I, 410–11.

the new state prison, and, from 1827, an active member of the Society for the Improvement of the Common Schools. Barnard paid his debt in eulogizing Gallaudet: "we may, if we follow his example, help rear up a generation of youth having sound minds in sound bodies." Gallaudet was fact; Mrs. Sigourney wrote fiction, and in her saccharine portrait of Madam L., the epitome of virtue, she sketched the antebellum ideal:

> Yet while we indulge in charitable feelings, we should be careful not to reward deceit, or cherish vice . . . .Benevolence is blessed in itself, but it must be associated with discretion, ere it can confer blessings on others. A Christian should seek not merely to relieve bodily want but to evaluate moral character.[19]

Such were the values. Even the men who had made their fortunes by their ingenuity, who had profited from trade, who had speculated wisely, who had not graduated from Yale—even they still attended the same church (although Horace Bushnell worried that their attention might wander to worldly matters during his Sunday sermons) and voted with the same parties. These enterprising Yankees were making fortunes, Daniel Wadsworth and William Imlay initially from trade, James Goodwin first from the stage and then from the railroads. But they were cautious in spending money and often suspicious of government. It was not that they dodged their Christian duty; they did good, but it was private. Amos Morris Collins well represented this leadership group of Barnard's youth. Horace Bushnell summed it up in his eulogy of Collins:

> There is almost nothing here that has not somehow felt his power, nothing that has not somehow profited by his beneficence. Banks, savings institutions, railroads, the singular anomaly of a large wholesale dry-goods trade which distinguished Hartford as an inland city, the city councils and improvements, the city missions and Sunday schools, the Asylum for the Deaf, the Retreat for the Insane, the high school, the almshouse, three at least of the churches—almost everything public, had his counsel, character, impulse, beneficence, and what is more, if possible, his real work incorporated in it.[20]

Bushnell failed to mention that Collins was twice mayor of the city.

It is certain, and significant, that Chauncey Barnard, Henry's father, never belonged to Hartford's elite or inner circle. Nonetheless, he was a successful, and perhaps canny, man whose children enjoyed comfort and

19. Henry Barnard, *Tribute to Gallaudet* (Hartford: Brockett & Hutchinson, 1852); Lydia H. Sigourney, *Sketch of Connecticut Forty Years Since* (Hartford, 1824), 68–69.

20. Trumbull, *Memorial History*, 669–70.

education far beyond anything that he had—especially the last, Henry, born on January 24, 1811, when his father was fifty. The Barnards belonged in Hartford. John, the Blacksmith, was living in the town in 1732; in addition to his trade he invested in land, buying parcels outside of the town six times in the next twenty years. His son John (d. 1814) married Hannah Bigelow, also of Hartford, and they had nine children; the fourth was Chauncey, born in 1761. He married Betsey Andrews, and they in turn had four children, Betty, Chauncey, John, and Henry—all born in their father's middle age. The mother Betsey died in 1816 and always remained a shadowy figure for her son; all he remembered was her funeral. Chauncey married again, but Henry scarcely mentioned and never addressed letters to his stepmother, Eliza Seymour.

Chauncey, senior, at first followed the sea, rising to mate and subsequently captain of a brig plying the coastal and West Indian trade. His logbooks reveal a highly competent captain, and he was proud of his sea-faring days, being addressed always as Captain Barnard. His cargoes were mostly horses and cattle down to the islands, molasses and produce back. Once, apparently during the Napoleonic wars, his ship was captured; years later his youngest son inquired of a lawyer cousin in New York whether any compensation could be claimed under new agreements with France. At some time early in the century the elder Barnard retired from the sea, built a comfortable house in the city (in 1806—he had a family now), and turned his attention to expanding his real estate. He bought a piece of 300 acres the year he built his house, an indication certainly of ample means, and even purchased land as far away as Utica, New York. He collected rent from a farm in Windsor and from an elderly aunt who lived in Guilford on Long Island Sound. He drove hard bargains over sums due him and even over an escaped horse that strayed onto his land. When he died intestate, his sons posted a bond of $12,000— probably equal to $160,000 in today's dollars. He was comfortable, if not wealthy. But he was not an educated man; his few letters to his wife are terse, formal, and minimal. He must have attended school for a time, but he was not a grammar school boy nor a Yale graduate. Nor was he ever an alderman, councilman, or even an active layman in his city.[21]

21. Genealogical table and notes in miscellaneous Barnard papers, Connecticut Historical Society (hereafter CHS). Probate Record, Hartford County, Bond signed by Chauncey and John Barnard, with Henry Barnard as surety, March 13, 1837. In the Fales collection at New York University (hereafter NYU) is a genealogical memo on Barnard from S. Judd, November 20, 1841. There was, apparently, another Henry Barnard living in Hartford at this time, perhaps a relative, although our Henry never mentions him. The other lived on Washington Street, and was elected to the Hartford Common Council in 1837, the only mention I have found of him other than the listing in the Hartford Direc-

In his old age, Henry claimed to recall visits to his family from John Quincy Adams, the Alcotts, and Daniel Wadsworth, but there is little evidence to support the claim, except, perhaps in the case of Wadsworth, a Hartford patriarch. The elder Barnard certainly made it possible for his children to rise above his station, but he himself seemed not to care. Business, family, for there were cousins aplenty, his sons' futures in particular, were enough, especially as he was growing older.[22]

The Barnard family homestead was a far cry from the simple Cape in which Chauncey had been born. It was a typical late colonial house of generous and graceful proportions; it was well built, for it still stands, now a convent, with a small plaque identifying its special place in local history. There was a large yard, surrounded by an ornamental picket fence; an enormous elm and fine weeping willows shaded the house. In his jotted memoirs Barnard recalled a gale in his childhood which nearly killed the great tree, destroying its characteristic symmetry, and he carefully copied the tree's obituary from the Hartford *Times* on November 5, 1892, after another fierce storm. The size of the house was not embellished by Barnard's nostalgia. When his surviving daughter moved into a more modest house after his death, she had to have all the furniture cut down to fit her new, much smaller, Farmington home.[23]

Henry seems to have led a healthy, happy boyhood. His family was a close and very affectionate one, and he, the youngest, never was able to break "the lengthening chain of attachment" formed in those early years.[24] He did chores, he played the usual childhood games, he swam in the river, he went sledding—on the sled given him as a reward for reading the Bible from Genesis to Revelations. As an old man he recalled parades,

tory. Once, however, Chauncey Barnard, the younger, erroneously called at the post office for a letter, thinking it was for his brother; letter, June 6, 1831, NYU, to Henry. It is probable that Barnard's use of the term second, or II, during the thirties and forties, the time of his political activity, was in an effort to avoid confusion with the older man.

22. Fragmentary letter to Mr. King, NYU. The only letter from Henry to his father in Henry's youth is dated May 3, 1827; clearly the sixteen year old had been sent to inspect a newly acquired house, and he sent back detailed dimensions.

23. A. E. Winship, *Great American Educators* (New York: Werner School Book Co., 1900), 44; James L. Hughes, "Henry Barnard: The Nestor of American Education," *New England Magazine* (July 1896), has charming sketches of the family house and of Chauncey's birthplace as well as pictures of Barnard at 24, 43, and 82. The account of the storm is from a fragment in the Barnard papers in the Watkinson Library of Trinity College (hereafter TC). Biographical details are culled from Lannie, Norton, Steiner, and Brubacher for the most part.

24. Letter from London, May 6, 1835, YU. Some of his effusions may be stylistic, but Barnard wrote home constantly as well as to friends, and he frequently complained about the lack of response.

for the peace in 1815, for Monroe in 1817—that one complete with the Horse Guards. Books did not play much of a role in his childhood. They weren't left "loosely around" the house, and a weekly paper, the book he won for punctual attendance at Sabbath school, and a few volumes bought by his older brother and a cousin were all that he could recall, and, of course, the Bible. Henry seems to have been a very sociable and active fellow, with plenty of playmates. Later in life, however, he expressed regret that his "boyhood was not spent among the sons of college graduates."[25] Chauncey may have been content with his place in Hartford society, but it seems that Henry felt some hurt or shame, not for his family whom he loved, but for their circumstances.

Of course, like all children, he went to school; the difference is that he had more schooling. Somewhere along the line Chauncey Barnard decided that this, his youngest son, was to have the best. First Henry attended Miss Benton's Dame School where he learned, among other things, to use the needle, and then he went to the local South District School. That particular school is gone, but many like it remain, and Barnard's later and often repeated comments give a clear description of it and hundreds of others—a small boxlike structure, with an entry and space for coats and wood, small windows, a smoky stove, planks nailed along the walls for desks, benches in rows in the center. Here forty or more children would crowd, sitting, wiggling, waiting to recite their letters. As a school reformer later Barnard would praise such a school as a "school of equal rights," but he hated his for its "miserable routine and cruel discipline." His happy memories were of snowball fights with the "gra-mares" (boys from the grammar school) and "perpetual feuds" between the scholars of the north and the south districts; the boys from the north came mainly from "uptown families and thought themselves to be a privileged lot."[26]

Perhaps Henry was bored in school, perhaps it was boyish bravado, perhaps it is a myth, but in any event, according to an oft-repeated tale, one evening, when he was twelve, his father overheard him plotting with a chum to run away to sea—surely not surprising for the captain's son. But

25. Fragments, "South Green, notes and sketch,", "Books, What and How to Read," and "Libraries. How to Start and Support," and "Books and Libraries and their Management, Fifty Years Ago," TC. There are four drafts of the last, a common, and moving, practice of Barnard's in his old age. See also Richard Knowles Morris, "The Barnard Legacy," *School and Society* 89 (November 1961): 393–96.

26. Henry Barnard, *The Old Hartford Grammar School* (Hartford: Brown & Gross, 1878; hereafter *OHGS*), 208–09; Morris, "Legacy." For descriptions of district schools see Russell, *"Up Neck"*, 90–104, and Warren Burton, *The District School As It Was* (New York: Carter, Hendee, 1833; repr., 1969).

the captain had other plans for his clever youngest, and the next morning gave him the choice: the sea or Monson Academy in Massachusetts.

> My going to Monson took me out of the miserable district school and away from companions (excellent fellows in many respects and especially in all boyish sports, but without a lover of books among them and without a single inspiration for intellectual culture) into the society of young men and women, gathered from many towns, because of their thirst (the very motive for being there) for intellectual improvement.[27]

Of course he was homesick at first but that passed, and it was with nostalgia that he later recalled his first view of the school and village of Monson, nestling in its lovely valley. At the academy he probably boarded with a family, in the company of other students. Their life was a pleasant one—in the free hours they roamed the surrounding countryside, visiting the farms of classmates and enjoying "the advantages of nutting, birding, and other motives which belong to the period of boyhood." In a romanticized fashion, Barnard always credited Monson with developing in him the love of the outdoors as well as his love of books and study. Under the guidance of the English master, Samuel Woolworth, who in later years was secretary to the New York State Board of Education, the lad explored the works in Principal Flint's library.[28] It was at the academy that he first had the benefit of "thoro" teaching and where he learned "how to study and how to use books."[29] He also became a debater and in his study began to read the great orators. Still, he never was seen as a bookworm, just very bright. A classmate, Mr. Trask of Springfield, in his old age, recalled Henry as "the boy who played all the time but beat us all at our lessons."

The idyll lasted only a year—it was not unusual to move from school to school with frequency in those days. It may be that Monson, with its English curriculum, did not fit with Chauncey's dreams, or maybe Henry wasn't quite as blissful as he recalled. Back to Hartford he came, to be

27. Letter to Abel Flint, January 17, 1890, TC. See also Morris, *Legacy*, and Hughes, *Barnard*. Barnard published a sketch of Monson in *AJE* XVII (April 1868): 563–73; the academy was charted in 1804 and opened two years later; the English Department commenced the following year, and the Female Department opened in 1819 although the ratio of students was almost always about two-to-one male; the head during Barnard's year was Simeon Cotton, a Yale graduate, and the school prepared most of its students either for Yale or Amherst.

28. Draft on libraries, TC. Note the influence here; there is no way of knowing what Woolworth talked about with his student, but it is plausible that some of the attitudes of the antebellum responsible citizen were introduced very early.

29. Unpublished manuscript on travel, TC.

tutored in Greek for six months by his pastor, Abel Flint, a Yale graduate. He passed a rather casual entrance examination (an interview by one of the trustees, a judge whom the youth found imposing) and was admitted to the prestigious Hartford Grammar School, "well prepared to profit by its exclusive classical training as for its vigorous games of football out of doors." The school was a small, oblong, white frame building (replaced by a brick one in 1828 after Barnard had left), topped with a "little belfry" with a fish weathervane. Inside there were individual desks and seats for the scholars, something of a luxury. The playground was large and unusually long, and excellent for games. A schoolmate of Henry's, A. L. Chapin, in 1859 president of Beloit College in Wisconsin, speaking then at Barnard's inauguration as the chancellor of the University of Wisconsin, recalled his colleague as "one of the heroes," a senior boy:

> I was lost in admiration at the fleetness of foot and dextrous hits by which Henry Barnard . . . drove the black ball before him or sent it flying over the heads of his antagonists to the extreme limits of the field, and to-day my admiration is just as profound for the rigorous and felicitous use of his higher facilities. . . . There must be a close connection between early, physical, and intellectual training.[30]

The school was Hartford's best, and attendance (about thirty-six boys attended in Barnard's day) almost guaranteed admission to college should the student persevere. Tuition was a mere $1 per quarter, and the curriculum included some English study as well as the classical works. The teacher, Master Holland, impressed the boys with his dignity and "brought to the school not only rare attainments as a scholar, but mature age and some experience as a teacher" and in addition had what so many teachers lacked, "good common sense, a knowledge of methods, and a faculty of interesting young persons in their studies." We must view this assessment with some skepticism—Barnard, writing in 1878, clearly spoke in the voice of the educational reformer. Holland had been the salutatorian of the class of 1824 at Yale, one of the "lights that lighted the academies and common schools of the time." He may have been older than twenty, for students sometimes were forced to take time off from college

---

30. *OHGS*, 215. Anecdotes in this work are admittedly the memories of middle-aged men, for Barnard had polled his classmates. Chapin's reply offers a fine example of the erratic nature of schooling in those days. First he attended a school run by the Misses Patton where he learned "sewing and knitting, reading, spelling, and . . . the Westminster catechism"; then to the district school where he sat under Mr. Talcott and the assistant Miss Rockwell (note the female assistant); it was the texts that he recalled—Scott for reading, Pickett for grammar, Dadoll for arithmetic, Woodbridge for geography "then a novelty among schoolbooks;" at ten he started the grammar school.

in order to earn tuition money, but that he was very mature or had much of a knowledge of method is doubtful. He probably taught as he had been taught in school and college—by recitation of assigned texts. He did, however, light a spark in his pupils, and he assumed they wanted to learn. He seems to have ruled more by reason and example than by force; the memory of his boxing the ears of two scholars remained fresh in the minds of their classmates for its exception. Holland left in the middle of the year (perhaps to go back to Yale?) and was followed by Ashbel Smith, also of the class of 1824; he left after a year to study medicine but remained a life-long friend of Barnard's.[31]

Barnard could not have been more than two years at Grammar School, for he entered Yale in October 1826, just before his sixteenth birthday. Presumably he had passed creditably the oral entrance examination, demonstrating his facility in Latin, Greek, both classical and Biblical, geography, and arithmetic. If he had been happy at Monson and happier at grammar school, he was the happiest at Yale. The college meant much to him. After graduation he returned frequently, beginning with the first year, for reunions, and in his eighties he took over the duties of class secretary; at his last reunion only two of the class attended. His letters to classmates ring with warmth of friendships and he passed on news of mutual friends, who was married, who was in good, or more frequently poor, health, who was reading what.

> Stanley is here in the Grammar School—yet—Grant passed through this city a short time since rather unwell—he was on his way home. [Nott?] is enjoying better health than he has done in 4 or 5 years. . . . Averill is still in New York—Schoan has been sick, Woodruff is treading out the law in long strides—Pond is shedding his venom on me through the paper; I shall pop him when he comes back from New York. Brancid is at Haddam—Cone is said to be casting wistful glances at the short leg of Miss Brewster . . . Landry was on the same track not long ago.[32]

31. *OHGS*, 207–21. The former students to whom Barnard wrote were an impressive lot, including Professor Seymour of Western Reserve University and Jonathan Brace, a Connecticut legislator and common school reform colleague. Smith had a distinguished career, first in the republic of Texas, as surgeon-general in the army and secretary of state; when Texas joined the union he was elected to the legislature and served in a variety of capacities; see *The Handbook of Texas*, vol. II (Austin, 1952).

32. Letter to Loomis, April, 1833, YU. Elias Loomis, subsequently professor of astronomy and mathematics at Yale was the author of many texts; with his mentor, Denison Olmstead, he was the first American to report Halley's Comet. Barnard, writing from Paris, jested: "it must have been a moment of exquisite pleasure when you first hailed the sojourner in the invisible and immeasurable depths of space. . . . But why could you not contrive to give him a greater depth of tail behind?", letter, November 19, 1835, YU.

It was expensive to attend Yale, even for the son of a comfortable Hartford family. When Henry left for college in September, he reported later, he had $977.90 from his father; his total college bills amounted to $493.67. At the end of four years he was proud that he left few bills (a comment on the debts of his peers), mainly, and characteristically, to Durie and Howe, the booksellers. He was never forced to take a term off, to teach school, in order to pay his tuition, and certainly it must have been the idea of a lark rather than economy that caused him and a friend to share a horse for a trip home to Hartford, one riding on a piece while the other walked, then in turn walking on while the friend caught up to the tethered animal.[33]

The curriculum that Barnard followed was essentially the one confirmed by the famous 1828 *Report on the Course of Instruction in Yale College*. Careful reading of the *Report* proves that it was not as reactionary a document as many have claimed it to have been. The object of the college course was to "lay the foundations of a superior education . . . and to provide both the discipline and furniture of the mind." Despite some innovations, the curriculum remained basically the classical one. Sophomores and juniors did receive some training in English composition, and the study of political economy was added the year before Barnard arrived, and geology the same year. If he had wanted he could have studied French, but not as part of the prescribed course of study, for the mastery of modern languages was seen as "an accomplishment rather than necessary acquisition," and in any case, they were so easy they did not count. The method of instruction was traditional—for undergraduates daily recitations under tutors and examinations twice a year; seniors heard lectures in chemistry, mineralogy, geology, and most important, Natural Philosophy. Barnard could have heard Benjamin Silliman's famous introductory lecture which was a justification of the recently challenged curriculum and an introduction to the challenger; Silliman, who inhabited two worlds, saw "Man . . . below the humblest intelligence of the Spiritual world," but he also summed up: "Knowledge is nothing but the just and full comprehension of the real nature of things, physical, intellectual, and moral." Here was expressed the tension between religion and science which occupied the best minds of the early nineteenth century; Barnard was not troubled by the issue at all.[34]

33. Brooks Mather Kelley, *Yale: A History* (New Haven: Yale University Press, 1974), 144; *OHGS*, 230; Bernard C. Steiner, *Life of Henry Barnard* (Washington: Bureau of Education, 1918), 12–13.

34. *Report of the Course of Instruction in Yale College* (New Haven, 1830), 6, 39, 55; Charles H. Smith, *History of Yale University* (Boston, 1900), 199–200; Kelley, *Yale*, 156ff.; Benjamin Silliman, *Introductory Lecture* (New Haven, 1828).

Nor was he involved in the famous Conic sections revolt of 1830, probably because he was a senior, and the forty-three ring-leaders were all sophomores. He had, however, been sent home during the 1828 Bread and Butter rebellion, as was the entire college; four years later he wrote: rebellions were "queer things to look back upon. They give me qualms, not of conscience, but of stomach." And cautiously, he added that when he had a son he would want him to be in the rank and file of an uprising, but not a leader. With his conservative and accommodating nature he did not feel constrained by the college acting as "a substitute for parental superintending," and he felt and maintained nothing but respect and esteem for President Day with whom he was still corresponding in 1865.[35]

Given the restricted nature of the curriculum and the later evidence of Barnard's wide reading, it is only natural to ask where he received the rest of his education. Student access to the college library was severely restricted; only juniors and seniors could borrow books, and other classes could use the place but once a week. The library, in any case, held a very limited collection. In the 1808 catalogue a total of twenty-eight pages were devoted to religious books; in 1823 there were thirty-nine. In 1808 six pages were history, including three commentaries on Gibbon, but no *Decline and Fall*; by 1823 Gibbon had been acquired, along with several other historians. Among the miscellaneous works were Addison, Burke, *Don Quixote*, Franklin, Locke, and *An Essay on the Amendment of Silver Coins*. But no light reading, and certainly nothing on current affairs or education. Where, then, did young Henry and his contemporaries turn? Noah Porter spoke for Barnard:

He has often expressed to the writer of this sketch, his conviction, that while he did not underrate that instruction in science and literature and that development and expansion of the functions of acquisition and reflection, which he had gained from the regular college course, he owed more of his usefulness in public life to the free commingling of members of different classes, of varied tastes, talents and characters, to the excitement and incentive of the weekly debates, to the generous conflict of mind with mind, and to the

35. *A Circular Explanatory of the Recent Proceedings of the Sophomore Class*, 1830, 13; *Report*, 6; letters, December 7, 1830, September 5, 1832, YU. Lannie says incorrectly that Barnard was suspended for his part in the rebellion; the entire college was rusticated to clear the air. According to Steiner it was while he was at home that Barnard first heard of Pestalozzi from talking with Dr. Eli Todd when the latter came to the house to attend Henry's sick sister. See *AJE*, XVI, xlii (June 1866): 126, where Barnard introduces a letter from Day (who must have been ninety) as "the old living graduate (class of '95) of the college, a noble representative of the golden style of temperance, learning and piety."

preparation for the discussion and decisions of the literary societies with which he was connected.

Again, from Barnard himself: "to books, libraries, and debate I owe much more than to school, college or professors."[36] The literary societies were in their heyday during the time Barnard was in college, and all undergraduates at Yale were either members of the Brothers in Unity or of Linonia; he was a Linonian, and he ever acknowledged his debt to the society. It was to the societies that students came for recreational reading, to peruse the journals of opinion, to debate historical or political topics, even to act in plays (which had originally been outlawed by the faculty). Barnard wrote at least one play of which fragments of two scenes remain; the style is pseudo-Shakespearian. Scene three opens with the Duke in soliloquy: "My sight grows dim and every object dances / I swim before one in the maze of death," and at the end of the scene Rudolph is directed to exit "with a rush and a furioso"—whatever that may be. At the society, too, he perfected his oratorical style. One impromptu performance was recalled by Linonians for years afterwards.[37]

It was the society's library that was most vital to Barnard. By becoming, first assistant librarian, and then librarian, he had the run of the collection; he even, it was said, turned over his salary to buy more books. He may well deserve partial credit for the fact that the society's collection increased from 662 books in 1808 to 3,505 in 1831. The listings in history doubled in the period; a new category, Politics and Laws, was added, as was a section on travel; and there were hundreds of novels and plays and biographies, even one of Mrs. Siddons. All of the major British journals are listed, and so are the popularizing works—the *Family Library, Elegant Extracts, The Library of Entertaining Knowledge*. In his old age Barnard recalled that he "had free use of the books for two years, and in that way enjoyed the advantages of a pretty large library and some of the disadvantages of its proving a diversion from my regular college studies." Through formal study Barnard mastered the literary tradition and was to some extent introduced to the new thoughts of the age, but by means of his own reading he was entertained, he wandered throughout the world,

---

36. *Catalogue of the Books in the Library of Yale College*, 1808, 1823, 1831; *Catalogue of the Books in the Brothers and Linonian Libraries*, 1808; *Catalogue of the Books in the Linonian Library*, 1831; Noah Porter, "Henry Barnard," *CCSJ*, II, 1 (January 1855): 7; Hughes, *Barnard*, 562. On student societies see James McLachlan, "The Choice of Hercules: Student Societies in the Early Nineteenth Century," in Lawrence Stone, ed., *The University in Society* (New York, 1974).

37. Fragment, TC, Hughes, *Barnard*, 9.

he encountered the brilliance of contemporary political argument, and he was introduced to the compelling issues of the day.[38]

Barnard's record at Yale was good one, although not as brilliant as some, himself included, tried to paint later. In a class many of whose members went on to real distinction, he stood in the upper fifth.[39] As a sophomore he had won the Berklenian Premium for Latin and English composition, and at his commencement, although not either the salutatorian (his friend and future correspondent John Whiting Andrews) or valedictorian, he was one of fifteen other orators at the ceremony. (Commencement took an entire day in 1830.) While classmates spoke "on Original Thought" or "on the Influence of Emulation on the process of Mental Improvement" or "on the prevailing neglect of Moral Science" or "on the union of Literary Pursuits with the duties of a profession," Henry Barnard was listed as giving a dissertation on the "Scepticism of Men of Genius."

That address no longer survives; another does, in Barnard's most florid hand. The commencement program might have been erred, or else there was another important occasion for a formal address, a Linonian Banquet perhaps; whenever it was delivered it is the only example we have of Barnard's thrust of thought at this time.

A

Dissertation

on

The Services rendered by Christianity

to poetry

The style is self-conscious and studied; the analysis superficial, only touching and never grappling with the issues which must have been discussed in many a Linonian gathering. According to Barnard between Christianity and the classics there simply is no contest.

The utility and moral beauty of the Christian religion, its superiority over every other in its power to invigorate the understanding and purify the affections are acknowledged alike by all. Sublime in the antiquity of its recollections which go back to the beginning of

38. Notes for draft of article on libraries, TC. Years later Barnard was to write that his first knowledge of the Prussian school system was from reading J. W. Adams's *Letters from Silesia* and H. E. Dwight's *Letter from Germany*, printed in 1828; he may have read them in the Linonian Library; see *OHGS*, 228n.

39. In notes for G. E. Plimpton, TC, Barnard as an old man claimed to have been a member of Phi Beta Kappa at Yale; I suspect he became an honorary member when he delivered the annual oration in 1852.

time, celestial in its ceremonies, it appeals to every feeling which can improve and dignify the human ear.

No matter that he is just plain wrong historically; what is striking is his uncritical acceptance of the early nineteenth century blending of the classics and religion, sliding over any inconsistencies, with none of the turmoil of, for instance, a Bushnell. There are some key words here however —utility, improve—which reflect his reading and alert us to suspect a philosophical and political orientation. The dissertation, too, displays Barnard's developing oratorical technique: the language is ornate, but the organization absolutely clear. He makes three points, two of which reflect his times and become constants. Christianity has enlarged the province of poetry by delineating the finer workings of the female heart.

The polished Athenian with all his Epicureanianism of taste could never justly appreciate the blended intellectual and moral beauty which now hold the stronger sex in bondage.

Then he moves to his second point; the nobler conception of nature, prevalent in contemporary verse, also stems from Christianity.

The grandeur of Homer and the pathos of Virgil fade away before the conceptions of Isaiah and the [frenzied?] lamentations of Jeremiah, and we listen slow to the sweet notes of David's harp as they were but the echos of heaven's own music.

The voice is clear. Romantic, well-read, uncritical, lofty in conception, convincing and even comforting to an audience that shared his views.[40]

Like many with a newly minted bachelor's degree, young Henry, at twenty, did not know what to do after graduation. Like many of them he tried his hand at teaching. He accepted an appointment, sent his way by President Day, as teacher in an academy in Wellesborough, Pennsylvania, albeit with some trepidation. In thanking Day, he added, "I should be pleased to receive your advice respecting the conduct I ought to pursue —for I am about to enter on a course of trial with which I have no experience." The image of a trial is a Romantic one, but teaching was indeed a trial for Barnard. He did not like it, and he was not particularly good at it. The school itself was a disappointment, more akin to the

---

40. Order of Exercises at Commencement, Yale College, September 8, 1830, YU; unpublished manuscript, TC. If this is the speech to which Hughes referred, I cannot agree that Barnard's "first public speech was in favor of women's freedom." A classmate, Sherwood Bissell, recalled in old age "you were very much the head in our college course and you have kept it up"; letter, December 24, 1889, TC; I suspect this was part of the growing legend.

South District school than his beloved Monson. Years later he wrote from vivid memory:

> *We remember*, too, when it was once our fortune to play the school-master. Against one side of the house was fastened a long seat. Of equal length, stood a six-legged slab for a writing desk, two legs at each end, and two in the center to keep it from what the boys called *tilting*. Back of the seat stood two loose windows. In front of it stood the stove, broadside. To save faces and eyes, the scholars used to erect a parapet of slates and books along the forward edge of the slab. This protected the face, but the brush of air through the crevices in the windows and the cracks in the floor kept their heads and feet as cold as the North and South poles of the earth, while the radiation from the stove poured, point blank, into their equitorial regions . . . [41]

It was not abstract theory that turned Henry Barnard into an advocate of improved schoolhouses, and his pounding away at the need for ventilation must have reflected the memory of many a headache.

It is likely, too, that his stress on the necessity of providing some preparation and support for teachers stemmed from his sense of frustration and failure. He probably wanted to teach like Holland, or as later he felt Holland had taught, but he lacked the gift. His letters do show that during his tenure in Wellesborough he thought a good deal about the process of teaching. Discipline should be "of moral rather than physical force" with few but strict rules. "I made them *feel* I was their friend," but "neither did I at all in sports, for I am convinced nothing will sooner degrade an instructor." Better to get to school early "to talk to them about their studies and reading." He claimed that he never employed physical means but noted an infraction, like the Lord High Executioner, in a little black book and applied a light punishment, warning the culprit of possible expulsion should he transgress again. For guidance during the difficult days he used the new *Lectures on School-Keeping* by Samuel Hall, but they were of little help. He lasted three months.[42]

It certainly did not help that the fastidious and slightly snobbish Barnard had a low opinion of his scholars and neighbors. They were the "dirty Pennsylvanians," and "Their only object is to propagate and rot." His brother Chauncey tried to encourage him to "keep up good spirits for the time" the younger man had agreed to serve, but soon reports from

---

41. *CCSJ*, I, 7 (February 1839): 71.

42. Letter to Loomis, January 27, 1831, NYU; for an outline of the contents of Hall's work, see *American Journal of Education* (henceforth *AmJEd*), IV, iv (July 1829): 342–46.

home added to his misery. His stepmother became ill, and in February Chauncey had to write that they had just followed her to her grave, exactly fifteen years after they had buried their own mother. No matter the depths of his affection for this second mother, Henry was bound to feel, given his affectionate nature, lonely and alone, and far away. He responded as he was to respond again and again throughout his career—he walked away from a tough job. "Fatigued and shattered in health," with an "incessant cough which gave [him] a pain in [his] heart," he rejoiced to declare that "the long agony's over" when he resigned despite the entreaties of the trustees that he stay.[43] James Lowrey of the Board of the Academy wrote a reference:

> This may certify that Henry Barnard has taught in this place the winter past; that as a teacher he has given universal satisfaction both to the Trustees of the Academy and his pupils, who have made rapid progress under his instruction; that he is a man of superior talents and acquirements, and of that kind which eminently qualify him for an instructor, and of good moral character.[44]

There is no way of discovering if in fact Lowrey was correct, that Barnard had the makings of a very good teacher, or whether Lowrey wrote the customary generous evaluation of someone he had been glad to be rid of. Barnard was correct that he was not temperamentally suited for teaching, and certainly he had no intention of returning to it. Like his peers he did not view school teaching as more than "a life of brief enjoyment and protracted troubles."

Apparently Barnard was not too shattered in health to enjoy his trip home that late April, and his journal reveals a high spirited and energetic young man, able to walk twelve miles to catch the canal boat because he had taken one going in the wrong direction and brushing off a bad fall (from a bridge to the boat below) with a quip—"thus was the doctrine of momentum illustrated." Travel was rough at times, and the accommodations dreadful; he complained about the food and the lack of wine in the Rochester House. His comments on the people he met displayed a

43. Letter to Loomis, April 6, 1831, YU; from Chauncey Barnard, January 18, February 4, 10, 1831, NYU; Chauncey had become an engineer in the Army Corps of Engineers and, in April, wrote that he was about to depart for Minnesota. Barnard in 1880 published (in the *AJE* XXX [1880]) an excerpt from his own biographical sketch in Duyckinck's "Cyclopedia of American Literature," III:27; significantly there is no mention of his time as a teacher.

44. Typed copy, sent to Barnard in Providence, November 25, 1847, NYU. I can only speculate as to why Barnard, at this late date, and when he was highly successful, wanted a reference; he was job hunting at the time.

sharp eye and an elitist nature. A Mrs. Hill was "of low parentage" and "dunghill nobility" and his canal companions "not of the first water." The Yankee peddlers he encountered along the way were "a disgrace to the land of their birth" because of their trickery, but he grudgingly admitted that they were "a shrewd set with a rich vein of humor." Out of duty he called on relatives in Rochester; they were not interesting.

The trip had its instructive side. This future reformer was deadly serious when he visited the new prison at Auburn, which he thought a credit to New York state; he took careful notes "for an elaborate [display?] on Tread Mills to appear in the next report of the Prison Discipline Society." He also ordered a coat made by the inmates—unfortunately it failed to fit. It was in Auburn that he encountered Charles Grandison Finney whose subdued delivery was a disappointment. Barnard probably meant that Finney was not a good show, because he was unsympathetic with revivals such as the powerful one he witnessed near Ithaca, and the evangelizing efforts of his fellow traveler, Mr. Ross "disgusted" him. Ross was too persistent in countering Barnard's restrained objection that the excitement of revival excesses was certain to pass, and argued vehemently and nearly violently, or tastelessly. Barnard could not stand it and rebuked his companion.

> I cannot consent that you should bore me both with your elbow and tongue . . . I am in your view a hardened reprobate, so . . . let me enjoy as much peace both of body and of mind as this villainous stage will allow.

A rather rude remark from the cultivated young graduate, and one which shows his contempt for such as Ross; certainly, the recording of the incident in his journal reveals a cockiness in Henry Barnard.

The high point of the trip was his visit to Niagara Falls. He viewed the spectacle from every angle, recording his impressions in typically Romantic metaphor, his "bewildering sensations" of the "emerald color of the unbroken sheets." He felt "the Deity upon the morning breeze," and, in a fragmentary final, he attempted poetry: "You must stand before that outpouring of the fountains of the great Deep . . . you must hear." His instincts to stop trying were right; he was a better observer of people than poet.[45]

And so he arrived back in Hartford. Teaching had not worked out —whether it was the actual job, the loneliness in Pennsylvania, or ambition for greater things we cannot tell. But what things? What did an

---

45. Journal, NYU. Lannie, *Barnard*, 5, says that there is a journal of his schoolkeeping days; I have not as yet located it.

attractive, sociable, well-educated young man, not quite twenty-one, with comfortable means do? Of course he could always visit friends, and during the summer he spent considerable time in Amherst with his classmate James Humphrey. He returned to Yale for commencement in both 1831 and 1832—perhaps he still hoped for a tutorship. Certainly there was real reserve, if not sour grapes, in his congratulations to Elias Loomis on *his* tutorship: "It eats, worse than rust, into the noblest mind."[46] Further study, not desultory but directed, was an obvious option. He read law in New York, with his classmate Alpheus Williams, under Willis Hall, a future attorney general of the state, but influenza drove him home. He intended to continue with his legal studies but because the law "was a jealous mistress," he decided to devote only two hours a day to it. For the rest he simply read, borrowing books from the generous patrician Daniel Wadsworth and the Hartford Library Company. He set himself some Greek and Latin every day, and in letters to friends he discussed Plato and Herodotus; he also dwelt on passages from the Bible. He mused, while reading about the early civilizations of the Nile, on the origin of the races, citing Strabo. Barnard was deadly serious in his scholarly pursuits and highly critical of those, like his friend Stanley, who pursued study for its own sake, with little concern for its value. "He is accumulating knowledge without getting the faculty of making it useful." Useful is a term he adopted from the Utilitarians, for his reading included the greats of the eighteenth and nineteenth centuries, the *philosophes*, the Scottish philosophers, Gibbon, Locke, and especially Brougham. He read novels, and poetry even, and had a preference for Wordsworth. His reading was so wide that Noah Porter, a few years later, asserted: "Few professional scholars among us at the age of twenty-seven, were so thoroughly familiar with the ancient and modern English literature."[47]

It was an easy, and desirable, step from literary study to literary production. In the summer of 1832 he published in the *New England Review* an unoriginal, predictable, and unimportant travelpiece, the account of an afternoon's excursion to Wadsworth's "Montevideo"—a summer spot, a cottage, with a wooden tower, and a pond, some ten miles from Hartford. There "the elegance, the exquisite taste, and the great amount of labor and attention that has been devoted to this delightful spot of earth

46. Letter to Loomis, September 5, 1832, YU.

47. Letters to friends, YU; Porter, *CCSJ*, II:8. Among the Watkinson papers is an undated "Memo ... G. E. Plimpton," an autobiographical outline. Under "II, Post-Graduate Studies and Professional Reading" Barnard listed: 1. General, review and additional, 2. Law-legislation; 3. Attendance at public meetings, lyceum, courts, club, debate; 4. Excursions—always objects; 5. Travels.

... make it the little Eden that it is." The small pond brought out the poet:

> I could almost imagine that the fabled sea nymphs had left their coral chambers to smile once more upon the inhabitants of this common place world.[48]

Evidently he was very proud of this piece, for he sent it around to friends and was delighted when they had read it.

Speech-making was another form of literary production, and Barnard had already proved he was good at it. Now he joined a young men's debating society, and he attended lectures at the local lyceum. An undated speech, delivered at the conclusion of a lecture series, probably is of this period, for it reflects his style and presages themes to come. Such lectures were of benefit to all:

> Thronged as your Hall has been by the young and the old, by men and by women, from every walk, occupation, and class of life among you, forgetting here the false and arbitrary distinction of fashion and pursuit in the enjoyment of a common pleasure—brought heart to heart and mind to mind, by the electric chain of sympathy, along which the speaker has sent those impulses of thought speeding which has made every bosom throb as it were with the common hear of humanity.

Here to him was democracy in the joint pursuit of self-education, all "in the cause of truth—the cause of justice—the cause of liberty—the cause of Patriotism—the cause of Religion."[49]

Good, traditional values these, Whig values, and a Whig he was becoming. He apparently was a delegate to the National Whig Convention in Baltimore in 1831; on July 4, 1832, he spoke to "a small audience" of the National Republican Young Men of Hartford, and was "well-received." The talk was a spirited and partisan attack on Jackson, especially for his stand on the bank and his attack on internal improvements, as well as for the calibre of his supporters and their means. The right thinkers, "the purest patriots . . . are hunted by the pensioned press" of the Jacksonians. In the name of "slumbering patriotism" the young Barnard exhorted his listeners:

> Unwed to all names, unmindful of divisions which grew out of controversies that time has settled and untainted with the deep prejudices of party feeling, they may unite heart and hand in renewing

48. Typed copy, TC.
49. Manuscript, TC.

the sullied glory of our country. They may unite in rescuing the government from the continued misrule of one who, whatever he might have been, is now a weak old man—and from the reversion of a reckless intriguer who was the first to bow the honor of our diplomacy in the dust.

The theme of regeneration and of rescue was a Whig one. So was Barnard's evocation of the spirit of Washington. There could only be one man he urged his fellow partisans to support—Henry Clay.[50]

In a small way, and in a small city, Barnard was beginning to be noticed; his education, his attractive personality, even his background made it natural. In time he could be expected to rise to civic leadership, and this seems to have frightened him. In a revealing letter he gave a hint of humility, or even a foreboding of a fatal flaw. "More is expected of me than I can realize."[51] Or maybe it was false modesty.

Politics or *Wanderlust*, or a conscious plan to continue his education in another direction soon enticed Barnard away from his native city. In the winter of 1833 he went to Washington. Much later, in his old age he reflected on the value of travel:

> Travel is part of a university education and really in itself is the flower and fruitage of all previous study brought to the realities of society as it exists and the institutions past and present.

Travel could restore health—he and his contemporaries always seemed on the verge of succumbing to illnesses; it was also "the great school of manners, the school of living politics, the theatre of all socialistic problems." The habit of traveling should be encouraged early with frequent local excursions, where a boy could learn to observe nature and cultivate a sense of beauty. Ample and careful preparation for travel was essential in order that a trip should be truly instructive; travel accounts and experienced travelers should be consulted so that "the real object should be associated with the geography, history, and biography of the places visited." Most vital of all, though, was the habit of diligent notetaking. "At all times of life the habit of observation should be cultivated and tested by oral and written accounts of the actual experience."

The bookish and ambitious Barnard had plenty of models in the travel letters and sketches submitted to the weeklies and monthlies he read;

50. Typed copy, TC. The copy is undated, and the year could be 1832; it seems reasonable to assume the later date is correct, as the meeting was called to select delegates to a state convention to choose electors for the coming national election. See Steiner, *Barnard*, 15ff., who gives 1831.

51. Letter to Loomis, July 8, 1831, YU.

perhaps it was too much to hope to rival a Dickens or a Martineau, but he could aim for publication in the Hartford *Courant* or the Boston *Atlas*. From Washington he asked his brother Chauncey to "get terms" and to "jog Chapman," the editor of the *Atlas*. He also worried that the family might discard his letters, over which he expended so much effort: "I hope you preserve my letters as they contain hints upon which I would like to comment, and of which I have no record." At twenty-two Henry Barnard was already anxious to instruct, even if he had failed as a teacher, and his class was only his family. And he felt ready to seek realities very foreign to old New England.[52]

Armed with letters of introduction and invitations from several class-mates (for Yale attracted Southerners, John C. Calhoun being the most prominent graduate), Barnard said his good-byes. He spent the New Year's holiday in New York where the parties and the young ladies were superior; he wrote archly to his brother, "you are a fool (pardon the words) if you don't leave the Hartford game and follow a different scent."[53] Then Barnard headed for Washington, riding from Philadelphia to Baltimore in the "cars" with his idol, Henry Clay. "I assure you my expectation of the man whom we both ardently supported has not been disappointed."

Once in the capital city he found a suitable boarding house where he "messed with eight or ten Congressmen," most from his home state. He became a diligent and earnest observer, subscribing to the Washington *Intelligence*, buying in pamphlet form the great speeches of the day, listening to the legislators' dinner table conversations, and most of all attending the Congress. "I am here a fisher of men." He recorded all his impressions in his journal and letters home, drafting and rewriting several versions of the same event. This was the time that the great debate over Nullification was raging, the time, too, when the mighty strode the stage of the Senate. But Barnard was disillusioned at first to discover that "the majority of both Houses of Congress are in no way remarkable for talent or industry." His heroes fortunately stood tall. The "collision" of the giants in debate was "tremendous." Calhoun, while looking "care-worn," used language that was "sinewy" although "his periods [were] rather short." Clay "was overwhelming," but his admirer also had to admit "unkind and

52. Letters to Loomis, April 3, June 16, September 18, December 14, 1831; the latter has a sharp attack on Jackson; notes on travel, TC. The manuscript is clearly autobiographical, one of many fragments written later in life, when the didactic tone had become habitual and the metaphor of the school predictable.

53. Throughout these southern letters there are frequent references to "the fair sex," the "young ladies." Henry and his friends were very anxious with women and equally anxious to be married, that "blissful state."

personal"; his "sneers" made "the hearers' blood run cold." Webster was the most impressive.

> He shivered to atoms the specious but frail structure which Calhoun had raised with infinite labor, with a few strokes of his battle axe.

Sometimes Barnard's comments are rhetorical or self-conscious attempts to emulate those he heard every day; on the tariff debate: "What a miserable fluctuation! What a base surrender of the public faith!" Often he was just plain wrong, or unduly hopeful due to his politics, as when he saw the Jacksonian party in shambles. But then he was vehemently partisan. The President was "the roaring lion in the Palace," the "most abandoned tyrant at heart on the earth" who "blusters away like a madman on the subject of the tariff." Barnard saw clearly the illogic of northern opposition to the tariff and was even more prescient in sensing the possibility of a complete rupture of the national parties and the creation of a solid South below the Ohio. (Perhaps he heard others talk this way, in his mess—though usually in his journal he identified the source of his opinions.)

Parties, social rather than political, occupied our young tourist's free time. The informality and intimacy of the Washington scene is striking to the modern reader. Despite his condemnation of the President, Barnard could not pass up a *levée* at the White House. "It was an old assemblage from every section of the country." He also could not resist a dig; Jackson's penury, or lack of taste, was obvious—there were no refreshments. Another evening, with his Congressmen friends, he attended a *soirée* at the French minister's. The occasion was almost a disaster, for on the way he discovered he had forgotten his glasses—back he went to fetch them, although it added three miles to his trip. At least then he could see clearly enough to be highly critical of the ladies who wore too much paint, easily visible under the glare of the sparkling chandeliers. He watched the waltz for the first time, "a very graceful but voluptuous dance, in which a lovely figure is displayed to the best advantage." Quickly, in the letter, he went on that at such parties you meet all the same faces, "it is rather a bore." This was a very serious young man, almost guilty when he relaxed; after all, he had come to Washington to learn. "I have a grand time here, much better than I ever expected—it will be of great value to me."[54]

54. Letters, to Chauncey, January—March, 1833, to Dr. Todd, February 18, NYU. Edited versions of these letters and of Barnard's journal were published by Bernard C. Steiner, "The South Atlantic States in 1833, as Seen by a New Englander, Henry Barnard," *Maryland Historical Magazine*, XIII, 3 and 4 (September and December 1918): 267–386. The letters to Barnard from Chauncey are full of family and political news; April 8 is entirely

Six weeks in the capital was enough. The great debate was over, and the novelty of the social scene fading. Henry asked his older brother if "Pa," who was footing the bill, would let his younger son travel longer and further. Early in February permission was secured, and Henry set off for the South.[55]

For the first time in his life he was venturing into a new land, encountering a new culture. He had *entrées*, it is true, welcoming letters from friends and numerous introductions to the best and powerful. But he was uncertain about Southern proprieties, and he sought advice and comfort, admitting to himself that at times he had "felt very foolish and very stupid." He inquired of Ashbel Smith (a native and older) what were the "orthodox" hours for calling (the answer: twelve noon). He met new or unexpected food, fried chicken "the best dish in the world," and an enormous bowl of strawberries in April. Somewhat disturbing was the luxury of Southern life. He had encountered slaves for the first time in Washington where they were "a marked feature in the appearance of the Street," and "a real convenience—they go and come at your bidding, and a kind word, or action, especially a 'small bit' now and then attaches them fast to you." He liked having his fire lit in the morning and his water brought, but he came to see slavery as sapping strength of the South, making the owner inhabitants indolent. The really enterprising men he met were all from the North, whether adventuresome entrepreneurs or aspiring lawyers.

Barnard was happiest with the families of his Yale friends or with transplanted New Englanders like the Mitchells, who kept very northern households. He admired, in chaste romantic terms, the southern belles, (although he was horrified at the "intolerable" local habit which condoned women taking snuff), but he remained at heart loyal. "Northern wives for management and the endearing qualities of a mother stand 75% above par, yet a pretty Southern girl with a large plantation is not to be despised." Even the James River, though "noble" couldn't compare with the Connecticut, lined as it was with charming villages. He noted social

devoted to the recent election. Chauncey also acts the responsible older brother; Henry had been using the frank to send his letters home; it worried Chauncey who didn't want a scandal. A comparison of the letters and the journal exemplifies Barnard's technique; he repeated the phrase "shivered to atoms" to his brother, to Dr. Todd, and in his journal.

55. Letters from Chauncey, February 6, to Chauncey, February—May, to Betty, March 15; Journal, January 19, March 30, NYU. The nature of Barnard's relation to his father is a mystery. He wrote to his brother, to friends, to older men such as Dr. Todd, never to Pa. Yet the latter clearly was a powerful figure in the background, and Henry was fond of him. Perhaps he was sensitive to the fact that his father was ill at ease responding to letters. Better to have them read aloud around the family hearth.

differences; to his sister, Betty, he reported that Mrs. Carter had nothing to do with setting the table. And, as always, he could be sharply censorious. After a call on a Mr. Samuel Robbins he exclaimed "The Lord deliver me from cousins of the fourth remove when I travel." But calls on another cousin, Mrs. Barnard, a widow of Charleston, were another matter. She was a "very superior woman and you [Chauncey] must do what you can to make her stay [in Hartford] agreeable." That Chauncey clearly did, for subsequently he married this charming cousin.[56]

Travel in the South brought Barnard face to face with the intensity of the positions he had heard proclaimed in the Congress. "The morbid sensitivity of the South on the subject of slavery can't be conceived by those who have not visited this part of the country." He became convinced that if the North interfered with the "domestic relations of the South," as was being suggested by northern publications, a convention would be held and the "question of Union be agitated and decided." The Carolinas were the core of the opposition; Charleston the "headquarters of Nullification." Even in Greenville, "a great *Union* district," Nullifiers, with their badges on their hats were numerous.

> Everything I hear confirms me in the belief, that some of the leaders in the late excitement still contemplate a disunion of the states and the formation of a great Southern Confederacy. The politicians are beginning to agitate the slave question, and the morbid sensibilities of the South upon that point. These Southern Nabobs would as soon part with life, as with the luxury of their slaves. They would die without them.

Barnard never mentioned the morality of slavery. Nor did he underestimate the strength of Southern resolve, especially after extended conversation with the strong-minded brother of his classmate Edmund Smith.

> They [the Nullifiers] would have fought with the courage of desperation—It was their intention if things actually came to war, to fight us as long as they could in the open fields—then if they were obliged to give way, to blow up their cities, and retire to their marshes and swamps and carry on a "guerilla warfare." . . .The affair is not over yet however—that attachment to the Union which was once so universal, and so sacred, is gone, and I fear gone forever.

Good reporting and shrewd thinking; the foundations might indeed be being laid for a political career in this southern jaunt.

56. Letters, from Greenville, April 20, from Augusta, April 25, from Charleston, April 30 and May 9; NYU.

Politics were not Barnard's sole concern, and he was a diligent sight-seer. He visited all the local marvels wherever he was, a gold mine (he carefully described the process of "washing"), the imprisoned Indian chief Black Hawk and his sons (the chief looked "as a well-fed eagle caged"), and countless "perspectives." He went to extreme lengths to view natural wonders. To reach the Peaks of Otter, the highest point south of the Delaware River, he rode, or scrambled, miles, crossed one stream twenty-seven times, and climbed the final mile nearly straight up. It was mid-night when he descended, and he had to take whatever lodging he could find. This for a young man who had several times confided to his journal his fear of getting lost! Of particular interest to him was touring the new college at Chapel Hill with the president, not because of a special con-cern for education, but as a loyal son of Yale. He noted the three build-ings, the chapel, and the "respectible apparatus," the five professors, two tutors, and the hundred students, and for the most part he approved of what he saw.

> It was for a long time doubted at the North whether any thing like college discipline could be maintained at the South, but I did not observe any difference between the habits of the students here and at Yale—except in this boasted land of refinement their manners are more rough and their dress, even more vulgarly plain.

The students at the University of Virginia, on the other hand, were "a set of pretty wild fellows generally" who bolted their food and even played at marbles.[57]

The trip had two high points. Early one morning he rode alone up the mountain to Monticello; unhappily the morning was misty, and the view completely obscured. He was about to turn back down in disappoint-ment when suddenly, for a few moments, the clouds lifted.

> O it was a grand sight to see the mist roll up from the side of the mountain and gradually unfold a more glorious landscape than was ever exhibited in any scenic representation. . . . When the bell for morning service at the University came floating up the mountain. I could not but contrast even the beautiful rotunda with the immense

57. Journal, April 8, 18, May 18; Journal and letter, March 25 and 26, letter, May 25, Journal, June 5. Barnard was not too censorious of the Virginia students; see Jennings L. Wagoner, Jr., "Honor and Dishonor at Mr. Jefferson's University: The Antebellum Years," *History of Education Quarterly* 26, no. 2 (Summer 1986): 155–79. In Washington, Barnard had visited the Catholic College where, grudgingly, he was impressed; "were it not for its Catholicism [the college] would be a very eligible situation for a youth 12–17," Journal, January 23. Note Barnard's anti-Catholicism and the ages of the young men he thought might be in this college.

temple in which I stood. . . . What need of speakers. I felt within my own soul a spirit too strong for words, proclaiming, that the Lord was indeed in his holy temple, let the whole world keep silence before him, and what a temple.[58]

The passage far surpasses the Montevideo one, and remains one of Barnard's best. Perhaps his talent for writing would be nurtured, if he chose that route. Change of mood was an element he had not yet mastered, though, and he abruptly shifted to describe the owner of Jefferson's magnificent home who appeared and urged Barnard to take breakfast with him. Barnard's luck and Southern hospitality had held, and he enjoyed a generous meal, profusely apologizing for his inappropriate attire.

Barnard had set himself the goal of calling on all of those men "whose opinions may be of value" on this trip and a few days earlier had been frustrated that John Marshall was away. After the Monticello treat, armed with an introduction from Thomas Grimké, and after dining at mid-day with Governor Barbour (a meal "in true Virginia style" which included that luxury, fried chicken), he presented himself at the house of ex-President Madison. Mrs. Madison, still lovely, received him graciously and ushered him in to her husband's room. The elderly Madison, then in his eighties, who was lying on his bed, greeted the young man warmly, his eye bright, his voice still firm despite his years. "He conversed with great ease and expressed himself with inimitable clearness and precision on every subject." After what Barnard thought was a suitable time, he excused himself and bade his adieux, only to find his horse already stabled for the night. The remainder of the evening with Mrs. Madison was a delight—she charmed the young man and put him at ease. Rising at seven the next morning Barnard found the President had already eaten, and the rain coming down hard. So he spent another three hours in talk before reluctantly taking his leave. With jubilation he reported to his brother that "my visit with Mr. Madison was worth the whole expense of my journey."[59]

58. Letter and Journal, May 26. The metaphor is strikingly similar to that expression when he saw Niagara. In another letter he described Weir's Cave which surpassed Niagara: "such a scene I never expected to see." On this particular trip Barnard's intrepid perseverance was again demonstrated: because he was twice left by the stage, he hired a horse; he got lost three times, and the total trip amounted to forty miles over rough roads; letter, June 1, NYU.

59. Letter from Thomas Grimké, May 10, CHS. Barnard made good use of a chain of introduction; see Grimké to his friend Lyttleton Tazewell of Norfolk, CHS; letters, May 11, 21, June 1, NYU.

Expense was beginning to weigh on him. "I am getting out at the elbow, and at that more essential part, the purse." And he had had enough of travel, of missed connections and jolting conveyances. Rail travel was bad; after the novelty had worn off, the discomfort took over. Steamboats were unpredictable: "I am tired to death of this miserable way of travelling at the South." Yet, when he opted for the brig *Laura* leaving Charleston, she couldn't clear the bar for days, and he watched with impatience and frustration as the steamer, carrying his attractive cousin, chugged by, bound for New York. He seemed weary, if still determined. To his journal he confided "to tell the truth I am very anxious to get back again among my friends" and home. And home he went after his visits in Virginia, stopping only long enough in New York to watch the Jacksonians parade. He must have been overjoyed to be back, among his friends and family, with lots to tell; certainly the memory of the strain and fatigue would pass, and the pleasures and privileges grow brighter. "I do think without exaggeration that this trip will be of more advantage to me than any two years I spent in college." He was already open to his friend Smith's advice, that he go soon to Europe. "If I only had the means I would go directly."[60]

Once home, he turned again to his legal studies, perhaps convinced that legal practice was the path to politics. He attended lectures at the Yale Law School, and, because study in the county in which one proposed to practice was required, he read law in Hartford with William Hungerford, a local attorney. He was admitted to the bar on October 27, 1834, and then seriously had to confront his future.[61] His friends proffered advice. James Humphrey urged him to come practice in Amherst; William Matson, although himself living in New Haven, suggested going South; Horace Barbour wanted him to investigate the prospects in Louisville. Barbour also showed sense and insight when he added "with your advantages I should never leave Hartford. You may get more money elsewhere—will you find more happiness?" With Ashbel Smith, his former teacher and now confidant, Barnard balanced the idea of moving West or embarking on a career in Connecticut. Smith urged him to stay at home and to get to know the leading men of the state because Connecticut needed "good men and true." And, added Smith, politics for Barnard involved little risk, "always having high professional distinctions your

60. Letters, March 15, 31, April 25, May 11, Wednesday but clearly early June; Journal, April 18, 25; NYU.

61. Letter from W. C. Storrs, Middletown, October 21, 1834, CHS. Typed copy of a letter of admission sent to Providence in 1844, NYU. Trumbull, *Memorial History*, chap. VI, "The Bench and the Bar," 130–31 states that in the decade 1831–40 there were only thirty new members on the list of practicing attorneys; Barnard was not among them, evidence that he actually never practiced law.

main object, on which to fall back."[62] Barnard's consultation with his friends and his careful weighing of all the alternatives reveals a cautious nature; it also disproves Lannie's assertion that Barnard never intended to practice law and Barnard's own insistence that his subsequent election to the legislature came totally unsought. Everything he had done, his studies, his excursion to Washington, his adoption of law, pointed toward a political career.

He continued his speech-making in the city. He addressed the American Colonization Society, Connecticut branch, and on July 4, he was, once again, asked to deliver the holiday oration, this time at the North Congregational Church. To be asked to deliver an oration on the national holiday was always an honor, a mark of community standing, and it must have been particularly gratifying to be speaking in the North, not the South, Church. He selected as his topic the vital importance of education to the nation.

> The only security for the highest and the wealthiest, is the enlargement of the understanding and the purification of the affections of every individual voter, juror, witness, legislator, and judge of legislation.

But education was not merely to guarantee the security of the elite. Nor was mastery of the rudiments by the masses enough. Education should lead to self-culture as well as to search for truth.

> Education then—universal education—& the universal education too of the whole human being—the heart as well as the intellect, becomes at once the only security, the highest interest & the highest duty of the state & of individuals.

A ringing peroration linked duty, truth, and the nation in the phraseology of early nineteenth-century ideals.

> Patriotism must be cherished as the moving principle of public duty, not that patriotism whose beginning and middle and ending is self, but whose whole scope is truth—This is the holy maxim which it has been assigned to our nation, and our age to fulfill—this is the scope and glorious consumption of an American system of popular education.[63]

62. Letter from W. N. Matson, November 29, 1834, from Horace Barbour, December 6, 1833, from Smith, February 7, 1834; NYU See also letter from A. P. Nott, July 18, 1834, TC: "But you will do better in Hartford where you have friends and influence and an already enviable reputation." Barnard did make a brief trip West in the summer of 1835.

63. *OHGS*, note 228. Barnard here says he spoke on the importance of schools to the Peace Society; one wonders. See typed notes, NYU, ms fragment, TC. *Connecticut Courant*,

In December he addressed the Connecticut Peace Society, this time on the "weight of Universal Popular Intelligence" in the settling of international disputes. In his public utterances at this time, Barnard evinced no particular interest in school reform. He repeated the general views of responsible men and orated like a politician.

It was Barnard's participation in the Peace Society that provided him with his next opportunity. He was elected a delegate, one of two, to the international peace convention called for the following spring in London. His father agreed to allow him to go, and on an extended grand tour afterwards. Henry made his arrangements carefully, and he displayed some audacity for a virtual unknown. He wrote to Ralph Waldo Emerson for advice and for Thomas Carlyle's address; he wrote to Governor Barbour; he even wrote to his idol, Henry Clay. Clay answered that few of his European acquaintances remained after twenty years, but he included three letters of introduction and a "general letter or passport." College friends were not much help, but Thomas Gallaudet was, describing Barnard in an introduction to an Edinburgh colleague as "esteemed at home . . . for his private worth and promise of a future respectable career." (In the context we can assume the former here means Barnard's inherent abilities not his wealth.) Gallaudet also expressed concern for his young friend's soul; just prior to the latter's departure he wrote "you will be grievously exposed. Have you made up your mind on religion?"[64]

Barnard was still a young man and still somewhat shy and anxious about propriety; he must have been relieved to be traveling in the company of an older and experienced man, also a delegate to the convention. Dr. Heman Humphrey was a Yale graduate, a man of the cloth, the president of Amherst, and the father of Henry's college friend, James; he had also been educated in the Connecticut common schools and had served for a time as a teacher. His position and experiences led him to an active role in the growing reform movement—a very suitable tutor and chaperone indeed. During Barnard's extended visits to the family home and on this trip, Humphrey must have exerted an influence on the young man.

July 8, where the group is called Whig. Typed summary from Connecticut *Observer*, December 29, 1834: "W. W. Ellsworth, Henry Barnard, and others spoke." In Hartford society, the North Church was the prestigious one.

64. Letter from Emerson, March 13, 1835, NYU; Carlyle in turn wrote to his friend John Jeffrey, June 11, 1835; CHS. Letter from Clay, March 6, 1835, CHS. Letters from Maxwell, Wilson, Andrews, Ackland; March, 1835, NYU. Maxwell didn't know anyone in Europe but promised to forward his request to the governor. Letter from Gallaudet in Cincinnati, March 9, 1835, CHS. The fact that Barnard still had so many letters in his possession suggests that he never used half those he had procured; after his trip he told Loomis that letters really were not very much use, letter June, 1836, YU.

As early as 1823, in his inaugural address at Amherst, Humphrey had spoken on education; it should begin early; a self-denying, hardy and enterprising youngster was the goal; the family was at the core. "In order to become good citizens in after life, children must be accustomed to cheerful subordination in the family, from their earliest recollection." They would thus be prepared "to yield prompt obedience to the civil magistrate, by habitual subjection to their parents." Humphrey may have rehearsed on shipboard the ideas which resulted in a series of articles, titled "Thoughts on Education," published in 1838 in the New York *Observer*, and reprinted by Barnard in the early editions of the *Connecticut Common School Journal*. The goals of schooling were civic and social, and the means obvious—better schoolhouses, gradation of classes, well regulated and governed schools, a longer school year, and, above all, more qualified teachers.

> Whether your darling child is to be an ornament, or a burden and curse to society; is to be saved or lost, may depend far more than you are aware of, or than you will ever know until the judgment, upon the character and qualification, the faithfulness of unfaithfulness of the schoolmaster.[65]

From Heman Humphrey Henry Barnard learned the litany from which he would never deviate.

The two delegates sailed March 24 and were nearly six weeks at sea. Barnard again kept a journal of his trip, and it remains marvelously alive and honest, even when the prose is stilted, the jottings of a somewhat romantic yet sensible young man, setting out, as he felt, almost alone, on the great adventure. His mood was mixed, excited, apprehensive, and nostalgic. He was "leaving the home of my childhood . . . and the country of my pride and love." In his farewell—and he saw this trip as a rite of passage—he noted his obligations and debts to his father, a "most fond and indulgent parent," and to his sister "an almost mother"—just a hint that he may have felt the lack of a real mother. He was seasick at first, but he was soon able to relish the ship "posting in the ocean"; at night he stood watch with the captain, a "situation . . . of great solemnity" with the "brilliant phosforesence . . . a milky way of a mimic heaven." His mood fluctuated as the voyage wore on. He felt so shy he could not bring himself to speak to the captain's wife, so he read, a "beautiful story" by

---

65. Typed fragment of speech, TC. *CCSJ* I, 1 (August 1838): 63. James Humphrey, the son, was a member of Congress in 1863–67 and was instrumental in the establishment of the Department of Education which his friend Barnard was to head. See also *AmJEd* VIII (August 1826), for review of the 1823 speech.

Miss Martineau, while he watched a "picturesque" scene of the "frolick-some passengers" who played at games; blindman's buff later seemed "ludicrous." His pedantic nature noted the fact that the Captain over-hauled the letterbag containing more than 6,000 letters and packages, a "striking illustration of the extent of commerce" between the country and England. He listened with interest to the sailors, noting especially one who had served on a slaver; "I intend to gather from his lips, a recital of the horrors of the middle passage." At long last, after a period in the doldrums, both he and the ship, he knew that they were approaching land, and excitement took over. He felt like shouting at the "newness of life—I am so nervous I can scarcely write." The travelers landed that night in Liverpool, and the next morning he got lost, walking in wonder about the city. He saw such numbers of children that it looked as if "forty or fifty schools had just emptied."[66]

Many letters record the rest of the trip. Barnard employed the same method as he had before, careful notes, repeated versions.

> I will transcribe word for word the notes which I took on the top of the mountain and after my descent. . . . It is my custom to do this every day so that when I return by merely consulting these notes I will recall the entire scene and the actual impression of my travels.

Four pages of notes were not unusual. It seems that his letters were pub-lished, in the Boston *Atlas*, and, according to Humphrey, much read.[67] At times some were formulaic as if taken verbatim from guidebooks (at Stonehenge he noted the diameter of the ring of the thirty stones as well as their height and width), but elsewhere he wrote with simplicity and feeling—of Wordsworth haying at Ambleside, of the spa at Baden. Over-all he was, from the first day in Liverpool when he bought a more modish hat and added an inch to the heels of his shoes, totally happy; again and again he spoke of his good health and his brown cheeks. Even blisters from several days of Highland hiking were improved by a pot of "good porter."[68]

The immediate goal of the journey was London which the travelers reached after visits to Chester, Bath, Bristol, Salisbury (where he stayed with a sister of Mr. Bache of Wellesborough), Stonehenge, and Stratford. In the great metropolis he "felt a childlike admiration" for all he saw, and

---

66. Journal, NYU. This thin volume only takes Barnard to Liverpool. In the Watkinson Collection there is another journal, numbered 5, in a similar notebook, which records Barnard's steps from London north and to Ireland; my thanks to Margaret Saxe who transcribed it.

67. Letter, September 16, 1835, YU. Letter from Humphrey, July 2, 1835, TC.

68. Letters, May 5, 6, 9, June 4, 26, 1835, YU.

he saw so much. He was impressed by the courtesy of the English, especially of the helpful police, by the convenience of the omnibus, by the enormous plate glass windows and the equally enormous cart horses ("I will make inquiries on the subject"), and by the letters delivered by hand; in Hartford you had to call at the post office. By hand came the official invitation to Henry Barnard, as Representative of the Connecticut Peace Society, to attend the Convention of the Society for the Promotion of Permanent and Universal Peace. Barnard was notably silent on the sessions of the convention—it was merely a good excuse for a trip to Europe. But he did address it once, in a properly deferential role, seconding a motion of Dr. Humphrey's. The motion had referred to the conversion of the Jews, the heathen, and the infidel, and Barnard soared in his remarks:

> And if the first announcement of the great principles of our Society "Peace on Earth" was hailed with songs of celestial spirits, how will the final anthem be celebrated! What anthems of gladness will roll through the heaven! How the morning stars will sing together and all the sons of God shout for joy.

Also at the Peace Society he met a Mr. Bevard, "one of the oddest men," who "wriggles like an eel when he talks."[69]

On his first day in London, Henry had attended the anniversary celebration of the British and Foreign Bible Society at Exeter Hall (where he was "bothered" by clapping in a religious meeting); later he went to the Royal Society and, introduced by Benjamin Silliman, the Royal Geological Society. William Crawford, a diligent advocate of good causes, called on him with a book on the subject of prison reform and an invitation to visit the Milbank Penitentiary; he also got Barnard an introduction to the Superintendent of the Lunatic Asylum at Harwell and promised to lend Barnard copies of the Parliamentary Reports on the subject. Barnard was concerned with the right issues and to meet the right people. Early in his visit he took tea with Thomas Carlyle; John Stuart Mill was a fellow guest, and politics and party realignment were the topics. Barnard toured Parliament, noting that a dwarf kept the door, and found the chamber "without elegance or convenience." In the Commons he was especially impressed by O'Connell's "ready talent at debate." He was not particularly awed by the Lords—the Peers looked all "like an ordinary collection of men" and the Hall was a "narrow, contemptible room." Lord Brougham did live up to his admirer's expectations, but Melbourne was "a confused speaker [who] looks like a lazy man and a good liver." Wel-

---

69. Letter from Bowers, May 16, 1835, CHS; speech, copy NYU, must have been delivered before May 28 when Bowers sent Barnard the proof. MS of speech, TC.

lington in the House was no better, but seeing him review the troops, "a splendid display," was a different matter. The Iron Duke was "a fine horseman and has an enormous visage and nose enough for two."

Barnard had a hard time with his conscience in London. His good republican soul rebelled at monarchy with all its trappings. The jewels in the Tower made him muse "both at the vast splendor and the utter uselessness of the display." It made him feel better to describe the old queen as "a homely, good-natured looking old woman," but his not-so democratic self was delighted that she smiled and bowed to him. The class system bothered him, even as he enjoyed some of its advantages. He loved the elegance of the crowds at the Epsom Races, yet "it stirs my bile that the people of England will any longer by ridden by nobility." He was, after all, an American, with ideals of the Puritan and the democrat; yet he was also developing a taste for the finer things.[70]

Over and over, Barnard emphasized the serious purpose of his trip. His object was "to see what was peculiar in the countries I am in." London was cosmopolitan, and he wanted to "try every mode of life in order to see the English people under every variety of aspect." So North he went, down the Thames by steamer, to Hull, then York with its magnificent minster "more the creation of his hands who fashioned the mountains, than the work of man." With his classmate, Brooks, he visited Fountains Abbey (a ruin inferior to Tintern Abbey) on the way to the Lake District. They hiked, more than thirty miles in two days, past miserable villages, talking to incomprehensible Yorkshiremen. Mr. Wordsworth did not disappoint them, nor did the majesty of Scafell and Great Gable, both of which they climbed. On to Scotland, where Abbottsford and the huge flocks of sheep got equal billing. The former was "a picture of his [the author's] mind," the "whole amount . . . a piece of Romance"; the sheep "the most singular and beautiful thing of the kind I ever saw." The hyperbole is delightful, and one can see Henry, increasingly liberated from obligation, bubbling with the newness of life. In a thoroughly romantic fashion, he and Williams, who had joined his classmates, sauntered along, reading *The Lady of the Lake*; Brooks always wanted to hurry. Some seriousness remained however. In Edinburgh he breakfasted with the Cruikshanks, "friends of all good objects," and he met DeQuincey. He loved the Scottish capital, "the most beautiful city I have seen . . . [it] surpasses London in its solidity." And the castle's brooding presence, was so picturesque.

70. Letters from Crawford, April 23 and May 29, 1835, CHS; from John Musgrave, June 2, 1835, giving tickets for the Lords, CHS; letters May 13, June 2, 4, 7, 10, YU. The republican response to aristocratic England was common; see for instance Jonathan C. Messerli, *Horace Mann: A Biography* (New York: Knopf, 1972), 388–92.

The young Americans' trip to the Western Isles was nearly a disaster. Iona was miserable, squalid huts and wretched children. On the way to Mull the steam burst, necessitating a walk across the island in the driving rain, and then a "timid boatman" refused to ferry them to Oban. It was a relief to arrive in flourishing Glasgow and to a warm bath. Barnard did not seem to notice the urban poor, but he was angered in Scotland by the landed nobility who lived off the labor of their tenants. "It makes me fiercely democratic to see how poor human nature is trod upon in this Old World." Poverty was worse in Ireland despite "magnificent Dublin," yet in all his comments he remained dispassionate and, as when he found some Irish beggars "amusing," aloof. He reflected New England puritan prejudice when he commented "nobody need be poor, who will work industriously," and nativism when he added that it would be a blessing to the United States if immigration of the "bellicose" Irish could be halted. Let his native land remain homogeneous, distilling the best of the old world, which he yearned to emulate, with the republican equality and small town simplicity he wanted to preserve.[71]

This young Barnard was very much an American abroad, for all he professed the wish not to consort with Americans. On July 4, nostalgically, he lifted a glass of wine, in the company of friends, to celebrate the national holiday. "My heart lept for joy at the sight of the Star Spangled Banner, floating from a ship from 'down East.'" He maintained a lively interest in news from Connecticut, especially political news. The Whigs had been roundly defeated in the May elections, and he was "appalled" that his state was to be represented in Congress by "such men" as the Jacksonians; "how downcast are the friends of goodness and good principles." When in England he sounded like a liberal: "Well, when I see how the mass of men in the old world are trodden down by the few, I could wish, and will strive . . . to secure a better lot for America." When he thought of home, he reverted to his innate conservatism.[72]

In some of his letters Barnard worried about his elderly father, and he assured his brother that he would return if needed. Nevertheless he picked up the pace of his trip and became wholeheartedly the tourist. He strolled through Oxford, with reflections on architecture and not education; he climbed Mt. Snowden, in the mist and fog; he returned to London where he felt very much at home; and then he crossed the channel (proud that despite the rough crossing he did not get sick) to the low countries. One myth about this continental tour, perpetuated by Barnard's early memorialists, must be immediately dispelled. There is absolutely no evidence

71. Journal, TC. Letters, May 6–7, June 4, 19, 26, July 7, 1835, YU.
72. Letters, May 6, 30, July 7, 14, 1835, YU.

that he went to Europe to study education. He may have discussed the topic with Brougham, although he never said that he did, but the only laws we know he studied were those on prison reform. He certainly did not have as his chief object a visit with Pestalozzi, as one biographer asserted, for the great educator had been dead for nearly a decade. Among Barnard's papers is an undated invitation to visit Hofwyl, and in his notes for his autobiography he said he visited Fellenberg, but he never mentioned such a visit in his letters home, even in one that speaks of Mr. Gibbs of Boston, who was about to leave his boys at the famous school. Barnard's only comment is significant: "for one, I would prefer to see an American boy educated in America—with an American soul—feelings and prejudices."[73]

If England had produced heady sensations in Barnard, Europe was positively intoxicating. All summer he toured, starting in Antwerp and ending in Italy. Now he was really in a foreign land, with the names, the languages, "the grotesque appearance" of the low country houses. As he had done on his southern tour, he wrote formal and stylized accounts, clearly intended for publication, and chatty, detailed ones for his family. A trip up the Rhine, in the company of an English "noble and his lady" was glorious, although "no where so majestic as the Hudson. It nowhere reflects the stern grandeur of the Highlands or lingers amid such soft green meadows as adorn the Beautiful Connecticut," and the "decayed and decaying houses" contrasted poorly with his "own smiling villages." A musical festival at Wiesbaden, with 500 instruments, was impressive, but it was "revolting" to see the ladies gamble at Baden. That spa had all the appearance of an American village, but "its moral and immoral accomplishments were altogether foreign. . . . I hope we shall never see that advance in civilization." All was folly and dissipation—yet he noted in minute detail every detail of the ladies' appearance, claiming "the manners of each may be studied in one view and lessons to avoid or follow can be obtained." Among other details he discovered national character in the eating habits of his fellow diners: the English were clannish and complaining, the French merely shrugged, and the Germans devoured everything. He did not like German food, finding it too greasy. But in Switzerland when he dined with the Count de Sellon, and his lovely daughter, the food was superb: soup, fish, beef, mutton, chicken, assorted puddings and pies, fruits from the count's own orchards, six wines, most from his vineyards; coffee was taken on the terrace with the view of Mt.

73. See Hughes, *Barnard*, 565. Invitation, TC, ms notes, TC. Barnard also said he visited Guizot and Thiers in France, which is possible as the journal from the time of his French stay is lost; one suspects, however, that in old age he claimed he had met the major figures in education very early on.

Blanc, illuminated by the setting sun. The meal surpassed the conversation, for the count, leader in the peace movement though he was, didn't speak much English. And Barnard knew no French.[74]

To his sister Betty he described Germany's lovely gardens and the German respect for public property. "It is the burning disgrace of our country that we cannot keep our fingers from spoiling what would otherwise remain a delight to see." He wrote of the houses and markets, and of the vineyards, full of women working at the harvest. "What a sight for a wine and woman admirer like myself." To his brother John he described an avalanche of pigs being driven past his inn window, squealing on their way to market. Brother Chauncey, the engineer, got a careful description of the Simplon Pass, forty-two miles, with over fifty bridges, six or eight tunnels, switchbacks, all beautifully graded. One can imagine with what expectation the family must have waited for the letters and with what joy they must have read them. None was to have a similar trip.

In Switzerland Henry climbed to St. Bernard's Hospice (which he spelled Barnard), and he was amazed to discover that the monks in that isolated spot already knew of the nativist riots in New England. Then down to Italy he went. Lago Maggiore's "quiet beauty sank with a holy influence upon our heads." He lived "a daily life" in Rome for a month, where he inspected the Dome (one assumes of St. Peter's), and visited Naples briefly. Italy was all "the beautiful and the graceful," even if the Italians did try to cheat him, and the customs officials at every border wanted a bribe. The record is sketchy for this section of his trip, for few letters remain, and the autobiographical fragment in the Trinity College papers is merely an outline with a tantalizing phrase ("sad incident" in Rome); there are even fewer records from Paris where he spent part of the winter. But he was already thinking of home, perhaps beginning to weary of the constant movement. First he said he would be back by Christmas, but Paris offered too much "for the man of the world and the man of science," enough "food for reflection for a life." He did arrange to have shipped home quantities of "extra old Holland gin of the most exquisite flavor and smell," and he ordered some "instruments"—surely surveyor's—in a superior case for his elder brother.[75] Then, after another trip to London, he finally sailed for home.

In Hartford, Pa was not well and was probably demanding. Henry

---

74. *Fragment du récit d'une visite faite au comte de Sellon* (Geneva: Impr. Bonnant, 1837). This was a translation of Barnard's account in the September 1835 Peace Advocate, a journal to which he sent a stylish account of his day with the count.

75. Letters, July 27, 28, August 1, 6, 9, 25, 29, September 17, 20, 25, 28, 30, October 1, 1835, YU. Letters to Chauncey, November 20, 1835, CHS, from John to Chauncey, February 28, March 6, 1835, CHS.

spelled John, in the nightly watches at the sickbed, and pondered his future. It was easy to fall into the old patterns, although some of his tastes, for wine for example, were new. There was ample time to write to friends and to read, and he had enough money to buy books, ordering boxes of them from his London agent; the house which in his childhood had nary a book was beginning to house a library.[76] These book orders reveal his interests. Five of the books on one list are on the theory and practical treatment of mental illness; there was a three volume summary of poor law legislation; a complete set of Bolingbroke and several histories (one of which the poor agent had to seek in over twenty bookstores); finally, the complete set of both the *Retrospective Review* and the *Westminster Review*. Absent are any works on education.

Although during this time Barnard fretted that law would bring "little pecuniary inducement" and considered going into business, he had enough money, even with his book purchases, to consider speculation in land. Ashbel Smith was cautious but suggested that Henry come to the southwest to survey the situation himself; E. P. Grant, on the other hand, guaranteed ten percent profit if Barnard followed his lead and invested in Ohio. Barnard's replies to these letters are gone, and so is any record of his financial or speculative dealings. He lived comfortably most of his life, expending large amounts and earning little, so perhaps he was a better businessman than later events seem to suggest.[77]

We cannot know if Chauncey, senior, quizzed his son about his intentions and prospects during those final six months; the father may have regretted that he was not to live to see his dreams for, and investment in, his youngest realized. But the issue of his future nagged Henry, and once again he turned to his friends for counsel. One tried to pry him loose from Hartford.

> Barnard, why do you stay there? Why do you hide your talents and energies under the miserable *peck measure* system of rascality that always has and always will disgrace the politics of your native State?

There were "hundreds of places to settle, great opportunities" in the West; why not "leave the ease of the East" and the literary life of home "for the

---

76. Letter from Vienna, J. G. Schwarz, July 1836, NYU; Schwarz promised to buy twelve dozen bottles of Tokay wine and twelve dozen of another wine, but a year later, May 28, reported the wine was of poor quality. Bill from Edward Rainford, London, August 16, 1836, NYU. Letter to Loomis, November 26, 1836.

77. Letter to Loomis, November 26, 1837YU; letters from W. M. Matson, November 19, 30, 1836, NYU; from Smith, September 27, October 31, 1836, NYU; from Grant, February 7, 1837, NYU. Grant also asked Barnard to send him sugar beet plants, mulberry trees and gooseberry bushes.

rough and tumble of a profession." But the young man would not go West; caution or duty, kept him in Connecticut. Another urged Barnard to be more active in politics, and more partisan. "Why not make a distinct and spirited appeal to the democrats in your papers? . . . Keep up the excitement and increase it," he wrote as the time for local elections approached. But even in his youth Barnard was not comfortable with the actuality of partisan forays, whatever his vocabulary.[78]

He seems to have considered starting a lyceum, and he resumed his speech-making. It had been the American Peace Society that had sent him to Europe, and quite naturally the board of that organization wanted to hear about the convention. They resolved that he should speak in Litchfield, Norwich, Providence, and Boston—his first efforts out of the state; it may have been through his speech-making that he was introduced to the schoolmen reformers of his neighbor states. Among his papers are notes for a lecture which he later said was given in 1836, to the Goodrich Association, a lecture he repeated in New Haven, Norwich, and Litchfield. He listed among the topics, the lack of professional preparation for teachers, especially the lack of instruction relevant to the national industries. The United States had nothing comparable to the French Polytechnical Schools or the Mining Schools in Saxony. These notes just do not make sense for this period of his life. He may well have lectured on his trip, but on it he had not visited any such schools; it would be nearly two decades before he would interest himself in technical education. I suspect that in his retirement he had begun to re-write his own history.[79]

What that history was to be was not clear in 1837. Here was a handsome young man, of smallish stature (recall the added inch to the boots), with rather deep set brown eyes, thick, slightly receding brown hair, a sensitive mouth, and rather carefully trimmed sidewhiskers, an attractive, even dapper, young man. He was of a warm and affectionate disposition, devoted to family and to his many friends. Occasionally he appears as almost rakish as when he stayed on for a weekend in Kingston, New York, at a party given by a "lady of an unspellable Dutch name" where he "enjoyed myself flirting with a belle of the most generous rotundity of person."[80] But seriousness, earnestness, dominated. He was well educated and well connected by virtue of that education; he had traveled rather

78. From J. W. Andrews, October 31, 1836, TC; See also letter from Matson from Washington, March 3, 1837, where Matson rails against van Buren and the weakness of the Connecticut Congressional delegation.

79. Resolution, CHS; Fragment, TC. Letter from Emerson, March, 1836, CHS; letter to Loomis, November 26, 1837, YU.

80. The party is described in a letter to Chauncey, December 18, 1837, NYU.

extensively in this country and abroad. He was a careful observer, better of men than events, and a glutton for information, for facts and details if not for nuance and depth. His opinions reflected his background; he was convinced and secure in his convictions. He seemed secure, too, in his material comfort. An uncomplicated man, perhaps, whose life had been as smooth as his face suggested. But not a man without purpose, only without a mission.

II

WHIG

REFORMER

So far back as I have any recollection the cause of education—of the complete education of every human being without regard to the accident of birth or fortune—seemed most worthy of the consecration of all my powers, and, if need be, of any sacrifice of time, money, and labor which I might be called upon to make in its behalf. (Connecticut Common School Journal, *n.s.,* II [1855]: 11n)

In April 1837, a year after his return from Europe, Henry Barnard was elected to the Connecticut legislature.[1] His election certainly did not come unsought, as he claimed, but under quite flattering circumstances. He received the largest vote of any of the four candidates put forward and, at the age of twenty-six, was the youngest man to be honored by the state electorate. He was a sensible choice—a well-educated and traveled native son, a lawyer, if untried, with a reputation as an excellent speaker, and a moderate interest in all the right things. He also was loyal to the Whigs and a worker; in February he had chaired the local Whig convention for the first Senatorial district.[2]

---

1. The well-known statement which begins this chapter appears in Amory D. Mayo, "Henry Barnard," *Report of the Commissioner of Education, 1896–97*, chap. XVI (Washington, D.C.: Bureau of Publications, 1898), 777, in Frederick C. Norton, "Sketch of the Life of Henry Barnard," *Connecticut Quarterly* IV, 2 (1898): 261, and is repeated in Anson Phelps Stokes, *Memorials of Eminent Yale Men*, vol. 1 (New Haven: Yale University Press 1914), 261. Thus can one trace the growth of the Barnard legend.

2. Letter to Loomis, November 26, 1837, YU; letter from Andrews, April 21, 1837, TC; *Connecticut Courant* (hereafter cited as *CC*), February 18, 25, April 8, 1837.

Connecticut had kept its colonial charter as its constitution after the Revolutionary War, and although the Hartford Convention of 1814 may be viewed as the dying gasp of Federalism on the national scene, men of that persuasion continued to dominate Connecticut politics for another two decades, despite annual elections, and in contrast to neighboring states. The constitution was reformed in 1818, chiefly due to the efforts of the Toleration Party, and the Code of Laws was revised in 1821; the most significant changes were the dis-establishment of the Congregational Church and the extension of the suffrage to virtually all white males. In addition the judiciary was made independent, and the state school fund, derived from the sale of the Western Reserve, was made perpetual and was designated for the exclusive use of the schools. Connecticut was obviously stirring, but it would be a generation before the Whigs would finally be defeated. For Barnard, identification with the Whigs came naturally, based on his background, his education, and his mentors. His rather anxious desire to be counted among the very best may also have contributed.[3]

Whigs stood for a personal and social ideal: in individuals, effort and discipline, in society, order and harmony, and in both, purpose. Whigs believed fervently in material progress, but they also shared a "mutual commitment to purifying American society, to making it moral."[4] Their vision of morality was that of the homogeneous and Protestant past from which they sprang. Cities were menaces and unfamiliar, too big, filled with newcomers, and, in Halttunen's word, confidence men.[5] With their dreams of harmony and unity Whigs seemed reactionary, but they were also very pragmatic. These lawyers, merchants, new industrialists, and even their ministers, welcomed change, as long as it was controlled. And they were inventors—of intricate new machines and of various new social institutions designed to liberate constructive energy while inhibiting and redeeming destructive forces. They advocated corporate charters for a range of economic activities and novel institutions for the reformation of society. Consistent with their vision of unity, these men insisted that they were nonpartisan even when embroiled in politics; they assumed that all, once properly enlightened, would subscribe to the Whig consensus. It followed that schools became vital among the institutions chosen as agents for social goals. Whigs shared a sense in the continuity of human

3. On Connecticut history of this period, see Purchell, *Transition*, 221–62; Morse, *Neglected*, 2ff.

4. Daniel Walker Howe, *The Political Culture of the American Whigs* (Chicago: University of Chicago Press, 1979), 201–02.

5. See Karen Halttunen, *Confidence Men and Painted Women: A Study of Middle-Class Culture in America* (New Haven: Yale University Press, 1982).

development; their emphasis on the value of past experience and on the inexorable unfolding of the future led to a strong interest in history and reinforced their optimistic view of man's story. It followed that schools became vital among the institutions chosen as agents for social goals.[6]

As a complete Whig and one of the more articulate members of the legislature, Barnard may have helped draft party statements:

> The party to which we belong are proverbial for their independence of thought and action. . . . They are highminded, virtuous men, governed more by patriotic feeling than by party policy—frank, manly, and honest, they go boldly up, every man to his purpose but acting without concert, they are usually beaten by disciplined office holders . . . We are strong in numbers but even stronger in the justice of our cause.[7]

And he must have applauded with enthusiasm when Oliver Ellsworth, the newly elected governor spoke of "free institutions, where industry and integrity are a passport not only to wealth and influence, but to places of trust and distinction."[8] Barnard and his colleagues were reassured to have the local ship of state piloted by such a man as Ellsworth—a lesser man would govern poorly. But responsibility carried a burden. In an early speech Barnard had echoed his idol, Lord Brougham: "Every man must make himself as good and as useful as he can, and help at the same time to make everybody about him and all he can reach better." The young legislator had come to feel that in a true democracy, education enabled all men to succeed, by their own efforts; he expected that then all would agree, without the spirit of partisanship which served only to contaminate public discourse and action.

> Men do not rise in society here at the smile of a monarch, nor sit preeminent in wealth and honor upon entailed estates and titles. Neither do our laws, so powerful as well as so just, allow the strong or the overbearing to oppress or terrify the peaceful or feeble. Men must rise, if they rise at all, mainly by the aid of virtue and intelligence and both are held in esteem, in a good proportion to their influence.[9]

6. Howe, *Whigs*, 21ff., 36, 70–71, 127ff., 181ff.; Sidney L. Jackson, *America's Struggle for Free Schools* (Washington, D.C.: American Council on Public Affairs, 1941), chap. IX.

7. *CC*, August 4, 1837. The occasion was the repeal of the Canterbury law.

8. *CCSJ* II, 1 (August 1839): 6. The governor's specific subject was support for the common schools and for Wesleyan College which had not until this time received any state funds, due to opposition from the intellectual and religious leadership of the state —the president and faculty of Yale which feared competition.

9. *CCSJ* I, 6 (January 1839): 50. Sidney Nathans, *Daniel Webster and Jacksonian*

The challenge of the times was that Connecticut, like the rest of the nation, was changing. The population was increasing rapidly, and immigration brought diversity. No longer was there ethnic unity, nor was Congregationalism the faith of all of the fathers. The newcomers and refugees from the faltering farms tended to concentrate in the swelling cities, attracted by jobs available in the new manufacturing concerns. Speculation, risk, expansion, were the order of the day, and the opportunistic entrepreneurs, who tended to be Whigs, flourished. The Erie Canal, that stupendous accomplishment, stood as a symbol of the new order and served as a stimulus accelerating the rapid economic change. The canal provided jobs for unskilled immigrants and also helped funnel men and women to the greener pastures of the West; six new states were added to the Union between 1810 and 1821, beginning to tilt the nation geographically, economically, culturally, and politically away from the Eastern seaboard. The West attracted; even Henry Barnard had toyed with the idea of joining the flow.

New interests and new men, startling evidence of a changing society, the impersonality of the city displacing the intimacy of the village, along with all these came confusion. Two major depressions, one in 1819 and another after the Panic of 1837, introduced modern economic dislocation, unemployment and poverty on a scale unfamiliar to those accustomed to the self-sufficient and self-contained market economy. Even that certainty, Puritanism, was shaken, within by the Unitarian heresy, without by a multitude of sects and a bold Roman Catholic Church.

Politics, too, were changing. The abolition of the property qualification in East, coupled with the expansion of the more democratic West, resulted in an enlarged electorate of white males, and many of these new voters had very different concerns than their Whig opponents. It was an intensely political time. Men not only argued; they voted, and consistently in large numbers. Connecticut ranked third in the nation in voter turnout, averaging over 77 percent in presidential years during this period. A new factor was the strength of the two party system. As Daniel Feller points out, "sectionalism gave way to partisanship by 1840." Prior to that time sectional loyalty largely determined political stance; now, increasingly, voters aligned themselves with one of the two emerging parties.[10] Elections were close and frequently bitter, and electors were stridently loyal to party, united by custom, and common fears and foes, more than

---

Democracy (Baltimore: The Johns Hopkins University Press, 1973), 41ff., emphasizes the polarity of the party of the wise and the party of the people.

10. Daniel Feller, *The Public Lands in Jacksonian Politics* (Madison: University of Wisconsin Press, 1984), xvi and chap. 8.

by ideals and platforms. Whigs stood, in the main, for social homogeneity and economic diversity, governmental intervention, and moral absolutes, while the Democrats believed, for the most part, in social diversity but a traditional economy, local authority, and governmental restraint.

The Era of Good Feelings was over, and the Age of the Common Man loomed. Reading the contemporary press, one is struck by the raucous rancor, the irresponsibility by most modern standards, of the party organs such as the Connecticut *Courant* (Whig) and the Hartford *Times* (Democrat). There was also a social dimension to this political change. After about 1840 the old Standing Order was replaced by a class of self-made entrepreneurs and dissenters; like their predecessors they sought political office, as Whigs usually, for they sought to belong.[11] Henry Barnard, the son of a former sea captain and certainly a self-made man, had more in common with this second group, the lesser elite, than with the Wadsworths and Sigourneys he cultivated.

The shift was an evolution, though, rather than a revolution, and politics in Connecticut during the antebellum period were in utter confusion. By 1832 the Democratic Party was ready to rival the Whigs, and in the next year Van Buren paid a visit to Hartford; perhaps his influence helped them to win the legislature for the first time that year. But the following year the Whigs elected the governor, and in 1835 they narrowly prevailed in the Congressional elections. The Democrats swept back, in both the state and national races, in 1836. Back came the Whigs to the legislature, with Barnard among them, the next year, and in 1838 they also elected the governor. The Whigs managed to control the state until 1842, when they were shoved aside, not to return to power until 1848. In some years national issues, the tariff in 1833, the bank in 1837, the Mexican War in the 1840s, were paramount; in others temperance, local improvements (such as a bridge over the river at Hartford), or school reform and the competing concern for local autonomy in 1842, swung the voters.[12]

Henry Barnard was returned to the legislature three times, between 1837 and 1839; unlike his contemporary, Horace Mann, after 1839 he never again stood for public office. He seems, with deference befitting a newcomer, to have played a minor role in the 1837 session. In the opening session he heard the Whig speaker, Stillman Wightman, extol

11. Robert Dahl, *Who Governs* (New Haven: Yale University Press, 1961), 2–30; this study focuses on New Haven, but Dahl's point is valid for Hartford and the state. See also Morse, *A Neglected Period*, 282–83; Meyers, *Jacksonian*, 149; Pessen, *Jacksonian*, 55–56.

12. For the political developments see Morse, *A Neglected Period*, 84ff., 19ff., 334–35, and Michael F. Holt, "Winding Roads to Recovery: The Whig Party from 1844–1848," in Maizlish and Kushma, *Essays*, 41ff.

the spirit of the age, justly celebrated for its benevolence, enterprise, love of liberty and ceaseless exertions for the promotion of the comfort and happiness of the human race.

Wightman called for a broad program of improvements, so that "the blessings of government" would fall "like the dews of Heaven" upon all. The Democratic Governor, Henry Edwards, adopted a less lofty tone, asking for reform of the law on attachments, a program of internal improvements, and a minerological and geological survey of the state; he also reported that the school fund was prosperous.[13]

The young representative from Hartford was placed on the special joint committee on the recommended survey and later that year accompanied the author of the study, when he was working in the Hartford area.[14] The only bill Barnard introduced was one on jails, and in his only recorded speech, delivered on May 23, he spoke for some forty minutes in opposition to an amendment to the constitution designed to limit the tenure of judges, a perennial Democratic position, and in his words, a "seminal principle of mischief." In the speech he displayed eloquence and some political savvy, deftly quoting Van Buren's position (in 1821) supporting an independent judiciary. He also gave a hint of the embryonic scholar—he traced the history of the judicial system from the acts of William and Mary, he quoted from the Constitutional debates of 1787, and he cited innumerable statistics.[15]

During this session neither the Whig leadership nor Barnard devoted anything but routine attention to matters of the common schools. General amelioration of society, Wightman's "ceaseless exertions for the promotion of the comfort and happiness of the human race," occupied them. Whigs were reformers, and reformers tended to be Whigs. One way to cope with the increasing sense of insecurity fostered by the rapidly changing economic and social scene was to try to stop parts of it, to return to the harmony and stability of the pre-modern era, while, ironically, fostering the very economic forces which were accelerating the social change. The Whig dream was of the idealized small, Protestant, New England town where virtue and reason prevailed. Their goal was to purge society, and to elevate the moderate, self-reliant, industrious, and moral citizen. Two means were utilized, persuasion and the voluntary benevolent organization.

13. CC, May 7, 1837.

14. Undated, typed reminiscence, TC. See letters to Percival, November 14, 1838, April 27, 1839, May 24, probably 1839, in which he agreed to an extension of the time for the survey, YU; Barnard would always need an extension.

15. Remarks of Mr. Barnard of Hartford, May 23, 1837, TC.

The humanitarian was preacher as well as social worker, dogmatist as well as pragmatist, and concerned with his own salvation as well as with the well-being of his fellows. Arthur Tappan, the highly successful capitalist, is a good exemplar. In addition to the enormous sums of seed money he gave to a variety of organizations, he was an officer in nearly a dozen worthy groups ranging from the American Education Society to the Society for the Promotion of the Common School in Greece.[16] Others were equally busy in as wide a range of causes, the relief of the poor, of seamen, of fallen women, for better prisons, new asylums, and libraries, supporting temperance, against the Sunday mails, for peace. All of the actors in the reform movement were totally and inextricably interconnected; the same men sat on the different committees, and, as a convenience, the dates of various annual national conventions overlapped. If you were for peace, as Barnard was, you were for prison reform, as he was, and usually you were also an abolitionist of some conviction, which he was not.

Connecticut, until about 1830, had been the center of reform movements, due to the combined stimuli of Yale and the Calvinism of the Second Great Awakening—a significant proportion of the reform leaders were ministers. Horace Bushnell was one of the last of the great preachers to indulge in abstract theological speculation, for more and more men of the cloth were turning their attention to life on earth. His contemporary, and rival, Lyman Beecher never seemed to forget that he had been a member of the Yale Moral Society as an undergraduate. In 1811, the year of Henry Barnard's birth, he began to agitate for the elimination of Sunday mails; in 1813, with Judge Tapping Reeve, he founded the Connecticut Society for the Promotion of Good Morals; by 1825 he was campaigning for total abstinence. Medical men and their allies among the clergy founded, in 1817, the Connecticut Asylum for the Education and Instruction of the Deaf and Dumb, and, in 1824, the Hartford Retreat for the Insane. Laymen moved from promoting religious instruction in the notorious Newgate Prison to agitating for a more humane one. Thomas W. Gallaudet was Hartford's premier reformer, the first director of the Connecticut Asylum, on the board of the Hartford Retreat, as he was of the Hartford Society for the Improvement of the Common Schools, founded in 1828; in the latter he was associated with such luminaries as Roger Sherman, the son of a signer of the Declaration of Independence, Joel Hawes, the city's leading divine, and Seth Beers, the trustee of the state's school fund.[17]

16. Bertram Wyatt-Brown, *Lewis Tappan and the Evangelical War Against Slavery* (Cleveland: Press of Case Western Reserve University, 1969), 51–52.

17. See Charles Roy Keller, *The Second Great Awakening in Connecticut* (New Haven:

Although leadership in the humanitarian reform movements was the province of the men of any community, women did play a role, and the opportunity offered to them was a vital impetus to the movement for women's rights. Women were particularly active in efforts for widows and orphans, in the temperance and peace movements, and increasingly in education. The Grimké sisters were perhaps the most renowned and persistent of the female reformers, and few were as active and public as they. More women labored behind the scenes, where institutions such as the Hartford Retreat had an auxillary ladies' society. Some have argued that the scope of these causes was consistent with the concept of the women's sphere and, combined with the private and subservient role accorded to women, served to perpetuate inequity. Such a view is unhistorical. Limited though the roles were, they did provide dedicated women with an opportunity to develop skills and confidence which would later be transferable to other arenas, and, in addition, these were the causes championed by men as well as women. Emma Willard did have to be content to have her speeches read for her as late as 1840, and Mary Lyon depended on the men who chaired her committees, but they and Catharine Beecher figured prominently in educational reform and were allies whom Barnard quoted and respected.[18]

Efforts to improve the schools of Connecticut had commenced as early as 1799 when the Reverend William Woodbridge, an instructor in a school for females, founded the Middlesex County Association for the Improvement of the Common Schools, dedicated to promoting "a systematic course of instruction, secure moral and religious principles" and to attempting to "elevate the character and the qualifications of teachers."[19] In 1816 Denison Olmstead devoted his master's oration at Yale to the "State of Education"; he found teaching poor and recommended institutions where teachers could be trained. Both of these men remained loyal to the cause for thirty years, and others soon joined them. Samuel May, another minister, James Kingsley and Hawley Olmstead, both professors

---

Yale University Press, 1942), chaps. VI–VII. Galluadet, like many concerned parents today, while active in educational reform, educated his children privately.

18. Ann Firor Scott, *Making the Invisible Woman Visible* (Chicago: University of Chicago Press, 1984), 38ff. Gerda Lerner, *The Grimké Sisters from South Carolina: Rebels Against Slavery* (Boston: Houghton Mifflin, 1967), 183ff. See *CCSJ* III, 5 (Janaury 1, 1841): 70–71, where Barnard quotes Beecher, and II, 13 (June 1840): 242–43, III, 2 (November 15, 1840): 29–30, and IV, 7 (March 15, 1842): 64, where he discusses Willard's work.

19. *AJE* IV, 12 (1858): 707–08, Barnard notes that the interest in the reform of education was motivated by the sale of the state's Western Reserve; the proceeds after long and spirited debate were allocated to the schools. See *AJE* VI, 12 (1859): 367ff., for more than twenty pages of debate, quoted verbatim.

at Yale, and Gallaudet all wrote and spoke on the condition of the schools during the twenties, and May was the catalyst for a state convention in 1826 at which the one hundred delegates agreed to form the Connecticut Society for the Improvement of the Common Schools.

Agitation by such respected leaders bore fruit; Governor Wolcott, who had cited the need for reform in his messages in 1822 and 1826, called for specific legislation in 1827: the granting of the power to tax to the school districts, the institution of the Lancastrian system in the common schools, and the encouragement of academies.[20] A legislative committee subsequently recommended that the position of the state superintendent of the common schools be created, but no action was taken. In 1828 Governor Tomlinson requested stronger state intervention to guarantee good schools: good teachers were key, he said, and they should be examined prior to assuming their duties and should be supervised by competent visitors. The supporting report from the Committee on Common Schools added a renewed call for a paid superintendent of schools but was printed, and ignored. Perhaps out of frustration, the Society for the Improvement of the Common Schools called another convention in 1830, with Noah Webster in the chair, which demanded better schools as well as better teachers. While some talked, others acted. Milo Jewett took to the lecture circuit, addressing parents and teachers in thirty-two towns throughout the state, and demonstrating new school apparatus and novel techniques. Four years later two principals, Theodore Wright of the Hartford Grammar School and John Brace of the Hartford Female Seminary, along with Gallaudet, offered a premium of $25 for the best design for new, adjustable schoolroom seats.[21]

Several points must be underlined at this juncture. One is the dominant role of the old Standing Order in this movement. The men who advocated improvement of the schools were members of the state's aristocracy. The issues were few, and had broad appeal, primarily the qualifications of teachers and the physical condition of schools, and the solutions proposed consistently required a stronger role for the state. The evolution of the movement was predictable and gradual; first came exhortation, then organization, and only when persuasion seemed ineffective, a resort to a call for action. Finally, Henry Barnard was not involved in any of these early endeavors. There was a well-founded movement for school amelioration, with an articulated agenda and effective leadership, in his native state before he adopted it as a cause.

20. Note that the governor saw no inconsistency in advocating state support of both public and private efforts.

21. Henry Barnard, *Normal Schools* (Hartford, 1851), 7 and note, *AmJEd* III, vi (June 1828): 381–82, and vii (July 1828): 443–44, summarize the Connecticut reform efforts.

It is legitimate to ask, as he might have done, why the demand for school reform at this particular time? Americans had believed always in education, for moral and social purposes; support for education for political goals was a legacy of the republican period.

> Our forefathers understood very well, that the institutions of civil liberty, and Protestant Christianity, . . . could not exist unless their foundations were laid deep and strong upon the firm base of popular education.[22]

During the antebellum period a new vision and a new urgency appeared. If America was ordained by God, if indeed progress toward the City on the Hill was possible, then, in the face of evident imperfection and immorality, education was ever more essential.

> A system of education which may give to every member of American society a portion of knowledge adequate to the discharge of his duties as a man and a citizen of the republic, is essential to the advancement of the private interest, the maintenance of public virtue, the due appreciation of talents, the preservation of a sacred regard to principle, and of a high tone of moral sentiment.

Note the easy mixing of the public and the private, and the use of the word "system." New to the discussion of the reformers in their political guise was the idea that there should be a methodical provision of education, that the states should do more than require the discharge of parental responsibility for education.

> The destiny of man is for activity and improvement; the destiny of states, that would maintain a respectable rank, is for activity and improvement.[23]

The state of Connecticut had long had schools, requiring them originally in 1650. As early as 1700 towns of over seventy families had been obliged to maintain a school, supported by taxation, for eleven months of the year, smaller towns for six. Legislation after the Revolution, in 1795 and 1799, created school societies, coterminous with the parishes, and defined their duties and the duties of the school visitors. Money from the sale of the state's Western Reserve in 1795 and from the national surplus fund in 1836 provided substantial support for the schools. Ironically, the size of the School Fund, which by Seth Beers's careful management had

22. *CCSJ* I, 4 (November 1838): 32, Judge Church speaking at the Litchfield County School Convention, October 30, 1838.

23. Walter R. Johnson, *Remarks on the Duty of the Several States in Regard to the Public Education* (Philadelphia: W. Sharpness, 1830), 2, 7.

more than quadrupled betwen 1800 and 1836, served to harm the schools; local authorities kept school only as long as the money held out, and a law of 1821 had ended the legal obligation of towns to tax for the support schools. Barnard later called this action "the most disastrous enactment ever placed on our statute book." As a contemporary observed, "With the ability to have the best schools in any state in the Union, it is acknowledged that they are surpassed by many others."[24]

It is indisputable that there were schools. In 1823, in New Haven's First School Society, there were eleven schools for children under eight, four for girls over eight, and two for "colored" children. By 1830, in addition to the college and Hopkins Grammar School, there was a Gymnasium, a boarding school for boys under ten, seven boarding schools for young ladies, a Private and Select Institution for Young Ladies, as well as a ladies' seminary, a Lancastrian school for boys and one for girls, three high schools, a "Practical Mathematics Seminar," and a Franklin Institution. Hartford, in 1836, had ten school districts, but less than half of the children of the city attended the common schools. Contemporary newspapers are filled with advertisements for private establishments, for Miss So-and-so's Female Academy, or with announcements that Mr. Blank, late of Something Academy, would be taking pupils. But still, at least two hundred children were in no school at all.[25]

None of these schools, public or private, was terribly good. Most were ill-housed in small and uncomfortable buildings, crowding in as many as eighty children of all ages, even as young as three, who came with great irregularity. All were victims of the seasons, in the winter prey to the inconstancy of parents charged with supplying wood and in the spring often emptied when chores called. Schools were kept, not taught, by youngsters often only a year or so removed from their own schooling, young men in the winter months, young women in the summer. None had any preparation for teaching, and few had much aptitude. "All was a round of haste, imperfection, irregularity, and the mere mechanical commitment of words to memory."[26] The unfortunate teachers had no equipment and no standard texts, for these were the days when teachers had to

24. Barnard, *Fifth Annual Report* (May 1850), 41. Emerson Davis, *The Half-Century* (Boston: Tappan and Whittemore, 1851), 56–58; *AJE* IV, vii (March 1858): 656–709, and XIII, xxxiii (December 1863): 724–36, "History of Common Schools in Connecticut to 1838".

25. See Butler, *Education*, 248, 260ff., 368ff., 391–92; Orwin Bradford Griffin, *The Evolution of the Connecticut School System* (New York: Teachers College Press, 1928), 28–29; Trumbull, *Memorial History*, II:631ff., quoting Barnard.

26. Catharine Beecher, *Suggestions Respecting Improvements in Education* (Hartford: Packard & Butler, 1829). The interlocking relationships among the reformers is concretely

make do with what books the children brought from home. Turnover of
teachers was high, for it was cheaper to hire a new, inexperienced one
than to give a raise to last year's, and, most teachers did not look on the
position as anything but an interim before embarking on a real career or,
in the case of women, marriage.

Then there was the matter of supervision and policy. Provision of
schooling was under local control, with power lodged in the several societies; these in turn could create districts, but under the restriction that
there could only be one school to a district and one teacher to a school.
Responsibility for hiring of teachers lay with the district committee which
also appointed the school visitors; these served without pay and provided
cursory supervision at best. Yet so strong was the tradition of local control that it was to prove a major hindrance to subsequent reform attempts.
Schools may not have been very good, but they were as good as most of
the population desired.[27]

In the 1830s a new urgency propelled the reformers. Beecher posed the
issue rhetorically: "Are liberty and intelligence, with the restraints of moral
and religious education, a blessing or a curse?" The answer was obvious,
but liberty and the moral order were in jeopardy.

> I put it to every one present, what is your security, that mob-rule,
> which has exhibited such frightful scenes of violence and lawless-
> ness in many parts of the country, sweeping before it barriers which
> have hitherto guarded the rights of property and the comforts and
> privileges of social and civil life, and mingle all in one common
> ruin? . . . Our safeguard lies in the institutions of religion and in
> our system of education.

Education could be a powerful force for the preservation of society. "There
is no defect in character, habits, or manners, but is susceptible of remedy
. . . if proper methods are made and proper facilties afforded."[28] Unanim-
ity as to the importance of education and the recognition of the inadequacy of schools were twin ideas carried forward in a common campaign
throughout the northeastern states. The problems persisted, said Daniel

---

exemplified by this volume in the Yale library; the inscription on the flyleaf is "To Mrs.
Arthur Tappan from T. W. G."—Thomas W. Gallaudet.

27. *AJE* III, xxx (March 1863): 23–144, and xxxiii (December 1863): 737–52, "Schools
as They Were Sixty Years Ago," reminiscent letters to Barnard.

28. Beecher, *Suggestions*, 43–44. She repeated these themes in her *Address to American
Women* (1845); after detailing the horrors of the French Revolution, in twenty-five pages,
she depicted mob violence in the United States. "Nothing can preserve this nation from
such scenes but perpetuating this preponderance of intelligence and virtue."

Barnard of New York, because neither the citizens, through spontaneous efforts, nor the government voluntarily, would assume the initiative for reform; what was called for was a series of associations whose members would be "literary men, actually devoted to literary avocations or pursuits" who would "make a public profession of their interest in the cause of learning and education" and "agitate, and agitate, and agitate." It was just such men who formed the Associations for the Improvement of the Common Schools in every state, leaders, struggling, in the words of Levi Woodbury, with "reasoning and action of every description . . . to improve the masses."[29]

Of course the enemy in all this was the people, volatile and unruly, speaking different tongues, professing different faiths, holding different values. The arch-enemy was Jackson and his party, always derisively labeled Loco Focos by the Whig press. It was no accident that common school reform came when it did. The extension of the franchise in the 1820s had given a political voice to nearly all white males, and the emerging Democratic party provided a voice and a forum, and the means for political competition, especially in the bustling cities. The opposition Whig politicians and reformers hoped that their efforts would fortify the dikes of the past against an inexorable tide of the future:

> educational reformers converted the limited enthusiasm with which men of conservative temperment witnessed the rise of democracy in the United States into a generous enthusiasm for democratic education. Their motives were obviously conservative in that the reforms they introduced were intended to protect the republic against the consequences of an excess of democracy. But the tendency of their thought was unmistakably liberal.[30]

For a brief moment, the Whigs and the Workingmen were allies on school matters before the leaders of the latter group came to see their interests more in economic terms, an alteration in perspective probably hastened by the dislocation and depression in mid-thirties. The result was political polarization, and the strengthening of the Democratic party, and usually the Democrats opposed school reform because they opposed taxation

---

29. Daniel D. Barnard, *Annual Address Delivered Before the Albany Institute* (Albany: Albany Institute, 1836), 36–37. Levi Woodbury, *An Address on the Remedies for Certain Defects in American Education, Delivered before Lyceums or Institutions for Education at Portsmouth and Exeter, New Hampshire, Baltimore and Annapolis, and Washington, D.C.* (Washington: W. Greer, 1842), 15.

30. Rush Welter, *Popular Education and Democratic Thought in America* (New York: Columbia University Press, 1962), 102.

and any weakening of local control, whereas the Whigs viewed schools and state intervention as prime means of social salvation.[31]

The role of the Protestant ministry should not be overlooked. Ministers preached reform and announced meetings from their pulpits; ministers served on school committees and as school visitors. The school movement owed much of its moral aura to their guidance, for, just as the eighteenth century preachers thundered against spiritual decay, their nineteenth century heirs organized against moral and civic decay. But, it must be added, their role contributed to the increasing bigotry which characterized the purportedly non-sectarian campaign; committed and narrow Protestant schoolmen were only more polite than the more violent Nativists.[32]

The Whigs believed in the common man, but it was the common man they had known, the sturdy, dependable farmers who had the sense to listen to their betters and the determination to work, to struggle, to strive to join them. The Whigs advocated education, because it provided opportunities for those seeking to rise and because it limited and channeled the forces challenging the familiar order. The Whigs supported the allied organizations dedicated to education, the lyceum movement and organizations for schooling, both common and Sabbath. Now, in Connecticut, in 1838, with control of the legislature and with a Whig governor, they were ready to act forcefully.

Henry Barnard was poised to play a more prominent role in his second session as a legislator. The partisan Hartford *Daily Courant* noted that his "character as a legislator was fully established last year, and he will undoubtedly sustain the high reputation which he had there gained." The lawyer in him again spoke against a constitutional amendment limiting judicial tenure, but the reformer in him described all county jails as "a disgrace to an enlightened, and virtuous, and humane community," and called for better ventilation and lighting in prisons as well as the segregation of juvenile offenders. As a member of the Standing Committee on the School Fund, in a highly political move, he proposed an investigation of the Fund, administered during the past ten years by the respected Democrat, Seth Beers. Barnard's greatest moment came, however, when he supported that part of the Governor's message devoted to the com-

31. Maris Vinovskis points out that in Massachusetts in 1840 the differences concerning educational policy were identified with the competitory political parties; see *The Origins of Public High Schools: A Re-examination of the Beverly High School Controversy* (Madison: University of Wisconsin Press, 1985), 26–27.

32. To Bishop Martin John Spaulding, "the system of Common Schools in this country is a monstrous engine of injustice and tyranny"; see *Common Schools in the United States Compared with Those in Europe* (Louisville, 1858).

mon schools. Editorialized the *Courant*, "The cause of common school education has been of late woefully neglected, and it will find in Mr. Barnard a most able and efficient champion."[33]

Barnard had now adopted the school cause. He had not been on the Joint Select Committee on the Common Schools in 1837, nor had he spoken in favor of the act "For the Better Supervision of Common Schools," which nearly passed. Perhaps it was the influence of Gallaudet and other schoolman reformers; perhaps he had been delegated by the Whig leadership to prepare for the coming session; or perhaps he was just opportunistic.[34] In any case, during the previous spring and summer he had done his research well, demonstrating that penchant for meticulous investigation which would become his hallmark. He visited numerous schools in the state and questioned knowledgeable reform-minded colleagues. Their replies were predictable. Reverend Hemingway of East Granby wrote describing the variety of schools in his town and their miserable state; he admitted he did not send his own children to the common school and had given up on his duties as a visitor. "I was obliged to recommend teachers wholly unfit to teach or provoke the displeasure of almost the whole community." Philip Ripley of Hartford had a simple solution: "some effective and uniform system is all that is wanted, to be put in operation by an energetic and practical Man."[35] Ripley's suggestion did not fall on unreceptive ears.

Given his activity prior to the session, Barnard must have been a member of the Joint Committee on the Common Schools, chaired by John Rockwell, for the historical and statistical thrust of their strong report reflected his work, and the words were his.

> How happens it that we are willing to pay price for the skill and labor bestowed on very many things which we deem essential to our comfort and gratification, that enables those who furnish this skill and labor, or trade in its products, soon to obtain a competency, and even to amass wealth, while the teachers of our common schools, who expend their time and talent upon what we profess to regard as the dearest to us of all that we can call our own, our children and youth, can never, *by that occupation alone* go forward in

33. Hartford *Daily Courant* (hereafter, *HDC*), May 5, 7, 8, 15, 17, 21, 25, 1838.

34. Gallaudet, in 1851, recalled that Barnard had consulted him thirteen years earlier about his career. *AJE* XXX (1880): unpaged but 199–200.

35. Letters to Barnard, April 14, 25, May 5, 1838, NYU. Despite Barnard's activity during this session, there is no evidence to support his assertion, in 1842, that he "had devoted three years of preparatory study" before undertaking the commissionership; see *CCSJ* IV, 15 (September 1, 1842): 193.

the world, support a family, and rise to fair equality, in point of property, with those around them.

The litany of faults in the schools was familiar. Too many children did not attend schools at all; teachers were poor and ill-paid; there was no classification of pupils, no "wise division of labor and of husbanding the time"; and schools were kept too briefly, "an incalculable loss to that portion of our youthful population who are too young to be otherwise industrious." The diversity of textbooks was "an evil of no small magnitude," and the deficiencies of the schoolhouses all too apparent. The committee, however, was rather circumspect in criticizing the private schools —probably a political compromise and one that later Barnard would not have favored.[36]

In a speech "of great power and eloquence," Barnard supported the report and the bill which the committee introduced. He stressed the vital importance of the quality of the teachers in the common schools. "It is idle to expect good schools until we have good teachers." Only after teachers were better trained "in the most creative art of teaching," should they be better paid and permanently appointed to their posts. Then, in a Brougham-like peroration, he introduced a theme he would repeat again and again, and one which he most fervently believed:

> and the common school will no longer be regarded as common because it is cheap, inferior, and patronized only by the poor, and those who are indifferent to the education of their children, but common as the light and the air, because its blessings are open to all and enjoyed by all . . . that day will assuredly come, and it will bring along a train of rich blessings which will be felt in the field and the workshop, and convert many a hope into a circle of unfading smiles. For one, I mean to enjoy the satisfaction of the labor, let who will enter the harvest.[37]

The speech, and Barnard's decision to adopt school reform as a cause, was noted and appreciated. Wrote one admirer "Go on, my dear friend, in your great and benevolent plans, and leave little things to little men."[38] He would go on, for another sixty years, devoted to a single cause, with singular enthusiasm and commitment.

The bill, which passed unanimously, was brief. It provided for a Board

36. *CCSJ* I, 1 (August 1838): 2–5.

37. *CC*, May 12, 19, 26, June 2, 9; for Barnard's speech, see *NS*, 13.

38. Letter from Henry Holmes, M.D., May 7, 1838, typed copy, TC; Holmes was writing to Barnard to remind him to nominate the doctor as one of the directors of the state prison.

of Commissioners of the Common Schools, consisting of the Governor and the Commissioner of the School Fund, *ex officio*, and eight others, one from each county. The Board was directed to submit an annual report on the conditions of the schools in the state to the legislature, along with recommendations for their improvement and better organization, "and all such matters relating to popular education, as they may deem expedient to communicate." School visitors were obliged to report to the clerks of several districts by April 1 of each year and the clerks to send the returns to the Commissioners by the tenth of the same month; no money from public funds would be available unless the society complied with the statutory obligations described. Provision was made for a secretary to the Board "who shall devote his whole time, if required" to Board matters, and who was to receive not more than three dollars per day and expenses.[39] Thus, the law was at best permissive and directive; the only provision with teeth in it was the one linking the payment of state money to the performance of the school visitors.

The new board, made up of the Governor, William Ellsworth, and the Commissioner of the Fund, Seth Beers, with Wilbur Fiske (the president of the new Wesleyan College in Middletown), John Hall, Andrew Judson, Charles W. Rockwell, Leland Howard, Hawley Olmstead, William P. Burrall, and Henry Barnard, was approved by the Senate on June 6 and got right to work, meeting in Hartford on June 15 and 16. First in order of business was the selection of the secretary; on Barnard's nomination Thomas Gallaudet was elected. He declined, according to Barnard because the salary was insufficient for a man with his familial obligations, whereupon his younger friend vowed to raise an extra amount from private sources. Gallaudet, however, remained adamant. The obvious second choice was Barnard, although he was loath to accept, partly because he had been offered a lucrative law partnership, and partly because he was concerned that some might view his sponsorship of the law as an act of self-interest. He did finally agree to serve for six months without salary, while the board completed its organization; at the end of that time he resigned, to be reappointed for another six months and then annually until the position was abolished in 1842.[40]

The appointment was doubly advantageous, for Barnard and for Con-

39. *CCSJ* I, 1 (August 1838): 6. *CC*, while noting the passage of the bill, devoted no editorial to it; such comment was continually directed to matters of partisan politics.

40. *HDC*, June 6, notes the confirmation of the board. On the back of a letter from John T. Norton, July 10, Barnard noted "My own connection with the Board is only temporary—six months at the furthest," NYU. For Barnard's account of Gallaudet's refusal see *CCSJ* V, 2 (October 1851): 46–47; and ibid. 4, (December 1851): 136–38, for Barnard's letter, April 26, 1850, to the Norwich Aurora.

necticut. He had found an outlet for his very considerable energy and intelligence, one which provided him with wide latitude and required diligence and a measure of gregariousness, as well as his proven skills of research. That the job also demanded organizational skills and political prowess, areas where Barnard was weak, only time would tell. The state, into the bargain, received the devoted service of a man who committed himself, and could afford to commit himself, to the betterment of her schools, and who in the process would lay the foundation for state action in education.

The newly appointed secretary had already been recognized as an orator of considerable skill; his new prominence made him even more in demand as a speaker. He again delivered the July 4 oration in Hartford and was invited to repeat the speech in the major centers of the state, New Haven, Norwich, New London, Middletown, and Norwalk. Here was a splendid opportunity to spread the gospel, and here we can discover Barnard's ideas on education. The Whig in him recognized the cities as vibrant centers of trade, of politics, of fashion, and of talent, but in the cities sharp contrasts dominated, between "high intelligence and wretched ignorance—overgrown wealth . . . and abject poverty." The remedies he proposed were those of the humanitarian reformer, designed "to elevate and purify": for the young criminal, a House of Reformation for Juveniles "where correct moral and industrious habits could be formed"; for the poor, the improvement of their lot by the provision of employment, not charity, and "through personal intercourse, by awakening their minds a self-respect and force of thought to begin to rise above the adverse circumstances of their lot"; for poor families, better homes, built by "men of property," for a fair return, of course, homes which were attractive and convenient; for the children, efforts to cultivate a taste for flowers and music; for all, rich and poor alike, "innocent and rational amusements" and a "broad, liberal, and cheap system of educational influences," including schools, books, libraries, lectures, and "cabinets," all of which "must be spread before and around every child, youth, and grown person in our cities."

As was fitting for the man recently appointed to leadership of the schools of the state, Barnard detailed a system of schooling for the entire community: primary schools for children under eight, with women teachers and moral goals; secondary ones, for children from eight to twelve, with trained teachers, male and female, as both influences were desirable "at this stage of moral education, and in the formation of manners"; and high schools, with two departments, a classical one and one which would at the same time "furnish an education preparatory for the pursuits of commerce, trade, manufacture, and the mechanical arts." In addition, there should be departments for "colored" children and evening schools for working ones. All the schools should have libraries "of useful and interesting books" and a variety of equipment such as maps and globes, so that the teacher "may be vivid, accurate, and practical," for it was only by the means of such resources that the teacher could provide instruction in every subject, and the student could be empowered to go beyond the teacher and the text. The entire system should be administered by a full-time superintendent, supported by an elected board, with annual taxation.[41]

Here is a detailed plan for public education in a comprehensive whole. Others had called for the gradation of schools, but Barnard outlined a sequence. Many were beginning to insist on the importance of women as educators and nurturers in the early years of schooling, but Barnard gave women an equal role, at least until the age of twelve, when most children left school in any case. His elitism and racism is clear in the proposal for separate schools for black and working children, but it is to his credit that he included them in his system at all. Although he certainly reflected a conservative consensus, when he spoke of moral goals and the formation of manners, he also struck a utilitarian note in calling for a department for the useful arts, parallel to the classical one. Here he reflected Whig pragmatism and concern for material progress, but he may also have been attempting to attract to the public sector students drawn to the English departments of contemporary academies or to the private schools, so common in the cities, which were devoted to commercial arts. Consistent with his practical thrust was his emphasis on pedagogical innovation; teachers should be vivid and interesting.

Perhaps the most provocative notion in the entire speech was Barnard's conception of a horizontal, community-wide "broad, liberal, and cheap" system of education. Fully as important as the schools to the community were the libraries, associated indirectly within the schools or located elsewhere, and the lyceum, with its classes to teach language and debate so students could acquire the English essential for employment and for participation in the public duties of the citizen (here he was thinking of the immigrant worker). Quite separate, but supplementary, would be lectures

> to supply interesting and profitable topics of conversation, stimulate inquiry, direct the reading of the community, bring all classes together in sympathy with the great truths and noble deeds, and

41. For an outline of this speech see *OHGS*, 231–32; Barnard may have embellished this speech before the 1878 publication, but the section of the speech on high schools is in *AJE* III, viii (March 1857): 185–87.

thus break down the prejudices which grow out of non-acquaintance, and cultivate happier social relations.

Rounding out the educational facilities for the community would be two collections or museums, one for Natural History, the other of Useful Arts, and a Gallery of Painting, Sculpture, and Engravings. Barnard conceded that many of his suggestions were already realities in various towns and cities, thanks to the efforts of individuals, but these were separate entities. He recommended that all should be "extended, perfected, and brought together under a more efficient organization." Only through such a broad configuration of education, based on the common schools of course, and united in some rational system, could men escape classification according to their employment.

Here is the quintessential Barnard; here are his leitmotifs. He emerges as high-minded, moral, and optimistic, a reformer, a pragmatist, and a democrat. Of the goals of education, the social one was paramount—the uniting of all classes. All children were entitled to the best schooling, supported by the community resources, and equal to that provided in any private school. But schools were merely the foundation stone for community-wide learning, for education should be continual and constant. Of secondary importance was the utilitarian goal of education; it should aid the citizen in his public duties, and the worker in his daily tasks.

There were, admittedly, limits to this vision. The community Barnard called on was certainly that of his youth; by stressing English instruction he probably had the immigrant in mind; assimilation was part of his agenda. The entire tone of the piece gives the impression that it was the young male whom Barnard sought to educate in his lectures and collections; although later he championed secondary schools for girls, he recognized limits to their opportunities. He accepted the current practice of segregation, and, in advocating evening classes, implicitly he tolerated the prevailing evil of child labor. But at least he attempted to make provision for these children at a time when contravention of the 1813 law, requiring minimal schooling for factory children, was rampant. In stressing the unique qualifications of women as teachers of the young, Barnard echoed Beecher and Willard, and significantly, at this time he did not advance the economic argument that female teachers were cheaper. A key failure here, and in subsequent works of Barnard, is what he did not discuss; he really was not concerned with what was learned in schools, so long as it was useful. Curriculum never was important to him, although pedagogy increasingly would be.

Such were the goals of the young secretary; with remarkable energy he set out to achieve them. His initial directive from the board was "to hold Conventions of School Visitors and Teachers, and friends of popular education generally in the several Counties . . . and to establish a periodical" devoted to education as soon as possible. But first, Barnard sought advice from an experienced (by one year) hand; he wrote to Horace Mann.

> The inability of Mr. Gallaudet to accept the Secretaryship of our Board has thrown upon me the duties of that most responsible office for which I feel myself poorly qualified. I am therefore very anxious to see you, who have been over the same ground in your state, which I must traverse in Connecticut.

Mann replied promptly. "I welcome you most cordially as a fellow laborer in the cause of education." He reported that the previous year he had gone "Paul Prying," searching for facts about education in his state in the same way that "Peter the Hermit" got Crusaders.[42] Thus was begun a professional relationship which was to develop into a friendship that lasted until Mann's death.

Mann was not Barnard's only ally, and he turned to other laborers in the cause. William Alcott, an exemplary teacher, late of Connecticut and now of Boston, wrote, "What can I do for you. . . . What can I do for the Cause of Education in Connecticut? I beg you to make any commands and demands you think proper." The Reverend Charles Brooks, also of Massachusetts, asked Barnard to participate in a Plymouth County meeting to plot strategy for the compaign for teacher training institutions —and to associate with such greats as John Quincy Adams, Daniel Webster, and Robert Rantuil "in this holy and philanthropic cause." The principal of the Andover Teachers' Seminary had a novel idea; as "a fair experiment" might not the state (Connecticut) legislature be persuaded to send some young men to Andover, either paying the tuition or advancing a loan to the students who would only be required to pay board. All during summer, congratulatory and encouraging letters flowed in, as Barnard's, seeking information, went out.[43]

The first official action of the Board of Commissioners of the Common Schools was to issue an Address to the People of Connecticut, obviously written by Barnard.[44] In it the commissioners essayed to allay fears, spurred by the Democratic forces, of unbridled state power. True, the

42. Barnard to Mann, July 7, MHS; Mann to Barnard, July 9, NYU, both 1838.

43. Letters from Alcott, September 14, 1838, from Brooks, September 20, 1838, from Coleman, November 15, 1838, NYU; there are literally dozens of letters from Connecticut reformers.

44. The address is presented in full in CCSJ I, 1 (August 1838): 608; also in HDC, August 10, 1838.

Board had powers "of no common magnitude," but "they are clothed
with no official authority, to make the least alteration in the System of
Common Schools now in existence." Only the people, through the legislature, could do that. It was imperative, however, was that the board
discover the true condition of the schools.

> Facts are what we want, and the sooner we can procure them, the
> sooner we shall carry forward with efficiency and increased success
> our system of Common School instruction, whether it remains in
> its present form or receives some partial modification.

To gather facts, the board directed the "intelligent and efficient Secretary"
to visit throughout the state, to send out circulars requesting "timely
information," and to call county conventions of all the friends of education in order "that a vigorous impulse will be given to the cause" of
school reform. The information thus gathered and the pressure group
then crystallized would be utilized in preparing for the next session of the
legislature. This was to be a campaign of no small dimension.

Toward the end of the Address the Board announced their intention to
publish, under their secretary, a semi-monthly journal.

> With an able editor . . . and published at a moderate charge, its
> great object will be to promote the elevated character, the increased
> prosperity, and the extensive usefulness of the Common Schools of
> Connecticut. It will be needed . . . as an organ of communication
> between the Board and their Secretary and the public. It will aim to
> give information on what is doing in other states, and other coun-
> tries with regard to public education. It will assist in forming,
> encouraging, and bringing forward good teachers. It will contain
> the laws of the State in reference to the Common Schools. It will
> assist the School Committees and Visitors in the discharge of their
> duties. It will be the means of ascertaining the real deficiences that
> may exist in the Schools, and of suggesting suitable remedies.—It
> will endeavor to excite and keep alive a spirit of efficient and pru-
> dent action on the subject of popular education, and to introduce
> upon its pages, from time to time, such other kindred topics as will
> subserve the promotion of this important end.

All the aims and the topics of this state organ and of the future monu-
mental *American Journal of Education* are here: comparative state and
national history and information, professional encouragement and development, specific means of remediation, and an open-ended promise.
There is no hint that Barnard had any idea that educational administration might have to compete with his editorial inclinations; from hind-

sight, in fact, it is apparent that even during the first heady six weeks of his secretaryship he really longed to devote more of his energies to his studies. For the time, though, he, for the Board, concluded with a suitable appeal.

> The Board, then, looking first to Almighty God, and inviting their fellow-citizens to do the same . . . feel assured that the public will afford them all needed encouragement and aid. Let parents and teachers; School Committees and Visiters [*sic*]; the clergy and individuals in official stations; the conductors of the public journals, and the contributors to their columns; the friends of education generally; the children and youth with their improving minds and morals; the females with their gentle yet powerful influences; and all with their good wishes and fervent supplications at the thone of grace, come up to the work. Then will we unitedly indulge the hope, that Wisdom from above will direct it,—an enlightened Zeal, carry it forward,—a fostering Providence ensure it success; and Patriotism and Religion rejoice together in its consumation.

The Address resonates with Puritanism and Whiggism in its message and echoes the reformers in the means; it is Barnard in its grandiose and youthful energy.

The first issue of the new *Connecticut Common School Journal* conveyed the message of the board to the readers; in the second Barnard directed a series of inquiries to the local authorities. Did the local board have a system for the examination of teachers? Was there classification in the schools? Were there libraries, apparatus, and convenient schoolhouses? Did the teachers see their positions as a regular profession? How was moral instruction communicated?[45] The task of surveying the state was arduous. Blanks had to be mailed to the clerks of the school societies; frequently they were lost, or the number sent was insufficient. Or worse, the secretary's requests were ignored because of local opposition. Barnard did have some clerical help, but for the most part he worked alone, and sometime during the winter of 1839, it became clear that the deadlines set by the reform law could not be met. On March 1, he announced, via the *Journal*, that the time the reports were due had been extended to the end of the month of April.[46]

Letters with suggestions flooded the Hartford office. Eli Hoyt wanted simpler legislation, defining the qualifications of teachers, and free schooling for poor children; Timothy Dwight, Senior, warned of local opposi-

45. *CCSJ* I, 2 (September 1838): 9.
46. *CCSJ* I, 8 (March, 1839): 97.

tion to the increase in state direction and stressed the necessity of tying reform to funding; David Field, while offering the usual menu of reform, urged caution: "It is much easier to point out defects in our schools than to accomplish them." But Barnard was indefatigable. With prodigious energy, he seems to have answered the masses of queries directed at him. Might Middletown consolidate its four districts into one? Could a private high school be reorganized and recognized as a teacher's seminary under public auspices? Should not the school committees be reformed into a board and be paid? What could a board or committee do if the teachers persisted in disregarding its directives? And, most frequently: please, couldn't the Secretary come to lecture, to inform, to inspire the troops?[47]

The board had announced its intention to hold a series of conventions, that common device of all reformers, in every county of the state. These were soon called, beginning on October 10 in Brooklyn, in Windham County. All the Friends of Education—committee members and visitors, teachers, public officials, and "the clergy of all denominations" —were summoned, and the clergy was "requested to present the notice from their pulpits, and to invite the attendance of the friends of the Common Schools." Barnard promised that he and at least one board member would be present.[48] These conventions were for both propaganda and pressure, designed to "form new bonds of sympathy, and channels of united effort in promoting" the cause, free from "distinctions of party and sect." The vehicle was a very familiar one, as was the format, and the actors were equally familiar. Andrew Judson, a member of the Board of Commissioners, chaired the Windham convention, and Seth Beers, the Commissioner of the School Fund, opened the Litchfield one. Each convention began with a prayer, and at each a permanent county organization, with a full slate of officers, was established. Henry Barnard always gave an address "filled with deep thought and delivered with impressive eloquence," dwelling mainly on the accumulating and devastating data on the condition of the schools. Usually he spoke at length, but at Hartford he apologized for his brevity; he had risen from his sickbed to come, and only "an imperious sense of duty" got him there.

The resolutions adopted at the sessions were strikingly similiar, and all bear Barnard's stamp. Schools were discovered to be not so good as formerly, the recent reform initiative was praised, the board endorsed, the

47. Letters, September 1838–June 1839, NYU.

48. For the convention schedules see *CCSJ* I, 3 (October 1838): 17, and *HDC*, October 25. Thomas Gallaudet frequently accompanied Barnard on these trips, but he seems not to have spoken officially, preferring to address the schoolchildren who customarily were assembled before the meetings started.

Journal supported. Other resolutions urged the gradation of schools and the institution of ones for the higher branches, the building of better schoolhouses, the provision of better textbooks, and the creation of libraries. All the conventions agreed on the vital importance of encouraging and training "young persons of both sexes, of right character and talent" through the establishment of teachers' seminaries, and on the necessity of rigorous examination of prospective teachers. After voting to create a permanent association and urging the several towns to do the same, each gathering dispersed with the customary vote of thanks to the faithful organizing committee. Thus for six weeks, until the November 22 convention in Hartford, education and school reform were discussed and debated throughout the state. The press noted each meeting, and Barnard summarized the proceedings in his *Journal*. The county conventions spawned, as was intended, conventions in many towns, in Canterbury, in Norwalk, in New Town, in Stamford, all within a two week period, inspiring one enthusiast to report that "at last we are aroused from our slumber."[49]

The climax of all this activity came the next August when a well-organized State Common School Convention was held in Hartford. The format was familiar, even to the ten o'clock commencement. After the customary prayer, a committee, moved by Barnard and including him, nominated the officers for the meeting. In keeping with the bipartisan spirit, Seth Beers, Democrat and Commissioner, took the chair; in his opening remarks he summarized the efforts of the friends of education to date and expressed his optimism for the future "happiest results." A spirited discussion of vocal music in the schools followed, with George Emerson of Boston, a Reverend Mr. Brewer, "late missionary to Greece," and Barnard participating. In the afternoon session Calvin Stowe spoke of the necessity for action, and Thomas Cushing delivered a lecture on "the division of labor as applied to the business of teaching." Barnard followed with a discussion of gradation in schools and the vital necessity of union districts. After adjournment for dinner Edward Everett read an essay, which had been prepared by Mrs. Sigourney, on the "importance of cultivating more widely a perception of the beautiful in our Common Schools." Leonard Bacon of New Haven was more pragmatic in explain-

49. For reports on the conventions: Windham County, *CCSJ* I, 3 (October 1838): 24, and *HDC*, October 19; Litchfield County, *CCSJ* I, 4 (November 1838): 32, and *HDC*, November 2; shorter accounts of the remaining conventions, *CCSJ* I, 5 (December 1838): 44–48, and *HDC*, November 10, 26. The quotation is from a letter, January 22, NYU. For a vivid account of a county school convention complete with prayer, elections, resolutions, and a lecture, see the journal of Mary Swift in Arthur O. Norton, ed., *The First Normal School in America* (Cambridge, 1926), 176–82.

ing the plan of a new school house, one designed "as it should be" in contrast to Barnard's subsequent "amusing description of 'the district school house as it is.'" Two of the Massachusetts reformers present, Everett and Emerson, portrayed the schools in their state, emphasizing particularly the graded system in Boston. The stage was thus set for an active discussion the next day; on Barnard's initiative the matter of providing preparation for teachers was included in the debates. A series of preordained resolutions, advocating gradation of schools, union districts, libraries in schools, the establishment of teachers' seminaries and associations, and the introduction of vocal music in the schools, was passed before the convention dispersed, well satisfied one assumes. Once again the reform agenda was clarified.[50]

During the winter of 1838–39 Barnard continued his visits throughout the state. In January he inspected the district schools of more than ten towns in Litchfield County and others in Fairfield. Only illness, a complaint that was to figure more and more in subsequent years, and work prevented him from doing more.

> We regret that we have been obliged to decline so many invitations to be present at public meetings of the friends of education, and examination of schools in this as well as other counties, in the course of the present month. We hope our friends, even though we do not in every instance reply to their kind invitations, will be assured that it is nothing but the pressure of engagements here at home, which keeps us away.[51]

Barnard may, even at this early date in his official career, have begun to discover that there were aspects of public service incompatible with his personal style or he may actually have attempted far too much. In any case, he hired two assistants, James M. Pierpont and Alexander Seston, to inspect the schools in the northeastern parts of the state; they received $1.25 per diem and faithfully reported back to the secretary in detailed letters.

From the very first issue the *Connecticut Common School Journal* was intended as a vehicle for communication with the friends of education, but Barnard sought a far wider audience. He challenged:

> Reader, will you at once subscribe to the Journal?—The expense is trifling; you will not feel it. Will you get your friends and neighbors

50. *CCSJ* II, 2 (September 1839): 35–36. Mrs. Sigourney's "beautiful Essay" was read again at the State Lyceum; see *CCSJ* II, 5 (December 1839): 83–84. The participation of Emerson, Stowe, and Everett should be noted.

51. *CCSJ* I, 7 (February 1839): 172; 10 (March 15): 120.

to subscribe? Will you take a few extra copies as your means allow you to do, for distribution among those, especially teachers of youth, who may feel as if they could not just now meet the expense? What you do will come back again in overflowing measure upon yourself, your family, your children, and all your dearest interests.[52]

The *Journal* certainly was not expensive, fifty cents a copy, payable in advance to the vice-presidents of the local common school associations or to the local postmasters who "can render the Journal essential service by acting as its agents." One such official was cooperative, forwarding money from five young men, all teachers, who had subscribed, but it was hard to drum up interest. In his second issue the editor appealed to other newspapers in the state to print notices of the *Journal*, and the faithful *Courant* did announce the next issues. Teachers, a prime target group, were encouraged to secure four subscriptions from colleagues, the fifth then would be free; and a subscriber who signed up fifteen others would be entitled to two free copies. By late August Jonathan Weston had twelve subscribers, but, he reported, the apathy was such "it was like attempting to raise the dead." Loyal supporters such as board member Charles Rockwell canvassed continually, but by the spring of 1839 the editor was in debt. With the commencement of the second volume he had to raise the price to a dollar a year and was forced to solicit funds. Fortunately, John Norton of Framingham came to the rescue, assuming part of the debt and ordering fifty subscriptions.[53]

Part of the problem was that Barnard was so anxious to spread the gospel that he gave away countless copies. Titus Bissell, a Yale classmate, and Governor Seward of New York both acknowledged, with suitable thanks, receipt of copies, and the Administrator of the Poor Schools of Virginia was delighted to get his. Barnard loved such communications but failed to attend to mundane details. The supportive Mr. Norton did not receive all the copies he had paid for; Reverend Linsley became very impatient with the continuing delays and the lack of response to his letters—despite the fact that he had taken eleven subscriptions. Another subscriber complained that he had just received twenty sets of the *Journal* after having got another bundle a week previously, and he returned the lot; he also objected to the reporting of the county association meeting, a serious problem for Barnard if the complaint was justified. He depended on local support, both for the distribution of the *Journal*, and for mate-

52. *CCSJ* I, 1 (August 1838): 1.
53. Letters from Jonathan Weston, August 29, 1838; Charles Rockwell, August 12, September 2, 1839; John Norton, July 2, 1839; W. P. Burrall, July 10, 1839, NYU; from Henry Brown, postmaster of Preston, n.d., TC.

rial; he could edit, but he could not be everywhere, and he had no staff. Despite all the confusion and delay, ultimately more than 60,000 copies of the first twelve numbers of the publication were distributed—an enormous, and ambitious, achievement.[54]

For anyone committed to the study of and service to education the *Journal* was a bargain. Barnard's standards were high, and the materials vast. Early issues carried a series of articles on "Female Teachers" by Thomas Gallaudet, copious selections from Jacob Abbott's *The Teacher*, and high-minded addresses by Edward Channing, Charles Brooks, James Hillhouse, and Barnard's old mentor, Dr. Humphrey. Calvin Stowe's *Report on the Course of Instruction in the Common Schools of Prussia and Wirtemberg* was printed in its entirety; commented Barnard, the promoter as well as the scholar, "The *Report* is worth a year's subscription to the Journal."[55] Two topics foreshadow Barnard's future scholarly interests. There were numerous short articles on desks, ventilation, and schoolhouses in general; most of the May issue, is devoted to the topic. And throughout the entire volume there were historical articles, on education in Connecticut, in South America, even among the Waldenses, subjects not guaranteed to attract a wide audience.[56]

Barnard did the lion's share of the work on the *Journal*, although Timothy Dwight, Junior, contributed a number of articles and hoped to become the editor himself—something Barnard knew he could not afford. Dwight found it very hard working for his friend and wrote rather petulantly in December: "I have heretofore been left entirely in the doubt most of the time," with publication times moved and topics requested and then not printed. He did share his friend's grand views, suggesting an enormous range of subjects—the morality of trade, sound and unsound views of history, how to teach the principles of agriculture and physiology, lessons in music. John Lovell, of the New Haven Lancastrian

54. Letters from Titus Bissell, April 15; Governor Seward, June 28; J. Brown, July, 1839; John Norton, February 6, May 2, June 13; all 1839, NYU. On the complaint, see *CCSJ* I, 7 (February 1839), where Leonard Bacon reports on the New Haven meeting. Barnard was following contemporary practice in sending the *Journal* to friends and colleagues in other states.

55. *CCSJ* I, 11 (April 1839): 121ff. In the first two volumes of the *Journal* most numbers were 16 pages long; in vol. III the pattern became one of alternation: 16, 8, 16, 8; in vol. IV the pattern was maintained but the numbers shortened: 4, 8, 4, 8. The number division was maintained even when an article occupied several numbers; W. A. Alcott's "Slate and Black Board Exercises" is spread over numbers 8 through 11 of volume IV.

56. *CCSJ* I, 12 (May 1839): 142–52. See *CCSJ* I, 8 (March 1839): 84ff., where the editor discusses education, focusing on normal schools, in Prussia, Holland, England, and Scotland. The intent was to teach: "This brief sketch of the School history of Scotland, is full of instruction for Connecticut."

School agreed to submit an article if the editor would promise that it would be printed in full; it was, nearly a year later, all seventy pages of it, including the number of minutes required for pupils to complete complicated mental computations. Masses of material came from John Norton, who had accumulated materials on a visit to Albany—the report of the New York Regents, the statutes of the Albany Academy, and a history of education in the city.[57]

There was something in the *Journal* from many a pen, but there was a great deal of Barnard. In frequent editorials he advocated, in hortatory but mild language, the party line. "A truly good school is a great benefit . . . every member of the community where one is found derives some value from it." Steady habits, industry, morality, even an increase in property values, all flow from good schools which are disciplined, patriotic, well ventillated, with suitable desks and new apparatus, which teach grammar and vocal music and drawing, and have well educated teachers. "Hints to Teachers" presented a bewildering array of novel and traditional methods—model lessons, reflections on possible arrangememts for the classroom, the importance of movement and activity, and of lower seats for younger children, as well as story telling and the singing of moral hymns. In addition Barnard promised to provide teachers with extracts from other educational publications in order to "acquaint our readers with the titles, authors, and some of the opinions of the publication which we consider worthy of their attention."[58]

If the *Journal* had actually been read by practicing teachers, it might have provided an invaluable service, but it never was, either because it was ponderous, dull, or inaccessible. In 1840 William S. Baker detected the problem. "I will only add if you wish to conquer the great enemy *Ignorance* you must shoot lower."[59] Barnard, with his fastidiousness and his own level of education, could not or would not comply. The *Journal* was intended to elevate as well as instruct, to raise the level of the teachers to that of the editor, who already saw himself as a teacher of teachers.

Everything Barnard read and much of what he published focused on the paramount importance of better preparation of teachers. In the second issue of the *Journal* he had outlined four ways a young teacher could be aided, and perusal of the publication was only one of them. Equally

57. Letter from Dwight, December 11, 1838; from John Lovell, August 27, 1839, see *CCSJ* II, 13 (June 1840): 231ff.; from John Norton, December 24, 1838, see *CCSJ* I, 10 (March 1839): 115ff. See also *CCSJ* I, 5 (December 1838): 40, 42.

58. *CCSJ* I, 3 (October 1838): 22–23.

59. Hendrik Gideonse, "Common School Reform: Connecticut 1838–1854," Ph.D. diss. (Harvard Univ., 1963), 97n; see also Mayo, "Henry Barnard," 790–91, who suggested that Barnard's literary style was lost on the average reader, or scared him.

important were "occasional instruction given by persons of experience," and "practical experiments under the direction of well qualified teachers," and, of course, Teachers' Seminaries. Here were all the components of a complete system of teacher education, periodic workshops, some sort of a practicum, full-fledged training, and a literature.[60] But the legislature had turned down a seminary, so the secretary attacked on another front—by establishing periodic training institutes for teachers. It is a bit difficult to ascertain precisely where the credit for the first teachers' class should be given, although Barnard later claimed to have sponsored it at his own expense in the fall of 1839. A brief announcement did appear in the October number of the *Journal*, signed by T. L. Wright, principal of the Hartford Grammar School, inviting young gentlemen intending to teach in the winter common schools to take advantage of "the liberality of benevolent individuals" to receive "gratuitous instruction" prior to undertaking their teaching duties. On the same page Barnard endorsed the course, noting it had already begun and "the time allotted . . . is short."

Twenty-three young men attended the sessions with the twin goals of improving "their acquaintance with the studies taught in our Common Schools and with the best methods of school government and instruction."[61] The roster of the instructors included some of Hartford's best teachers and individuals recruited from afar. Wright himself handled the topics of grammar and school management; one of his teachers taught the rules of arithmetic, while Professor Davies, of West Point, heard recitations in higher mathematics. The Reverend Barton, from the Andover Seminary, covered reading and natural philosophy, and Gallaudet explained how to teach composition and how to use slates. The principal of the Hartford Female Seminary, who in the spring would give a similar course for female teachers, lectured on the principles of mathematics, geometry, and astronomy, and demonstrated the use of globes. An opportunity to observe a veteran teacher was provided by Mr. Snow, of the Center District School, who welcomed the young men to his class; visits were made nearly every day to other schools in the city. Thus this first teachers' class combined further education, methodology, and field observation—the components of all future teaching training.

Henry Barnard appeared as a guest lecturer, speaking on the relation

60. *CCSJ* I, 5 (December 1838), is especially representative.

61. *CCSJ* II, 4 (October 1839): 52, where Barnard gives full credit to Wright, whereas in his later *Normal Schools*, 16–17, he takes the credit. See *JRIII* I, extra II (November 26, 1845), where Barnard repeats that the class was his initiative and paid for by him; Wright was "in general charge." In an article, unsigned but listed in the index as Barnard, *AJE* XV, xl (September 1865): 387–88, Barnard gives essentially this same account.

of teachers to the school system, to parents, and to pupils, as well as on the laws of health in schools and the means of forming teachers' associations. His presence had its impact on one of the young men attending the course, David Nelson Camp. Camp, whose dreams of further education had been frustrated by ill health and family responsibilities, had taught in the common schools of Connecticut for a number of winters. The teachers' class was ideal for youngsters such as he, and shortly after its conclusion he wrote to Barnard.

> I take this opportunity to express my sincere thanks for the instruction I have received in the city through your instrumentality and shall ever feel it a pleasure to do what little I can to aid in the object in which you are engaged.[62]

Camp thus became the first of the legions of Barnard devotees, and he lived up to his promise; within a few years he began his thirty year's service as loyal lieutenant to general Barnard in the cause of education.

By this time Barnard had served over a year in his new position. In April he had been re-elected to the legislature in a Whig sweep, once again garnering more votes than anyone else on the local ticket. The Whigs had approved all of the school reform measures, castigating the Loco Foco opposition as an attempt "against liberty" designed to "keep the people in darkness." Governor Ellsworth, in his annual address, singled out Barnard who had "devoted himself assiduously" to the work of the school reform.

> Who that wishes the rising generation to be blessed with knowledge, and especially those indigent who have no other advantages besides common schools, will look to this generous and Christian effort, with jealous feelings?

The Governor also praised Barnard's first report, "a work of much observation, critical examination, and reflection, well worthy of your attention."[63]

The *Report* may not now read as a "bold and startling document" as Chancellor Kent described it, but it certainly was "founded on the most painstaking and critical inquiry," and throughout it was orderly and slightly cautious.[64] The first matter mentioned was, significantly, the *Journal*.

---

62. Letter from Camp, November, 1839, NYU. See David N. Camp, *Recollections of a Long and Active Life* (New Britain, 1917), 12–13, for a description of this class or institute. Barnard noted in a later publication, that prior to "separating, the members of the Teachers' Class published a 'Card'" expressing their gratitude; see *NS*, 17.

63. *CC*, February 16, April 6, May 4, 1839.

64. For the report see *CCSJ* I, 13 (June 1, 1839): 155–91, quote 155; see Mayo, "Henry

More than 60,000 copies of the twelve numbers have been circulated . . . and as it has kept aloof from the disturbing influence of
party or sectarian differences, it has, it is hoped, in some measure
been serviceable to the cause it was established exclusively to
promote.

Barnard accounted for his activities in minute detail: over the year he had
heard from more than 1,200 schools, inspected 200 of them, delivered
more than 60 lectures, and talked to teachers and visitors in more than
two-thirds of the state's school societies. His work was bearing fruit;
school associations existed in more than fifty towns; public examination
of teachers was a reality in at least forty; and in some teachers had formed
societies for mutual improvement. Lest critics say that this was not much,
he countered:

No one can be more sensible than myself of the little which has
been accomplished compared with what is needed to be done. But
this emphatically is a work in which all sure progress must be slow.[65]

The secretary then summarized the major weakness of the Connecticut
schools, particularly the lack of uniform standards; far too much was left
to the discretion of the local committees. Because "public opinion will
not long remain in advance of the law," corrective revision of the school
law was "indispensable." Legislation should permit the gradation of
schools, and the employment of more than one teacher in a single district, and the visitors should be paid. Support for the schools should fall
on the property of the district rather than the parents, thereby ensuring
that the schools would indeed be common. Even if all his proposals were
to be adopted, ample support and flexible organization would be ineffective without good teachers; the remedies were "pecuniary inducements"
and the simplest of solutions: a Teachers' Seminary. Barnard gave twice as
much space to this final recommendation as to any other.

With good teachers, properly trained, and employed under more
favorable circumstances than now, and sustained by the respect and
adequate compensation of the public, the common schools can be
made . . . to give as sound moral and intellectual culture to all the
children of the State, as can be had in the best private schools.[66]

Barnard," 789–91 and Gideonse, "Common School Reform," 81–83. The quotation from
Kent is in *CCSJ* V, 5 (December 1851): 124.

65. *CCSJ* I, 13 (June 1, 1839): 156.

66. Ibid., 176.

What can be made of this *Report* and its twenty-seven-year-old author? The Henry Barnard who emerges is no surprise. The young Whig had worked hard and faithfully, and he produced comprehensive, if predictable, proposals which were well documented and argued. The document detailed the condition of the schools in fourteen pages of appendices —the most meticulous data, derived from the school returns of each district school, county by county, its teachers, pupils, texts, with abstracts of reports from visitors and teachers—the wealth of information is daunting. No legislator could complain that he had insufficient information on which to base corrective legislation. Barnard here stood in the vanguard of those who would conduct massive studies on all social topics as a prelude to reform measures. The *Report* was also scholarly; here the historian was at work. It was conservative in its classification of children —those of the reckless and vicious, those of the poor and ignorant, and the colored children—and in its tone.

> The whole field of moral education is almost abandoned. . . . the tendency of the present course of instruction is to give undue precedence to the intellectual development, omitting, if not checking, the growth and expansion of moral feelings. . . . No child should grow up to the responsibilities of active life, to the exercise of all his rights, and to the discharge of all his duties, as a citizen, and a member of society, a stranger to those motives which ought to guide and govern all human activity.[67]

From this passage it is clear that Barnard still thought, as did the vast majority of his peers, male and female, that the public sphere was exclusively male. He also was racist; blacks should be educated, for not to do so ultimately cost the state, but in separate schools. He supported equal pay for the female teacher because of her unique abilities with younger children; only by paying her well would the schools be able to attract a superior type of female teacher—here is an argument usually advanced for male teachers. Finally, when he came to discuss the content and the methodology of schools, Barnard sounded surprisingly progressive.

> The course of instruction (in our common schools) will be radically defective, unless it embraces the harmonious development of the whole nature of the child—the physical, intellectual, and moral powers, and till it shall end in a preparation for the real business of life—not for any particular pursuit, but for any and every pursuit.[68]

67. Ibid., 169.
68. Ibid., 165–67, 169. In discussing education for blacks, Barnard advanced the social

The Board endorsed the *Report*, advocating four modifications in the school law. Districts should be allowed to hire more than one teacher or to combine with another district to create a union district; districts should be able to appoint two of their committee members to serve as paid visitors; the school taxes of the poor should be abated by the towns; and the law should be revised to make more specific the specifications for school houses. There were no recommendations concerning the qualifications or training of teachers. A bill was, however, reported out of the House Committee on the Common Schools appropriating $5,000 to the Board to use in the preparation of teachers; at its second reading the Secretary characteristically spoke at length. "Give me good teachers, and in five years I will work not a change but a revolution in the education of the children of the State." The "sum should be so expended as to reach, if practicable, every teacher in the State," by conventions or institutes where each would absorb practical hints and could buy and read works on the theory and practice of teaching. Again, Barnard's peroration soared: "Though the prospect is dark enough, I think I can see the dawning of a better day, on the mountain tops," when a change will "pass over the public mind, and over the public order," when the common system would no longer be regarded as cheap, inferior, and attended only by the poor, but truly common, and for all.

There was no dissent to these sentiments, but the bill was ultimately lost in the Senate which referred it back to the Board for "a specific plan of expenditures."[69] It was probably the failure of this aspect of his total plan that led Barnard to the support of the teacher's class discussed above. Still he could look back on this his first year in office with satisfaction. A major piece of legislation concerning schools had been developed, although he had not had time to prepare the revised draft of the school code; that piece of business lay ahead, as did the question of the teachers' seminary and matters of pedagogical reform. All in all, he could agree with a learned contemporary, that "The present age may be truly characterized as the era of Education."[70]

---

cost argument: Negroes made up only one-twentieth of the population of the state but accounted for one-sixth of the crime.

69. *CC*, June 1, 8, 20; for a summary of the bill see *CCSJ* II, 1 (August 1839), 6–7. *CC* June 1, debate on the bill. For excerpts of Barnard's speech, see *CCSJ* II, 1 (January 1855). See *AJE* XI, ii (June 1862): 563–72, for quotation from this address which, Barnard reported, was repeated in over fifty cities. In a letter to Mann, December 21, 1838, MHS, Barnard outlined a proposed issue of the *Journal* devoted to European innovations in teacher education, especially to Stowe's *Report* "if I shall be able to lay hands on it." See also letter, January 16, 1839, MHS.

70. *CCSJ* I, 12 (May 1839): 148, quoting Mr. Justice Story addressing the opening

More than school matters occupied him during these eighteen months of tremendous activity. Barnard had been a delegate to the National Lyceum Convention in 1831, where resolutions were passed praising teachers and advocating training schools for them, and he seized on the idea of lyceums as allies in his reform campaign.

> The increase of active and well educated lyceums in this State . . . is much to be desired, as one of the most direct and effectual means of directing the attention of the people to the importance of improving the schools.[71]

In the spring of 1838, he was one of the catalysts in the formation of the Hartford Young Men's Institute, a local lyceum, and he worked diligently arranging a series of lectures.[72] His letter to his friend William Tully, down in New Haven, was probably similar to all the invitations he sent, although the tone may have been a bit more frivolous. After explaining that the Society was "for the purpose of securing a Library and a Course of popular lectures," he added: "The audience will be miscellaneous and (as is very proper considering our name) will contain a goodly portion of the fair sex." Unfortunately Tully declined to cooperate, but others agreed to deliver lectures scheduled for Fridays in the coming fall and winter. Denison Olmsted said yes, Alpheus Williams promised to speak on hygiene, supportive Heman Humphrey suggested two lectures, one on "the importance of moral character and how it is won and lost." Charles Brooks offered three topics, and his lecture on elementary instruction in Prussia and Holland subsequently appeared in the *Journal*. Of course many refused, Daniel Barnard and Benjamin Silliman among them, and some failed; at the last moment Barnard himself had to give the initial lecture.

That the series was intended as a vehicle of education is clear from the topics, although it is a bit hard to detect the vital importance of "Patronomatology, or the Philosophy of Surnames" which Charles Wil-

---

session of the American Society for the Diffusion of Useful Knowledge.

71. *CCSJ* I, 5 (December 1838): 39–40. *HDC*, May 19, June 11, 1838; *CC*, June 3, 15, 1838, for notice of first annual meeting at which Barnard presided. *CCSJ* II, 5 (December 1839): 81ff., for Barnard's report of the executive committee of the Institute, whose success was no longer "problematic." See Carl Bode, *The American Lyceum: Town Meeting of the Mind* (New York: Oxford University Press, 1956), esp. 8, 23, 57, 101ff.

72. *HDC*, June 16, announcement of the Institute; October 5, report and announcement of the lecture series. A poster advertising the lectures is among the Barnard papers in the collection of the Connecticut Historical Society. Comparing its list of speakers with the letters indicates he often must have been disappointed, or else he was overly optimistic when he had the schedule printed.

liam Bradley of East Haddam wanted to deliver; Barnard seems to have put him off. Professor Davis spoke on Science; James Hillhouse (who finally came after failing twice), urged the necessity of a national litera-ture "to give the nation more sons of consummate education" and "to arm them with that moral heroism" that was necessary to fulfill "the holy mission which has been assigned America." Reverend Pierpont's lecture on Constantinople might have been a disappointment, but by the time of his second lecture the crowds were so large the series had to be moved from the Center Church to the larger Second one.[73] The young society was a great success, with 350 members by October, the popular lectures, a debating class which met weekly, and a library, for Barnard had been able to secure permission from members of an older, private one to transfer their books to his new institution. He also had begun conversations with the Daniel Wadsworth which would eventually result in Wadsworth's endowment of the Athenaeum in Hartford.[74]

Barnard had time during these busy days for another organization, the Connecticut Historical Society. This society had originally been founded in 1825 through the impetus of Thomas Robbins, a minister and antiquar-ian. Its thirty incorporators represented the Standing Order—fifteen law-yers, seven doctors, six clergymen, mostly Yale men steeped in the classi-cal and Biblical heritage who could still recall familial anecdotes of the glorious Revolutionary past. They feared that with the death of the few remaining "grey-headed men" the state would be bereft, with only "the uncertain echo of a remote tradition." Hence the need:

> It shall be the duty of every member of this Society, to obtain and communicate information relative to the civil, ecclesiastical, and nat-ural history of this State, and of the United States.[75]

Unfortunately, after presiding over four meetings in five days that first year, John Trumbull, the president, moved to Detroit, and the new group languished for more than a decade. In March 1839, Edward Herrick, one of the charter members, approached Barnard about the possibility of

73. *HDC*, November 27, December 7, 10, 18, 24, 28, 1839. Letters, winter, 1838–39, NYU.

74. In the report of the executve committee of the institute the total number of vol-umes in the library, with the addition of those from the Hartford Library Company was 5,000, a sizable number, and money was set aside for further purchases. Various letters on the library transfer are in the NYU collection.

75. Connecticut Historical Society, *An Address to the Public*, 1825; Christopher P. Bickford, *The Connecticut Historical Society, 1825–1975* (Hartford: Connecticut Historical Society, 1975), is the source for much of this discussion; see also *CCSJ* II, 11 (June 1840): 180, for Barnard's summary of the Society's history; there are also miscellaneous documents both in the Society's archives and in the Sterling Memorial Library at Yale.

re-incorporating the Society—Barnard was a natural choice, a local legis-lator known to have an interest in history. On May 20, he introduced the petition of thirty-nine signatories (fifteen of the originators of the group), and the legislature confirmed the original charter by resolution. The revived Society met on June 1, in the rooms of the Hartford Young Men's Institute, which had just received its charter, and elected Thomas Day, a judge and for twenty-five years the secretary of the state, as president. Henry Barnard became the corresponding secretary, a position he held until 1846.[76]

One of the duties of the corresponding secretary was to seek out his-torical materials and information, a task perfectly suited to Barnard. He wrote to the publishers of all of the periodicals in the state, requesting that they forward to the Society all copies of their issues; he circularized the ministers, much as he had the school visitors, asking them to respond to a series of questions: what were the names of the parish officers, from the time of the gathering of the congregation to the present? what were the dimensions of the parish edifices, inside and out? what other interest-ing information could they supply? would they forward any valuable doc-uments? He sought memorabilia, he requested collections of papers, he welcomed busts of native sons. He must have relished a letter from Rever-end Chapin discussing the Druids, and somehow relating them to the Hebrews, Adam Bede, Tacitus, Pliny, the Persians, Hume, and of course the Bible. Both his native pride and love of statistics were satisfied when Governor Ellsworth promised from Washington to forward a digest of all patents granted to Connecticut citizens or to those born and educated in the state. Professor Kingsley alerted him to the Hopkins School papers and some manuscripts of Samuel Johnson's, and his counterparts in other states sent him their materials.[77]

One of Henry Barnard's proudest moments came in April 1840. The Historical Society had long wanted to mount a celebration, and the tri-centennial of the colonial charter provided the opportunity. Barnard orchestrated a splendid event. Noah Webster, the state's grand old man, agreed to be the day's orator, provided the party was held off until after the bad winter weather. Invitations were dispatched to everyone: Jared Sparks and Daniel Webster were too busy, Roger Sherman, Justice Storey, and Washington Irving just said no, but Richard Henry Dana, writing from "Shipboard" promised to attend. Thomas Robbins regretted that "a

76. Bickford, *Historical Society*, 21ff.; *CC*, May 25, 1839; miscellaneous fragments, Ster-ling, YU.

77. Circular, Sterling, YU. Letter from Bacon, January, 1839, CHS. See Bickford, *His-torical Society*, 25. Letters from Ellsworth, April 3, 1840, CHS; from Kingsley, September, 1840, CHS, and February 3, 1841, NYU; from Chapin, November 18, 1839, NYU.

good work of grace among the people of my charge" prevented his attending but rejoiced that anecdotes of the past would not be lost due to the efforts of the Society. Some who declined sent toasts to be read in their absence; one was Daniel Dewey Barnard's: "Connecticut—emphatically the land of steady habits—and of habits not more steady than virtuosity, politic, and wise."[78]

The celebration began on the evening of April 20 with a gala reception at the home of the president, Thomas Day; the guests wore period costumes, and those of the ladies were fully described in the press. "It seemed as though the old portraits on some high walls of pomp and power had suddenly walked out of the frames." The grand banquet took place the following day in the Old State House, in a hall elaborately decorated with portraits of the state's former greats which Barnard had borrowed. (Joseph Trumbull had lent ones of the first governor and his oldest son, the colonel, and then added that colonel's wife "thinks you uncourteous in not requesting to take the Old Lady also—as they lived together on good terms while in life, she hopes you will not separate them now.") Webster orated, a Centennial Hymn was sung, three Odes were delivered, and endless toasts proposed, including one to the Charter Oak. Barnard offered his:

> Let us honor the virtues of Public Spirit, Patriotism, Justice, Religion, which were substantial virtues in those days, and let us not forget the other names and events which have shed a lustre over later pages of our history.

The dinner began at two in the afternoon, and after many hours, Day, who was elderly, rose to leave; when the assembled guests seemed about to follow, Barnard quickly assumed the chair and assured them that the day was not yet fading, that the evening bells had not yet rung eight, and that there was more to come. It is not recorded when the evening ended.[79]

The business of the Historical Society occupied Barnard off and on for the rest of his life. He served as its president from 1854 to 1860 and as vice president from 1863 until 1874; he was chairman of the library committee for years, and, ever consistent, he regretted that the library was not accessible to the general public.[80] This leadership of the Historical Soci-

---

78. Letters from Webster, December 3, 5, 23, 1839; from Sparks, April 4, from Daniel Webster, April 7, from Storey, April 13; from Irving, April 12; from Marsh, April 11; from Doane, April 7; from Barnard, April 10; from Robbins, April 9; all 1840, all CHS.

79. Letter from Joseph Trumbull, April 19. *Supplement to the Courant*, May 9, 1840, YU; notes on party, CHS.

80. It was to Barnard as president that Thomas Seymour wrote from Russia in Sep-

ety was Henry Barnard's sole civic honor; he was never a board member or officer in any other philanthropic or benevolent organization in his native city, poignant evidence that he failed to become a member of Hartford's inner circle. Late in life he pictured himself as a key figure in the development of Hartford's cultural resources, the man who persuaded Daniel Wadsworth to endow a building which would include the gallery, the Historical Society, and the Young Men's Institute, with its library, all under one roof; he may well have made a practical suggestion for the construction of the structure, but he did not contribute to the subscription which supplemented Wadsworth's largess.[81]

Barnard took his undeviating loyalty to his native state, and to its Historical Society, with him when he was commissioner in Rhode Island. He became aware that the state was interested in acquiring the vast library belonging to Thomas Robbins, and, unwilling to let the resources slip away to a rival, if neighbor, state, he initiated negotiations with the wily minister and persuaded him to return to Connecticut with his books. When Robbins needed more than argument, Barnard started a subscription to raise a suitable salary, himself guaranteeing $300. This, plus the fact that Robbins had offended certain female members of his congregation, worked, and he returned to Hartford, an enthusiastic and disorganized librarian of the Society until his death in 1856.[82]

Sometime after his appointment as Secretary to the Board of Commissioners, Barnard joined the American Institute of Instruction, a society dedicated to the improvement of education which, despite its name, originated in Boston and for most of our period remained a New England organization. The early leaders of the Institute were men of impeccable credentials, friends of education of long standing such as James Carter, George Emerson, Gideon Thayer, William Channing Woodbridge, and William Russell, all of whom would be prophets and sources for Barnard in his professional career. They were college graduates and learned professionals; if teachers they came from the prestigious private academies; and

---

tember 1858, sending a sprig of pressed flowers and reporting that in the university library which he had visited he had seen volumes of the *American Journal of Education* on the shelves.

81. Bickford, *Historical Society*, 33, 41, 46; see also biographical fragment, TC. Letter from Seymour, September 13, 1858, CHS. Barnard's role in the Society introduced him to national historical circles; he was elected an honorary member of several state societies, a usual quid pro quo, and he was one of eight from Connecticut elected in June 1844, to the National Institute, letters, CHS.

82. Letter from Robbins to Barnard, July 15, 1844, NYU, where the former mentions the figure of $300. *AJE* III, i (March 1857): 279–83, for obituary of Robbins and Barnard's eulogy; Bickford, *Historical Society*, 35–41.

all were "gentlemen of good moral character."[83] The Institute was and remained the most elite wing of educational reform in the antebellum period.

The presentation and subsequent publication of "valuable lectures and the discussion of interesting topics related to popular education," rather than political pressure, was the original aim of the organization. But, as Barnard rued, few from Connecticut had ever patronized its meetings, much less joined or read the published proceedings. In 1839 he urged his state colleagues to attend the upcoming sessions in Springfield, to prove "that Connecticut has not gone to sleep in patriarchal self-complacency over the good deeds of other days," and he promised to publish valuable extracts from the Institute's volumes. Barnard certainly went to Springfield although from the newspaper reports he did not figure in the discussions.[84] So he must have been exhilarated and flattered to receive a letter from Thomas Cushing the next year, asking for a lecture at the annual convention in Providence. But Barnard does not appear to have gone to that meeting, for his name does not appear in the *Proceedings*, and he makes no reference to it in his *Journal*. He was, however, elected a Counsellor of the Institute, a position the duties of which were vague and the occupants many.

Barnard was again asked, this time by William Russell, to speak to the 1841 convention in Boston, and George Emerson, the chairman of the Committee on Arrangements wrote to set the time of the lecture and to ask, repeatedly, for a title. Barnard sounded as if he planned to go, referring to a "half-promise to lecture," and Horace Mann hoped to entice him away to Nantucket for a holiday afterwards. "Shall not we school boys deserve a recess," he wrote. At the very last moment Barnard reneged, and his excuse was weak. He had been on holiday in New Hampshire and Vermont and "fell in with a party of friends"; when the brother of one of the women was forced to return to Hartford, Barnard "took his place by way of guide, companion & friend of the ladies." The illness of one of them, and the comfort of their carriage, as compared with his horse, persuaded him that his duty lay in Vermont. To Mann he wrote:

> I fear I cannot be at Boston. I have prepared *mentally* my lecture or talk which is "the present condition and improvement of the common school system of New England." If I am booked for a lecture I

---

83. See Paul H. Mattingly, *The Classless Profession* (New York: New York University Press, 1975), chap. V. especially 84–104; quotations 90, 94.

84. *CCSJ* II, 1 (August 1839): 13–14; *CCSJ* II, 5 (December 1839): 83. At Springfield Barnard heard, among others, and approved of, Gideon Thayer; see *CCSJ* III, 5 (January 1, 1841): 57.

must throw myself on your generosity to help me out of this scrape. . . . I am chagrined at the position I find myself. . . . I am very anxious to contribute my mite toward the object but I fear I cannot be there without appearing to desert a part of duty voluntarily assumed . . .

Emerson forgave him and asked for a copy of the lecture so that it could be included in the forthcoming volume of the *Proceedings*; it never appeared, certainly because it had never been written.[85]

This episode shows Barnard, who longed so for prestige and recognition, failing a group which had the power to bestow just that status; it also presents him unprepared and ready to produce a hackneyed piece, if at all; and it reveals him in a frivolous light, for it is hard to believe he was the only one on whom the ladies could depend. Maybe one of them had attractions he did not admit. The entire episode suggests that, much as Henry Barnard was devoted to the cause of school reform, he remained a gentlemanly and leisurely reformer.

His name appeared on the list of counsellors of the institute until 1844 when he was elected one of the more than twenty vice-presidents. Mattingly points out that this was an honorific position, a recognition of national status in the field of education, and that many of the holders never attended any meetings. Barnard apparently did but played a relatively minor role. On one occasion, when a speaker failed (did he blush with shame?), he moved that the group discuss the organization of schools in cities; on another, he was appointed to the committee to oversee the balloting. At the 1845 convention, in Hartford, he gave the closing lecture, in Northampton in 1850 he gave the opening one; neither was published, nor were any substantive remarks of his. His name gradually moved up the list of names of vice-presidents until 1866 when he was second; for one year, 1875, when his career and that of the Institute were in decline, his name headed the list, but he was never president. After 1875 his name disappears from the *Proceedings*.[86]

During his second year in state office, Barnard and the Connecticut Board worked well together. He continued his school visits, during the winter 1840–41 examining, he claimed, more than a thousand schools —certainly he had uncredited assistance; one disciple wrote:

85. Letters from Cushing, July 29, 1840; from Russell, February 1, 1841; from Emerson, July 17, August 12, 16, 18, 24; from Mann, May 21, July 26; all NYU. The letter of August 16 was sent to Barnard in Brattleboro, Vermont. Letter to Mann, Lannie, *Henry Barnard*, August 15, 62–63.

86. *Proceeding of the American Institute for Instruction*, 1844, 1845, 1849, 1850, 1866, 1875, 1876. See *AJE* II, 1 (August 1856): 242, for Barnard's listing of his activities in the AII, 1845–53.

You know I am to some extent your protegy in these matters, for it required an infusion of yr. hightoned zeal to induce me to the neglect of my other avocations (& hobbies) to make myself work & toil & battle in our hyperborean storms for the magnificent compensation of $2 a day![87]

Reports from towns throughout the state had to be compiled, in itself a huge job. "It will require a month of *solid labor*, with the assistance of a clerk, to make such an abstract of them as to be of any value to the legislature." Nonetheless the next year he asked the visitors to forward more of their "views in a series of connected remarks" on school organization and upon possible revisions of the school law.[88]

The secretary published most of the school reports in their entirety; those from the First School Society in Berlin, the district of Kensington, are of particular interest, for they introduce Emma Willard. Willard had been born in Kensington and commenced her teaching career there in 1804; it was later, when she was on a visit home, already the distinguished head of the Troy Seminary, that she met the young Barnard, then a student at Yale. In 1840 at her native village's annual school meeting, her ideas on schools were read by Elihu Burrit, one of the local committeemen; they made such an impression that she was unanimously elected superintendent of the common schools—the title and the action are unique for the time. Willard presided over four summer schools.[89] One of her innovations was the selection of an elder girl in each of them to serve as an assistant teacher, a modified monitorial system used at Troy, and she held an informal teachers' class in her kitchen for the four teachers and assistants. Throughout this time she wrote Barnard frequently. She complained to him about the poor quality of the books available in the schools and expressed the need for a clock, and she begged him to undertake a careful inspection of her schools, staying at least two days. The inspection did take place one day, a "festal" gathering, from nine in the morning until six-thirty at night, with only an hour's break, and "with-

87. Letter from Henry Randall, December 4, 1841, NYU, Barnard was an official school visitor in Hartford in 1840; see *OHGS*, 239–41.

88. Reports from towns: *CCSJ* II, 10 (March 1, 1840): 149ff.; 11 (April 1, 1840): 165ff.; III, 4 (December 15, 1840): 49ff; 7 (February 1, 1841): 81ff. For Circular to School Visitors, with fifteen topics: 8 (February 15, 1841): 97ff.; 9 (March 1841): 108ff.; the circular repeated in 14 (July 1841): 177ff., with responses. Examples of communications from towns, Clinton, April 5, Deep River, April 6, Middletown, May 3, NYU. The fragment of the chart on which Barnard compiled the data is in NYU.

89. It should be recalled that summer schools were primarily for girls, and therefore it is not quite as extraordinary that a woman should preside over them.

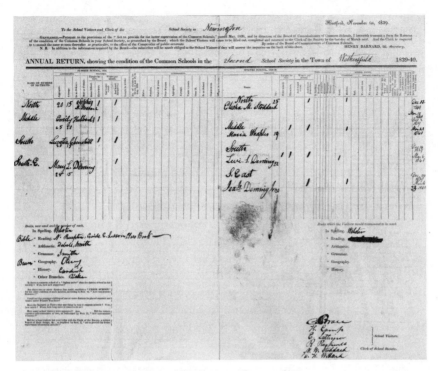

School Visitors Return Form, Newington, Connecticut

out the slightest abatement of interest on the part of the numerous assembly, or of weariness on the part of the children."[90]

On that same day the women of Kensington formed the Female Common School Association, open to all women of the district.

> We are moved hereto, by considering the vital importance of elevating by right education the common mind—by the endearing ties which bind us to the children of our own school—by the knowledge that it is the proper sphere of women, to take care of young children,—and by the consideration of the deficiencies heretofore experienced, and the need of united and efficient effort, as well as of some additional pecuniary means for supplying those deficiencies.

90. *CCSJ* III, 2 (November 15, 1840): 30; 4 (December 15, 1840): 54; *AJE* VI, 16 (March 1859): 153ff., "Memoir of Emma Willard," by Henry Fowler who points out how extraordinary it was that a woman who could not vote was elected to public office. See David N. Camp, *History of New Britain* (New Britain: W. B. Thompson & Co., 1889), 225ff., for another biography by one who may have met Willard. Alma Lutz, *Emma Willard: Pioneer Educator of American Women* (Boston: Beacon Press, 1964), chap. 14, describes the relationship between Willard and Barnard.

The role of educational reformers such as Willard and these nameless women is too often ignored by historians. Women frequently formed auxillary associations such as the Kensington one, predecessors of the PTAs of a century later. Barnard approved heartily:

> From the outset of our labors in this field, we have been sensible of the vast influence for good which the mothers of the district or society might exert by more active individual or associated efforts, in behalf of common schools.

He only regretted that Mrs. Willard did not remain in Kensington long enough to put her plan into action, and that the fathers, too, were not involved, for parents were vital supporters of schools.[91]

The *Connecticut Common School Journal* dominated Barnard's mind and time, and by 1840 it was more and more difficult to separate his activities as secretary from his as editor. So, too, he used his agents in a dual capacity. David Camp was hired to visit the towns of Guilford and Madison, delivering copies of the *Journal* to the school society clerks, soliciting subscriptions, and inspecting schools; although ever eager, he was not too successful. Elsewhere William Baker fared no better, and he advised that

> the Third Volume of the Journal be more adapted to the wants of men whose minds have not been highly cultivated & who *will not* take the pains to examine any thing unless it come clothed in a garb *attractive*, peculiarly *attractive* to children. They are in fact but children in knowledge.

And even among the intellectuals of New Haven, Denison Olmsted discovered, the Journal was "too pale." "The good to be done will . . . not depend so much on the quality of the matter as upon the kind being such as will particularly interest the common people.[92] But Barnard refused to compromise his standards, and he had to struggle to make ends meet. After "much hesitation" he had raised the cost to $1 a year in August 1839, and in the final number of the second volume he implied that it was to be the last; despite the indispensability of such a journal, its circulation did not warrant its continuation, and he had already expended too much

91. See *AJE* XV, xl (September 1856): 612–16, "Female Common School Associations"; William J. Reese, *Power and the Promise of School Reform* (Boston: Routledge and Kegan Paul, 1986), chap. 2, "Municipal housekeepers," details similar activities in the Progressive period.

92. Letters from Camp, August 14, October 2, 14, 1840; from Baker, October 2, 23, 1840; from Olmsted, September 8, 1840; all NYU. *CCSJ* II, 1 (August 1839); IV, *Fourth Annual Report*, 187 mentions the visits of Camp and Baker.

of his own time and money. It was an empty threat, however; he lowered the price back to the original one and delayed publication for three months, but by December, he still had only some three hundred subscribers, well over half of them in Hartford County alone.

> This to be sure is rather a mortifying exhibit of the financial prosperity of the Journal, and is another evidence of the little reliance which can be placed on the promises of cooperation in this cause, which are so freely given, but so lamely redeemed.

The complaint was decidedly unfair to all those who gave concrete assistance and advice which Barnard stubbornly refused to heed.[93]

Barnard's ineptness as publisher compounded his problems. Subscribers frequently failed to receive what they had paid for, and one supporter wrote to demand an immediate reply to his repeated letters: "Considerable dissatisfaction has been expressed." William Alcott never seemed to get his issues, and when one finally came, it was badly paginated. As a contributor he had another complaint: Barnard had not paid him for his articles; he finally settled for a complete set of the *Journal* and $15.00 but protested "it is quite an unusual way of doing business." Cyrus Peirce returned proof commenting that it had "lots of errors and the punctuation is very faulty." Thomas Webb remarked that he saw much of Mann's "property" in the Journal without "any mark of ownership," although Mann never protested and repeatedly forwarded additional material—it was common practice for editors to pirate from other publications. Favorites of the editor's persuasion, such as Dr. Humphrey, Miss Beecher, and William Channing, figure with regularity. One issue (volume II, number 14) contained extracts from the *Annals of Education*, the *Quarterly Register*, the *American Almanac*, the census of 1830, and countless primary documents. The March 1841 edition carried four addresses to the Institute for Instruction, all delivered ten years previously, and Horace Mann's *Fourth Annual Report*. In addition to culling brotherly publications for material, Barnard relied on his friends for help. Timothy Dwight searched out examples of school apparatus, and William Bishop negotiated for drawings and prices of drafts of school house plans.[94]

There was no question, in the minds of Barnard's fellow travelers,

93. *CCSJ* II, 1 (August 1839): 5; 12 (May 1840): 181; III, 1 (November 1, 1840): 5ff., for a self-justifying editorial; 4 (December 15, 1840): 56, list of subscriptions; 5, January 15, 1841. The legislature did help some of the circulation problem, appropriating a small amount to send copies of the first two volumes to the districts; *Fourth Annual Report*.

94. Letter from Butterfield, November 26, 1840; from Peirce, January 5, 1841; from Alcott, June 2, 13, August 10, 1840, but on October 26, 1841, he offered to sell Barnard his *Slate and Blackboard Lessons* for $100—they appeared in the final issue of the *Journal*;

about the value of the *Journal*. The assessment of George Combe so pleased the editor that he quoted it:

> It was a very ably conducted, useful, and cheap periodical, but it did not discuss politics, nor theological controversy, not news; it was full of his moral and practical information relative to the importance of education.[95]

This was precisely what Barnard intended, but there was a real question whether those for whom he pledged to make the publication "as serviceable as possible" actually read it. Certainly there were masses of practical hints, on how to teach reading, spelling, penmanship, map drawing, and how to keep an orderly school register, and there were model geography, arithmetic and music lessons. Alcott's entire *Slate and Blackboard Exercises* was published, monopolizing four issues. In fact, almost the whole of volume IV is devoted to the concrete needs of teachers.

The message implied in all of the suggestions is pragmatic and progressive, with a larding of moral overtone. "Education not only begins earlier than most persons imagine, but it continues much longer." In school children should always be asked to do and to verify what they learn from their own observation. Every child has a "natural curiosity" to know, but what is taught, to be really learned, should be linked with daily experiences. Tasks and even the arrangement of the classroom should be varied from child to child, from day to day. The source is patently clear: Pestalozzi.

> No person is fit to be a teacher who is not, by original reflection, or careful study, made himself familiar with the Life and principles of Pestalozzi.

Barnard was not original in trumpeting the message of the great Swiss educator. During the previous decade his ideas had been publicized by predecessor publications and in innovative schools such as those of Bronson Alcott in Connecticut and Boston and Neff in New Harmony. Barnard, however, was to be a leading apostle of Pestalozzi for the next twenty years.[96]

---

letter from Dwight, January 27, 1841; several from Bishop, from Providence, March, 1841; all NYU.

95. *CCSJ* IV, 3 (January 15, 1842): 30, where Barnard listed periodicals devoted to education and quoted some who have pronounced the *Journal* as dead and admitted that it "has indeed announced its own expected mortality several times."

96. *CCSJ* II, 4 (November 1839): 55; III, 9 (March 1841): 116–18; IV, 3 (January 15, 1842): 29. See *AmJEd* III, xi (September–October 1828), xii (November–December 1828):

On the surface the ready adoption of Pestalozzian principles by the schoolmen reformers, social conservatives that they were, seems extraordinary, but the principles and methods responded to their pragmatic natures. Classrooms modeled on the Swiss educator's ideas *worked*, and results mattered. Barnard demanded a teacher who taught rather than kept school, and he stressed the art and skill of teaching. His insistence on the necessity of more comfortable school houses, "with a seat and desk, of appropriate height and easy access" matched the efforts of entrpreneurs such as Samuel Colt to have factories suitable to the tasks of the employees.[97] The use of cheap and simple apparatus and "modes of communication based upon and adapted to them"—a sand desk, an abacus, a globe, an arrery, charts, outline maps, even "a plan of Jerusalem"— would enable a well-prepared teacher "to communicate more accurate knowledge in a school of four months than is usually done in twelve months when the articles are not provided." Then, too, better texts and active methods made the pupil happier and more responsible.

> Occular evidence . . . is often indispensable for correcting the imperfections of language. . . . Other things being equal, the pleasure which the child enjoys in studying or contemplating is proportioned to the liveliness of her perceptions and ideas.

Barnard favored Pestalozzi's methods because they made schools more pleasant and more efficient.

The members of the Board commended their secretary in their *Annual Report*, and endorsed his suggestions, for school libraries, for normal schools or departments in academies, for more female teachers. They asked for legislative support for the Journal and for more than the proposed $5,000 for a normal school, and, while expressing appreciation for the recent legislative action, they sounded a warning as if they heard a tolling bell:

> should the Legislature, however, interfere to sanction unnecessary or systematic disregard of the requisitions of the school of law, the efficiency of the whole system would be destroyed.

Barnard was less appeasing; there could be no rest.

751–52, IV, ii (March–April 1829): 97–107, for a "concise but clear and satisfactory account" of Pestalozzi's methods.

97. On better schoolhouses see *CCSJ* III, 9 (March 1, 1841): 105–19, where Barnard described the new school in Windsor, anticipating issues he subsequently discussed in *School House Architecture*; on texts and equipment, including catalogs, see *CCSJ* III, 10 (March 15, 1841): 121–28.

Windsor Schoolhouse, *Connecticut Common School Journal*, March 1841

Much of the ignorance with which every person comes into the world, is scarcely touched by the feeble and irregular means employed to enlighten it. Much of the talent of the State is virtually buried for want of the quickening spirit of education, to breathe into it the breath of life. Much of the moral nature of every human being, which if cultivated, would have adorned public and private life, and dried up the sources of violence and injustice, is left a waste, or what is far worse, is covered with growths of the most monstrous vices.[98]

Barnard still found his days occupied in responding to pleas for advice and assistance. He continued to received countless invitations to speak, on any topic; to the New London Young Men's Institute he repeated his standard talk on the "Moral and Educational Wants of Cities." R. H. Hotchkiss asked him to come to Woodbury to talk about school houses, as the town was about to build a new one, and the secretary advised on

98. The *Second Annual Report* is in *CCSJ* II, 13 (June 1840): 197–218. The appendix, "Education in Other States and Countries," takes up numbers 14–16 (July–September 1840): 245–336.

every stage of building the new school in Windsor. He also served as an informal placement agency for teachers. Jonathan Edwards, bearer of a famous Yale name and a recent graduate (just ten years after Barnard —did he empathize?) wanted a position teaching Latin and Greek, and came highly recommended by Benjamin Silliman; Maria Cowles, an Ipswich Seminary product, with eleven years experience, wanted a job, and from Worchester Mr. Washington wrote on behalf of his sister. Towns sought teachers. Norwich, Southington, and Thompsonville all wanted male ones for seven to fourteen year olds, men who would "keep a good school." In Thompsonville the candidate would have to agree to a class of fifty to sixty in the day and four evening sessions a week for youngsters who could not attend by day, all for between $22 and $24 per month plus boarding around. Perhaps some of the young men on whose behalf H. E. R. Rockwell wrote took those jobs, but Rockwell was concerned that at the end of his school's term so many of his students were unemployed.[99] The net result of all of these requests to the state's education officer was the subtle strengthening of the role of the state in school matters.

Then there were countless miscellaneous matters. Harper and Brothers sent a School Library Series and sought an endorsement from the secretary; there was a bill for school apparatus. Both Gideon Thayer and Barnard's cousin Roswell Carter, of Auburn, wanted advice on suitable boarding schools for family members. From Louisville came an inquiry about poor houses, from J. M. Peck, of Rock Island, Illinois, a request for Barnard's first two reports. In March 1841, with Samuel Gridley and George Emerson, he visited the Massachusetts Normal School at Lexington and another at Barre; he agreed with Howe that the lack of a model school was the Barre school's only weakness.[100] He still had Historical Society business and the task of getting lecturers for his Young Man's Institute. A Yale acquaintance, Dr. John Robertson, who was also a school visitor, agreed to lecture on "Ancient Cathedrals," and Horace Mann

99. Letter from Edwards, July 22, from Cowles, November 1, both 1840; from Hotchkiss, June 18, from Thomas Douglas, February 13, 15, March 14, September 15, from Washburn, October 9, from Wells, January 4, from H. E. Rockwell, October 28, requests April 14, July 22, October 2; all 1841, NYU. On Barnard consulting with school building projects, see CCSJ III, 9 (March 1, 1841): 105; for lecture see IV, 2 (January 1842): 23. Douglas wanted an Episcopalian to speak—evidence that Barnard became an Episcopalian prior to his marriage to a Catholic. Note that Rockwell was training teachers.

100. Letter from Harper, January 15, 1841; bill, January 29, 1841; letter from Thayer, September 23, 1841; from Carter, September 15, 1840; from Howe, March 28, 1841, NYU; Arthur O. Norton, *The First State Normal School in America* (Cambridge: Harvard University Press, 1926), 34. Barnard addressed the students at Lexington, CCSJ III, 11 (April 1841): 143.

repeatedly promised to come but finally had to cancel because at the time the entire reform movement was in danger in Massachusetts. "Last year we had to weather a religious squall—this year a political one."[101]

Barnard was facing his own political storm, for there were signs that the reform coalition in Connecticut was beginning to fracture. Board members were less conscientious, and between May 1840 and 1841 two resigned. Samuel Church explained:

> the existing spirit of partisanship is a variance with every principle and project, and what is done by one administration must be undone by the succeeding one, irrespective of merits. This is the equal fault of the present-day parties.

Even that stalwart supporter, Denison Olmstead quit after May, 1841, while still giving enormous credit to the secretary for his "persevering, self-denying, and judicious efforts to diffuse the light of knowledge over the whole community."[102]

More serious for Barnard was the evidence of Democratic opposition which surfaced during the legislative session—although the secretary did not realize just how formidable it was. The Democratic controlled Committee on Education directed the comptroller of the state to audit the accounts of the Board of Commissioners in an obvious effort to discredit the secretary; fortunately for Barnard, all expenditures were allowed, and he was exonerated. In the three years ending May 31, the board had expended an average of less than $1,590 annually, and not one cent of the School Fund had been contributed to board operations. No member had been paid for his services, and Barnard, during the same period had received just under $1,000 annually, being paid on a per diem basis. His annual expenses averaged about $590, but he had contributed, from his own resources, $3,049, most of it for the *Journal*. The Committee concluded its Report:

> It appears further, that the Secretary has, of his own accord, and to promote what he supposed to be the prosperity of the common schools, expending more than the whole amount of his compensation.

Barnard, conveniently forgetting that as a novice legislator he had joined in a call for an audit of the accounts of the Democratic Commissioner of

101. Letter from Robertson, signed Yale '29, March 23, 1841, TC; from Mann March 2, 7, 21, 1840, NYU. The next year Mann signed a March 9 letter "your fellow-laborer, but who I hope I shall never have for a fellow-sufferer." He was so wrong.

102. Letter from Olmsted, May 11, 1841; from Perkins, May 1841; from Olney, January 4, 1841; all NYU. Letter from Church, April 1842, TC. On developing political opposition see Gideonse, "Common School Reform," 118ff.

the School Fund was infuriated and insulted by the attack on his probity and published his defensive reply.

> The committee will, I trust, excuse the personal character of this communication. It is unavoidable, from the nature of their inquiries. And however painful it has been to me to speak of my own labors and to spread out an account of the expenses voluntarily incurred in which the public can be supposed to feel but little interest, it seemed necessary to rescue my motives for laboring in this field, from suspicion and distrust. I assumed the responsibilities of a new, difficult, and delicate office, with a settled purpose to expend every farthing I should receive in promoting what I believe to be the true and enduring good of the common schools. I have continued in this office only at the repeated and urgent solicitations of the Board. I shall retire from it with the satisfaction that I have asked no one to do what I have not shown a willingness to do myself, and with no other regret than that I have not had more time, more ability, and more means to devote to this course, which holds every other good cause in its embrace.[103]

Barnard's reaction, after the battle, was to claim persecution, exhaustion, and illness; he had written to Mann "we are now in the midst of our troubles," prey to "violent" attacks in the partisan press; later that he had been "sick for a month" and was completely "jaded out," unable to finish his annual report. In late June he fled to upstate New York where he stayed with his cousin Roswell. Another letter to Mann was showed him rapidly restored:

> My excursion was delightful & has proved serviceable to my health. If you ever go to that region, don't fail to explore the ravines and water falls about Ithaca. New England can't show anything so picturesque. I have seen nothing out of Switzerland surpassing Goodwin or Taghcanick Falls. I was induced to visit them by reading the "Country Rambler", vol. IX, of the School Library, Juvenile Series.

A month later he was on another holiday in Vermont, and in November he was in Detroit where he may have met his future wife for the first time.[104]

Barnard's performance suffered under the stress, however. The June

103. Appendix to the *Third Annual Report*, *CCSJ* III, 12 (May 1841): 221–24. See also Porter, *Barnard*, 21–24.

104. Letters to Mann, May 26, June 5, July 3, August 13, 1841, MHS; letter addressed in care of Williams, Detroit, November, 1841, NYU.

number of the *Journal*, in which reports of legislative activities had appeared in other years, is simply verbatim extracts from the reports of other states; in July he produced a forty-page summary of the school returns and the Board's report. This *Third Annual Report* of the Board is an utterly confusing document which begins with the draft of the revised school law, followed by the letters on the audit; a fifteen-page "Remarks on the History and Present Condition of the School Law," precedes the actual *Report*. It is fairly easy to reconstruct the state of Barnard's mind when he put the issue together. The attack on the Board and more directly on him distracted him; the material he had at hand would do. And when he came to print material pertaining to the Board, his own defense, as supplied by the letters on his expenses, and his achievements, as exemplified by the draft of the school law and his article on the history of school law, were of paramount concern to him.

The political pot came to a boil in 1842. The Democratic opposition regarded the educational reform movement as a party question, inaugurated by the Whigs, for the benefit of the Whigs. The Board necessitated an unnecessary expense; the thrust of the reform legislation served to diminish the powers of the local governments and hence was undemocratic; worse, the whole program was a foreign import, the "Prussianizing" of a sound American institution. In February the Democratic party convention passed a resolution demanding that the Whigs show cause that the general education of the people of the state had benefited sufficiently to justify the expenses incurred.[105] The Whigs, of course, *knew* that they had acted in the best interests of the people and that the people had benefited and would benefit more if they would only follow the selfless leadership offered; it was hard for the party to believe that anyone would or could doubt their motives. Barnard mirrored their smugness:

> The only real satisfaction of being in office, is the opportunity it gives of carrying out more effectually, than can otherwise be, sound views of public policy and social improvement.[106]

To Mann, though, he revealed his discouragement and concern.

> I am sick & sad. The school movement is now in the whirl of political vortex & I am the target of all sorts of mean & false representa-

---

105. *CC*, February 18, 1842. Gideonse, "Common School Reform," 134ff., quotation 139; see also Porter, *Barnard*, 19–20. Michael B. Katz, *Reconstructing American Education* (Cambridge: Harvard University Press, 1987), 32ff., calls such opposition "democratic localism."

106. Porter, *Barnard*, 12n; I have not located this quotation elsewhere and surmise it came directly from Barnard.

tions. I am naturally sensitive to the injustice of such proceedings, & now that I am worn down by labors, & by some troubles all my own, my nerves are quite bare. I dread to take up a party paper. This is weak, but I can't help it. I am obstinate enough, & were it not for that, I don't know what would become of me. But go on. You have some noble spirits to sympathize with you & you must keep the flag flying as a rallying point of the friends of the good cause everywhere.

Mann, who was a far more astute politician, urged Barnard to stand fast, to fight and save the "Ark of God from the hands of the Philistines."[107] But fighting was not Henry Barnard's forte.

Barnard misinterpreted the nature of the attack; it was political rather than personal. He did not, however, underestimate the danger. The Whigs were roundly defeated in the April elections, when the Democrats achieved a majority in both houses of the legislature and elected Chauncey Cleveland, a man whose constant carping criticism had been anathema to the Whigs for the past four years, as governor. ("Madman" had been one of the *Courant*'s milder epithets.) Cleveland hit hard in his inaugural address. Under the preceding administration "an officer had been employed at considerable expense" on school business with few notable results. The Governor recommended repeal of much of the reform legislation, especially the sections granting increased powers to the school committees and payment for visitors. The new Committee on Education of the House was, according to Barnard, "selected with reference to crippling" the reform movement, and seven of its nine members were "as radical & ignorant as demagogues, and as utterly unfit to legislate on the subject as could be selected out of a very ignorant & bitter minded Legislature."[108] Strong language indeed for a high-minded man who professed to be above politics.

The repeal bill passed both houses by a majority of more than two to one. In a letter to his "Dear Friend" Mann Barnard moaned: "vandalism of party has swept from our Statute Books everything which was calculated to give efficiency to the administration of our school system"; the result could have been different "if there had been but one adroit friend of education in the Legislature." He claimed that he had done "everything which he could to reverse the ruin which had gone forth from the despotic cliques of politicians who rule with a rod of iron the party of

107. Letter to Mann, March 2, 1842, MHS. Letter from Mann, April 25, 1842, TC. A letter from Chauncey, March 1, gives a hint of family business: tenants were in arrears, the joiner needed to be watched, the clover needed to be sown.

108. *CC*, April 9, May 14, 1842; letter to Mann, May 29, 1842, MHS. For excerpts of Cleveland's message, see *CCSJ* IV, 4 (December 1851): 25–26.

which they are leaders . . . ," but he had not, and he could not. The party
of the right thinkers, the advocates of service and of efficiency, had been
outsmarted and rebuffed, and the secretary had not lifted a finger to prevent its defeat.

Characteristically Barnard complained that he was run down and
confined to his bed with sickness, and then he went off to the Springs for
a rest. He was also open to various suggestions for his future, to Mann's
that he come to Massachusetts, perhaps to head a normal school, and to
the idea of a voluntary association for the support of education in Connecticut. "I love old Connecticut & regard this as emphatically missionary ground, and with any prospect of success I should be willing to labor
on without pay for five years to come."[109] There is an odd dissonance
here, between the exaggerated and stereotypical expressions of despair
and a matter-of-factness. One suspects that disappointed as Henry Barnard was he was not devastated; he was not a passionate man, and his
equanimity was stronger than his anger.

The Whig majority of the Board did not go out with a whimper. In an
"Address to the Public" they reviewed their achievements and concluded
with words which leave no doubt as to the author of the piece.

> All of these improvements a spirit of vandalism has prostrated; and
> while our sister states are carrying forward the system which we
> had adopted, with the most cheering hopes for success, Connecti-
> cut, with her immense funds, has made a retrograde movement.[110]

The Board submitted a *Fourth Annual Report*, reviewing their activities during the past year, which had been minimal; no returns had
been requested although some had been received. Several documents of
importance that had been prepared by Barnard for the legislature,
but that body, consistent in its spirit of economy, refused to print the
two most recent ones, on schools in cities and on normal schools. In
summarizing their expenses, the Board stressed that no member had
ever received any compensation and that the secretary "had been paid
for his services the sum authorized by law, and on the same principle,
that members of the Legislature, and every per diem officer in the
employ of the state or national government is paid." They concluded
with their "conviction of the beneficial results of the measures of the

109. Letter to Mann, June 11, July 3, 1842, MHS; John T. Norton of Farmington, one
of the Board's most stalwart supports, opposed any private efforts which he felt would
only provide the legislature with an excuse for doing nothing; he advocated a campaign,
once again, to "stir up the people"; letters June 4, TC, July 15, NYU, both 1842.

110. CC, June 25, 1842. Note the repetition of the word *vandalism*.

Legislature, in the cause of general education" and gave generous credit to "the indefatigable exertions and ability of the Secretary of the Board":

> His labors will long be felt in our schools, and be highly appreci-
> ated by all who entertain just and liberal views on education; and
> whether appreciated or not, he will assuredly have the satisfaction
> of having generously, with little or no pecuniary compensation, con-
> tributed four of the prime years of his life, to the advancement of a
> cause well worthy of the persevering efforts of the greatest and best
> of men.[111]

The Barnard myth was begun.

Barnard's own final report is a curious document, because it was not the one he had intended to write. The Board had

> thought it advisable to review the grounds we had gone over during
> the past four years, as a sort of landmark, after the flood of popular
> error & party madness had subsided, as well as an ark to process the
> good seed for future cultivation.[112]

He began each section with "prior to 1838" or a similar phrase, and reviewed his actions in a rather indiscriminate fashion; much is repeti-tious, with echoes of previous reports and speeches. The tone through-out is cautious, conciliatory, and self-serving, and he stressed that a true evaluation of his work was yet to come.

> The full effects of the measures of the Board, if persevered in, can-
> not be seen, until at least one generation of children have grown up
> under the influence of a more enlightened, liberal, and vigorous
> public opinion in relation to this whole subject.

But to set the record straight he listed what had been accomplished. Attendance at school meetings was higher, there were new and repaired schools throughout the state, and in many of them uniform sets of books had been made available; visitors were more attentive, there were graded schools in more than one hundred districts, with a woman in charge of the younger children and a man of the older ones; teachers were employed for longer periods and at higher salaries, and some had a small measure of preparation. With some satisfaction Barnard could sum up his four years of effort:

111. *CCSJ* IV, 15 (September 1, 1842): 172–92, especially 175.

112. Letter to Mann, May 29, 1842; Barnard said that once he knew what the Governor planned to say he had to rewrite his report.

Wherever the common schools have been improved, the number attending them has increased, and the attendance and expense of private schools has diminished; and thus the advantages of a good education have been made common to rich and poor. And as at once the evidence of the past, and the pledge of future improvements, parents and men of education and influence generally, are found more frequently visiting schools, discharging with zeal the duties of school committees, conversing and reading on the subject, and acquainting themselves with the efforts which are making this and other countries to give a more thorough and complete education to every human being.[113]

Henry Barnard had not changed; if discouraged at times he was not bitter. He still wanted common schools for all, and he still believed that the duty of their leadership lay with the men "of education and influence." He had proved that he was not skilled, or interested, in political maneuvering during the past year; Horace Mann would have played out the scenario quite differently. What he had demonstrated, in his brief tenure as secretary, was his effectiveness as an agent for school reform propaganda. He had also planted the seed of state initiative and intervention in school matters, previously the exclusive right of the local government. Certain weaknesses were obvious in his performance as an editor, and as an administrator he was largely untested. But during the four years he had risen to prominence, within the state and within educational circles of the nation, as a spokesman who could stand with any. Full credit was given him by one of his elder mentors:

> No public officer, that I have ever known in the State, has done so much of labor and drudgery to prepare his field, expending at the same time *more* than he received, and seeking his reward in the beneficent results by which he was ever expecting to honor himself and the State.[114]

The question for Henry Barnard in the summer of 1842 was precisely the one he had faced twelve years earlier when he had graduated from Yale: what was he to do? The difference now was that he was certain of one thing. He had elected education as the chart on which to plot his course. What the route and the eventual destination should be was not clear.

113. *CCSJ* IV, 15 (September 1, 1842): 192.
114. Horace Bushnell in a lecture, 1843, to the Hartford Young Men's Institute; *CCSJ* II, 1 (August 1843): 62.

III

SCHOOL

ADMINISTRATOR

*The cause of true education, of the complete
education of every human being, without
regard to accidents of birth or fortune, is
worthy of the concentration of all powers,
and if need be, of any sacrifice of time,
money, and labor we may be called upon to
make in its behalf. (Farewell to the Teachers
of Rhode Island, 1849)*

During the early summer of 1842 Barnard was busy winding up
his business in Connecticut. His supporters sent comforting letters of
appreciation and regret and sought guidance as to what next step the
friends of education should take; to them the ex-secretary was still the key
figure. Even two years later, when the legislature was again in Whig hands
and again resolved to appoint a commission to investigate the condition
of the schools, the governor wanted Barnard to act as chairman, but by
that time he was occupied elsewhere.[1] Others now sought his services.
Although I have found no substantiation for Norton's claim that Barnard
was offered the superintendencies of Boston, New York, Cincinnati, and
New Orleans, an acquaintance in New Orleans did make a tentative
inquiry whether Barnard would be interested in some appointment. And
Senator Albert Picket begged Barnard to come to Ohio to combat oppo-

---

1. See letters from John T. Norton, June 4, William Eaton, June 9, Eli T. Hoyt, June
30, Richard Smith, July 7, 1842; from R. S. Baldwin, September 24, 1844; all NYU. In
Barnard's very old age he received a letter from Charles Marseilles of Exeter, New Hampshire, who claimed that he was not the only one under the "delusion" that Barnard had
declined election to the Senate of the United States; "in the interest of *correct history,*"
Marseilles begged the old man to set the matter straight. Unfortunately he did not, or we
have no record that he did. Letter from Marseilles, January 20, 1899, TC.

sition to "the exertions of the few friends deeply interested in the holy cause" of common school reform.[2]

One option was for quite a different position within the common school reform movement. Horace Mann wanted his friend to become head of one of his state's normal schools.

> Connecticut is not the place for you now. Let Cincinnatus leave Rome, and in her distress, she will send for and implore his return. I look upon a change in public opinion in Connecticut as certain, within a period not distant. With New York on on [sic] side and Massachusetts on the other, her frozen heart will be warmed into life.

For some inexplicable reason Barnard felt in a strong bargaining position and both negotiated and temporized. He was weary and discouraged, he feared he was not the man for the job; yet he wanted the school moved from Barre to Springfield, a site nearer to home, and he wanted to be guaranteed a model school and assistants and sufficient time free from duties for his extensive correspondence and scholarly activities. In the end, he declined the offer, or let it lapse. But more than eight months later Mann wrote that he had "not abandoned all hopes of you yet" and, as the political climate had not improved, he urged Barnard "Come to Massachusetts who will show her appreciation of your qualities and powers of usefulness."[3]

Barnard published additional numbers of the *Connecticut Common School Journal* and two small books after his dismissal, although neither bears his name on the title page. *Hints and Methods for the Preparation of Teachers* was copied verbatim from the *Journal*, a technique he would employ frequently in the future in an effort to secure a wider readership among teachers for his work. The second publication, entitled *The Legal Provision Respecting the Education and Employment of Children in Factories*, had been prepared for the Board and appeared in the *Journal* after the legislature refused to print it. The report contained masses of information —from Massachusetts and Rhode Island, from England, Russia, Swit-

2. Frederick C. Norton, "Sketch of the Life of Henry Barnard," *Connecticut Quarterly* IV, 2 (April–June, 1898): 130. Letter from Albert Pickett, October 6; from Andrews June 19, August 14, October 3; from Recorder Baldwin, November 3; all 1843; from committee in Columbus, January 3, 1844; all TC. All of these letters come after Barnard's Western trip, not before.

3. For the negotiations see Mann's letters June 23, July 27, August 9, August 19, September 13, 1842, NYU, and Barnard's replies June 11, July 30, August 8, August 19, 20, September 3, November 22, 1842, MHS. On the change of site see letter from Heman Humphrey, August 2, from Mann, August 9; in letters July 27 and August 19 Mann begs

zerland, Austria, and France, as well as Connecticut. Barnard included extracts from Mann's *Fifth Annual Report* and abridged an article on the "Elevation of the Working Classes" from the *Westminster Review*. An article on the factory system in Lowell and the city's educational facilities was awash with statistics and cited as a model; "the richest and the best educated parents are glad to avail themselves of these public institutions."[4] Even at this early stage of his career as an educational editor, Barnard abdicated editorial judgment; he simply printed it all, with a few characteristic comments.

With his desk now cleared, Henry Barnard could do what he loved most, travel. He was able to afford it, for he was a man of means, the proprietor, it seems, of sizable property. In *Armsmear*, the memoir of Samuel Colt which Barnard published in 1866, there is a map of Hartford's South Meadow which identifies two valuable parcels of land as belonging to Henry Barnard, one of fifteen acres and another, along the river, of forty; once Colt had built his famous Dutch dike these holdings became very valuable. In addition, when Barnard died, his daughter sold some acreage, "a wood lot," in West Hartford. Henry Barnard had also increased his patrimony by investments, even speculation—in Michigan (Williams used the term "your mill") and in Texas. He was a frugal man in a way, who refused to loan Williams money for a newspaper, which seems surprising, or to Grant for a cooperative venture. But he spent lavishly on his own schemes and pleasures, especially to indulge his greed for books as indicated by the numerous letters in his correspondence from his London agent detailing orders and shipments.[5]

For the next fifteen months this personable young bachelor toured the country, visiting friends and lecturing.[6] In the fall he went to Detroit to

---

for answers, for a date on which Barnard will meet with the normal school visitors; by August 24 a date was settled, and Mann urged his friend "not to fail."

4. *Hints and Methods for the Preparation of Teachers* (Hartford: Tyler & Porter, 1842); cf., *CCSJ*, IV, 3 (January), 13 (July 1842). *Legal Provision Respecting the Education and Employment of Children in Factories* (Hartford: Case, Tiffany & Burnham, 1842); cf., *CCSJ*, IV, 13 (July), and 15 (September, 1842).

5. *Armsmear: The Home, the Arm, and the Armory of Samuel Colt* (New York: Alvord, 1866), 58. Letters from Williams, September 2, October 4, 1843, August 9, 1844; from Grant, December 6, 1843, TC; from Rainford August 15, 1843, January 3, 1844, NYU.

6. Letter to Mann, November 22, 1842, MHS. Porter, *Barnard*, 65; see also *AJE* XXX, unpaged but between 198–201. Barnard claimed to have addressed six legislatures and interviewed the governors and leading citizens of most state and large cities, and to have established a network of correspondence which "in subsequent years led to the building of schoolhouses, the introduction and modification of systems of public schools, and the employment of teachers in nearly every State." The 1842–43 letters do not support quite such a lofty claim.

stay with Alpheus Williams for a month, a time which "passed indeed delightfully" but was not long enough for "uninterrupted talks" and "time to mature future plans." Williams pressed his friend to settle on an occupation. "You have now sufficient means to take hold of any business . . . and secure yourself in easy independence." Spending and laboring "to make our children wiser" was a thankless task; better to stay in Detroit and make money.[7] But Williams argued in vain, for even as he wrote, Barnard was on his way. He went to Ohio, stopping in Canton, Columbus (where he addressed the College of Teachers) and Cincinnati; then on to Kentucky where in Lexington he lectured to the city council. Soon he was in Mobile and then New Orleans—he lingered with Ashbel Smith nearly another month. He returned home via the south, spending time during May in Charleston, and making an extended visit in Albany with Henry Randall before returning to Hartford.[8]

Henry Barnard's capacity for friendship is exemplified on this trip. He was a gregarious person, a delightful companion, and a loyal and warm friend. Henry Randall was certainly responding to his friend when he wrote, "Yes, we do, as I trust 'understand' each other. I give you my hand in return for yours; let our league be perpetual." Williams, in the affectionate letter already quoted, closed, "I have felt very lonely since I left you . . . I feel as if your visit was not half finished and that I was letting you go much too soon." With his friends, in letters as well as on visits, Barnard discussed everything from Fouirerism to Goethe, and his romantic impulses emerged when he talked of his reading; his rendering of a work by Piccolomini during an Albany visit was so affecting that Randall reported he could not longer bear to read the poet himself.

The friendship with Samuel S. Randall had conscious overtones of the great German romantic relationships. In mid-1843 Randall wrote with some formality, "by what fortunate chance have I continued to elicit and secure so deep an interest in my welfare, from one comparatively speaking a stranger?" A year later, after Barnard had made another visit to Albany, Randall wrote, "Your pale sad face, as it looked in our last sit up, haunts me like a specter." What could be the cause of such unhappiness: certainly not "pecuniary reverses" which would not "raise a ripple on

7. Letter from Williams, addressed in care of Andrews in Columbus, December 19, 1842, NYU.

8. Letter to Mann, February 13, from Louisville, March 26, Baton Rouge, 1843, MHS. Barnard called Mann "my guide, my home, my friend, my fellow laborer and fellow sufferer." According to Barnard (*AJE* XV, xi [September 186]: 400), after his lecture in Columbus he had a lengthy interview with Judge Ebenezer Lane, the result of which was the establishment of teachers' institutes in the judge's home town of Sandusky and the "complete reform" of the schools.

your calm, expansive intellect"; nor the loss of a job; could it be love? It might in fact be just that. Williams had written to Barnard in Frankfurt that he, Williams, had not had a chance to see their "incipient flames," for Miss E. M. was away and "Miss J—D— not seen nor heard from." In October he could report that "Miss D. is a good and worthy a person as ever." Whether Barnard was in love, these are the first clear references to his future wife. Perhaps he was ready to take Randall's advice to "keep your heart open to the influence of woman's love," but it was to his male friends that he expressed deep affection.[9] These friends remained until their, and his, dying days.

Although pleasure, and the desire to see his country, was the prime motive for Barnard's travels, research was another. He had begun to collect materials for a project that was forming in his mind, the writing of a history of schooling, and he sought information from every quarter. That grand old man of educational reformers, James G. Carter responded that he had always been "very careless and slovenly" about his papers, but in order to set the record straight and with "the historian now at my heels," he would try to answer Barnard's queries.[10] Francis Bowen sent an almanac from New York and promised to put some required information into a summary table for Barnard's use; Sam L. Harris, up in Augusta, Maine, reported that he had sent out circulars to seventy towns seeking the information his friend sought and would forward the results to Hartford. Barnard collected primary documents in vast quantities and compiled factual information in minute detail, and indiscriminately, displaying the fascination with statistics so common in the thirties and forties.[11] What

9. Letters from Grant span the years 1843–63, TC; letters from H. Randall, November 30, 1843, TC; July 16, 30, 1843, January 1, April 25, May 17, 1844, NYU; from C. P. Bordenave, November 11, 24, 1842, January 5, 1843; from S. S. Randall January 4, December 8, 1843; from Williams, February 7, October 4, 1843; all NYU. See *AJE* XIII, xxxi (June 1863): 227–31 and frontispiece for a "Memoir of Samuel S. Randall," who "endeavored to the best of his ability, to incorporate with, and infuse into the system over which he presides, the ideas and principles & the best and most enlightened educators of the age." Randall, an Albany reformer was the Superintendent of Schools in New York City from 1854 to 1870.

10. *CCSJ*, n.s., II, 1 (1855): 65–66. Letter from James G. Carter, October 30, 1843, TC. Carter showed some pique: "I confess that I have sometimes thought that some of my contemporaries have made rather indecent haste to cover up my tracks in their glorious careers."

11. Letters from Bowen, July 27, August 14, 1843; from Harris, October 14, 1843; NYU. The correspondence of 1843 and 1844 is full of replies to similar queries; S. S. Randall, October 20, 1844, complained that he had submitted the same answer six or seven times. For an absorbing account of the contemporary fascination with statistics see Patricia Cline Cohen, *A Calculating People: The Spread of Numeracy in Early America* (Chicago: University of Chicago Press, 1982).

was he to do with such masses of material? Randall was encouraging: it was Barnard's "duty" to publish; and then to get a good agent to introduce the book—Randall grandly promised that the New York Department of Education, and the generous Daniel Wadsworth, would sanction it.[12] Wadsworth and the world had to wait, however, for Barnard's skills and energy were about to be pressed into service elsewhere.

On December 6, 1843, Governor Fenner, of neighboring Rhode Island, issued a circular to the people of the state, announcing the appointment of Henry Barnard "to collect and disseminate in every practical way information respecting existing defects and desirable improvements" in the schools of the state. Thus came the famous summons: "It is better to make history than to write it."[13]

Before examining Barnard's career in Rhode Island we must survey, as he would have done, the state to which he would devote much of his time and attention for the next five years. Rhode Island was a New England anomaly, a tiny state, with a history of religious toleration, political conservatism, and rampant individualism. It was a land of small farms and, because it was blessed in its location, increasingly active shipping. Like Connecticut, this smallest state had clung to its colonial charter after the revolution; the governor and the bicameral legislature were elected annually by the property holders of the commonwealth. The legislative sessions were held twice a year, in each of the five largest towns in succession, and two delegates from each of the towns sat in the assembly, whatever the size of the community. Fear of centralization and a concentration of power were almost pathological among the conservative citizens.

But Rhode Island had changed drastically in the first three decades of the century. Partly because of the embargo and dislocation of the War of 1812, and because of advances in technology, the state's economic base shifted from the sea to the land. A textile industry, centered on the abundant water power, prospered; by 1832 capital investment in factories was three times that in shipping—so much had commerce declined. The state's population grew apace, more than doubling between the revolution and the Civil War, and concentrating in the major towns. Two phenomena associated with rapid modernization appeared: social dislocation and political inequity. Conditions in the new factories were, of course, appalling; the work week was as long as seventy-eight hours, and over 3,000 children under twelve worked in the mills. With factories came urbanization. In 1841 40 percent of the white male population lived in

12. Letters from S. S. Randall, June 2, October 11, 1843, NYU.
13. I have found no substantiation, other than Barnard's statement, of Fenner's remark.

Providence; they paid two-thirds of the taxes, yet in the assembly they had only one-twentieth of the representatives. The rapidly declining rural villages continued to enjoy equal representation; one hamlet of 665 citizens sent two delegates as did the largest city.

It was in this setting of social and political fragmentation that a democratic movement, led by Thomas Dorr, challenged the standing mercantile elite with its agrarian base. The Dorr Rebellion is a fascinating story, complete with major themes—the challenge of a new order to a dying way of life, the democratic impulses of the common man, and a flawed hero.[14] Thomas Wilson Dorr was the son of a prosperous Providence manufacturer, a Harvard graduate, a lawyer, an Episcopalian, by nature and inheritance a Whig, and a reformer. He served on the Providence school committee, and in the assembly, from 1834 on, he stood for regulation of banking, of the debtor laws, of education; he was also an abolitionist. Within four years he had left the Whigs and allied himself with the Democrats; by 1840 he chaired that party. Soon he became the leader of the new People's Party, and in May 1842 he was inaugurated governor under the recently ratified, and highly controversial, People's Charter, one of two competing fundamental laws. To some he had inherited "the sacred mantle of 1776"; to others he was a renegade or, worse, a traitor. For a time the state had two governments, and the issue of the legitimacy of each was debated endlessly in the partisan press.[15] The matter was resolved when, late in May, Dorr led an abortive attack on the Providence arsenal, an event which Henry Barnard would later describe, in good, hyperbolic, Whig fashion: "The State was converted into a camp, every village and hamlet resounded with the din of military preparation."[16] Dorr's resort to force alienated most and, equally telling, made him look ridiculous. He was arrested, tried for treason, and sentenced to life in prison. Ultimately the issue of the legitimacy of his action and of the People's government and taken up by the Supreme Court which repudiated Dorr; redress of any grievance, said the Court, lay not with the justices but with the state's political processes.[17]

---

14. The most recent work on the rebellion is Marvin E. Gettleman, *The Dorr Rebellion: A Study in American Radicalism, 1833–1849* (New York: Random House, 1973); the author's basis is implicit in his title.

15. Gettleman, *Rebellion*, 72. The details of the People's Constitutional Convention, the adoption of the two constitutions, and the existence of two competing state governments are unnecessary here; so too is the comic opera tale of Dorr's abortive military venture.

16. *North American Review* 67 (July, 1848): 251.

17. Gettleman, *Rebellion*, chap. 7, presents the legal and constitutional aspects vividly; Arthur May Mowry, *The Dorr War* (Providence: Preston & Rounds Co., 1901), 297ff.,

Dorr's flirtation with violence strengthened the law and order elements in the state, but the grievances of the people were recognized. A compromise constitution, which contained a bill of rights, reformed and extended the franchise, and reapportioned the Assembly was ratified by a small number of voters in April 1843. Although the towns maintained their equal representation in the state senate, the ten rapidly growing northern ones now held a majority of the seats in the lower house. And a key clause imposed on the legislature the duty of promoting education. To the Whigs such action was essential.[18] As a result of this mandate a law was passed authorizing a state-wide survey of schooling; such a survey had to have an agent. We are now at the point when Henry Barnard will once again step onto the stage.

The pattern of education in the colony and state of Rhode Island presents the familiar one of small dame schools, a few village ones, a collegiate Latin school, and independent school masters; support came from individual donations and fees. There was no provision for the public support of schools prior to 1800. In that year, responding to the agitation of the Providence Association of Mechanics and Manufacturers, the General Assembly passed an Act to Establish Free Schools, "to contribute to *the greater equality* of the people, by the common joint instruction and education of the whole."[19] The act required towns to support one or more schools, the number being dependent on the size of the community, for an equally varied length of time, for the benefit of children between the ages of 6 and 20. Providence immediately established the maximum the city was allowed: three school districts with terms of eight months each. Villages such as tiny Middletown maintained one school for a mere four months, and most towns protested or ignored the law.

There were sound historical reasons for the opposition to the state support of schools, no matter how minimal. First was the traditional devotion to civil liberty and individualism; then there was the heritage of religious toleration and the presence in the state of a number of sects, many of which did not require, and even suspected, an educated ministry. In addition the political organization of the state resembled a federation of towns which clung tenaciously to their independence. Finally, a practi-

---

echoes Webster: "Agitation, not revolution, was the proper course to take." Dorr was subsequently pardoned and released after a brief time in prison, a hero to some.

18. Elisha R. Potter, *An Address delivered before the Rhode Island Historical Society* (Providence: G. H. Whitney, 1851); see also *JRIII* II, 1 (July 1847): 1–32, "Discourse of the Hon. Job Durfee to the Historical Society."

19. *JRIII* II, 2 and 3 (August 2 and 15, 1847): 37–38. See also Charles Carroll, *Public Education in Rhode Island* (Providence: E. L. Freeman Co., 1918), 78.

cal consideration was the fact that the state held no Western lands which in Connecticut had supplied the financial base for the state's initiation of educational reform. All this resulted in an aversion to any expenditure for schools or the slightest encroachment on town autonomy. In the words of one of the political leaders, "if we have not been the most educated, we have been the most free."[20]

The school law was repealed, in 1803, with no debate. Matters far more pressing for a maritime state, embargo and war, and conflict with neighboring states over boundaries, diverted the legislature's attention from matters of schooling. After peace was restored, amid growing social dislocations, an effort was made in Providence to ameliorate the city's schools. In April 1828, a committee, chaired by Francis Wayland, visited Boston to investigate the schools. They reported that in a republic it was incumbent for the rulers to provide education and valuable, useful education, for all; graded, primary schools should be scattered throughout the city; because of the dearth of good teachers, a monitorial system was a necessity, even in the secondary schools; in all schools record keeping, improved texts, and supervision should be introduced. The authorities in Providence acted on their committee's recommendations swiftly, and by summer a high school, with male and female departments, opened.[21]

This stalwart group of Providence reformers was joined by the state's opposition newspapers in a campaign for school legislation. A bill was passed in the fall of 1828 providing that the avails from all lotteries in the state and from duties on auctions should be returned to the towns, in proportion to the population under sixteen, for the purposes of education; the amount was not, however, to exceed $10,000 although the towns in turn could raise by taxation up to twice that amount. The act appropriated an additional $5,000 to establish a permanent school fund and authorized the creation of school committees in the towns, without specifying their duties. Although this law differed from the 1800 one in providing more money in grants and by the creation of a school fund, it did not require the towns to supplement the state money, and it limited the amount a town could raise. An ardent advocate of education and of state intervention, John Howland, did not view this as a great improvement, calling the law one "for the discouragement of schools."[22]

20. *JRIII* II, 1 (July 1847), "Discourse of Job Durfee," 31. See also *North American Review* 67 (July 1848): 240–56, esp. 248, quoting Updike.

21. *AmJEd* III, vii (July 1828), "Report of the Committee on Public Schools for Providence," 385–90. The same volume, 427–39, noted with approval the opening of the Providence High School Female Department.

22. The passage of the bill is noted in *AmJEd* III, iv (April 1828): 253; see *JRIII* II, 2 and 3 (August 2 and 15, 1847): 41–49, for debate on the school act, especially the remarks

Howland was too pessimistic. This law, unlike its predecessor, was not repealed; a principle and precedent were accepted. In 1831 another group of friends of education, again under Wayland, sponsored a survey of the schools of the state conducted by a veteran teacher, Oliver Angell. Angell's report, issued in 1832, made two findings: private schools outnumbered public ones, and there was considerable inequity between communities in the provision of schooling. Most towns provided a form of rudimentary training for the youngest children although frequently these were not free, and the majority of private schools housed older children. In Newport there were two public common schools, serving 400 students whereas the thirty-two private ones catered to a total of only 900. Providence, of course, with its developing system, was the exception having eight common schools, each averaging over 100 pupils; still the seven academies enrolled a total of some ninety scholars.[23]

In 1836 the income from the state's share of the federal surplus was distributed to the towns for educational purposes; within two years this amounted to over $18,000 in addition to the $10,000 annual grant. The towns were also required to report their expenditures to the secretary of state. In 1839 an attempt was made to codify all the scattered educational legislation and to define more clearly the statutory responsibility for the provision of schooling. A permanent school fund of $25,000 was created, and state money was allocated only for the provision of instruction, for teachers. Town school committees were given expanded powers, but towns were limited to raising double the amount received from the state. Finally, in a characteristic Whig action, a law of 1840 required that all child laborers receive at least three months schooling—like similar laws elsewhere this last was largely ignored.[24] Thus, contrary to later interpretations, Rhode Island did, in fact, participate in the educational reform movement prior to 1842. Sporadic legislation, based on the same ideology as that of the leaders in neighboring states, had addressed the same evils; reformers had data on which to base their invectives and the examples of successful achievement elsewhere. True, action had been piece-

of Joseph Tillinghast, a perennial reformer. In these pages Barnard reveals his research method; he cites pamphlets, reports, and newspaper accounts, quoting without comment. See also Carroll, *Education*, 87–102, where he emphasizes the role of the press in securing favorable action on the bill.

23. For selections from the report see *JRIII* II, 2 and 3 (August 2 and 15, 1847): 49–50; Carroll, *Education*, 102–06, largely based on Barnard's work.

24. Peter J. Coleman, *The Transformation of Rhode Island, 1790–1860* (Providence: Brown University Press, 1963), 218; see *JRIII* II:51–53 and Carroll, *Education*, 115–19, for abstracts of the official returns.

meal on the state level and successful for the most part only in Providence, but the seeds were there.

What was lacking was a sense of crisis and inspiring leadership; within the space of two years both appeared. It took the disturbances of the Dorr uprising to convince the state political leaders of the necessity of pressing ahead with the matter of the education of the masses. As a result, the Constitution of 1842 gave to the General Assembly the duty of promoting public schools "by all means they deem necessary and proper" and granted towns the right to tax for the provision of education.[25]

Early in the 1843 session Wilkins Updike, of South Kingston, a Yale graduate, a Whig, and a friend of Barnard's, introduced yet another education bill, this time one to ascertain, again, the condition of the schools of the state. Echoes of Barnard are striking in Updike's speech:

> Pass this bill—sustain the agent who may be appointed—act upon his recommendations when they are sanctioned by the facts and sound arguments—engraft upon our system the tried improvements of other states—and enlist the people, the whole people, in this great work of elevating the schools, where all the children of the state may be well educated, and this little bill of three sections will be the beginning of a new era in our legislation of the subject of education.[26]

The bill was actually harmless—basically the state wanted to know how its $25,000 was being spent. An agent was to be employed to survey the state, to visit schools and collect information in order to make recommendations for the "improvement and better management of the same." Governor Fenner knew exactly whom he wanted in the job, and in November, Thomas Burgess wrote to Henry Barnard to sound him out about it. He would be paid three dollars *per diem* plus expenses and he was to start immediately. According to the Barnard myth, he was reluctant to accept the position, but, prior to the passage of the bill, at Updike's invitation, he had addressed the Rhode Island legislature "On the Conditions of a successful system of public schools," and he readily accepted Governor Fenner's famous challenge.

Barnard at first saw the job as one of short duration. "I go to Rhode

25. Frank Tracy Carlton, *Economic Influences Upon Educational Progress in the United States, 1820–1850* (Madison, 1908; repr. New York: Teachers College Press, 1965), especially 110–12, makes this point convincingly.

26. *JRIII* I, 7 and 8 (March 1 and 15, 1846): 109. For very similar accounts of Barnard's activity in Rhode Island, see *CCSJ* IV, iv (December 1851): 131ff., and *CCSJ*, n.s., II, 1 (January 1855): 65ff.

Island to labor for the winter. I shall be back in January," he wrote to a friend. He knew that the Governor hoped for an early report, after which its author could return to Hartford, to write and to arrange the schedule of lectures for his Historical Society. In fact, Barnard was seldom in the neighboring state for very long; he was still listed in the Hartford Directory as residing on Main Street, and most of his letters during the winter of 1844 are addressed there. Updike wrote to him in despair in January only to find that Henry was in Albany; in April Updike claimed that "Everybody here wants to see Mr. B. We are very lonesome and look for you every day," and Barnard's horse was getting fat in his pasture from lack of use.[27] In the winter of 1844 the potential of the position in Rhode Island was not apparent, not even to Henry Barnard.

In making an effort to evaluate Barnard's activity and contributions in Rhode Island, it is important to attempt to isolate his contributions from those of his colleagues. A later historian would write of "Mr. Barnard's school law," yet a political opponent would complain in 1848 that the commissioner was never in the southern part of the state and was not worth his salary.[28] The truth must lie somewhere in between crediting Barnard with all educational initiatives and asserting that he was ineffectual. As had been the case in Connecticut, he could rely on a strong, although small, base of supporters led by Updike and Nathan Bishop. The former had lobbied for Barnard's appointment and continued to do yeoman service in the cause. Bishop, an exact contemporary of Barnard's, a former tutor at Brown, and now the superintendent of Providence's growing school system, was the author of several editorials lauding his friend's appointment and may well have been the source of many of Barnard's pronouncements on urban education.

The fact that the appointment of the school agent was part of a continuing program advocated by a contingent of reformers is clear from measures passed before Barnard even had submitted his first oral report. In January 1844, the legislature repealed all laws not included in the newly revised statutes except those pertaining to education; these were to remain in force until 1845, and the school agent was directed to prepare a revised school code. Another law gave extensive powers to the school districts for the improvement of schoolhouses, and to impose taxes for those pur-

27. Letter from Barnard to Rev. C. W. Bradley, November 30, 1843, YU; letters from Updike, April 5, 18, May 13, June 1, August 5, and October 31, 1843, NYU. Updike mentions "your Miss Leach"—Barnard had been in Rhode Island long enough to have a social life!

28. Thomas Wentworth Higginson, *A History of the Public School System of Rhode Island* (Providence, 1876), chap. VIII, 63. Providence *Journal*, June 28, 1848, in scrapbook, Rhode Island Historical Society (hereafter RIHS).

poses. Subsequently, in the October session, the school agent was directed to prepare a document to assist the district committees in carrying out the mandate on school buildings; this publication was, of course, the genesis of Barnard's *School Architecture* which will be discussed below. Thus it is impossible to give Barnard all credit for action taken during the first months of his tenure in the state.[29] What we cannot assess is how much influence Barnard exerted in private conversations with his colleagues. He was officially merely a school agent; other powers were to come.

Barnard set to work immediately, utilizing the same strategies he had employed so successfully five years before in his native state. He held a series of meetings; the first, held in Bristol on December 16, was widely reported in the press and provides us with the pattern of subsequent gatherings. The "State Lecturer on Public Schools" spoke for an hour and a half, outlining his scheme for universal schooling: each town should have as many elementary schools as could easily be reached by small children, each should have secondary schools, two probably being sufficient, and ideally a high school, open to all youngsters, of both sexes, with a curriculum designed to prepare for a useful life. All of these schools should of course be comfortable and pleasant places. Barnard concluded with "a powerful appeal" to the citizenry to engage in the noble cause of school reform.

A few days later Barnard was in Woonsocket where in "plain, homely, direct, earnest talk," adorned with no flourishes but the "powerful eloquence of truth" and the "utmost courtesy of manner," he spoke for two hours. He began with a brief survey of European education lauding especially the "unequalled Prussian system." Next, perhaps because he anticipated antipathy when he advocated the measures of an authoritarian state, Barnard examined the motives for a system of schools. It was necessary, in a republic, to educate the citizenry for political reasons. But education was also "to open the treasures of books" to all. Although he quickly added a comment on the value of the reading of the Bible, his point here has the ring of warm and personal conviction. From the why he moved to the where of schooling and asked his audience to compare the local churches, edifices in which the congregations spent at most an hour and a half each Sunday, with the schools in which the children of the community suffered daily for hours. He gave a "thrilling view of the philosophy and importance of ventilation" and a lengthy disquisition on oxygen. Next, while criticizing most teachers, he admitted that there were some

29. *JRIII* I, 7 (March 1, 1846): 111–12; for the pamphlet see ibid., Appendix xii, 11 and 12 (May 1846).

excellent ones, but he emphasized that they had only become so "by experimenting on your children." To counter the argument, strong in Rhode Island, that the provision of schooling was expensive, he advanced the standard Whig response; it was more economical for the state to educate the young than to meet later the costs of pauperism and crime which resulted from ignorance. He concluded: "The fact is no tax is made on the principle of *private accommodation but of general good*."[30]

This speech was certainly repeated countless times, by Barnard himself, and similar ones were delivered by his allies. For, although he later would claim to have conducted 1,100 meetings and school visits, the record indicates that he was counting totals and not his efforts exclusively. Barnard depended on an army, or platoon, of loyal soldiers in the cause; Wilkins Updike was the captain whose name appears in the accounts of many meetings. But Barnard, the agent, also employed, as he had in Connecticut, an agent, William S. Baker.[31] Baker was a highly successful teacher who utilized his skills as an advocate of education when his duties in the winter terms allowed. Throughout 1844 and 1845 he toured the southern part of the state, visiting as many as twelve districts in a given week, and working himself to the point of exhaustion. Something of a Johnny Appleseed of education, out planting the seeds of schools, he cut a figure both ridiculous and effective.[32]

The governor had expected a report from his agent in time for the spring legislative session, and in April Bishop wrote to Hartford that the agent's presence was required within the week. Barnard was, once again, elsewhere. He had accepted Francis Dwight's invitation to attend a convention of county supervisors in Rochester, New York, and there he praised the state's system of supervision which was, he felt, far superior to anything in New England. The "fifty or sixty intelligent" supervisors were able, conscientious, and paid.

> This admirable structure rises harmoniously with the political organization of the State in other respects, through towns and counties, till it finds its natural head in the State.[33]

30. Scrapbook, RIHS, clipping December 16, 1845, probably from the Providence *Gazette*; clipping December 29, 1845, Woonsocket *Patriot*, December 29, 1843.

31. Edwin Martin Stone, *Manual of Education: A Brief History of the Rhode Island Institute of Instruction* (Providence: Providence Press Co., 1874), 32–33, says that Baker was employed as an agent by the Institute—"his name will ever be held in honor."

32. Letter from Updike, April 5, from Baggs, April 15; both 1844, NYU; see also Kingsbury in *CCSJ*, n.s. II, 1 (1855): 67. For Barnard's biography of Baker, see *AJE* XIV, xxxvi (September 1864): frontispiece and article 592ff.

33. Letters from Dwight, April 4 and 12, 1844; account of the speech in *Common School*

This speech, which characteristically lasted over two hours, was Whig in tone and substance. In it Barnard endorsed the idea of centralization, and gave a hint of the ideas he was formulating for Rhode Island. He closed with the ringing phrases which were to become his hallmark—that schooling should be cheap enough for the poorest and good enough for the best.

In June Updike had to prod his friend, "trusting" the school bill was at the printer. The friends of education were marshalling their forces and consolidating their position for a new assault, and they were convinced that the presence of Barnard was key to the success of their campaign. To Updike there could be no difficulty "if only you will keep at our head."[34] Here again we are confronted with the enigma of Henry Barnard, and the perception others had of his value. The Rhode Island reform leaders were all eminent men in their state, Wilkins Updike a senior member of the assembly; Elisha Potter, Jr., who joined the ranks in 1844, was the son of one of the state's leading political figures and had served in the legislature, then as a congressman for two years before he went back to the assembly. One plausible explanation might be Barnard's affability, for everyone liked him; another might be the fact that he was an extremely effective speaker. Then, too, Barnard's reputation was not confined to a few small New England states. His opinion, judged by the letters he received, was constantly sought on any number of subjects—once, when he had been away for six weeks he returned to find nearly 100 letters awaiting his attention.[35] Barnard himself seems to have shared, and even encouraged, his colleagues' high estimation of his contribution, for even while he remained in Hartford and delegated many of his duties, he complained about his compensation. Updike apologized about the size of the "grant" and promised to improve upon it; "Rhode Island will be true to her engagement" he promised—whatever that was.[36]

There is an additional, hypothetical explanation, not of Barnard's self-satisfaction, but of the local reformers' insistence on his importance and value. The state had recently been racked by civil discontent and disorder and had only just settled down under the new constitution. Politics were volatile, and the Whigs were wary. Some reformers, like Potter, had origi-

---

Journal (Massachusetts) VIII, 14 (1845): 212–17.

34. Letter from Bishop, April 14, from Updike, June 1; both 1844, NYU.

35. Letter to Asa D. Lord, May 22, 1848, collection in the library of Rhode Island College, (hereafter RIC); this college is the successor to the first Rhode Island Normal School, founded in 1854, after Barnard left but owing him a deep debt; Barnard Hall sits in a prominent location on the new campus.

36. Letter, May 13, 1844, NYU.

nally been conservative Democrats but after the Dorr War had become a law and order Whigs; moderate Democrats and moderate Whigs alike supported school reform. It was clear to them that social stability and successful progressive legislation depended on attracting the widest possible support and arousing the least controversy. Henry Barnard filled the bill. Twenty years later Potter, reflected on the "complete regeneration" of education effected by Barnard during a time of "intense political excitement" and credited him with political skill.

> he so managed as to secure the support of all parties and many of his most zealous friends were among the Dorrites and the democrats of that day.[37]

It is more probable that the fact that Barnard was an outsider and neutral made him an attractive candidate to lead the state's reform efforts.

That reform was moving forward was clear. In the May 1844 session, the revised school law was introduced and debated. It is odd that with all of the adulation heaped upon Barnard for his work in education, there is little mention of his authorship of this important piece of legislation. There is no doubt he wrote the bill; he had been directed to do so, and he clearly stated in its introduction that the bill "was prepared by the State Agent." It was, after all, a very suitable task for a well-trained lawyer, and one for which his previous experience in Connecticut was ample preparation. Although his assignment had been to survey the condition of schools in Rhode Island, the report on schools was presented *after* the proposed school law was adopted; a consensus on the necessity of reform did not depend on the accumulation of data on the deplorable conditions existing in the state. Barnard's role in Rhode Island was less to convert than to codify, and then convince the legislature to adopt his codification, with its considerable changes.

Barnard testified before both houses of the assembly for two days during June. His preparation was substantial, and his explanations, subsequently printed in the *Journal of the Rhode Island Institute of Instruction*, were masterful and restrained. He referred to precedent and practices in other states and in local communities, and he emphasized usefulness and uniformity. But the bill itself was assertive.[38] Significantly, the first chapter dealt with the state's role. "For the uniform and efficient administration" of the act, provision was made for a Commissioner of Public Schools, an

---

37. Letter, January 10, 1867, NYU.

38. For the proposed bill with Barnard's remarks, see *JRIII*, I, appendix viii, 113–36. The subsequent bill is in appendix ix, 136–47. In note 112, Barnard itemized the differences; his first draft was even more centralized than the one he printed; see 559–92.

official appointed by the governor, who "should be selected with special reference to his knowledge and experience in all matters relating to schools." Considerable powers were delegated to the commissioner. He was authorized to apportion the money to the various towns, and in return to request information from them. He was to visit the schools and appoint county inspectors; he could certify teachers and recommend textbooks in an effort to achieve excellence in the former and uniformity in the latter. He was directed to establish Teacher's Institutes and at least one Normal School, after further action by the legislature. And he was empowered to "adjust and decide without appeal" all controversies under the act that were submitted to him by the towns or districts. What Barnard was here proposing was nothing more or less than a state system of education. Funding, the resolution of disputes, and the approval of teachers were all to emanate from the state, through its agent, who had to report to the legislature annually. The goal was "uniformity in the administration of the system" and a measure of accountability.[39]

The second section of the act was uncontroversial, for it confirmed the appropriation of $25,000 for the "encouragement and maintenance of public schools." Barnard recognized that some voters still held out for local support of schools, or none at all, and he reasoned with them.

> But from the best consideration I have been able to give to the subject, it does not seem to me to be a matter of so much importance from what source the funds are supplied as it is that they are supplied in liberal measure, and so appropriated as to stimulate public and parental interest and equalize the privileges of education among all the children of the community.

If the cost were to be borne entirely by the state the burden would be too great, yet placing total responsibility on the parents would benefit the "intelligent and the wealthy" to the detriment of the children of "ignorant, vicious, reckless, and intemperate"; those children would be deprived of "that moral and mental culture necessary to fit them for present usefulness and immortal destinies." The towns were too unequal in means, determination, and liberality to be allowed to retain their exclusive role. Hence a system of shared responsibility, with the state providing half of the cost of schooling, an amount reserved for teachers' salaries. The stipulation that towns which did not comply with the requirements of the act would receive no money from the state added teeth to the law.

39. The reforms promulgated by Barnard are consistent with the model proposed by Michael Katz and styled incipient bureaucracy, although he does not use Rhode Island as an example; see *Reconstructing American Education*, chap. 2, 41ff.

The powers and duties of the towns were itemized in the next chapter of the act which, for the most part, strengthened them at the expense of the districts. Towns could establish districts, with the approval of the state commissioner, and different grades of schools were encouraged. Towns had the power to tax for support of schools, provided that the tax was equal to one-third of the state grant. Towns maintained the right to elect the committees that ran the schools; the law gave no new powers to the committees but more clearly defined the existing ones—of examination and inspection, of regulation and suspension. The apportionment of the state money, which was to be used solely for teachers' salaries, was determined by a dual standard; half was given in equal amounts to the several towns, and half was in proportion to the population of children under the age of fifteen. In a provision which Barnard saw as "of first importance," towns were also authorized to establish school libraries "for the use of the inhabitants generally."

The powers of the local districts, defined in chapter three, were essentially administrative, for Barnard saw districts as impediments to efficient school administration. The trustees of each district had custody of the school and were obliged to build, repair and maintain it:

> *Provided* that the erection and repairs of the district school house shall be made according to the plans and specifications approved by the school committee of the town, or by the Commissioner of Public Schools.

If a district refused to establish a school and employ a teacher for at least seven months, the town was empowered to do just that. The district committee members still could hire teachers and visit the schools, and they were directed to provide school books for such pupils whose families did not supply them—consistent always with state policy. Barnard was insistent in his testimony on limiting the size of the class a teacher could hold. Fifty scholars were "by far too large a number for one teacher" and defied "all classification, discipline, and thoroughness of instruction."[40] Better to have two, graded, classes.

In his original draft of the bill Barnard had included a section on secondary schools, asserting that "One thing is certain, this class of schools will exist." If the state declined to act, then the private sector

---

40. In his remarks Barnard noted that more than forty districts in the state had held no school at all during the winter 1843–44, and some had none for two years. In a district the rule was one teacher one school; by limiting the size of a school to no more than fifty Barnard was moving to the regularization of class size.

would, and only the few, the wealthy, would benefit. The legislature was not ready for such a step and omitted the high school clause from the final law; Providence remained the only locality in the state to provide advanced schooling at the public expense.

To introduce a strongly worded chapter on teachers Barnard quoted his fellow school reformer, Charles Brooks: "As is the teacher so will be the school." Barnard proposed that no teacher should be paid by public money who did not hold a certificate signed by the town committee chairman (good for one year), or by the county inspector (good for two years), or by the commissioner (valid for three years), and all teachers were required, first of all, to give proof of "good moral character." Competence "in English language, arithmetic, penmanship, and the rudiments of geography and history" and the ability to govern a school were necessary; the qualifications to teach included "not only knowledge, but the power to impart that knowledge."

Among the miscellaneous provisions of the law was section XXIII which, in Barnard's own words, asserted

> the cardinal principle of a system of common and public schools,
> by placing the education of all children, the rich and the poor, on
> the same republican platform, as a matter of common interest, com-
> mon duty and common right.

No child should be deprived of schooling because of the inability of the parent or guardian to pay the school tax—here was a clarion declaration of the common right to schooling. But it was considerably weakened by the entire omission from the final law the existing provision which guaranteed to any child laborer under the age of twelve a minimum of three months schooling a year.

The bill, despite such compromises, was a strong one. It created an embryonic state school system headed by an appointed bureaucrat who wielded considerable power. It established a chain of supervision and direction from the commissioner through the towns to the districts, and a reversed chain of reporting up to the commissioner who reported to the legislature. It mandated a shared responsibility for the support of schools and guaranteed free education to poor children. This emphasis on the strengthening of the educational apparatus of the state, with provision for increased supervision and the establishment of standards, was characteristic of the Whig antebellum school reformers. The common school revival should perhaps more accurately be titled state initiative or interference, and the Whig leaders knew it. Wilkins Updike, while aware of weaknesses in the proposed law, led the debate in its favor.

Let us have an organization to begin with, so that our efforts will not be thrown away, and our money squandered as now. Let us have a law by which good schools can be established if we can convince the people that it is in their interest to establish them. Let us have a law by which none but qualified teachers shall be employed . . . Let us have a law by which the enormous evil and expense arising out of a constant change of school books shall be remedied; and all new school houses erected after judicious plans and directions . . . Let us have an officer whose intelligence, experience, and constant oversight shall give efficiency and uniformity to the administration of the system . . . Let us have a State pride on this subject.[41]

The bill was passed by the House in June; the Senate considered it and then ordered it circulated among the populace—a common practice and a expedient move in a state so devoted to individuality and to the popular will and with such a recent fracturing of the social and political consensus.

Henry Barnard, in the meantime, returned to Hartford to work on his long-overdue report and the pamphlet on architecture, and to wait. He had essentially written himself into a job in his draft of the school law, but final passage was not a certainty. He was, as he wrote, in a thoroughly romantic lament, "drifting, drifting, drifting." He must have itemized his complaints to his attentive friends: the money he had spent, the recognition he had not been granted, the expense and the ill-health he had suffered. Francis Dwight, an extremely close friend and fellow school reformer, wrote to console him.

I know how it has been with you—you have lost money doubtless in your school movement, and I regret it much. But you have some fame—for the sake of which you played.[42]

Barnard constantly sought and depended on such reassurance from his friends.

The reform bill had been approved by the October legislature by the time Barnard had submitted his report, on November 1, 1845. There had

41. For Updike's speech, see *JRIII* II, 2 and 3 (August 2 and 15, 1847): 53–56. Albert Fishlow's essay "The American Common School Revival: Fact or Fancy," in Henry Rosovksy, ed., *Industrialization in Two Systems* (New York: Wiley, 1966), 40–67, deserves inclusion in all discussions of the common school movement; see esp. 49ff.

42. Letter from Bishop, May 20, from Dwight, May 5, 1844, both 1844, NYU. Dwight was the editor of the New York District School Journal, a member of the executive board of the State Normal School at Albany, and responsible for Barnard's being invited to the supervisors meetings in 1844 and 1845; a year later Barnard was to note his friend's "untimely death" in the only obituary published in the four numbers of his Connecticut journal or the three of the Rhode Island one; *JRIII* I, extra iv (January 1846): 40.

never been any doubt among his allies that he was the man for the commissionership: Updike was certain that passage of the law would surely "work an entire change in the state"—but only if Barnard would take the commissioner's post. Otherwise "all will be as if thrown away. . . . You must keep at our head, direct our movement, and we shall triumph." Apparently the governor agreed with the school reformers and offered Barnard the opportunity to create the system he had proposed.

Barnard claimed he had delayed in submitting his report until the *Act respecting Public Schools* was secured, for "many suggestions for the improvement of schools contained" in the document were based on provisions in the law.[43] The logic is faulty. Fenner had requested a report on the conditions of the schools; recommendations for their improvement would be a natural corollary. That Barnard waited to place his proposals within the parameters of the recently enacted legislation reveals his cautious nature. He did not want to be caught in political controversy, and he wanted to get off to a good start.

The *Report* is a lengthy document organized under five "heads": Modes of Ascertaining the Conditions of the Public Schools (pages 5–7); Measures Adopted to Interest and Inform the Public Mind and Prepare the Way for a More Complete and Efficient System (pages 7–16); Defects in the Laws Relating to Public Schools as They Were, with an Outline of the System as it is at Present Organized (pages 17–27); Conditions of the Public Schools with Suggestions for Their Improvement (pages 27–80); and Other Means of Popular Education. Some general observations can be made from a cursory reading. For starters, there actually is no section five; suggestions for the means of education appear only as part of other recommendations; this is only the first instance of Barnard's Tables of Contents not matching his text. A second impression is how familiar all the material is. Next the reader is overwhelmed with Barnard's passion for an orderly presentation. There is a constant listing of numbered points, confusing to the reader; paragraph 4, Classification, makes perfectly good sense internally but follows a point 8 four pages earlier, which is succeeded by a new list of graded schools, beginning with point 1. The argument flows, but the itemization confounds. Finally, despite the overall organization, Barnard did not follow the heads he indicated, and he omitted material he promised by implication. Suggestions on methodology, uniformity of textbooks, the qualification of teachers, and the matter of supervision "will be deferred to another opportunity."[44] Barnard had

43. See *JRIII* I, 1 (November 1, 1845): 5–16, continued in 2 and 3 (December 1 and 15): 17–48, and 4, 5, and 6 (January and February 1846): 48–80.

44. *Report*, 66–67.

lots of ideas, and he attacked his research and writing with energy and dedication—at first. But he became hasty. There was a good mind there, but one which seemed to wilt under prolonged activity. The inability to finish a task was to become a Barnard hallmark.

The new commissioner had brought to his survey a well formulated view of state responsibility for the provision of schooling, and his survey of the condition of education in Rhode Island reflected his Connecticut experiences.[45] Because he believed that popular acknowledgment of the true conditions of the schools was a necessary prior condition for any widespread acceptance of school reform, he had "aimed to disseminate as widely as possible, by all agencies within my reach," that information. He, and his unnamed allies, had delivered 500 lectures on at least twenty-five subjects; the list of topics demonstrated the controlled and directed nature of the school campaign. Some were:

> The advantages, individual, social and civil of a more complete and practical education of every child in the state, and the necessary connection of ignorance, or misdirected education with insanity, pauperism, vice and crime.
>
> The peculiar advantages enjoyed by Rhode Island for an efficient and complete system of public instruction.
>
> The moral and practical uses of music and drawing, as branches of education in every grade of schools.
>
> The necessity of providing in every system of public schools, for the professional education of teachers by the establishment of Teacher's Classes and Normal Schools.[46]

And the "evils" of inadequate schoolbooks and poorly constructed schoolhouses and the constant turnover of teachers; included in the latter topic was "the importance of giving permanent employment to well qualified teachers of both sexes in the same school."

Barnard had also arranged for the printing and distribution of a series of Educational Tracts, and "upwards of ten thousand copies" were bound with the almanacs of that year—an ingenious publicity device. Rhode Island farmers might not have been highly motivated to learn the details of the condition of education derived from the census of 1840 or to study a system of popular education designed for manufacturing communities or to share in hints for the teaching of the common branches, but the

---

45. For the circulars directed to the towns and districts, see *JRIII* I, appendix 1:81–84. The scrapbook contains Barnard's working sheets on which he assembled the mountains of date, all by hand.

46. For the lecture topics, see *JRIII* I, appendix ii:86.

state's schoolmaster was determined to educate them.[47] The series lapsed after seven numbers due to "want of time and the pressing nature of other duties," but Barnard optimistically persisted in his efforts to instruct the citizens of Rhode Island. He had "nearly completed arrangements" for a library in every town which would house educational journals, pamphlets, and books and would also serve as a repository for state laws and reports. Naturally, such libraries would mount lecture series.

> By creating a taste, and forming habits of reading in the young, by diffusing intelligence among all classes, by introducing new topics and improving the whole tone of conversation, and imparting activity to the public mind generally, these lectures and books will silently but powerfully help in the improvement of public schools, and all other educational institutions and influences.[48]

The bulk of the report focused on the schools of the state and Barnard's suggestions for their improvement.[49] All children, including and especially those of "ignorant, negligent, intemperate and vicious parents," those who had missed out—the clerks and apprentices—and the deviants, all had to be schooled in order to break up the "moral jungles" and to reform the "infected districts," particularly of the cities. Barnard recognized the value of private efforts, but when those failed the state had to intervene, to tame "the young barbarians" into "the manners and habits of civilized life." For those utterly recalcitrant, untouched by voluntary efforts or the public schools, there would be Reform Schools. Finally, because the political preservation of the nation demanded an educated citizenry, the "right of suffrage should be withheld from such as cannot

47. For a list of the tracts, see ibid., appendix iv:90. The tracts are bound, in the edition in the Yale collection, in *JRIII* II, following 400, beginning with 1, "Education in the Relation to Health, Insanity, Labor, Pauperism and Crime"; this is unattributed but is Barnard's reprinted from the Connecticut journal; 2 is his "School-House Architecture pamphlet"; 6 and 7, published in 1846, are methodological treatises on the teaching of English composition and grammar.

48. *Report*, 22; for libraries, see *JRIII*, appendix v:9@1–92 and vi:92–96. Barnard announced his "intention" to prepare an index of the libraries.

49. *JRIII* I, 10 (April 15, 1846), appendixes x and xi, 149–64, "Statistical Tables" (which include summaries from other New England states and details from Massachusetts); 11 and 12 (May 1 and 15), appendix xii, "School-Houses," 165–226 and appendix xiii, "Books in Use in Public Schools," 227–28; 13 and 14 (June 1 and 15), appendix xiv, "Public Schools in Cities and Large Villages," 219–40. Barnard's reference to specific counties and districts suggests that the data might not have been complete and also reveals a weakness in his argument stressing the need for public support to prevent recourse to private schooling; when the public schools were in session 21,000 attended, and only 3,000 sought private instruction.

give the lowest evidence of school attendance and proficiency."[50] Society could not allow anyone to remain uneducated.

Provision of schooling, vital though it was, was not sufficient; proper records must be kept, for there was a close connection between attendance and achievement, as well as a link between attendance and school organization. Gradation of classes was vital, for a mixing of students was sure to lead to inattention, distaste for learning, and truancy, and presented insurmountable obstacles to effective learning. In some cases, however, an older boy might be advanced if he was too chagrined to be retained among the smaller ones—an early hint at social promotion.

Teachers in charge of each grade should be selected according to their suitability for the age, and the most suitable teachers for younger children were female. Female teachers were cheaper, often by half, than male ones, but to Barnard the advantage in hiring women was not to save money; rather the schools could be kept open longer, sometimes as much as two months at no extra cost. More important was the superiority of female teachers who had "more gentle and refined manners, purer morals, stronger interest and greater tact, and contentment in managing and instructing" the young. In a suitably graded system, female teachers "whose hearts are made strong by deep religious principle," should teach "habits of attention" and "the rudiments of language," and awaken a desire to "cultivate the mind" in the younger children. However, "before the superior efficiency of women in the holy ministry of education" could be felt, their "education must be more amply and universally provided for" and particular provision for "some special training in the duties of a teacher" made. In secondary schools, both female and male teachers could instruct in the broader branches "which lie at the foundation of all useful attainments" and are "indispensable in the proper exercise and development" of "the faculties of the mind and to the formation of good intellectual tastes and habits of applications."[51] High schools, where the instructors were male, should be open to both boys and girls who would study a comprehensive curriculum, modified according to the "sex, age, and advancement and, to some extent, future destination of the pupils." For the boys the program was the contemporary English one, preparatory for all walks of life and only secondarily for higher education; for the girls study was to develop "a well-disciplined mind, high moral aims, practical views of her own duties."

Common education had its limits, after all. Barnard was sincere in his advocacy of higher education for females, especially those who intended

50. Ibid., 45, 48–51, 57ff., appendix xv, "Rules and Regulations," 241–52.
51. Ibid., ii, 50.

to be teachers, but his hierarchical conception of gradation and its resultant differentiation in curriculum, contributed to the limitations imposed on antebellum women and ultimately led to the second-place status of women in teaching and of the institutions which trained them. Of course the most prominent female school reformers of the day—Willard, Beecher, and Lyon—held precisely the same views and in all probability influenced him.

Finally, Barnard recommended the formation of permanent teachers' associations which would offer the isolated young teacher a modicum of instruction in skills and an opportunity for some companionship. "The attainments of solitary reading will thus be quickened by the anchor of a living mind." He also pleaded for "at least one Normal School," and to buttress his request, he dropped a hint.

> I have good reason to believe that any movement on the part of the state . . . would be met by the prompt cooperation of not a few liberal minded and liberal handed friends of education, and the great enterprise of preparing Rhode Island teachers for Rhode Island schools, might soon be in successful operation.

Apparently in February Thomas Hazard had pledged to raise money for the normal school from among his wealthy friends, but unfortunately, nothing came of the suggestion until after Barnard had left the state.[52]

Echoes of Barnard's Connecticut days are loud in his first Rhode Island report, but there is a subtle change and a new note of authority. Despite his insistence that "the framework of the old system" was "substantially preserved," Barnard had created the potential for an articulated system of public schooling. Previous voluntary and local efforts had proved to be irregular, insufficient, and unequal; of necessity, therefore, the state was forced to intervene to provide schooling that was universal (except for blacks), compulsory, and rationalized, designed for the age of the pupils, their status, and their predictable future. Teachers in the system should be trained and in appropriate positions. The entire structure, from the primary district school to the yet-to-be-inaugurated normal school, should be under centralized direction, in the hands of the enlightened and responsible few. The state would set the standards, the towns would establish and support the schools, and the districts would manage them. Barnard's key words were efficient, useful, moral; his negative ones were vice

52. See *JRIII* I, extra, xii, (July 1, 1846): 189ff., for an "Address on Education" delivered before the Washington County Association for the Improvement of Public Schools, January 3, 1846, 169–70. Hazard was a typical reformer, a manufacturer who had time to publish essays on language, temperance, and on the "causes of the Decline of Political and National Morality."

and ignorance. Only with education, directed and guided, could righteousness prevail, and previous means of providing that education had been found wanting. There was a void to fill and an opportunity available, for the state to play a dominant, although never exclusive, role. The arrangement Barnard developed was one of shared responsibility, and he chose to share its leadership with his fellow reformers.

Barnard's career in Rhode Island, and his success, was from the very start mixed with and dependent on, the Rhode Island Institute of Instruction. In September, 1844, a group of the friends of education had met in convention in Washington County under the chairmanship of Wilkins Updike. Barnard, the new state agent, was among the speakers, and he also served on the committee which drafted a constitution for the new local association (although his name is not among the signatories of the final report). The report rings with the sound of Whig ideology:

> Let us on this subject forget all differences of opinion which divide and distract society on religious and political questions, and unite heart and hand in promoting that cause which holds every other good cause in its embrace.[53]

Even prior to the formal organization of the Washington County Association, the founding committee arranged to hold twenty-seven meetings throughout the county, nearly one a day during the ensuing month. These meetings were the means through which the public lectures mentioned above were delivered, although Barnard does not admit the link. Nor does he share credit in two other particulars. From the association's circular, it is obvious that it served as the agent for the distribution to its membership of Barnard's publications, and it was the county teachers, probably at the close of one of the meetings, who organized the first Teachers' Institute of the county. Similar associations were formed in 1845 in other counties, and the Smithfield and Cumberland Institute held ten meetings over the winter.

The next year, following a pattern common for reform organizations, the county leaders united into a state-wide Rhode Island Institute of Instruction which, as Barnard readily granted, rendered "very important co-operation and did essential service in the cause of educational improvement." In his mind the Institute's meetings were his forum, and its journal was his voice.[54] There is evidence, however, of a contrary interpretation.

53. Scrapbook, poster announcing the Washington County meeting, January 3, 1845; *JRIII* I, appendix iii:8@6–90.

54. *Report*, 10; appendix iii for the Institute's constitution, 88–89. See *AJE*, XIV, xxxvi (September 1864): 559–92.

The executive committee of the new organization, vowing "to shun partisan and sectarian illusions" in the common goal of school reform, listed three goals: to circulate educational material, to employ an agent, and to conduct teachers' institutes. In their view, the arrangement was a reciprocal one. William S. Baker, whom Barnard called his agent, was employed by the Institute "under the joint direction of the Commissioner and of the Special Committee" as agent to carry the message of reform, and the Institute sponsored the first state Teachers' Institute in November 1846, although again in cooperation with Barnard.

The implication is clear, and intriguing—the Institute viewed itself as a full partner with the Commissioner in the cause of educational reform. Here was a possible model for school leadership akin to Michael Katz's idea of paternalistic voluntarism in which worthy and responsible men of vision took a responsible role in the reform of schooling. In this case the partnership was with a man appointed and employed by the state. Just as schooling was supplied by both public and private means, so, too, could the leadership in the school movement be shared. Decisions on major policy issues could rest with the private individuals, as well as with the legislature, and implementation with the public official who in turn could rely on volunteer participants. It is hindsight that blinds us to the potential of such an arrangement, and it is conceivable that had Barnard and the Institute maintained and expanded their relationship this model could have dominated nineteenth century school policy.[55]

The character of the periodical that Barnard edited in Rhode Island bears out this view; it was the *Journal of the Rhode Island Institute of Instruction*, not of the state nor of the commissioner. The editor spelled out his ambitious plans for the publication in an initial issue which appeared just two weeks after the reform law went into effect; there were to be two numbers a month, with a single volume of twelve numbers; each number would be "at least sixteen pages in octavo form," and Extras "containing official circulars, notices of school meetings, and communications respecting individual schools, and improvements in education generally," as well as Educational Tracts "devoted to the discussion of important topics," would be supplementary. Barnard promised that each volume would consist of at least three hundred pages and cost only fifty cents; for those seeking a bargain, or willing to distribute the periodical within the com-

55. *JRIII* II, 6 and 7 (October 1 and 15, 1847): 153–61, "Annual Report of the Rhode Island Institute of Instruction"; see Katz, *Reconstructing*, 25ff. The founders of the Institute represented all elements of contemporary schooling: John Kingsbury was head of a private girls' school, Amos Perry of a grammar school, Nathan Bishop superintendent of schools in Providence, and others were school committee members and senior teachers.

munity, ten copies could be obtained for three dollars. He was listed as the editor, and Thomas C. Hartshorn was the business agent. In this way the Institute maintained supervision over the publication, and Barnard was freed from annoying business worries.[56]

The joint undertaking was neatly demonstrated in the very first number of the *Journal*: it commenced with the consitution of the organization and moved to the October 1843 act that appointed Barnard as school agent. Barnard's report to the legislature then ran without pause through number 6.[57] The remaining numbers of the first volume, 7–14, were all appendices, and for the most part contained the documents and statistical data the Commissioner had referred to in his report. But he could not resist including, with no explanation, five pages of factual information gathered from the New England states and New York. Numbers 11 and 12 were devoted to the pamphlet on schoolhouses, and the final two appendices were all miscellaneous addenda, a report of public schools in large cities and the by-laws of the Providence schools. There may be an explanation for the lack of originality in these final numbers as well as for the absence of any number in May in the apology of the business agent, at the close of the June 1 Extra, that "the illness of the Editor, and other causes which he could not control" had prevented the regular publication of the *Journal*. He promised that as soon as Barnard was recovered, the regular numbers not already sent would go out.[58]

Barnard, as was his habit, prepared an index for the first volume, but a rather idiosyncratic one listing such items as "Amusements, taste for." Subscribers also received a series of Extras, the first of which was issued November 6, 1845, or before the *Journal* itself. Each Extra was headed with a Prospectus, signed by the Institute committee, which announced "a series of Teachers' Institutes or temporary Normal Schools."[59] These Extras had two purposes: to serve as a vehicle of easy communication, a sort of newsletter, and to provide Barnard with an excuse, under the guise

56. *JRIII* I, 1 (November 15, 1845): 3; for the Institute on the *Journal* see *JRIII* II, 6 and 7 (October 1 and 15): 155.

57. A subscriber might well have been somewhat confused when his numbers 2 and 3 (December 1 and 15), ended in mid-sentence on the word "which" and he had to wait until nudmbers 4, 5, and 6 (January and February 1846), appeared to complete the sentence "spring from a sense of social, moral and religious obligation . . ." One suspects that after the first number of the requisite sixteen pages, Barnard issued the rest of his report simultaneously.

58. Ibid., Extra xi (June 1846): 102.

59. Ibid., Extra 1 (November 6, 1845): 1ff. The prospectus was reported in numbers i–viii, (November 1845–March 1, 1846), and x–xiii, (April–June 15, 1846); there is no number ix.

of disseminating information, to publish some of the vast store of material he collected.

The Institute, in its annual report, had expressed the need for a second volume, and Barnard's intention, to employ his most-used word, was to publish on the first and fifteenth of each month, or "on such days as may suit the official engagements of the editor," and to produce a volume of at least four hundred pages. The business agent, doubled the price for a single copy, and all subscriptions had to be paid in advance; any correspondence with the publication had to be post paid.[60] The publishers were attempting to put the *Journal* on a better financial footing, something Barnard never achieved in any of his periodicals.

The new volume began with a single number in July, a reprinting of a speech by Justice Durfee on the civil policy of the state. The legislature had ordered Barnard to print three thousand copies of this speech for distribution *gratis* throughout the state, but he decided to print excerpts in his periodical, charging the usual price. He added a note that it was his "aim" to distribute the entire speech, with no mention of the legislative mandate. He also inserted an editorial comment, that there was "a greater omission" in the speech, for Durfee had failed to mention public schools. An odd criticism, indeed, considering the fact that the author was reviewing the history of the colony and calling for the creation of a sensitivity to history and the state's past! Nonetheless, Barnard, ever true to his mission, redressed the balance by printing, in the next numbers, an unsigned article, originally from a temperance journal, on colonial schooling, and the remainder of the August number was devoted to school legislation up to 1845.[61] In the September 1 issue, Barnard reproduced, apparently verbatim, the school reports submitted by three towns pursuant to the requirements of the new school law.[62] Thus the subscriber to the Journal would have in these four numbers, a useful reference, some contextual background, an interpretation, albeit biased, of the condition of education, the recent legislation, and some model reports. The *Journal*, in relaying useful information, served the same function as a professional publication today.

The remainder of volume II, for the most part adhered to this practical plan. In number 5, Barnard printed material which focused on heating

60. *JRIII* II, 1 (July 1, 1847); the Prospectus in this volume is signed by Charles Burnet, Jr.

61. Ibid., 2, for the legislative resolution; Durfee's speech, 3–32; the other speech in 2 and 3 (August 2 and 15): 33–37.

62. Ibid., 57–88. All three reports are for the year 1847, yet it was only September when they were published.

and ventilation, complete with diagrams of complicated apparatus information designed to assist the committees charged with the care of the schools. The catalogue of a school library in number 7 provided similar guidance for any committee that had the funds for such purchases.[63] The information in numbers 8 and 9 must have been truly invaluable to committeemen confused about the provisions of the new school law. In response to a suggestion from Potter, Barnard printed all recent school legislation, the law of 1845 and amendments passed the following two years, with an index, and he devoted twenty pages to a very straightforward explanation of the powers and duties of the school officials and their relation to the state commissioner. His explanations illustrated vividly his view of his office: he was the source of authority. In addition he created various forms "not prescribed by law" but safe precedents to utilize in certifying the appointment of school trustees, teachers, and inspectors, in drawing up contracts with teachers and builders, and in preparing tax forms.[64] As many of the districts of the state were entering the arena of public education for the first time, with inexperienced and ill-prepared elected officials, this guidance was vital in order to prevent waste and inefficiency, twin horrors to the reformer schoolmen. That it reinforced the role of the state may have gone unnoticed.

In the final numbers of the volume Barnard presented miscellaneous information, on the Institute's annual meeting, on the Teachers' Institutes, and on the "Progress of Education in the United States"; the latter concentrated on New England although there were extracts from some Ohio and Indiana reports. The editor was conscious of gaps in his information, of the scarcity of material form the South, and he also had "intended" to print reports from Michigan, "but the space allotted to these notices is now exhausted."[65]

Had Barnard maintained the conceptual framework and emphases of volume II, or had anyone equally talented and more disciplined succeeded him as editor, the Rhode Island *Journal* could have evolved into a truly professional periodical, providing at regular intervals vital information and imparting a sense of unity to the teachers and policymakers throughout the state. To expect such an actuality was perhaps premature, and in

63. Ibid., 5 (September): 89–130, followed by 137–52, which quoted reports from school superintendents in New York and the New England states "Lest the author should be thought to exaggerate the deficiencies of school-houses"; 7 (October), library catalogue 170–200.

64. Ibid., 8 and 9 (November): forms 225–303. I assume it was a conscious decision to make these materials available to the school authorities before the commencement of the winter schools.

65. Ibid., 306–52, especially 346, 352.

any case Barnard lost steam. Volume III, when it did appear, was not a periodical at all but a corpus of reports from 1845 through 1848, sewn together with no clear rationale. Neither the word *Journal* nor the name of the Institute appear on the title page. Half of the volume is devoted to Barnard's *School-House Architecture*, and the catalogue of the Pawcatuck Library, organized by subject and by author, takes up nearly one hundred pages. Barnard had, once again, "intended" to submit a final summary of his various oral reports to the legislature, but he had "not health sufficiently vigorous to renew the work" before leaving the state, so it was "presented in a far less condensed and elaborate form than it was his intention originally to prepare."[66] He did have the strength, however, to create an elaborate index to the three volumes. The prefatory report to this volume was actually Barnard's valedictory to Rhode Island—but that jumps ahead of our story.

The *Journal's* circulation was probably exclusively among the members of the Institute, but they and Barnard knew that the key to all progress lay with the teachers.

> If the teacher has the proper sense of the importance of his position, and conducts himself accordingly, he will secure to himself the affection and respect of the people of his district, by exerting his utmost power to protect the moral and intellectual advancement, not only of his scholars, but of the community around him.[67]

Teachers were only as good as their character and education allowed, so training, in some form, was imperative. The leadership of the Rhode Island Institute of Instruction was proud of the fact that the state had been the first in the union "to sanction Teachers' Institute by legal enactment," and Barnard's very first official act was to call for a series of "Teachers' Institutes, or Temporary Normal Schools" for anyone, male or female who intended to teach that winter. He saw these institutes as "among the most important agencies which can be worked for the immediate improvement of the schools by inspiring the right spirit and increasing the practical knowledge of teachers . . . ," and he expended a good deal of his energy during the fall of 1845 in arranging institutes to meet those twin goals.

Institutes differed from the public, inspirational meetings in a number of ways, and in time a regular format developed. Generally an institute

66. *JRIII* III, *Report*, iii–iv. The October 1848 session of the legislature authorized the printing of the material. Barnard had chaired the committee which set up the Westerly library, and his correspondence is full of letters asking about libraries. Note the word "leaving."

67. *JRIII* II, 8 and 9 (November 1847): 258. Note the masculine pronoun.

extended over several days, with daytime sessions directed at a restricted audience of teachers and evening ones open to parents and community members. The sessions for teachers focused on the specific and practical and provided opportunities for "inquiry, discussion, and familiar conversation" among the assembled teachers. Instruction in the common branches and in the methods of teaching them, as well as of governing a school, was given by imported experts. Support came from those attending, usually $2 for the entire period, and from those local dignitaries who chose to underwrite the endeavor; participants frequently boarded with members of the community who in turn attended the evening sessions, drawn by the promise of lectures by luminaries. Institutes, thus, became a form of community educational activity and served to strengthened public resolve and support, as well as to train teachers.[68]

A typical one was held in Scituate, November 17–22, 1845. Henry Barnard himself was in the chair, and after the opening prayer, he addressed the assembled crowd on his favorite themes. He could not resist giving a brief history of institutes, slyly noting that the first had been held in Connecticut under the leadership of the man who was now the commissioner of the schools in Rhode Island. He outlined the topics to be covered during the sessions, and he assured his audience that an "opportunity would be given for addresses, discussions, and the familiar conversation" on a wide variety of topics. He then introduced Mr. Salem Town, the principal in charge, commenting on Town's extensive experience, and listed the other lecturers. Barnard spoke again the following day, cautioning the teachers against a too hasty adoption of a new pedagogy. "The sudden abandonment of an old method, and adoption of a new, is one of the most common causes of failure in a certain class of teachers."

Barnard next addressed the Centreville institute, urging teachers to be moral, punctual, and mannerly, atune to the physical comfort of their charges and to the needs of their own health. "Much of the punishment of our schools comes from the bad digestion of the teacher." It was not just a matter of exercising to avoid headaches; teachers need mental exercise as well. Neither the Institute, nor visits to other schools, nor regular teachers' meetings could serve as a substitute for "thorough study and practical training." In conclusion, the Superintendent bade the assembled

68. *AJE* VIII, xxi (June 1860): 673ff.; *JRIII* 6 and 7 (October 1847): 156, quoting from the Rhode Island Institute of Instruction *Annual Report*; the author went on to lament the absence of any state allocation and to emphasize that members would no longer bear the cost of the institutes. See *JRIII* I, Extra 1 (November 6, 1845) for Circulars 1–4, repeated in II, 11 and 12:353–54. See also *AJE* XV, xl (September 1865): 387–414, 504–11.

teachers to "be of good cheer—stand by the cause, and the cause would uphold them." Such a sermonlike admonition probably was of far less value to the teachers than the methodological instruction and the opportunity for the development of an *esprit de corps* among the young men and women attending—but inspiration helped.

For the most part Barnard left the bulk of each institute's program to the "Board of Instructors" of experienced lecturers which he had assembled, for he never saw himself in the role of an expert on pedagogy. Judging from a letter W. H. Wells wrote him, the division was a successful one.

> Your institutes left the places where held in a red-hot glow. Your separation of practical professional work with teachers in your day sessions, from popular addresses to parents and the public generally in the evening, is most judicious. Your placing teachers, as well as your speakers and helpers, in the families of the place, where the work done and to be done was sure to be talked over, is a stroke of genius. Your educational tracts scattered broadcast before and after the meetings, your provision for educational addresses in all the neighboring towns during the week preceding and during the session of the institute, was inspiring work of the best sort.[69]

Institutes must have required an enormous local support to organize, but there are no accounts of those activities. Barnard's correspondence, however, is full of letters recording his efforts to secure instructors for the fall sessions. It was not easy. William Russell, a highly experienced teacher who was at the time inaugurating a teachers' seminary in Merrimack, Massachusetts, offered frequent and helpful advice, and a great load must have been lifted from Barnard's shoulders when Russell's son, Francis, agreed to assume the leadership of several of the institutes for $25 per week. Charles Northend did promise to send a selection of hymns for use in the institutes' ceremonies, but many others disappointed Barnard; the dependable Updike declined, pleading illness, and Thomas Gallaudet said he was too old and infirm. Elisha Potter agreed to open the Pawtucket institute, and the venerable Josiah Holbrook, after lengthy negotiation, lectured for $3 a day. William Fowle was booked for Woonsocket but sounded petulant:

69. Letter from W. H. Wells, November 26, 1845, NYU; Salem Town had led over twenty institutes in New York so was truly a professional teacher educator by this time. Given the number of references to Barnard's appearances, it is hard to know what to make of his statement in *JRIII* II, 11 and 12 (December 1847), that his health and other engagements required "a temporary suspension of his official labors" and that he had attended only one institute. See the memoir of Wells, *AJE* VII, xxi (June 1860): 535.

So my pay can be great & I can do some good I beg you to have as little to do with other teachers as possible. I do not ask any assistance.[70]

The question of finances was a persistent problem; raising money was burdensome and accounting troublesome. Barnard seems to have underwritten some of the costs, for on at least two recorded instances he was publicly thanked at the conclusion of the sessions "for his measured liberality in assuming the expenses of the Institute."[71]

Like all of the school reformers, Barnard viewed institutes at best as temporary substitutes for normal schools.

The Institute thus illustrates imperfectly the benefits of a Normal School, or a course of systematic and practical training for a proper length of time, under experienced teachers, and with a workshop as it were, attached, where an apprenticeship in the art of teaching can be served.[72]

He had unsucccessfully recommended the establishment of a normal school in his first report. That he was pondering the curriculum of such a school is suggested by a curious document in his scrapbook. Pasted on a page dated 1843 is a "Scheme of a School" (*opposite*), surely a design for a normal school. The three-year curriculum and the combination of the common school subjects, teacher demeanor, and morality reflects with precision the common normal school program. Suggested, too, by the topics for the third year is the final year of collegiate education in which the president held forth to the seniors on the lofty subject of moral philosophy; apparently Henry Barnard held high ambitions for a normal school.[73]

The vast quantities of letters directed to Barnard prove that he was

70. Letters of refusal from Northend, July 17, from Welles and Emerson, September, n.d., from Davies, September 13; from Potter, September 21; from Updike, September 27; from Gallaudet, November 25; from William Russell, September 16; from Francis Russell, October 1, 20, 24, November 13; from Fowle, October 26; from Holbrook, October 13, November 1, 14, 20; all 1847, all NYU.

71. See resolution of the Pawtucket Institute, *JRIII*, II, 11 and 12 (December 15 and 25, 1847): 366. A letter from Robert Allwyn, East Greenwich, November 13, 1846, NYU, gives a detailed accounting of the expenses of the Institute there and concludes he is owed $14.30.

72. *JRIII* II, 11 and 12 (December 15 and 25, 1847): 253–386, especially 354–55, 358, 366. An analysis of the lists of participants is instructive. At Centreville there were fifty men (four Tillinghasts) and twenty-eight women; a week later at Pawtucket there were forty-four women and thirty-eight men; at Bristol the numbers were nearly equal.

73. A normal school almost became a reality in 1847 when Charles Potter of Providence made the "munificent offer" of a building for a school if the legislature would

Scheme of A School
Classes of Studies

1st class
acts and arts
1 manners
1 standing   2 walking   3 sitting   4 talking
2 simple acts
1 Reading   2 spelling   3 speaking   4 singing
3 Compound acts
1 arithmetic   2 penmanship   3 composition   4 disputation

Second Class
arts and sciences
1 necessary
1 agriculture   1 architecture   3 mechanical
2 convenient
1 geography   2 history   3 policy
3 elegant
1 eloquence   2 philosophy   3 poetry

Third Class
Duties and Blessings
1 Personal

Duty	Blessing
1 Purity	Light
2 Temperence	Health
3 Patience	Triumph

2. social

Duty	Blessing
1 Truth	Peace
2 justice	order
3 Kindness	Comfort
4 Prudence	Plenty

3 Divine

Obligation	Privilege
1 Reverence	Approbation
2 Submission	acceptance
confidence	Forgiveness
gratitude	Complacency

indeed a busy man during the Rhode Island years. Under the law of 1845 the commissioner was granted substantial advisory power, and it was to him that the school committees turned in times of confusion or dispute. Was a district complying with the law in enumerating only weekly? what was required when a school was relocated by the vote of the town, or when two districts voted to merge? was a certificate issued in 1846 still valid in 1848? Once he was asked to come to settle a boundary dispute —and deliver a lecture in the evening. Some of the questions addressed difficult matters of policy such as what rights of appeal did a farmer have whose land lay in two districts and was thus subject to double taxation. Then there were applications from teachers for jobs, and requests from districts for teachers, as many as three inquiries in one day when the season of the winter schools approached. Book agents sent sample copies in the hope that Barnard would recommend them, and school trustees wrote asking his opinion on the selection of texts. Many of the letters are plaintive, asking the same question for the second, or even the third, time, an indication that Barnard was overworked, or inattentive. And many of the letters were addressed to him in Hartford, rather than to the Mansion House where he boarded in Providence; he never seems really to have committed himself to the service of Rhode Island.[74]

It had always been Barnard's practice to delegate responsibility for tedious chores, and he continued to do so during his tenure in Rhode Island. William Baker roved the state, leasing a horse from Barnard to ease his travel, and complaining constantly. J. A. Goodwin inspected ten schools (two of them private) in five towns, delivered lectures at eight public meetings (replacing Updike at one), all in the space of eight days in 1848—he apologized for the fact that a storm held him up one day; after that busy fortnight he returned to his own school to teach.[75] Barnard could not have been effective in his position without the constant support and activity of scores of others, and it is not to his credit that he never publicly recognized their contribution.

The demands of administration never distracted Barnard from his principal love, research and publication. His major work during this period was *School Architecture or Contributions to the Improvement of School-Houses in the United States*.[76] He had lectured and published on the scandalous

---

establish a permanent fund to cover the annual expenses. See *JRIII* II, 6 and 7 (October 1 and 15): 211.

74. Letters on these topics are too numerous to cite; the similarity with Connecticut requests is striking.

75. Letter from Goodwin, October 4, 1848, NYU.

76. All succeeding references are to *School Architecture, Jean and Robert McClintock,*

physical condition of the schools since the start of his career; major chunks of the future book had appeared in the *Connecticut Common School Journal*, and he had published a pamphlet on school architecture in 1842. Many of his letters during this period were replies to his requests for plans and wood cuts of schools, especially of those recently constructed in the large cities such as the Philadelphia High School and the schools of the New York School Society. Barnard was becoming something of an expert on school construction, and he contributed a section on school-houses to a contemporary how-to book, *The Builder's Guide*.[77] A comparison of the various versions is time-consuming; what counts is the commonality of all them, for any one provides a window to Barnard's mind and methods.

From his earliest days, and from his teaching ones, Barnard had been acutely sensitive to the physical discomfort under which scholars and teachers alike suffered, and his repeated visitations to contemporary schools confirmed his personai distaste for their condition; his research revealed means of improvement. *School Architecture* combined personal insight, modern technology, and Barnard's evolving conception of the ideal common school. On first and cursory reading, the book seems to be a miscellaneous compilation of materials on schools with a strong dose of moralizing; on closer reading the line of argument becomes clear. Schools, as they were, were poor; schools could be better. One way was to improve their organization, and in chapter 3 Barnard repeated the taxonomy of gradation he outlined everywhere. Given the purposes of schools and an ideal system, how should such schools be built? The core of the book was in chapters 4–6 where the author detailed plans, pedagogical possibilities, and his passion—means of heating and ventilation. And finally, once there was a school, it had to be governed, hence a final chapter on Rhetoric and Rules.

To all reformers education was the highest moral duty imposed on the individual and on the state, and the school was society's agency. How could the school impart the lofty vision of its mission amidst decay and decrepitude—the answer was by architectural symbolism. Small wonder that Barnard began with a Greek Revival facade when he designed a new school in Washington County, Connecticut, in 1839. Schools were to be models of "taste, comfort, and convenience," but most of all they should be temples to learning, places where there was nothing

eds., Classics in Education (New York: Teachers College Press, 1970; hereafter *SA*).

77. Ibid., 2, note, and 337–38, "A Note on the Text." Chester Hills, *The Builder's Guide* (Hartford: Appleton & Co., 1846).

"to defile the mind, corrupt the heart, or excite unholy and forbidden appetites."[78]

The school served a second purpose; it guaranteed and nourished the conscience of the community in which it stood. Ideally it should protect and maintain the elements of the nation's rural past, both the sense of intimacy and cohesion and the actual physical elements of trees and flowers. No school should stand on a dusty crossroad but, along with the church, in the very center of the town or village, an oasis of culture and learning for all. In addition to the handsome building, the site should welcome, with borders and groves of trees (native, of course) and garden plots, designed to enhance but in addition to provide a natural laboratory for the children, and a place to play. From George Emerson's *The School and the School-master*, Barnard reprinted an elaborate perspective of a "rustic" Roman Revival School House; the plot is huge, ringed with trees, with ample greensward where children were depicted playing discretely, and with two carefully landscaped outhouses down a flowered path at a suitable distance from the school.[79]

Once a community had completed the building of such an edifice it was only fitting that it be opened with ceremony, "a public and joyful commoration."

> In prayer, and in praise to the Giver of all good and the Author of
> all being—in song and hymn and anthem, and in addresses from
> those whose positions in society will command the highest respect
> for any object in whose behalf they may speak, and in the presence
> of all classes in the community, of pupils and teachers, of fathers
> and mothers, of old and young—the school-house should be set
> apart to the social purpose of the physical, intellectual and moral
> culture of the children who will gathered within its walls.[80]

These occasions provided an opportunity for elegant orations which repeated the maxims of moral and civic duty and educational responsibility favored by the Whig reformers; creeping in, too, was another theme. Barnard excerpted with transparent approval a dedicatory discourse by

78. Ibid., 31, 123–28, quotation 128. See 140 for Gothic Revival school in Providence, and 192 and 195 for Greek Revival elevations at two Massachusetts normal schools. Barnard's design for a school in Windsor, 120–21, repeats *Builder's Guide*, 90 and 95. An odd feature is that the floor plan has two entrances, one for boys and one for girls, but the front elevation has a single door.

79. Ibid., 128ff., especially design, 130–31. Despite Barnard's concern for the necessity of education in the cities, his designs and descriptions were for rural schools; he included some urban plans but never discussed them.

80. *JRIII* III (1848): 402. See *SA*, chap. 7, 300, for identical speech.

Francis Wayland in which the Brown president gave to education the credit for the fact that Rhode Island cotton was coming to dominate the world market, that the era of manufacture and railroads was at hand, and that "bountiful Providence" was guiding prosperity and even luxury.[81] Schools could contribute to economic as well as spiritual welfare.

The construction and design of schools, then, was driven by the highest of motives, and the exteriors conveyed those ideals. Schoolhouses were also places where large numbers of young scholars gathered to learn; schools had to work. All of the plans were designed to make the school rooms functionally efficient—behind the Greek or Roman exterior lay working classrooms able to accommodate the numbers of children thronging to school. Effective learning depended on the teacher's mastery of technique, on how he or she arranged the room and what equipment was provided for the room, fully as much as the zeal for learning depended on the projection of an ideal. The mode of instruction, whether recitation, simultaneous, or mutual (Barnard's term for Lancastrian system), should dictate the classroom layout, just as different grades of schools necessitated different classroom organization. In every school, whether the one-room district one, or the elaborate three-floor Gothic structure of the Free Academy of New York, it was details that mattered. A big, overhead lantern light provided less glare and was, incidentally, less easily broken; strong, durable, and comfortable seats made pupils more attentive, and saved the district money in the long run; good stoves and proper flues were essentials.[82] Teachers could read about pedagogical aids and compare the apparatus available to them with the array listed in Barnard's book; school committees had addresses of manufacturers of school equipment and even comparisons and evaluations of different models.

Sadly, the work is marred by Barnard's personal failings as an author. The final chapter, "Rhetoric and Rules," logically completed his argument. But once again he seemed to have lost interest. He quoted at length two dedicatory speeches, and printed the detailed rules of an assortment of schools, public and private. The common thread in all this material is the connection between morality and student behavior. It was absolutely necessary that students scrape and wipe their boots before coming into the classroom because, in addition to keeping the schoolroom clean and free from mud and dust, such tidy action trained the students. Neatness, cleanliness, order, punctuality, in instruction and in the routines of the

81. *JRIII* III (1848): 408–14, especially 412. Wayland must have been speaking at the dedication of the Gothic Revival schoolhouse in Pawtucket illustrated in *SA*, 148–49.

82. Compare *SA*, 118, design for a one room school with 181–91, design for a multi-story school. Note that all school rooms were for more than sixty children.

school were vital; so were cooperation and consideration, and a decent respect for the school's property. Anything else was pernicious. To paraphrase Charles Brooks, "as is the school, so is the pupil." The cumulative message of *School Architecture* reflects Whig philosophy; morality was linked to education, and education to utility; progress depended on all three.

Barnard's correspondence in 1847 and 1848 reveals his methods of research and the amount of time he spent on the book. In addition to his usual sources, the annual reports of friends and of school committees such as the Providence one, he consulted the works of the generalists, like George Emerson, and of the rising professional architects. One was Thomas A. Teft who had been a teacher at the age of seventeen, before apprenticing to a builder and then attending Brown University. Barnard also borrowed designs from the manufacturers of furniture (teacher and student desks), schoolroom apparatus, stoves, and furnaces. Details concerning the publication of the book are endless, and the publisher, A. S. Barnes, driven nearly mad by the author, warned, "The succession of delays is detrimental to the Book."[83] Plates and proof did not arrive on time, and Barnard never responded promptly to letters although he wanted instant attention when he did write. The book was finally published in August, at the cost of seventy-five cents, and Barnard turned to its promotion.

The most effective and usual method of distribution of such works was through the states. The Connecticut legislature appropriated funds to purchase copies for the local school committees, and the commissioner of education in New Hampshire hoped to be able to order enough copies for every district in the state; that state ultimately would not pay. Another way to distribute the book was through the teachers' organizations, and the faithful Baker was pressed into service as an agent. W. H. Wells wanted to sell it to his Essex (Massachusetts) Teachers' Association, but no copies arrived on time. Charles Northend received ninety-six copies, but did not know how much to charge, or what to do with any surplus; fortunately he was able to dispose of them all. In fact, the book was an enormous success, going into a second printing in October. Barnard intended to revise it before the new issue, but as he said in the preface, his time was "too much absorbed in the immediate and pressing

83. Letters from W. H. Wells, March, June 8, August 26, 30, October 25, November 3; from Joshua Bates of Brimmer School, July 18; from Gardiner Chilson on stoves, September 22, 28, November 14, 15 (he was installing one in a school); from Barnes, January 24, April 21, 26, June 22, 27, July 10, August 4, October 5, 7; all 1848, NYU. On Teft, see *JRIII* III (1848): 305ff., and *SA*, 146.

duties of his office, to admit of his doing anything beyond a general superintendence of the publication."[84]

Even while he was engrossed in his duties in Rhode Island and with his authorship, Barnard turned his eye to a broader scene. Sometime during the winter of 1844–45, before he was sure of the Rhode Island appointment, he had suggested to George Emerson an ambitious "design of a mission in favor of the common schools." Emerson had gathered pledges amounting to $1,200 if Barnard would go spread the gospel to Vermont and Maine; more support was guaranteed if Barnard were to prove as successful as a school advocate in the northern states as he had been in Rhode Island. In May Emerson forwarded $600 and asked for a careful accounting; Barnard was to begin in July.

> You shall enter upon your general mission for the Common Schools, devoting yourself . . . to the work of enlightening the public mind and exciting the right spirit, wherever you may be called upon to go.

Somehow it is hard to imagine Barnard contenting himself with such a minor role, that of an itinerant agent like Baker, and there is no evidence that he ever actually took up the call. Nor do we know what he did with the money. Such a dereliction of duty did not prevent Emerson from writing in the fall that the Boston School Committee was looking for a superintendent, and "eyes are turned toward you." He added that the salary was much more than Barnard could have dared hope for from the New England plan, and that subscribers to the mission would not object to Barnard's making a choice in favor of the Boston position.[85]

There were other opportunities. Horace Mann wanted Barnard to serve on the building committee for the new Normal School at Bridgewater, and he turned down countless requests to participate in teachers' institutes. Henry Randall in New York summed it up: "I tell you what it is Barnard—you are getting a standing in this state you little dreamed of," in New York and elsewhere—national service might come next.[86]

---

84. Letters from Beers, July 3; from Barnes, August 4, October 5, 7, November 17; from Wells, August 26, October 25, 30; from Northend, November 7, 27, 30; from Mayhew, November 9; from Whitcomb, October 19, all 1848, NYU; from John Beard, Tallahassee, who ordered a copy, September 20, 1849, NYU.

85. Letter from Emerson, January 13 (to Hartford), January 25 (to Providence), May 18 (to Hartford), October 31 (to Providence), 18, 1845; from Andrews June 19, August 14, October 13, 1843, January 3, 1844, TC. In a letter to Mann in 1846 he did mention that he had committed himself "to attend some of the Institutes in Vermont," August 17, 1846, MHS.

86. At the 1845 meeting of county superintendents Emma Willard was also present,

As early as the fall of 1845, moreover, James Bunce, a perennial school reformer in Connecticut, had urged Barnard to return to his native cit and state. "Come out of the wilderness—I mean no disrespect to our brave little neighbor—and help your own birthplace and state, at least by your advice." Barnard declined while writing a detailed letter, laying out a program which included the establishment of a high school and the furthering of Teachers' Institutes. The two men agreed to offer a "Premium for a Practical Essay on the necessity and mode of improving the Public Schools of Connecticut, and of adding to the schools in cities, a department of instruction in the higher branches of education." The prize was won by the young Noah Porter who undertook the assignment "on the urgent solicitation of . . . and after full consultation with" Barnard— or so Barnard said. His heart, and concern, obviously was still in his home state, and the schoolmen there continued to look to him. But it is doubtful that Barnard wrote Seth Beer's reports as commissioner between 1845 and 1849 as he later claimed.[87]

Still he was on the lookout for another job. In the summer of 1846 he lectured on the common schools in Ohio, Michigan, and Wisconsin, and he negotiated with his friend, Asa Dearborn Lord, about the possibility of a lengthy sojourn in Ohio as a participant in the school reform movement there. Barnard's initial response to Lord was entirely favorable. "The *cause must go forward,* unless the law which hitherto governed the progress of society utterly fail," he wrote, and he dispatched proposals by now thoroughly familiar, for gradation, for institutes, for a journal. At first he saw Lord as the leader, but Lord urged Barnard to undertake the task; so, too, did Andrews who was trying to raise money for the enterprise. "We can raise much more to keep you here I think than in anticipation of your coming." Barnard implied that he would accept the challenge but emphasized that it would be "without any ambition after office & with the explicit understanding" that he would take none, that he would come only as a "friend of the cause" for a year, if his health permitted.[88]

---

and S. S. Randall painted an amusing picture: "I should have liked above all things to have seen you all assembled, semi-circularly no doubt around Mistress Willard, intently listening to her voluminous harangue—relating her early experience—and no woman I wot of has had more—& telling you all what good boys you had been & how much better and wiser and all that sort of thing, you might live to be. When she had concluded, I suppose, she gave you all, beginning at the east & ending with the Greatest—his Holiness of course—a nice slice of plumb pudding—& told you to go out two by two & not fall out by the ways." Letter May 28, 1845, NYU. See also *AJE* VI, xvi (March 1859): 165.

87. *AJE* XV, xl (September 1865): 391. The account is Barnard's; there is no corroboration in the letters.

88. Ibid., 390 note, mentions lectures in Chicago, Milwaukee, Madison, Detroit, Ann

Characteristically Barnard was full of plans. First of all Lord would have to have a job, while he continued with the vital task of editing his Ohio education journal. Head of the as yet nonexistent high school would be suitable, or if not that, superintendent of the Asylum for the Blind, a post for which Lord's "intelligence and moral value" qualified him. If the salary of either of these positions was insufficient, Barnard grandly assured Lord of help. "We propose to supply the deficiency of salary out of our individual means." A week later Barnard wrote in rather more dictatorial terms. He had become "morally certain" that he would go to Ohio, and Lord was the man he wanted to work with; perhaps Lord could be head of the Columbus schools or, more important, principal of a Teachers' Institute "to be got up in every part of the State." Lord was to continue to edit his journal *but* under Barnard's supervision; Barnard insisted that Lord consult with him before printing his second volume or any other material. "Don't let us cross each others paths."[89]

At the end of one of his letters to Lord, Barnard congratulated his colleague on his good fortune in having a wife who could sympathize with him in his labors. Barnard himself was not so blessed. "My fate is almost worthy of a Wandering Jew—whose song Wordsworth has woven into touching English verse." But his fate was soon to change. An early biographer says that he met his wife in the fall of 1846, but Barnard, writing to Mann after his marriage, said that "it was nearly five years ago," and there were clear references to J. D. in letters written in 1842. Barnard, good Romantic and reformer that he was, idealized the nuptial state, and by the time he was thirty-six, he longed to be married. Yet in the letter to Mann announcing his impending marriage, he devoted a long opening paragraph to school matters and asked for material for publications before broaching what must have come as a stunning surprise. He was to be wed two days hence, and his bride was Josephine Desnoyers of Detroit, whose "chief attraction" was "a heart full of all feminine affections." They had met by chance, on one of Barnard's many visits to Detroit, and he had been attracted, he said, by her "unobtrusive acts of kindness & charity to a poor family in Detroit." Years passed, whether Barnard was too preoccupied with his work or because there were serious religious complications, we cannot tell. He certainly was apologetic to Mann on the subject of his intended's faith.

Arbor, Sandusky, Cleveland, Columbus, and Cincinnati. Letter from Barnard to Asa D. Lord of Kirkland, Ohio, November 19, 1846, RIC; see also letters of November 4 and 27.

89. Letter from Barnard to Lord, November 17, 1846, RIC. Note the interchangeable roles; a reformer could reform anything.

I hope it won't shock your philosophical or theological *prejudices* to know that Miss D. is a Roman *Catholic*. In its atmosphere she was born & has lived & has been living & in its faith, for all I shall do to disturb it, she will continue to live & will die.[90]

Although Barnard here professed an intention to attempt to convert the future Mrs. Barnard, one suspects this was for Mann's benefit. Despite his earlier expressions of anti-Catholicism, Barnard's religious reservations were never as intense as Mann's and in any case, he was an Episcopalian.

The couple were married on September 7, 1847, and settled down in Barnard's hometown with only occasional stays in Providence. It is impossible to paint any picture of Josephine Barnard. The new husband wrote to a friend that his wife was "gentle and loving, intellectual and pious" —hardly a rhapsody after only three days of marriage. Captain Morgan referred to "your darling wife," and added in a parenthesis, after asking the couple to visit, "don't forget her." Perhaps the captain was jesting, or perhaps the bluff man suspected that Barnard could forget his wife.[91] The marriage lasted forty-four years, or until Mrs. Barnard's death in 1891, and five children were born from it. The first, a daughter, was born in the summer of 1848, for on August 17 Josephine Barnard wrote her will leaving all her worldly goods to her husband and appointing a guardian for her daughter Mary, and in September George Emerson sent his regards "to Mrs. B. and to Miss Mary."[92] The only son, a lawyer like his father, died in 1884, but two unmarried daughters survived their father, the youngest, Emily, dying in 1919.

By the winter of 1848, the task of administering the Rhode Island system had a dreary sameness to Henry Barnard. He spent an increasing amount of time away from Providence, and Elisha Potter, who minded the office when he could, wrote of mail piling up and complaints from those who found Barnard not available. Potter warned early in the winter that reappointment for another term was in no way certain. "In such a situation as yours a man's enemies increase every year." The locked office and the commissioner's absences were noted, as was his failure to submit regular, written reports.[93]

90. Letter to Mann, August 5, 1847, MHS. In this letter Barnard said he had tried to see Mann in West Newton, why he did not say.

91. Letter from Hills, September 11, from Morgan, December 28, both 1847, NYU.

92. Probate records, Connecticut, there is no other will. Mrs. Barnard's estate was appraised in 1891—300 shares of the Eureka Iron and Steel Company of Michigan, worth $300.

93. Letter to Mann December 16, 1846, MHS; letter from Potter, February 23, 1848, NYU.

It was no wonder people complained. Barnard was more interested in the progress of the new high school in Hartford than in matters in Providence. In March he had addressed the Young Men's Institute on the necessity of training "all youth for the service of the country, for active usefulness, and for domestic life"; one way to do this was to establish a high school. The citizens agreed, authorizing the school on March 8, and Barnard was asked to furnish a plan "of a suitable building," to suggest schools the founding committee could visit, and to recommend teachers. Finally, on December 1, he took part in the dedicatory exercises of the recently completed building.

It was natural that he spoke of the architecture, of the "spacious, convenient, and attractive structure," and of the content, "the physical, intellectual, and moral training of the pupils" which rested "on the solid basis of thorough systematic teaching in the schools below." He continued with one of his few specific discussions of curriculum, commending the school's program which combined classical and practical studies with a new emphasis on science:

> It meets the demands of our age for an education in science which shall make the wind and the stream, and the still more subtle agents of nature, minister to our material wants, and stimulate in all directions, the inventive pictures of man, by which mere muscular toil can be abridged, and made more effective. At the same time it does not ignore these apparently less practical studies, especially the mathematics and classics, which the gathered experience of successive generations of successful teachers, and the profoundest study of the requirements of the mind of youth, and the disciplinary and informing capabilities of different words of knowledge, have settled to be the best, although not, as I hold, the only basis of a truly literal scheme of general or professional educators.

Thus, as early as 1849 Barnard anticipated the comprehensive high school. In addition he vowed that "the highest advantages of public education" offered to "youth of the same age, of both sexes, and of every condition" the opportunity to master the same knowledge, and to develop comparable mental habits. Still he could not escape his limited vision; the things girls and boys should study were vastly divergent—girls needed knowledge of sewing and domestic economy, boys of practical matters around the farm or shop.

In this speech of celebration Barnard continued his battle with the private sector in education and showed his concern about the competitive founding of academies and colleges by corporations or religious bodies.

If throughout the nation, efforts to expand public education similar to those of the citizens of Hartford were not undertaken

> then will higher education—everything beyond the merest rudiment, pass into the irrevocable keeping of religious bodies and adventure schools, over which the public will exercise no control, and parents can have no guarantee of the value of the education their children will receive.

Barnard abhorred the idea of "a rival system," and feared the loss to the public sector of the children, destined by birth or aptitude, for the professions. He wanted Whig children to attend the common schools.

At the close of his oration, convention and his character, mandated a rousing peroration:

> I have no misgiving as to the future—it rises bright and glorious before me and on its forehead is the morning star—the herald of a brighter day than our schools have yet seen.

The High School would always stand as a monument,

> a shrine at whose altar-fire many ingenuous minds will be kindled with the true love of science, a fountain of living waters whose branching streams will flow us with ever deepening and widening current, which will bear on its bosom noble argosies, and nourish all along its banks, trees, whose leaves will be for the healing of the nations.

Barnard may have embellished this speech in the quiet of his study before publishing it, as a comparison with a similar one delivered in 1856 indicates, but the ideas and style are constant. He stressed access and quality, the democratic and meritocratic aspects, and the view that a high school would complete a system of schooling while at the same time exerting an influence on the lower schools. As he wrote later, the high school "will thus become a band of union, a channel of sympathy, a spring-head of healthy influence, and a stimulus to the whole community."[94] Yet he accepted a static view of society and opportunity; the high school might open the door, but only to a suitable and pre-determined space.

---

94. *OHGS*, 249ff., speech 251–53. In a note, 251, Barnard ascribed the speech to "notes recently recovered" on which he had jotted "Used at the dedication of the Public High School at Hartford Dec. 1, 1847 and at the opening of the Free Academy at Norwich in 1856." The two speeches are essentially the same although the later one is more florid. The Norwich speech is in *AJE* III, xiii (March 1857): 205–08; he repeats his 1838 rationale, 185–89. See also *AJE* XV, xxxix (June 1865): 279–83, where he summarizes the advantages of a community high school.

Barnard's efforts on behalf of the high school were realized, and Providence had lost its appeal. He claimed, to Lord, to be terribly run down, nearly convinced that his usefulness to the cause of reform was over, so off he went, alone, on a "tour of recreation & of health" to Virginia and the Carolinas in the spring of 1848. The trip proved restorative, and he returned to Providence, to "set things in order." But in the summer he was contemplating a trip to Europe, and to Lord, he spoke of plans for another vacation, in the late fall, before he left Rhode Island for good.[95] Repeatedly in Barnard's correspondence, especially in this period, the issue of his health is raised. After only a year on the job he had written to Mann that he was "sick, jaded out" with a headache and "a swollen face," alone in the hotel in Providence; in 1846 William Fowle had reported to Mann that Barnard was "unwell, worn down." Two years later Barnard moaned, "My health gave way this winter. But now I am much better." John Stedman sympathized. "You have abused, cruelly, cruelly abused yourself." Samuel Randall always fretted about his friend and urged him not to overwork *"foolishly and wrongfully."* Yet Mann wrote, perhaps only partly in jest:

> You have talked about being sick & about giving up and going to the sexton, etc., etc. more times than the boy cried "wolf." I hardly know what to make of it. Yet you always look rubicund and rotund.[96]

Barnard may have suffered from some recurring ailment, from migraines, chronic indigestion, or gout, or even depression. But one suspects that he often cried wolf. Some measure of psychosomatic illness must have figured, for talk of health problems all too often coincided with periods of difficulty in his official duties; equally often, after despairing about his ill health, he was able to undertake an arduous journey. And he lived to a very old age. Barnard did not like drudgery, nor political pressure, nor the hint of failure; they made him ill, and they also made him search for greener pastures.

One job he seems to have hoped for in 1848 was that of successor to Horace Mann who had recently been elected to the Congress. Barnard wrote Mann directly about the position and also approached George Emerson who temporized in his reply. If Barnard was really ill, said Emerson, he should do nothing at all until he was fully recovered; in any case

95. Letter to Mann, April 4, MHS, from Mann, July 10, 1848, NYU; from Randall, February 13, from Allston, March 27, both 1848, NYU; to Lord, May 22, 1848, RIC.

96. Letter to Mann, December 7, 1844, September 24, 1846, MHS; letter from Emerson, March 13, from Stedman, March 20, from Randall, March 14; all 1848, NYU; from Mann, April 4, October 4, 1848, Lannie, *Barnard*, 93 and 95, the latter also TC.

he was still an official in Rhode Island; nevertheless, Emerson agreed to "pass on" Barnard's letter. The superintendent was bound for disappointment, for in September Mann wrote on a subject "not an indifferent one" to Barnard; someone else, Barnas Sears, had been elected to the post. Barnard was at least content that someone "orthodox" on educational matters was Mann's successor.[97]

Another dream was appointment as a professor of education. In the standard versions of Barnard's life it is asserted that he was invited to take up two professorships and three city superintendancies after he left Rhode Island.[98] An examination of his correspondence only proves that he negotiated for the professorships, and in vain. He was still, of course, very much a loyal son of Yale, and a recognized one. In August 1845, he had delivered the Phi Beta Kappa address, an honor and an opportunity, on a well-known topic—"the wicked neglect of moral and physical education and the consequent results of disease and crime."[99] So it was natural to turn first to his alma mater, and to his friend Noah Porter. Porter wrote that the Prudential Committee was in favor of creating a chair in education, with Barnard in mind, but that the hindrance was the question of an endowment. The Corporation was opposed to any professorship that was not funded, and Porter urged Barnard to lobby among his friends for contributions. The impasse remained until November when the committee voted unanimously that a professor of education should be appointed and that Henry Barnard was "the most suitable and desirable" candidate. The Corporation would not budge, however, and the matter came to naught. At the same time Barnard was exploring with his friend Potter the thought of a similar post at Brown. Potter did not know how to proceed, but he promised to sound out President Wayland. Apparently nothing came of this attempt either.[100]

Poor Potter. Not only was he asked to act as the embassary to Wayland, but he had to mind the store while his friend was away, a task he tried to fulfill faithfully. He wrote endless letters, conveying detailed bits of busi-

97. Letter from Emerson, March 13, 1848, NYU; to Mann from Barnard, May 19, October 1, MHS; from Mann, September, NYU. In October Mann was still hoping Barnard would get some job in Massachusetts.

98. See Porter, *Barnard*, 76; Barnard was the source. Norton, "Sketch," 130 repeats Porter verbatim—thus are legends born.

99. Letter from S. Richard, September 23, 1845, TC. I have not located this speech, but it certainly was identical to his educational tract on the same subject.

100. Letters from Porter, April 13, July 24, August 21, November 20; from Potter, April 28, May 3; all 1848, NYU. A professorship of didactics was established at Brown in 1850, and S. S. Greene, the superintendent of schools, was the first incumbent; see *AJE* XI, xxvi (March 1862): 285–86.

ness to Hartford and elsewhere. He also, in the same week that he met with Wayland, had to steer Barnard's renomination through the legislature, even though he knew that Barnard was half-heartedly interested at best. Potter was successful in the latter and reported to his friend that the only real debate was on the subject of the commissioner's salary, which the Senate, in June, refused to increase; Barnard was chagrined.[101]

So Henry Barnard was once again, officially, the Superintendent of the Public Schools, but Rhode Island got precious little from him during the summer of 1848. Letters on school business had to be forwarded or attended to by an unidentified "Anthony" (certainly a clerk) and the faithful Potter. At one point Potter, worried at the number of times inquirers had found the commissioner's office locked, asked if he could advertise that it would be open two specified days a week, and he would try to cover if Barnard was unavailable. Even William Baker was concerned and wrote that there was "not a little hard talk from friends & foes because of your absence."

> Allow me once more to say I hope you will hasten back immediately. Your business demands it—your interest demands it—the cause demands it.[102]

But Barnard was then in Detroit with his wife, and in early September he was in Maine, for the annual meeting of the American Institute.

He had determined to resign. By October Potter was certain of it, and even requested that Barnard speak to the governor recommending his deputy as his successor. Yet oddly, in December Barnard was only "threatening to resign." Potter kept writing, imploring his friend to be available, to report to the legislature, not to be away for more than a fortnight, all so as not "to give any ground for complaint."

> Think of these things. It is the only plan by which you can get along without complaint. Whether these complaints are reasonable or unreasonable, you would not like to leave the state with the popular clamor against you.

Potter was a politician, which Barnard was not, and he was trying to make certain that Barnard went out a hero and that he, Potter, would be able to orchestrate the kind of farewell he knew Barnard craved. But Barnard was not pleased by his friend's tone and must have sent some testy

---

101. Letters from Potter, February 23, May 6, 23, 30, July 13, 1848, NYU. In his explication of the reform bill, Barnard had emphasized that the legislature retained control over the commissioner through its power to set his salary; here he was hoist on his own petard.

102. Letters from Potter, July 13, 20, from Baker, August 9, 23; all 1848, NYU.

replies to Potter, valiantly toiling in the cold office, too busy to come to Hartford when summoned. Potter apologized for his "careless remarks," assuring his demanding friend "you have done so much for the state."[103]

The decision was finally made. Barnard tendered his resignation to Governor Harris and, citing the utter failure of his health as the reason for his resignation, delivered his last, oral report to the General Assembly.[104] According to Noah Porter, the report was "most elegant and impressive, and was listened to for nearly two hours, with almost breathless attention." It was not printed subsequently among the documents Barnard included in the final volume of his *Journal*, so probably it was never written, but one can imagine what he said. He might even have repeated the ringing conclusion of an earlier speech, that Rhode Island could be "truly an Empire State, ruling by the supremacy of mind and moral sentiment." Or he may have ended with the more simple phrases of his preface to the final volume of the *Journal*:

> With these explanatory remarks the document is committed to your hands, with the best wishes of the undersigned for the continuing prosperity of the Public Schools of Rhode Island, and with the most grateful acknowledgements for the uniform kindness with which he has been treated by the people of the State, and for the official co-operation which he has received from the Legislature, from school officers, teachers and the conductors of the public press, in the discharge of his numerous and arduous labors.

Barnard left the state amid applause, not thunderous perhaps, and with an eight hundred dollar bonus, negotiated no doubt, by the asiduous Potter.[105]

Barnard never mentioned any official tributes, the "proper complimentary resolutions" Potter had hoped to attain, so he must have been disappointed in them. Francis Wayland referred to Barnard's "remarkable abilities," and Potter was formal: "The State of Rhode Island owes you a debt of gratitude. . . . You understood the needs & peculiar character of the State." John Kingsbury, the president of the Rhode Island Institute of Instruction, spoke in measured tones for his colleagues, emphasizing their collegial relationship with the commissioner.

103. Letters from Potter, October 10, December 1, 2, 5, 18, 19, 24, 1848, January 1, 6, 1849, NYU; Mrs. Barnard wrote Potter December 14 saying that Barnard was ill, and was seeing people in his room, would Potter come.

104. Barnard, *AJE* XIV, xxxvi (September 1864): 275, dates his resignation January 1848; "It was a sore trial for Mr. Barnard to resign before he had fully consummated his plans and agencies." The date is wrong by a year.

105. *JRIII* III, iii–iv; letter from Updike, August 30, 1848, NYU; from Potter, March

Mr. Barnard was peculiarly happy in securing the cordial cooperation of every class who take an interest in education. None rendered
him more willing aid than those whose ample fortunes enable them
to sustain every benevolent enterprise. Mr. Barnard, I have reason
to believe, never appealed to this class in vain.

The reform leaders had appreciated the ally they had in Barnard, although
it is clear that in the end they still viewed him as a partner in the enterprise, not the messiah.

The state's teachers, on the other hand, were more appreciative. They
voted Barnard a silver pitcher and forwarded an effusive commendation,
noting with special warmth, the commissioner's efforts on behalf of the
institutes and for better schoolhouses. Barnard responded with his valedictory sermon, which contained the words which began this chapter. He
went on:

Ever since the Great Teacher condescended to dwell among men,
the progress of this cause has been upward and onward, and its final
triumph has been longed for and prayed for, as well as believed in,
by every lover of this race. And although there is much that is dark
and discouraging in the past and present condition of society, yet
when we study the nature of education, and the necessities and
capabilities of improvement all around us, with the sure word of
prophecy in our minds, and with the evidence of what has already
been accomplished, the future rises bright and glorious before us.
. . . The cause of education cannot fail unless all the laws which
have heretofore governed the progress shall cease to operate, Christianity prove a fable, and liberty a dream.[106]

Others were not so sure. "In fact, Sir, we make but slow progress in the
new and beautiful system of public education," wrote one school com-
mitteeman. For in truth Barnard had made only a beginning, and it was
left to his faithful lieutenant, Elisha Potter, to develop and solidify his
predecessor's innovations.

The work of Mr. Barnard was after all only the preliminary work.
He created the system, but it was in a community so unequally
prepared, and in many regions so unprepared, that he could not
carry the organization beyond a certain point.[107]

30, 1849, NYU.

106. *Proceedings* of the National Teachers' Association, hereafter cited as *NEA*, 403–04;
Tribute, unsigned, TC; Porter, *Barnard*, 67; letter from Potter, February 11, 1849, NYU.

107. Letter from School Committee, Charlestown, November 6, NYU; Higginson,

That schooling in Rhode Island had improved vastly during Barnard's stewardship was clear. As an early authority boasted, "the decisive battle had been fought and won." Whereas in 1844 only three towns levied school taxes, in 1847 only three did not. Over $120,000 had been spent on new schoolhouses, each with vastly improved accoutrements, and graded systems had been introduced in the larger localities. The question is, how much of this reversal can be credited to Barnard. Early scholars, beginning with Porter, heaped praise upon him; Frank Tracy Carlton was more wary and more accurate. "The really significant fact is that in the early forties the long struggle for a constitution and broader suffrage qualifications ended."[108] Consensus had been achieved, to a large extent, on the matter of the state's role in the provision of schooling, and Barnard built on that consensus. And, as in Connecticut, in Rhode Island he had corps of dedicated fellow reformers, older statesmen and younger teachers who preceded and would follow him.

Nonetheless, in the small ocean state, Henry Barnard may well have reached the pinnacle of his powers. He had conceptualized a system of public schooling and had initiated the steps necessary for a centralized, public state system. He turned legal empowerment into administrative fact, inaugurating a commissionership which exerted considerable centralizing force. He had been instrumental in the organization of teachers' institutes which had the potential to evolve into more permanent training institutions. He had introduced a utilitarian element into the content of schooling. And he had helped to make education a matter of high priority, among his allies in the reform movement and also, albeit to a lesser degree, among the citizenry of the state. All of this he had accomplished in something over three years—with, certainly, the constant buttressing of the coalition that had brought him to the state in the first place. But again, as it had before, a fatal flaw had intervened to curtail Barnard's effectiveness. He was not content to remain an administrator, charged with the day-to-day, month-by-month, oversight of the emerging system, or he was bored by it; he saw himself in grander terms, and he longed for the prestige and applause he felt was his due. A larger stage, or failing that, his beloved Connecticut was what he sought.

History, 80–84.

108. See Carlton, *Economic Influences*, 70ff.

IV

TEACHER

EDUCATOR

*No man is so insane as to employ a work-
man to construct a valuable or delicate piece
of mechanism, who is to learn how to do it
for the first time on that very article. No
one employs any other than an experienced
artist to repair a watch. No parent entrusts
the management of a lawsuit involving his
property or his reputation, to an attorney
who has not studied his profession and given
evidence of his ability. No one sends for a
physician to administer to his health, who
has not studied the human constitution and
the nature and uses of medicine. No one
sends a shoe to be mended, or a horse to be
shod, or a plough to be repaired, except to
an experienced workman; and yet parents
will employ teachers who are to educate
their children for two worlds.* (Connecticut
Common School Journal *I, 4 [November
1839]: 65)*

"You must be perfectly happy—and free of care—back again
in your beloved Connecticut among its eminently pious people," wrote
Elisha Potter from Providence to Barnard. Ever loyal to his friend, Potter
attended to the unfinished business Barnard had left behind and acted as
the intermediary in negotiations with the governor and the legislature
over Barnard's final stipend; $800 was eventually appropriated, enough,
thought Potter, for his friend "to feel rich for a time." Typically Barnard
promised more than once to come to Providence to submit his final
report; characteristically he failed, moaning about his health, even as he

visited New York and Boston. By July Potter, who had been appointed commissioner, pointed out that if the previous year's report was not forthcoming, neither would be final payment; he also sent a list of specific issues requiring Barnard's attention and even offered to meet him in New York to discuss them. Still, as late as November, Potter was reiterating "seriously" that there would be real trouble if the report did not appear.[1]

Much as Henry Barnard loved Connecticut, he thought now of moving to Detroit. There was talk of his being appointed Superintendent of Public Instruction in the city; the job, unfortunately, went to another. Nonetheless, Barnard began to build a house there, with his brother-in-law, Peter Desnoyers acting as his agent. The cellar was dug in March, and by July the foundation was laid; Barnard promised to send out plans, procrastinated, and then vowed to bring out an architect. Mrs. Barnard did spend the summer in Detroit, and Barnard was there sometime during September. Whatever happened to the house is not clear; it may have been continued with an eye for investment once the possibility of a school position fell through.[2] Barnard was building four houses in Hartford on speculation at the same time.

During this period of uncertainty Barnard seemed somewhat changed to his friends. One old friend was even rather sharp: "You are not growing, but grown old, you grow fat without laughing and that will be the death of you." He added, with a touch of bitterness, that Barnard had only written because he wanted a loan of $500—which was declined. As was his wont when things failed to go smoothly, Barnard hoped to flee. The supportive Samuel Randall commended his friend "to a total abandonment of Normal Schools, Schoolhouse Architecture, & Common Schools in general, and to a Substitution for three months at least of Normal Comfort, Domestic Architecture, and Common Sense (in the Pickwickian acceptance of the term)."[3] Captain Morgan suggested a trip to London. Instead Barnard turned to the delayed history of education, writing near and far (as far as the new state of California—he received a map from an acquaintance out there) for information. He also negotiated

1. Letters from Potter, February 23, 24, March 9, 30, April 13, 25, May 10, July 15, October 2, November 3, 25, 1849, NYU. Potter sent letters to Barnard for his attention: from N. Munroe, March 29, 1849, requesting payment for services at an institute, from W. H. Perry, June 19, complaining that a library, which had been paid for and had not been delivered; Gideon Chilson, the merchant of school stoves, sent bills—in some cases, according to Potter's notes, for stoves that did not function.

2. Letters from Desnoyers, March 24, July 28, from George Hand, May 25, from Williams, October 1; all 1849, NYU.

3. Letter from R. Sanford, January 29, from Williams, February 12, from Morgan, February 9, from Randall, April 25, all 1859, NYU.

for support for the projected publication. At the summer meeting of the American Institute of Instruction, where he delivered two lectures, it was announced that Henry Barnard contemplated writing a history, and a resolution of support was passed. A committee was appointed to confer with him, which it probably never did, and which he assuredly would not have welcomed. What he sought, more concrete assistance, was not forthcoming.

The projected history was once again delayed, as Barnard was drawn more and more into school affairs in his native state. He refused, he reported, to become the head of the new Hartford High School, but other matters were brewing. It had been politics that had driven him from office in 1842, and now it was politics which provided him a second opportunity to serve Connecticut. Seth Beers, the highly competent and long-term Commissioner of the School Fund, had served as Barnard's successor, and whereas Beers was not as fervent an advocate of the common schools as his predecessor, and certainly was lower keyed, he did not preside over the disbanding of all progress in educational matters as his political foes had anticipated. That simply was not feasible, nor politic, and Beers was a better politician than Barnard.

For the most part, during the mid-forties, elections in Connecticut swung more on national issues than on local ones despite the strength of party loyalty.[4] The election of 1844 had been fought mainly on the tariff although school matters were also raised, and the victory of the Whig, Roger Baldwin, in the gubernatorial race assured the reformers that their cause would not languish. During the legislative session a committee of the customary eight was appointed, to investigate the condition of the schools for yet another time; it was instructed to submit specific suggestions for reform by the following session. In the spring the committee reported that "the true economy of the state . . . would be promoted by the establishment of a Normal School," noting that the increased cost would be a mere five cents annually per child in the state. No action was taken during the session, presumably because the political balance was so unstable. The next year the Democrats elected the governor, Isaac Toucey, who made no mention of education in his address to the legislature. There was, however, sufficient bipartisan support for school improvement to allow passage (by a concurrent vote) of the principle features of a plan, including provision for a normal school, submitted by the Joint Standing Committee on Education. The legislature did demonstrate some caution

4. See *AJE*, XIV, xxxv (June 1864): 262ff., for a summary of developments in Connecticut prior to Barnard's return. See Gideonse, "Common School Reform," chap. V, "Reawakening."

in voting to have the plan distributed to the school visitors throughout the state for their response.

The wisdom of this strategy, and the existence of a consensus is proved by Beers's report the next year. He repeated almost verbatim the planks of the Whig platform of a decade before; he endorsed the idea of a Board of Education, town-wide supervision of schools, and a Normal School; he supported teachers' institutes and associations, and an educational journal. Much later Barnard was to claim credit for Beers's report:

> The compiler of this article has the best authority for stating that the First, Second, and Third and Fourth Reports of the Superintendent of Common Schools of Connecticut, from 1845 to 1849, and all circulars relating to the School Returns and Schools for Teachers, were prepared by Mr. Barnard during his connection with the schools of Rhode Island.[5]

This from a man who could not complete his own reports! The truth of the matter was that years of agitation were finally paying off, and school reform had come to be seen as a democratic and proper measure by members of both parties.

The emergence of such a favorable climate and the election of a Whig governor marked 1847 as an auspicious year. Governor Clark Bissell referred in his address to the normal schools and seminaries in Massachusetts and New York and expressed the fear that Connecticut was falling behind her neighbors; he urged the legislature to create a Normal School. Beers concurred, noting in his report that the issue had been "long before the people" of the state, and he paraphrased, precisely as Barnard would have done, the usual arguments: what was necessary for teachers was "a thorough knowledge of what is to be done and the practical skill to do it." The proposed school would provide the opportunity for teachers to acquire that knowledge and skill.

> If the legislature would pledge the means to sustain the annual expense of such a school, on an economical scale, for a period long enough to give the institution a fair trial, it is believed that there are towns in which it should be located and individuals ready to provide the necessary buildings, furniture, and apparatus.

Not a ringing call certainly, but a careful recommendation, entirely consistent, in its emphasis on economy and local action, with Democrat phi-

---

5. *AJE*, XV, xl (September, 1865): 393n; *CC*, April 16, May 16, 1846. Barnard credited Beers's probity in *AJE*, VI, 2 (June 1859). For the political developments see *CCSJ*, V, iv (December 1851): 138ff., and *AJE* XIV, xxx (June 1864): 262ff. See also *Normal Schools and*

losophy. Beers had read his audience and the political climate better than Barnard and urged that the school be allowed "a fair trial." Debate on the measure was spirited. Loren Waldo, a perennial supporter, summarized the arguments with good Whig phraseology:

> Either the public must educate the character of the State, or the great Adversary of all good will educate them for his own purposes.

Most members concurred that the Assembly was not moving fast enough and voted for still another committee to sit during the recess to devise a plan for the new school.[6]

The demand for improved preparation of teachers was one of the initital planks in the platform of the early schoolmen reformers; antebellum schools were equated with teachers, and if one were improved, so would be the other. One of the canons of educational history is that Massachusetts led the way in 1839, and in fact the first public normal school was established there in that year, but the story leading up to its founding is far more complicated. Barnard himself tips his hat to Elisha Tichnor for introducing the concept of normal schools in an article published in 1789, although he rapidly goes on to stress Connecticut's role in innovations in teacher training. Denison Olmsted, a former teacher in New London's Union School, titled his 1816 Yale master's oration "The State of Education in Connecticut" and advocated an Academy for Schoolmasters. In 1823 William Russell, then the head teacher in the New Township Academy in New Haven, published his "Suggestions on Education" including a call for the better preparation of teachers; he re-issued his remarks in 1826 in the first number of the *American Journal of Education* which he had begun to edit. The previous year had seen the almost simultaneous appearance of a spate of critiques of education, all of which in some way addressed the question of teachers. Thomas Gallaudet in Connecticut, James Carter in Massachusetts, and Walter Johnson in Pennsylvania led the chorus.[7]

Gallaudet sketched the proposed institution in some detail: it should

---

Other Institutions, Agencies, and Means Designed for the Professional Education of Teachers (Hartford: Case, Tiffany & Co., 1851; hereafter cited as *NS*), 23–26.

6. *CC*, May 8, June 26, 1846; *NS*, 25. *JRIII*, II, 10 (December 1841): 329, states that John M. Bunce and colleagues raised $10,000 which they offered to the state for a normal school if the General Assembly would appropriate an equal amount—as Dwight had done in Massachusetts—but the cautious legislature declined to act.

7. *AJE* XXV (1875): 479–81; summary of background of normal schools, *AJE* XIV, xxxvii (December 1864) and xlii (March 1866). Barnard publicized the views of the proponents of teacher training from the very beginning; see *CCSJ* I, 8 (February 1839): 91, for a speech by Governor DeWitt Clinton on the "Education of Teachers."

have two or three professors, a library with the major works on education
("theoretical and practical, in all languages"), and suitable teaching apparatus; connected with it should be a model school. The seminary should
be supported either by the public or by magnanimous individuals, and its
clients should be young men preparing for a career in teaching who would
receive a diploma upon the completion of the course. Gallaudet's goal
was both the preparation of teachers and the elevation of their status.

> Why not make this department of human exertion a profession as
> well as those of divinity, law and medicine? Why not have an Insti-
> tution for the training up of Instructors for their sphere of labor, as
> well as institutions to prepare young men for the duties of the
> divine, the lawyer, or the physician?

The young men who would see themselves as missionaries, working "for
the advancement of the Redeemer's kingdom" and their object would be
to "prepare the rising generation for usefulness and respectability in life,
and to train them up for a better and happier existence beyond the grave."
The mission was lofty: "Is a *shoe*, or a *bonnet*, to be put in competition
with *an immortal soul?*" Gallaudet counseled small beginnings, perhaps a
course of lectures for teachers, or a modest school whose trained teachers
would attract notice by their excellence; he was certain that the public at
large would be willing to bear the cost once the value of the product was
demonstrated.[8]

Reforming statesmen read Gallaudet's and similar essays. Among them
New York's Governor Clinton became a standard bearer; he made education the focus of his 1826 address and advocated the establishment of a
seminary for the training of teachers—the first governor to do so—but
the legislature refused to heed his call.[9] Thus, as early as the 1820s the
ground was being prepared from which the normal school movement,
spurred on by the European example, was to spring.

Gallaudet had counseled small beginnings, and in fact there were a
number of experiments in teacher training prior to 1839. Schoolmasters
such as Henry Rockwell, who offered to instruct *gratis* ten "worthy and
indigent females" desiring to teach, frequently attempted to prepare their
more advanced pupils to assume teaching duties. Josiah Holbrook, of the
Lyceum fame, in the winter of 1824–25 established an academy at his
farm in Derby, Connecticut, where "one prominent object was to qualify

8. Gallaudet, Plan, 4ff. Note that Gallaudet thought of teachers as male.

9. See *AmJEd*, I, vii (July 1826): 434; the editor commented "Nothing surely can be
more beneficial to the interests of our state, than the establishment of a seminary which
may furnish a constant supply of well educated teachers."

teachers." Up in Vermont, beginning in 1823, Samuel R. Hall presided over a small, private seminary for the training of teachers ; he was called from there by Phillips Academy at Andover in order to create a department "to afford the means of a thorough scientific and practical education, preparatory to the profession of teaching and to the various departments of business." It was Hall who issued the rallying cry: "GIVE TEACHERS A PROFESSIONAL EDUCATION."[10]

New England's initial efforts were replicated in Ohio. The Western Literary Institute petitioned the Ohio legislature in 1834 to establish a permanent institution "with collegiate privileges" to be called a Teachers' Institute. This Western innovation anticipated both the New England teachers' conventions and the demand for a state supported teacher training school; the word college also suggests a connection with more general dreams of higher education, part of the educational boosterism of the period.[11]

Ignored by conventional historians of the normal school movement are the efforts of contemporary women who emphatically belong in the front ranks of the founders of teacher education. Emma Willard, Catharine Beecher, Zilpah Grant, and Mary Lyon all saw teaching as an honorable profession for women who, according to the emerging canon, were uniquely endowed by the Creator with characters suited for the task of nurturing the young. In urging women to train as teachers, these pioneers were offering the challenge of higher education, for the training of teachers always incorporated the study of the higher branches of learning as well as exposure to educational thought and pedagogy. Women had the intellectual capacity for advanced study, said Beecher, and women could save the nation. Anne Firor Scott is entirely correct in noting that Merle Borrowman, in *The Liberal and the Technical in Teacher Education*, "seems never to have heard of Troy or Mt. Holyoke." What Scott does not underline is the fact that the efforts of these women *predated* most of the popular agitation on the subject and all of the early action.[12] The first significant

10. Letter from Henry Rockwell, September 27, 1839, NYU; on Holbrook see *AJE* VIII, xx (March 1860): 248, note A; he had between fifty and sixty pupils of both sexes, but the school only lasted one year. For Hall's lecture see *AII, Proceedings*, 4 (Boston, 1834), 242ff.

11. *Proceedings of the Western Literary Institute* (1834), preface. See *AJE* XIV, xxxvii (December 1864): 739–49; Barnard delivered an address on "Conditions of a Successful System of Public Schools" to the Institute's annual convention in 1842.

12. Scott, *Invisible Woman Visible*, 69, 85n7. Barnard frequently referred to these women and published their biographies, but he chose to ignore their importance in the early training of teachers. See *AJE* VI, xvi (March 1859): 125ff. (Willard), and X, xxv (June 1861): 670ff., (Mt. Holyoke).

group of teachers specifically prepared for the profession were women, from Hartford, Troy, Ipswich, and especially from Mt. Holyoke, a corps of dedicated apostles of schooling and virtue, who radiated throughout the nation in a hidden but substantial network.

There is another, unnoticed, predecessor to the normal schools. In New York State during the first third of the century Stephen van Rensselaer was the greatest of the Hudson Valley patroons and also an enlightened public servant. Legislator, chancellor of the state, regent of the school system, commissioner of the Erie Canal, president of the Board of Agriculture; there was nothing that did not bear his stamp. His particular interest was science; he commissioned geological surveys, especially along the route of the canal, and he worried about the popular ignorance of modern science and the lack of qualified instructors to teach science in the schools. In a grand, and characteristically antebellum, fashion he resolved to rectify the situation, by creating a new institution "to qualify teachers for instructing the sons and daughter of farmers and mechanics . . . in the application of experimental chemistry, philosophy, and natural history, to agriculture, domestic economy, the arts and manufactures." The Rensselaer Institute opened in 1826, providing free tuition to students who would "go out to the world as an army of Teachers for at least one year." The new school was as innovative in method as in design; the students served as apprentices, demonstrating through experimentation and explanation their mastery of any given material. Teacher training was not to be theoretical, and instruction in science was not to be rote.[13]

Rhetoric and scattered experimentation characterized the discussion of teacher education during the twenties; strong and consistent pressure to that end came to be exerted during the thirties. William Russell's new publication, the *American Journal of Education*, paid careful attention to the topic, reviewing the essays of Carter, Gallaudet, and the others, and summarizing the 1825 report of the Massachusetts committee which advocated normal schools. The editor also featured exemplary teachers, and the *Journal* was the voice of the Lyceum, an organization which had the improvement of teachers among its original purposes. This excellent journal was read by the well-educated and high-minded men of the American Institute of Instruction, and the two went hand in hand, in print and in addresses at the annual seesions, mounting a campaign for teacher education.[14] Both strove to raise the standards of instruction and to ele-

13. Palmer C. Ricketts, *History of the Rensselaer Polytechnic Institute* (New York, 1895), 6–11, and 33–34 for the act of incorporation.

14. *AmJEd* I (1826): Prospectus; see I, viii (August 1826): 485ff.; I, xi (November 1826): 678–79, 684–85; III, iii (February 1828): 78ff., and III, viii (August 1828): 497, on lyceums.

vate the status of the teacher, "by making him feel how high and noble is the work in which he is engaged, how extensive and thorough must be his preparation, and how entire his devotion." The October 1836 meeting of the Institute, for example, resolved that "the business of teaching should be performed by those who have studied the subject, as a profession."[15] It followed that the place for such study was an institution designed for that specific purpose. The Institute twice memorialized the Massachusetts legislature, in 1836 and 1837, proposing a superintendent of the common schools and means of improving teachers; on the specificity of the means they were unclear, for they concentrated on the evil rather than the means to repair it.[16]

It took the single-minded insistence of Charles Brooks, a Massachusetts minister and reformer, to popularize the notion of the normal school. According to him, a chance encounter on a European tour in 1835 introduced him to Dr. Julius, a Prussian reformer, who, during a tempestous Atlantic crossing, convinced the American of the distinct advantages of two features of the Prussian system, a state mechanism for supervision and a series of normal schools. Brooks readily admitted, "I fell in love with the Prussian system . . . I gave my life to it." For at least the next two years he worked with almost fanatic devotion for the cause. His oft-repeated message became a slogan: "As is the Teacher, so is the School."[17]

The Prussian system which Brooks so admired became familiar to the wide audience of American educational reformers through the English translation of Victor Cousin's great report on Prussian education and through the widely distributed *Report on Elementary Public Instruction in Europe* by Calvin Stowe, first published in December 1837, and re-issued subsequently many times in educational journals. Stowe had been commissioned by the Ohio legislature to investigate the European systems of education and to report to them—another example of the simultaneous activity in common school reform in the Midwest. Among his other conclusions, Stowe observed that the proper training of teachers was the very crux of the Prussian system, for a "superintendent of schools without a Teachers' Seminary, is a general without soldiers."

15. George B. Emerson, *History and Design of the American Institute of Instruction* (Boston: Tichnor, Reed & Fields, 1849), 4ff.; note the word *him*.

16. For the memorial see Barnard, *NS*, 103–10; cf., Mattingly, *Classless*, 108–09. That the Institute did not give up on its campaign is clear; one session of the 1839 convention was devoted to normal schools, with the usual participants, *CC*, August 31.

17. Letter from Brooks, November 8,1850, NYU. Brooks was a typical reformer, a founder of a Reading Society, the Old Colony Peace Society, and The Plymouth Bible Society, an incorporator of the steamboat line to Boston, a charterer of the Hingham Savings Bank, and the first to use anthracite coal in his section of Massachusetts.

> To attempt to train practical teachers without [a model school] would be like attempting to train sailors by keeping boys upon Bowditch's *Navigator* without ever suffering them to go aboard ship or handle a rope-yarn.

Stowe carefully spelled out the details: the course should be three years in duration, students should be at least sixteen, the curriculum should consist of lectures and recitations on all branches of learning as well as on the science of education and the art of teaching, and senior students were to be instructors in the companion model schools, an absolutely essential aspect of the training. The expense required for such an institution would be more than matched by the improvement in the quality of the instruction in the schools.[18]

Stowe's report found some receptive ears, but there was considerable opposition to such "Prussianizing" of that dearly held pillar of democracy, the Common School. The new ideas were foreign, in a time of cultural nationalism, they were bound to be expensive, in a time of economic depression, and they threatened the very core of the republic, the locality. What was more, they were unnecessary, or so the opponents thought. Teaching, after all, took no particular talent or skill — any smart youngster could do it, and few remained long in the classroom anyway. But the enthusiastic advocates were well organized and highly vocal, a match for any recalcitrant opponents. To reform came to mean to adopt aspects of the Prussian system, and most especially means for the improvement of teachers. The only real question was the nature of the projected institution; should it be a department in an existing school or academy, on the Andover model, or should it be an entirely new seminary. New York opted for the former, Massachusetts for the latter. The committee appointed to study the matter in Connecticut had to determine which course to follow.

The list of the interim committee read like a roll of honor in the cause of educational reform and included Thomas Gallaudet, Loren Waldo, and John T. Norton, as chairman. They worked diligently, visiting the normal schools in Massachusetts and academies in New York; Barnard probably attended some of their meetings. In the end the committee opted for a normal school, and in April the chairman placed an advertisement in the papers calling for proposals from towns interested in hosting the proposed institution.[19] The re-election of Governor Bissell and his

---

18. Stowe, *Common Schools*, 5ff., 83ff., quotation 88. See *CCSJ* I, 11 (April 1839): 134ff., and 12, (May 1839): 137ff.; also *NS*, 123ff.

19. *CC*, May 16, 1846, May 8, 15, 22, 29, June 26, July 3, 1847, for responses; one from Samuel Hart of Berlin for a seminary and one from the Centre Academy in Manchester

strong advocacy of education ("The cause of education is indeed fundamental to every interest in the country.") and, more significantly, of a
normal school, was a good omen. The report which Norton's committee
presented to the legislature was replete with concrete details: an appropriation of $2,500 annually for four years for the support of the normal
school, and the creation of a board of trustees, appointed by the legislature, to determine the location of the school and make the rules for it.
The bill passed the Assembly but was lost in the Senate—precisely the
fate of the first (1837) reform bill.[20] Partisan skirmishes over whether to
appoint an assistant commissioner of the School Fund, the successor
designate to Beers who was about to retire, occupied more of the legislature's attention than did the normal school bill; still the near-miss must
have been disheartening to its stalwart supporters.

Henry Barnard, of course, watched these maneuvers from nearby, and
he reported to his Rhode Island readers on "the healthy state of feeling in
Connecticut." Even if disappointed in the defeat of the bill, he must have
been gratified that the same body which refused to appropriate $2,500
for a normal school did vote exactly that same amount to buy and distribute to the school committees a work on school architecture—most
assuredly his.

The following spring Beers gave only a brief history of the previous
attempts to secure passage of a normal school bill and of the support for
it throughout the state. "It would be an insult to the common intelligence of the people of the state to suppose the subject was not understood." Debate in the Assembly centered, oddly, not on the merits of the
normal school but on a peripheral issue: whether the bonuses, required
of three banks seeking state charters, should go to the support of the
projected school. Some members (certainly Democrats) wanted the
money to go instead to the struggling Wesleyan College of Middletown;
some thought the idea of bonuses at all was a sign of corruption. In the
end both the bonus and an Act for the Establishment of a State Normal
School passed easily and were approved by Governor Trumbull on June
22.[21]

The law established one school whose purpose was

> not to educate teachers in the studies required by law, but to receive
> such as are found competent . . . and train them in the best meth-
> ods of teaching and conducting schools.

---

for a teachers' department.

20. *CC*, May 6, 13, June, 1848; *NS*, 25–26.

21. *CC*, April 7, May 12, June 2, 16, 23, 1849; for the bill see *NS*, 27–29, quotation from

Control of the school was vested in the trustees, who were to be appointed by the legislature and to serve without compensation; they had the power to locate the school, establish the curriculum, set the rules, and appoint the teachers; they could even "as they deemed best for the interest of the said school" move it from time to time. The principal of the Normal School was expected to conduct Institutes throughout the state, and he was an *ex officio* member of the trustees and Superintendent of the Common Schools. The size of the school was limited to 220 pupils, and each school society was entitled to nominate four individuals, two of each sex, on the basis of "their age, character, talents and attainments." All candidates were required to sign "in their own hands" a statement attesting to their intention to teach in the state in return for free tuition, and provision was made for a model school.[22]

The first normal school in Connecticut, then, was to be a separate institution, a professional school, and a form of higher education, admitting students who presumably had completed the schooling available in their communities and who had probably already done some teaching. The creation of the school can be viewed as a further step in the gradation of the common schools, and in the development of the state system of schooling. Elementary schooling was to be provided in the small district schools, higher studies in the union or high schools of the larger towns; those students who were ready to advance to another level, and who had not prepared for the classical college, could now attend the normal school. That school was part of the public provision of schooling in a state in which tertiary education was provided solely by private institutions; unlike the midwestern states which had created, at least on paper, universities, the New England states had no public ones. The New Britain Normal School established a Connecticut precedent for public higher education as well as for state teacher training.

Henry Barnard was the unanimous choice of the committee to head the new institution:

> His distinguished ability and zeal in the cause, coupled with his entire self-consecration, and large experience, constitute the surest guaranty of the successful discharge of the duties of the appoint-

---

Beers, 26. One legislator did observe sourly that the "only good" to come from a teacher training school was "to fit young ladies to be married." Jesse Olney, always a sturdy supporter, countered that one easily.

22. The provision for the moving of the school may have been thrown in as a sop to those disappointed when the trustees decided on the location of the school; it also established a vague precedent for the creation of additional normal schools in other parts of the state at some future date.

ment, and that no effort will be lacking on his part to give to the institution efficiency and vitality.

On September 6, Francis Gillette, the chairman of the trustees, wrote Barnard the news of his appointment, and everyone, even the Democratic papers, approved. Barnard received a number of congratulatory letters from his colleagues, but none was as florid as one from a teacher in Norwich:

> Sir,
>
> That, under your administration, *Education* may be the *guiding star* of Connecticut, giving light to her sister states, the loss of which would be deeply *felt* in the *moral world, as the annihilation* of the Sun in the natural, and that *boarding round, poor school houses, poor* teachers, and *disinterested* parents, may be among the things that *were* and *are not*, and that *thou mayst at last* be *recompensated* for thy *arduous labors*, by meeting the *smiles* of *an approving* God and hearing the welcome message, "Thy work is *done*," and *well* done
>
> is the wish of
Sarah M. Upham

One suspects that Miss Upham had attended one of the institutes Barnard immediately held in all eight of the counties. It was precisely his task to reach such teachers, through the institutes and through instruction in the as-yet-to-be-inaugurated normal school. As yet he had none of the powers which he had wielded in Rhode Island, and there was no mention of any extension of "direct state action" in the new legislation. The focus was solely on the training of teachers.[23]

Nearly all of Barnard's letters during the fall deal with the eight teachers' conventions he was obligated to hold before the commencement of the winter schools. Institutes had become a permanent feature by this time; Beers estimated that three-fourths of the winter teachers had attended at least one prior to the winter schools of 1847. He had established the institute schedule for 1849, but his successor was responsible for the staffing. Francis Russell again agreed to conduct the one in Bridgeport, but it was hard to get speakers for the other seven. Horace Mann reneged on a promise to come, and even the faithful Leonard Bacon declined to appear at Meriden. But David Camp was quick to volunteer, filling in at Meriden, and again at Suffield; unfortunately, a bad cold

23. Letter from Gillette, n.d.,TC; from Upham, November 2, NYU; see Gideonse, "Common School Reform," 243, who sees the normal school bill as a shrewd Whig move to reestablish state supervision.

prevented his conducting the Essex institute. Camp also was anxious to assist in establishing a state teachers' organization.[24]

Some 750 teachers, most of whom were already hired for the winter terms, attended the fall institutes, and Barnard spoke at six of the eight, enjoying the opportunity, he said, of "renewing a personal acquaintance" with the teachers of the state. The following fall fourteen institutes—as Barnard pointed out six more than the eight required by law—were held with a total attendance of nearly 1,200. The gathering at Willimantic, for example, had attracted ninety people. Whatever the fortunes of the new normal school, its two hundred students, if they all came, would be a tiny minority of the teaching cadre in the state. The popularity of the institutes, however, presented a problem of expense. The $400 appropriated by the parsimonious legislature was totally inadequate, "imposing a heavy pecuniary burden on the Superintendent and subjecting other individuals to large sacrifices of time for the common benefit of the schools of the State."[25]

In his capacity as Superintendent, Barnard was authorized to exert the "general supervision" of the schools of the state, and there was a myriad of specific queries and requests to which he had to respond—questions about the validity of certificates, pleas for teachers, inquiries about the construction of school houses. The Salisbury committee sought advice on texts and maps and the proper method of teaching arithmetic, and the Norwich School Committee had a dilemma: did two Indian boys dwelling in the township have a legal right to attend school, and if they did, would not all Chickasaws enjoy the same right? A sensitive, and thoroughly modern, issue was brought to Barnard's attention by a father from Bridgeport: was it legal for his son to be expelled from school for refusing to read the New Testament?[26] Thus, by means of such requests for advice and his responses, Barnard was offered an opportunity to extend the supervisory writ of his office, just as he had in Rhode Island.

Henry Barnard had matured as a politician, and caution dictated that he should act "on the principles which my predecessor had sanctioned in

24. Letters from Russell, October 3, 8; from W. P. Bunall of the Housatonic Railroad, who guaranteed half-price fares for the teachers attending this institute, October 22; from James Houghton, October 25; from Bacon, October 25; from Mann, November 3; from Camp, September 29, October 24, 27, November 27; all 1849, NYU.

25. *Fifth Annual Report* (May 1850), 3–5; *Sixth Annual Report* (May 1851), 3–4, appendix, 1–52, for detailed accounts of each institute. The fact that Barnard numbered his reports consecutively shows his desire to obliterate the years between his terms.

26. Letter from Norwich, November 20, 1849; from North Haven, December 5, 1850; from Salisbury, March 15, 1850, unsigned letter from Bridgeport, August 2, 1850; all NYU.

similar cases." That same caution was reflected in his report of 1850; there was absolutely nothing new, nothing unexpected, only a reasoned rehearsing of the familiar pleas.

> The plans which I have above suggested, seem to me practical, although their successful prosecution will involve much labor, and many agencies. It will require pecuniary aid from the state, but the expense, when compared with the amount of work to be done, and the agencies to be employed, will be inconsiderable.[27]

Barnard's limitation of vision, and his static view of his job, are obvious in the *Report*. His "first and main object" was to ascertain the condition of the schools, and the means he suggested, inspections and official visits, were identical with the ones he had employed nearly a dozen years earlier. He had come to realize, however, that such visits provided an opportunity to re-introduce "in a limited and imperfect manner . . . some of the advantages of a county inspection . . . despite the want of an official authority." To assist him, or to take over the drudgery, he delegated his authority, hiring "several experienced teachers and school officers" to visit at least two schools in each society and to deliver the expected lectures—here were the seedlings of a bureaucracy. More was impossible, for governmental structure in antebellum Connecticut was minimal; Barnard's office was a tiny room under the leaky State House roof.

Thomas K. Beecher, Albert Smith, David Camp, and E. B. Huntington all served as agents; they received the customary stipend of $3 per day and were expected to submit summary reports to the boss. Beecher toiled from September 2 to November 9, visiting 140 schools, giving 54 addresses to audiences which often numbered well over a hundred; he reported that he had walked a total of 220 miles and had traveled between 70 and 90 miles by train. Huntington visited all but one of the 26 school societies in his area and gave speeches in 23 of them; the voluminous detail in his report must have delighted Barnard. All of the agents reiterated the same dreary tale of deplorable conditions, and all agreed that the cure for the evils witnessed was, in Beecher's words and style, "THE THOROUGH TRAINING OF TEACHERS FOR THEIR PROFESSION." Barnard concurred. A primary focus of the inspections was the teachers.

> The great object is to prevent incompetent persons from gaining admission to the profession, and exclude such as prove themselves unworthy of its honors and compensation.[28]

27. *Fifth Annual Report*, 7.
28. *Sixth Annual Report*, 7–8, General Supervision; 57ff., the reports of the agents.

The standards for the emerging profession, all the agents agreed, should come from the state even while the powers of appointment remained with the local committees.

It was characteristic of Henry Barnard that less than a year after his appointment he wrote in his annual report, "Apart from my official connection . . . I felt it to be my duty as Superintendent of Common Schools to work for the Normal Schools." To buttress his own image he was turning the legislative mandate upside down—the creation of the proposed normal school was, after all, the task for which he had been hired. He worked hard on the school's creation. He wrote to William Russell of the new Merrimack Normal School in New Hampshire and to the New York State Normal School, for its brochure. The matter of the location of Connecticut's school was pressing. At first the trustees received only one bid because of persistent local apprehension that the new institution would in fact be a moving institute; but the publication of detailed specifications for the school's building, to be constructed according to Barnard's plans, and a guarantee of a minimum of four years continuous occupancy was reassuring. Four towns competed for the honor of hosting the first state normal school, New Haven, Farmington, Southington, and New Britain. Jesse Olney extolled the virtues of Southington as the site—it was in the geographic center of the state, it had a healthy climate and "unsurpassed natural beauty" and a "moral and industrious people," it was accessible by railroad, and it had an elegant and suitable building, the academy. The trustees finally settled on New Britain, however, and they exalted in their first step. "The nascent germ . . . is destined to become, not only the crowning ornament of the beautiful village in which it flourishes, but the ornament of the entire state."[29]

The process of the selection of the site is revealing, for it illustrates aspects of institution building in the period, and it also demonstrates the success of a decade of educational effort in Connecticut. New Britain in 1820 was a village of just over a thousand souls, but the completion of the railroad between New Haven and Northampton in 1848 put the town literally on the map. By 1850 it had trebled in size. It had a consolidated, or central, school district made up of the town's three smaller districts and a graded system consisting of a high school, an intermediate school, and four primary schools, all free. More than 400 of the town's 670 children attended the Central District schools. The town also had a benefactor, Seth J. North. North was a self-made man, a blacksmith, who began creating elaborate works in brass and peddling them about the country-

---

29. Letter from Russell, August 13, 1849, and January 8, 1850; from Olney, December 31, 1849; NYU. *First Annual Report of the Trustees of the State Normal School* (1850), 27–29.

side; so successful was he that he eventually established an iron and brass works to his and the town's mutual benefit. As Barnard later said, "He made the village." In 1849 North promised to subscribe $6,000, half the required amount, toward the proposed school, if the town would match his donation. The town did, and more; the New Britain Educational Trust raised $16,250, assuring that the New Britain Normal School would indeed become a reality.[30]

If there was to be a school it had to have a staff. Barnard's appointment was as principal, but he explored with William Wells the possibility of taking on the position. Wells wisely felt that such a substitution would constitute "an evasion of the manifest intent of the law."[31] There is dispute on this point. According to an early historian of the state, in an unattributed quotation, Barnard had originally accepted the position on the condition that he would have an assistant to take over the day-to-day teaching in the school, so that he could give "such attention to the institution as should be found compatible with the general supervision of the common schools of the State."[32] Although unsubstantiated, this account rings true, for it is the arrangement which Barnard desired. He had made the same request of Mann previously, and he had never seen himself on the decks but at the helm of the ship of schools.

Within a year of its founding, there was a normal school. It opened in temporary quarters in the New Britain Town Hall on May 15, 1850, with only 35 pupils in attendance, but by the end of the first term there were 67, 37 women and 30 men. The Reverend T. D. P. Stone ("late of the Massachusetts State Reform School") was "in charge"—Henry Barnard had his assistant after all. The aims of the school were to "truly educate and thoroughly train" the young teachers by giving them an opportunity to review or learn all the common branches and to expand their knowledge into new fields, such as vocal music and physiology, or even, for a few, some "agricultural chemistry and domestic economy." In all cases subjects, not texts, were to be studied. The pedagogical side of the curriculum included lectures on the history of education, the art of teaching, the theory of discipline, the principles of school architecture, and the legal position of teachers. By means of observation in the town's four district schools and through actual service in the school of practice, the neophytes could become acquainted with the use of the blackboard and other

30. David Nelson Camp, *History of New Britain* (Hartford: W. B. Thompson & Co., 1889), 23ff., 228ff. *AJE* VI, xvi (March 1859): 104, for biography of North, written by Barnard.

31. Letters from Wells, January 17, February 6, 12, 1850, NYU.

32. Trumbull, *Memorial History*, II:652. See also *CCSJ and Annals of Education* II, 1 (January 1855). Barnard was the source for both.

Connecticut State Normal School, New Britain, circa 1910

suitable apparatus, "not only that these studies may be more vividly appre-
hended, but that the teachers may be prepared to use means of practical
and visible illustration whenever the chance shall be furnished." Thus it
was clear from the start that the new school was to fulfill two functions: it
was to be the highest rung on the ladder of the common school system,
providing advanced study for the qualified students, and it was to play a
vital role in the development of qualified teachers.

> It is applying to the business of teaching the same preparatory study
> and practice which the common judgment of the world demands of
> every other profession and art.[33]

The teachers who were to be trained at the Normal School were to be
models for the entire profession. They would staff the better schools,
serve as instructors in the institutes, and provide the core for the embryonic teachers' associations; their very expertise would increase the demand
for excellent teachers. Note that in the quotation above Barnard says that
teachers should receive the same training that "common judgment . . .

33. *First Annual Report of the Trustees of the State Normal School*, 1–32; *NS*, 35–41; see
also *Fifth Annual Report*, 14–24. Barnard's notes (handwritten) for the section of the
report on general plans and aims in the Trustees' *Report* are in the Trinity College archive,
evidence that the report was drafted by him.

demands of every other profession and art." Demands but does not yet get. Academic professional training was not firmly established in any of the learned professions during the antebellum period. Barnard's own legal training had been for the most part courses of reading under an experienced lawyer, and academic legal education at the time was available only in a few small proprietary schools. Theology was the only profession which had established distinct, and separate, seminaries for its initiates during the antebellum period. The common school reformers were modeling their training institutions on the seminaries, not only because they saw their cause as a mission, but also because the theological seminaries were the first, and for the most part, the only professional schools.

During the first year of the Normal School's operation the Trustees created an institution. A building, four stories tall, with nine classrooms, was built; in it there were three study halls, a large room for lectures, a laboratory and a library, and offices. Two terms were scheduled, one from May 15 until October 1, 1850, the other from December 4 through late January, 1851; the January term and the first six weeks of the summer were to be devoted to review of the common branches, a sort of crash course for beginning teachers. Originally the Trustees designed a three year sequence, with a junior, a middle, and a senior class, but, being realists, they concluded that such an extended period of study was impossible for most teachers, and they welcomed students for any period at all. They were gratified that due to the "cordial reception" of "this young and truly meritorious candidate for public favor," a total of 154 teachers attended the school at some time, and of these, over a hundred stated that they intended to return for further study in future years, after a period of teaching. Unhappily the Trustees had exceeded their budget of $16,000 by $7,000.[34] Really it was Barnard, with his grandiose plans, who had exceeded the budget.

The dedication of the new building and school on June 4 was a festive affair orchestrated by the principal. The Connecticut Life Guard and a brass band accompanied the members of the legislature to the Hartford station where a special train waited to carry them to New Britain. There

34. *First Annual Circular of the State Normal School*, October 1, 1850; *Second Annual Report of the Trustees of the State Normal School*, 1851, 3–7; NS, 57–60. Essentially the same material is in NS as in the Annual Reports but in a different order. For a comprehensive history of the Normal School see *AJE* X, xxiv (March 1861): 15–58; the plans for the school, 51–54; legislation, 55–56; constitution and by-laws of the New Britain Educational Fund Association, 57–58. The deficit incurred was partly made up by assigning $4,000 of the bonus from the City Bank of Hartford charter to the New Britain Literary Fund; a proposal for a direct subsidy of $1,000 was defeated in the legislature; *CC*, June 28, 1851.

they were met by the New Britain Greys who led a parade to the "noble edifice" which was the new school. All stood outside for a welcoming speech from Selectman Marcellus Clark, and then Vice-Principal Stone conducted them into the large hall in which were gathered the 450 children of the model school. A young lad "declaimed . . . and a glee was sung." Then "in an effect which was very good" the doors to the new hall were thrown open, revealing a class of demure young ladies intent upon their studies. After a suitable prayer by E. A. Andrews (Yale class of 1810), Francis Gillette accepted the building on the behalf of the Trustees, and Henry Barnard spoke. He traced the history of education from "the earliest history of the Christian Church" and dwelt on the growth of normal schools in Europe and the United States; he then outlined the proposed full curriculum. His speech lasted nearly two hours, and the newspaper reporter regretted that he had "no space for any further sketch of this address. "A "splendid collation" followed, and then Horace Bushnell delivered a lecture on Connecticut. This was equally verbose, for the legislators returned at 11 rather than on the projected 9:40 train. Bushnell spoke of his younger colleague

> I remember with fresh interest, today, how my talented friend, . . . consulted with me as many as thirteen years ago, in regard to his plans of life; raising, in particular, the question of whether he should give himself wholly and finally up to the cause of public schools . . . He made his choice; and now, after encountering years of untoward hindrance here, winning golden opinions meantime from every other State in the republic . . . in almost every nation of the old world . . . he returns to the scene of his beginnings and permits us here to congratulate both him and ourselves, in the prospect that his original choice and purpose are finally to be fulfilled. He has our confidence; we are to have his ripe experience; and the work now fairly begun is to go on . . . till the schools of our State are placed on a footing of the highest possible energy and perfection.[35]

Barnard, the hero of the hour, must have basked in Bushnell's hyperbole, and another chapter in the myth was written.

Eager young teachers did apply to their local school visitors for appointment to the school, and the visitors made their selections, guided presumably by the *Hints to School Visitors respecting Applications to the State Normal School* written by Barnard and Stone. This brief document is an excellent exemplar of the moral dimension of teacher training. The first criterion was "purity and strength of moral and religious character"; good

---

35. *AJE* XXX (1880), unpaged but 199–200.

health and "a fund of lively, cheerful spirits" were sought next. Good manners, a love of children and a general competence and talent for teaching, as well as some experience, were desirable of course, for the Normal School could not create teachers but merely improve them. Above all else, a dedication to the Common School spirit must be present; "if need be, a martyr spirit, to live and die, for the more thorough, complete, and practical education of all the children . . . ," an education, defined as Barnard always defined it, as "good enough for the best and cheap enough for the poorest."[36]

The rhetoric far surpassed the reality during the first years of the Normal School. The trappings existed—a building, a curriculum, even undergraduate societies reminiscent of the Yale ones of Barnard's day, and a graduation. In September 1851, consciously imitating the collegiate institutions of the era, Barnard conducted the "semi-annual" (and first) examination and exhibition of the State Normal School and the School of Practice. Principal Stone (note the title) addressed the graduating class on Sunday, a baccalaureate in fact if not in degree. On the next day Barnard delivered an address to the class and to the State Teachers' Association, which was holding its first annual meeting at the same time, on the "Life and the Character of Thomas W. Gallaudet," a talk which was the basis for his later *Tribute*; three others, including William Baker, also spoke. Tuesday was the equivalent of Class Day, in which the two student societies, the Barnard and the Gallaudet (the latter wearing mourning armbands out of respect for their recently deceased namesake) held their public exercises, "which were listened to with deep interest by a large audience, composed of citizens and teachers from every section of the state." On that day and the next all of the students in the school were examined in the common branches, in drawing, in vocal music, and compositions were put on display "for inspection in view of the chirography which they exhibited." Finally, in an afternoon "devoted to orations, dialogues and compositions" by the graduates, three men and two women received their diplomas from Barnard. Leverett Camp was the valedictorian and delivered a discourse on "The Teacher as Philanthropist."[37] His sister was also in the class, and his brother David must have been as proud of them as Barnard was with this, his first graduating class. The younger Camp was later as effusive in his thanks to Barnard as his elder

36. *NS*, 61.

37. *CC*, September 30, October 11, 1851; the exercises in *CCSJ* V, iii (November 1851); Camp, *Recollections*, 34ff. Barnard's speech is in *CCSJ* V, ii (October 1851): 45–52; he repeated his stock phrases, "The cause of true education, of the complete education of every human being" and "Ever since the Great Teacher condescended to dwell among men."

brother had been a dozen years earlier, and as nostalgic as any college graduate.

> I trust we shall ever look back upon that time as a bright era in our lives, and that we shall remember *thee* as "Our Friend" in the cause we have espoused and that we have resolved to spend our lives and efforts to promote. May we through the Grace of God be as worthy children who shall arise up and call you blessed.[38]

We should pause and consider the various meanings of this rather pathetic little celebration. An obvious one is the conjunction of the graduation with the meeting of the new teachers' association. Barnard wanted to emphasize the unity of the profession; the graduates were teachers, the teachers belonged at the New Britain school. All were to participate in exercises of solemnity a well as celebration, forging a band of brotherhood (and sisterhood, for remember that there were two women graduates), through the induction of new members to the priesthood. That word is chosen with care, for the second element to note is the continuation of the missionary theme, exaggerated perhaps by Camp but still a dominant image; professionalism may have been coming, but teaching had not yet become secularized in the minds of its leaders. Camp's letter, too, reminds the reader in its terminology of the mode of address used by the students of Cyrus Peirce in Massachusetts; the element of paternalism in teacher training cannot be overlooked. And, finally, the replication of collegiate exercises, specifically of Yale's, buttresses the view that Barnard saw his new school as an institution of higher learning. Teachers, kin to ministers in dedication, were to share with them a collegiate education; they were to become members of a select persuasion, a profession. However, the antebellum conception of a profession was not the same as that held by a later generation, and although educational reformers such as Barnard consistently, in endless speeches and erudite articles, called for professionalization, what they envisioned was a state of mind, a sense of belonging and exclusivity, rather than of organization and specialization.

A tiny minority of the teachers attended the Normal School, for academic study as a requirement for entry into any profession was only a gleam in the reformers' eyes, and Teachers' Institutes dominated teacher preparation. The Normal instructors were obligated to conduct institutes when the school was not in session and in so doing served as an important link within the "profession." The format for gatherings was highly

---

38. Letter from L. Camp. December 31, 1851, NYU. For David Camp on this period, see *Recollections*, chap. V; in the first three years, thirteen men and nine women graduated.

TEACHERS INSTITUTE,
FOR SPRING OF 1851,
AT WILLIMANTIC MAY 5 TO MAY 9.

CONDUCTED BY

MESSRS. STONE, CAMP AND GUION,
OF THE NORMAL SCHOOL.

RHETORICAL READING, Grammatical Analysis, and Arithmetic will occupy most of the time, mingled with Discussions and Lectures. Board gratuitous to teachers in attendance.

This place has been selected as being central and easy of access from all parts of the State.

It is hoped that all who can do so will avail themselves of this opportunity of social conference, and of mutual instruction, and encouragement.

The first lecture of the institute will be delivered on Monday evening, May 5th, at half past seven o'clock. The lectures and other exercises will be open to the public.

Teachers are earnestly requested to be present from the first exercise to the close.

By direction and in behalf of

HON. HENRY BARNARD,
Superintendent of Common Schools.

T. D. P. STONE.

State Normal School, New Britain, Ct., April 16, '51.

Brown's Pioneer Press, New Britain. Ct.

Teacher's Institute,
Willimantic, Connecticut,
1851, broadside

regularized. Institutes were called in the fall, in each county, in preparation for the winter session, with usually one held each week; in 1850 they ran from September 23 to November 11, when the final one closed in Greenwich. Each began on a Monday evening, often with an address by Barnard, who employed these occasions to stimulate public support for the common schools, and closed Friday, after four days devoted to inspirational and practical lectures.

Barnard always displayed a keen sense of his audience and varied his message enough to make it palatable, even comforting. In New Preston, a remote, rural area, he emphasized the continuing value of an agricultural society but noted that the countryside suffered from an educational disadvantage; schooling should be modified to deal less with books and more with the real objects from the world around; a love of nature and observation of its laws should be cultivated in the child soon to become a farmer. On the other hand, at Essex, a bustling mercantile center, after noting that the first teachers' organization in the nation had met in the same county in 1799, he dwelt on the deficiencies of schooling in the seaport as compared with "properly classified and thoroughly taught" schools in nearby Deep River, with its factories lining the river. In Norwalk and in New Haven he talked about the particular challenge posed by the growing cities where schools should be centralized and classified into grades, so as to provide an education that would serve to equalize the social discrepancies between sections and families within the city; here he anticipated the later arguments for the comprehensive school.[39]

To staff the institutes, Barnard did not have to rely on the out-of-state eminences as he had formerly. The bulk of the instruction fell on his assistants, Stone and Camp, both instructors in the Normal School, asssisted by stalwart supporters such as Thomas Beecher and William Baker. In brief, he began to have a faculty, but he remained in charge. "In accordance with your views," reported Stone, after several successful sessions, he had scheduled fewer topics and devoted more time to practical matters, and to meetings of the local teachers' associations.

At the close of each institute the participants were listed and their names published, thereby giving credit to the more conscientious and committed teachers, and providing a roster of qualified teachers from which local districts could make their selections. A scrutiny of the lists tells us about the teaching force in Connecticut in mid-century. At the Norwalk institute 45 men and 26 women attended, at Essex 30 men and 24 women, whereas at Naugatuck there were more women than men. Gender was not a significant factor among those who were most serious about teaching. Frequently three or four members of the same family would attend a given institute; the Camps, with four siblings who taught, and diligently attended, were not unique.[40]

Institutes were expensive, far more than the parsimonious legislature had anticipated. "Each cost the Superintendent part of his salary," Barnard pointed out, adding that more institutes had been held for less money during the past two years than in neighboring Massachusetts. He recommended that each of the scheduled institutes be allotted $100, rather than the paltry $400 total, and he requested that he be allowed to hold additional, more frequent ones, especially in the larger cities.[41] No matter how high his hopes were for the Normal School, their realization, he knew, lay in the future. For the present the average teacher would have to receive his or her specialized training closer to home and for shorter periods of time.

39. *CCSJ* V, i (September 1851): 25, for list of institutes; summaries, 34–36. Barnard's schedule was daunting, especially considering the difficulties in transportation. He spoke in Stafford October 7, in New Preston October 10, in Colchester October 14, in Naugatuck October 20, in Essex October 21, in Norwalk October 25, in Glastonbury October 28; see 54–80. He could not have spent much time at home.

40. *CCSJ* VI, v (May 1852), 225ff., report on institutes, 1851.

41. Ibid., 226–27. In 1850 the total expense was $738 for 17 institutes, whereas Massachusetts spent $2,000 for 12.

Barnard's lectures to the institutes addressed a variety of topics which he repeated and clarified in a comprehensive fashion in his *Sixth Annual Report*, published in May 1851. The ideas and even some of the phrases ("The right of suffrage should be with held from such as can not give the lowest evidence of school attendance and proficiency.") are nearly identical to those in his Rhode Island reports, and his litany of the elements for school amelioration becomes tedious. The concept of a community-wide system of education was innovative in 1838; here it is repetitious. There was some refining of his views, an expansion and repetition of themes first advanced in the Rhode Island years. Schooling should be "framed and constructed" with "reference to the future social and practical wants of the pupils." All should go to school, but not all should go to the same school. The curriculum should be differentiated, not just for the sexes, but also for the life, present and projected, of the students. In agricultural districts, limited resources prohibited the employment of "teachers or professional men of the highest order of talents and achievements"; these instructors should offer instruction not based on books but on "the real objects of nature around—more with facts and principles which can be illustrated by the actual business of life." On the other hand, in the manufacturing districts and the cities, where there was a "quickness of intelligence, an aptitude for excitement, an absence of bigoted prejudice for what is old, and a generous liberality in expenditures," there was a demand for an education to counter societal flux, the omnipresent "corruption and vice" and the "admixture of people of different nations."

Barnard never saw education as dynamic, nor as offering the means for social advancement. It was, instead, designed to improve the quality of life for individuals who would then be content with their destined roles—in a sense he anticipated the determinism of twentieth century tracking. And in his advocacy of a centralized urban school system, with an elected or appointed board and superintendent, he sounded almost like a turn-of-the-century administrative progressive. Barnard had an inventive, active mind, and he at times was able to break out of the bonds of his background to benefit from and reflect on suggestions gleaned from his wide reading and valuable associations. But those instances are the exception rather than the rule, and are at best episodic. Henry Barnard was a first generation schoolman, and, like them he saw schools as agents for the salvation of society, for the preservation of the existing order.

> Let not the Christian, intent on the reformation of the soul, and its fitness for another state, forget that the soul is tied to the body, and

that through the body, and in these various ways it can be acted on for its own good.[42]

Social, moral, and intellectual progress went hand in hand with material prosperity, and the agents were many; paramount were the traditional New England family and the local school which together enabled the child (here Barnard employed the masculine pronoun) "to compete so successfully with the muscles of the foreign laborer."

Barnard was consistent in his insistent emphasis on the necessity of teacher certification. He devised a three-tiered certification system, similar to his Rhode Island proposal and based on education and experience, with the highest certificate being granted by the state to persons who had completed the Normal School and were thus the master teachers of the state. His scheme contained the germ of differentiation, in which the type of certificate would dictate the level of service; given the pervasive sexism of the times there was no question that the result of the proposed system would be to the detriment of the female teachers, confined to their exclusive role of nuturers of the youngest charges, but Barnard did not anticipate this.

In each of his previous terms of office Barnard had utilized a house organ as a means of communication and inspiration, so it was entirely to be expected that he would resume the publication of the *Connecticut Common School Journal*. He announced his intention at the annual meeting of the state teachers in September 1851, and the first number of volume five is dated September 15. The prospectus sounded familiar:

> The Journal will be the repository of all documents of a permanent value, relating to the history, condition and improvement of the public schools, and other means of popular education in the state. It will contain the laws of the state, relating to schools. . . . It will contain suggestions and improved plans for the repairs, construction and internal arrangements of school-houses. It will aim to form, encourage, and bring forward good teachers; and to enlist the active and intelligent cooperation of parents, with teachers and committees, in the management and instruction of schools.

The journal would publicize meetings relating to education and inform its readers about developments in other states and countries in order to "help keep alive a spirit of efficient and prudent action in behalf of the physical, intellectual and moral improvement of the rising and all future

42. *Sixth Annual Report* (May, 1851) 1–48, esp. 10–11, 14–15, 19, 25–28, 31–33; quotation, 40–41.

generations in the State."[43] It would be, in short, all things to all readers. Barnard projected four numbers for the fifth volume, to fill out the remainder of the year, and promised that the sixth volume would have twelve "to be issued as far as practicable" within the first week of each month. In addition the editor vowed to publish "as his health and official duties shall allow" a series of educational tracts or documents authorized by a legislative resolution; these would be distributed to the teachers and school officials of the state.[44] Barnard's editorial intentions had altered no more than had his policy ones.

During 1851, in addition to the *Journal*, Barnard produced two of the required reports, *Practical Illustrations of the Principles of School Architecture* and *Normal Schools and Other Institutions, Agencies, and Means Designed for the Professional Education of Teachers*. The book on architecture was a new edition of his 1848 book, with a slightly different intent, but the two volume study of normal schools marked Barnard's debut as the historian he dreamed of being. A massive history of education was still his goal, and what would perhaps have constituted a chapter in such a survey became a monograph. The author's grand conception is obvious from the title; he promised to cover all means for the preparation of teachers and to include, in the first volume, the United States and British America, in the second all of Europe. In fact in the United States there were but six, Connecticut, Massachusetts, New York, Pennsylvania, Rhode Island, and Michigan, and only 28 of the 224 pages were devoted to the last four; the British Provinces received one page. The European volume was somewhat more inclusive, although equally skewed, with a bit over a quarter of the work given to Prussia, a quarter to the rest of the continent, and nearly half to England and Ireland.

Barnard's purpose was admittedly didactic, to convey "the matured views and varied experience of wise statesmen, educators and teachers" in order to give "valuable hints and reliable information" to the toilers in the vineyards of the common schools. His scope was limited by the availability of his materials and his linguistic abilities, as well as by his inclinations. He made no claim to originality nor did he attempt to mask his reliance on authorities of compatible viewpoints.[45] He had made a serious attempt, "with much diligence and by extensive correspondence" to conduct research beyond the official documents he had received. He wrote to Oliver Peirce, the state superintendent of New York, to Walter Johnson

43. Prospectus, *CCSJ* V, i (September 1851): 7.
44. Prospectus, *CCSJ* VI, in V, iv (December 1851). The words of this prospectus are identical with that of volume except briefer.
45. Circular, vol. II.

of Pennsylvania, who sent a collection of his pamphlets, and to Asa Lord in Ohio for any information at all—somehow Ohio got lost in the final product. He exchanged a series of letters with Charles Brooks in November and repeated almost word-for-word Brooks's account of his previous activities in Massachusetts. Nicholas Tillinghast sent a very frank appraisal of the normal school at Bridgewater.[46] Material for the second volume could not be easily sought from such personal acquaintances, so Barnard depended on the accounts of William Woodbridge, Calvin Stowe, and Alexander Bache. He read a history of Austria, published in 1850, an *Account of the Dutch and German Schools* (1840), the *Education of the Poor in England and Europe* (1846), and vast numbers of English journals and reports. The volume is a splendid collection of items selected from the vast corpus of antebellum intercontinental liberal reform, an archive for future scholars.

In fact, volume two actually comes close to what we consider a history, closer than any of Barnard's earlier work; nearly every national section commences with a survey of education and schooling in the particular country before giving a summary of current educational provision. Yet critical analysis is missing. As one might expect, tables abound, including a complete statistical summary of French education in 1843. In a three-page extract of Bavarian educational facts Barnard included the detail that 5,284 schools, out of a total of 6,065, had a mandatory nursery-garden. Many of the entries are tantalizingly incomplete. In the account of education in the Grand Duchy of Baden, for example, Barnard promised to follow a condensed version of the plan for primary education with an outline of the curriculum at the Carlsruhe Normal School, which he never did.[47]

Elisha Potter, while praising the work, expressed the wish that Barnard had found time to include a greater number of his own ideas. Potter may have only skimmed the book, for more than occasionally Barnard does venture an interpretation or a comment such as it "is a given that education is essential to a people"—hardly a startling observation. Again, "every system of education, to be successful, must be adapted to the institutions, habits and convictions of the people." The French Revolution was in no small measure, "the result of the neglected education of the great mass of the people," an opinion entirely predictable from a reformer Whig. Education must be for all, and even the highly praised school

46. Letters from Lord, April; from Peirce, July 6, November 12; from Johnson, August 29; from Brooks, November 2, 8 (cf. *NS*, 125–26); all 1850; from Tillinghast, December 19, 1851; all NYU.

47. *NS*, I:53 (chapter on Massachusetts); II:127–29, 135, 199, 220–24 for tables.

system of Prussia was guilty of ignoring the education of girls, thus opening "a chasm, broad and deep, between the intelligence and intellectual
capabilities of the two sexes." New England was doing much better, "giving to every girl, rich or poor, and whatever may be her destination in life,
an education which shall correspond, in amount and adaptation, to that
given to boys in the same school."

Barnard praised the school system of Holland for an early classification
of teachers, an emphasis on method, and the careful selection of books,
but he felt that professional training was of limited value for it merely
"produced routine rather than intelligent teaching."[48] Teacher training in
Austria was also deficient, although systematic, for it gave "a routine
knowledge of methods, but does not secure the mastery of principles, or
that formation of the pedagogical character" which "a regularly constituted Teachers' Seminary is so well calculated to give." Throughout Europe
schools were becoming good through improved teachers and because the
schools were open to all, and, most important of all, because of a system
of inspection. "The soul of the whole system is inspection, or in other
words, active and vigilant superintendence,—intelligent direction and
real responsibility."[49] Barnard selected for praise and emphasis those elements which authenticated his policies.

In summary, *Normal Schools* was not a work on normal schools; nor
was it good history. It was a formidable, if incomplete, record of the
state of education in the mid-nineteenth century in some of the northeastern states and in northwestern Europe; it concentrated on the administrative aspects; it introduced a historical perspective to the discussion; it
relied to a large extent on original documents. Judged by modern standards, the technique is faulty. There is no clear chronological sequence
either in the narrative or in the order in which some of the documents are
printed; citation, when available, is very incomplete, lacking pagination,
and commentary is often mixed in with the source. The use of political
divisions, states, leads to constant repetition and prevents careful analysis.
But the overarching weakness is conceptual: Barnard had no thesis
although he had a purpose. He failed to stick to his subject and to omit
material not relevant, and he never posed critical questions. He produced
a convincing compendium of information, carefully culled to present a
picture to buttress the views and policies he and his colleagues promul-

48. Charles Leslie Glenn, in *The Myth of the Common School* (Amherst: The University
of Massachusetts Press, 1988), 109ff., discusses the influence of the Dutch system on
antebellum reformers.

49. Letter from Potter, February 17, 1851, NYU; see *NS*, 107, 145–46, 188–89, 195, 204,
207.

gated. Finally, in his selection of his materials he created an interpretation, and by doing so he inflated his role as interpreter—the former was no mean achievement and has endured, whereas the latter did not survive its creator.

Despite the pressure of his duties in Connecticut, about which he complained constantly, and his scholarship, Barnard had the time to be very much involved in a new national educational organization. Partly because of its New England, even Boston, bias, and partly because of internal strife, the American Institute of Instruction had declined in importance in the late 1840s. In December 1848, Barnard was asked by Alfred Wright and Samuel Randall if his name could be included among those calling another convention, tentatively scheduled for late in the following summer. The instigators of the new group aimed to attract some of the second generation of schoolmen, the superintendents of the state and city systems, and men from a broader geographic area.

The first Convention of Friends of the Common Schools and Universal Education finally assembled in Philadelphia, December 17–19, 1849, under the gavel of Horace Mann. Barnard's name was not among those listed in the call for the meeting, although in his account he says that he was, nor was he elected one of the officers who included, in addition to Mann as president, five vice-presidents and four secretaries.[50] Barnard did introduce the idea of an active role for new association, suggesting to the convention the appointment of a general agent (who can doubt whom he had in mind), and he was made the chairman of a committee, consisting of Elisha Potter, Joseph Henry, and John Whitehead, of New Jersey, to study the matter. Two days later he outlined a national scheme: it was to consist of a museum, a journal, a system of educational exchanges, tracts, and an agent—obviously he had come to the convention well prepared with a plan which replicated actions already implemented for the most part in many individual states. There was some exploration of this idea, but no action was taken, nor was it discussed in subsequent sessions. The educational world was not ready for Henry Barnard's grand national design.

Barnard was charged with the arrangements for the next year's convention, and he was diligent in his preparations. In a transparent effort to

50. See letters from Wright, December 5, 19, 1848, January 24, March 17, September 12, November 19, 1849; the vice presidents—Joseph Henry of Washington and the Smithsonian, John Griscom of New Jersey, Samuel Lewis of Ohio, Alonzo Potter of Pennsylvania, and Greer Duncan of Louisiana—represented both generations of reformers. A copy of the call in NYU does not include Barnard's name; see *AJE* I, i (August 1855): 1–136.

broaden the base of the Friends and to increase attendance, he wrote to countless associates, urging them to attend, and he attempted to arrange reduced train fares for the teachers, and to sell blocks of tickets to his Connecticut and Rhode Island colleagues. He even inserted an advertisement in the Hartford papers offering excursion fares to those willing to go.[51]

It was natural that Barnard's expertise was sought by the Friends in two areas where he was indeed skilled: school architecture and school law. At the August convention a committee on school architecture submitted a report by Elisha Potter; in it Potter briefly summarized the various publications on the subject and then gave a précis of Barnard's work which the author had prepared at the committee's request. The convention voted to have the report published, providing an opportunity for a broader circulation of Barnard's work than had been achieved in 1848 and reinforcing the reputation of its author as an authority on the subject. And by writing a summary Barnard found it easy to comply with the Connecticut legislature's directive to publish a series of essays on school topics; he had the pamphlet sent to every member of the Connecticut General Assembly.[52]

Barnard played a major role in drafting the constitution for the new American Association for the Advancement of Education, as it was called, and was appointed to the Standing Committee in 1851 and 1852 when Bishop Potter was president. He was an active participant at every session for the next four years, and in 1855 he was elected president, an honor which placed him once and for all among the inner circle of mid-century national educational reformers. The Association was a transitional organization in the evolution of the education profession, national where the American Institute had been regional, and broader based, with superintendents attending in addition to the ministers and lawyers of the preceding evangelizing reform groups. It was in design, and even in title, similar to the more prestigious American Association for the Advancement of Science, which was founded in 1847. Both, as Thomas Haskell argues convincingly for the latter, were exemplars of the emerging professions

51. Letters from Thomas Rainey, Cincinnati, March 31, April 7, July 8; from Mann, August 9; on tickets from Amos Perry, August 4, R. I. Cooke, August 8, W. B. Fowle, August 8, John Johnson, August 11, L. L. Camp (who agreed to go), August 11 and 13; from Benton, Iowa City, May 3, June 12; all 1850, all NYU. Benton added the comment that one of the future conventions should be in a slave state "to avoid local feeling."

52. Letter from Potter, July 4; from Potter to Biddle, July 22; from R. L. Cooke, July, n.d.; all 1850, NYU. For the committee report see *CCSJ* V, Appendix, "Practical Illustrations of the Principles of School Architecture."

and of the antebellum search for authority in a rudderless world. But the educational association was short-lived, and it was not a teachers' organization at all. These remained, where they existed, localized in the states.[53]

Barnard spent parts of the winters of 1851 and 1852 in Detroit, leaving the mail to pile up in his office and the faithful William Baker to go on circuits of inspection throughout the state. The Barnards may again have thought of settling in Michigan; their second child was born there, and Barnard invested more than $10,000 in an insurance company.[54] He must have impressed men of affairs in Michigan, for in July his name was advanced for the presidency of the state university. Oddly, during precisely the same time, Barnard was negotiating with the university in neighboring Indiana about its presidency. He either declined or never was actually offered either position, but it was probably in the context of the dealings with the two universities that Barnard was awarded his honorary doctorates. His most active promoter in Indiana had promised in one of his letters to suggest to Benjamin Silliman that Yale bestow the LL.D. on their illustrious graduate, and he also wrote to Bishop Potter requesting his assistance in securing a like honor from Union College; after all, a university president should have such a badge of scholarship. There may be a connection between the matter of the honorary degree and the fact that Barnard, responding to the request of President Woolsey, gave the Phi Beta Kappa address at Yale's commencement the fall of 1852. He received the degree from both colleges in 1852, and ever afterwards he was referred to as Dr. Barnard.[55]

Perhaps because he expected to resign to assume a new position, or because he felt he had realized his agenda in Connecticut, Barnard completed his *Seventh Annual Report* in good time. His tone was almost valedictory. During the past autumn nine institutes had attracted over 900

53. *AJE* I, i (August 1855): 1–15. Thomas L. Haskell, *The Emergence of Professional Social Science* (Urbana: University of Illinois Press, 1977), esp. 68; Haskell does not see the parallel with the AAAE.

54. Occasional glimpses of Barnard's business affairs appear in his letters. In June 1850, his sister-in-law wrote to her husband, Chauncey, about Henry's "affair," adding that there was no settlement and Henry wouldn't pay; a few days later she wrote that Josephine was in town and had called on Louisa Barnard but had said not a word about "us"; "I hope you have settled with Henry, but I know him so well I don't anticipate anything conclusive or decisive until compelled to it." Apparently Barnard could ignore family as well as official demands when he wanted to do so.

55. Letters from Read, June 21, 24, 1852; from Woolsey, July 6, 1852. There is no mention of Barnard's degree in the newspaper accounts of the commencement, and Yale records only list the members of the graduating class. The biography of Barnard by Porter, 80, incorrectly states that Barnard received the university job offers and the honorary degree in 1851 rather than 1852.

teachers; for once he publicly acknowledged the efforts of Stone and Camp who had spent five weeks of their vacation "gratuitously" instructing the attending teachers, and he thanked the ministers of the state who had discussed the necessity of educational reform from their pulpits. He noted the countless "school celebrations," the meetings of teachers, pupils, and communities, which had been conducted mainly through the "tireless" exertions of William S. Baker. He regretted that his plan of publishing ten separate educational pamphlets had not gone forward as he had hoped, but attention to his official duties, "correspondence and personal interviews," and time consumed in preparing for and attending institutes, as well as his duties at the Normal School, had left "but little time for study and composition."[56]

Barnard devoted the bulk of the report to his proposed modifications in the school law, calling them a "restoration" of the former system. Subtly, however, Barnard had incorporated his vision of the expanded state role into the recommendations. He advocated the usual, gradation, classification, and especially better teachers; he justified property taxation for the support of schools on grounds of community interest; and he insisted that the apportionment of state money was to be based on actual attendance rather enumeration. School visitors should be appointed by the Superintendent and paid by the state, and the authority for a three-tiered system for the certification of teachers should lie with the state.[57] Barnard strove to advance the cause of public education in order to counteract the privatization of schooling, which he felt was undemocratic, and to improve the processes of teaching which he knew to be backward. In closing, despite his inherently optimistic nature, he ended on a note of discouragement.

> The progress of school improvement, dependent as it is on so many influences and complex interests, is slow and difficult enough under the most favorable circumstances, but when it is opposed, or not even aided, by those unto whose souls the iron of avarice has entered, and by others, who have not enjoyed or felt the want of superior advantages themselves, are satisfied that what was good enough for them forty years ago is good enough for their children now, but by those who have shown their opinion of the necessity of improvements by withdrawing their own children from the common schools, it is a hopeless, despairing work indeed.

56. *Seventh Annual Report*, in *CCSJ* VI, vi and vii (June and July 1852): 257 ff., esp. 260, 266.

57. Barnard estimated a cost of $631 per annum, whereas neighboring Massachusetts expended $2,500 annually for two agents; the low estimate was clearly a political ploy.

He need not have despaired. The act which he proposed was supported by the Democratic governor; despite a preliminary defeat in the assembly, it was reconsidered and passed on June 25.[58]

Barnard continued the publication of his *Journal* with the bulk of the first four numbers devoted to Thomas Gallaudet. The death of the distinguished reformer in the autumn of 1851 had moved the younger man, and he had eulogized his mentor to the State Teachers Association recalling him as a friend "whose intimate and almost parental council [*sic*] he had so long had the happiness and advantage of enjoying," and reminded his audience that it was Gallaudet who was among the first to call for the professional preparation of teachers.[59] Barnard was later asked to deliver the formal eulogy of Gallaudet at the civic memorial service, a recognition of his long professional relationship with Gallaudet and of his reputation as an orator. This speech lacks the spontaneity of the one to the teachers, but his picture of Thomas Gallaudet is essentially the same, that of the quintessential antebellum reformer—methodical, punctual, economical, cautious, benevolent, "friend of the poor and the distressed." Not all who were listening could be privileged to serve as Gallaudet had served, but all could, with "fidelity as teachers, educators and friends of education" help steer the young along the proper path, away from "moral jungles," by "education, economy and industry, into homes of comfort, peace and joy." There was another lesson to be learned from the life of Gallaudet.

> The greatest service rendered by him as an educator and teacher . . . is to be found in his practical acknowledgment and able advocacy of the great fundamental truth, of the necessity for the special training, even for minds of the highest order, as a prerequisite of success in the art of teaching.

The entire memorial service, along with several of Gallaudet's sermons, was published by Barnard the following year as his *Tribute to Gallaudet*.[60] It is a small volume, characteristically with an appendix of nearly two hundred pages, primary documents all. Both Barnard and the Gallaudet family were much concerned that the book should have as wide a distribution as possible, and Thomas Gallaudet, the younger, was delighted at the reception it received, especially that it rapidly sold out in New York.[61]

---

58. *CC*, June 26, July 24, 1852. See Gideonse, "Common School Reform," 287ff.; the author errs slightly in the chronology of the session.

59. *CCSJ* V, xi (October 1851): 45–52.

60. *Tribute to Gallaudet: A Discourse in Commemoration of the Life, Character and Service of Thomas W. Gallaudet* (Hartford: Brockett & Hutchinson, 1852).

61. *CCSJ*, VI, ii and iv (March and April 1852) which repeats verbatim all the material

With his work in Connecticut completed, Barnard was anxious to make a trip to Europe, and for the first documented time he had a legitimate reason of health. In early June, 1852, the day after the meeting of the American Association, he had been thrown from a wagon and sustained "a bruise & injury to [his] head and wrist" which required a "rest" all of July. Although Josephine Barnard wrote to Horace Mann that her husband's condition was not as severe as first feared, he still could not read or write without a "confused feeling in his head," and the doctor would allow no work.[62] In fact, Barnard wrote Mann, the doctor had "ordered" him to go abroad, for he was "overworked and a good deal damaged by my fall." He planned to sail on July 10, and spend a month or six weeks in England, with people "it will be pleasant for me, an invalid, to see." He wanted to meet Sir Kay-Shuttleworth, a noted British student of education, and he planned to visit institutions for the deaf and dumb in Dublin and Edinburgh—an interest sparked by his work on Gallaudet during the previous winter. He did go first to Dublin, then Edinburgh, perhaps to Yorkshire, and he spent some time in London; he may have gone to Paris and he considered going to Germany. In each locale he visited the specialized training schools and was received as an honored guest, an American educator of stature.[63] From this trip came the core of the material for his next long-delayed major volume of educational history.

Josephine Barnard did not accompany her husband on this trip, and her few surviving letters to him offer poignant evidence of their relationship. She wrote frequently to her "dear, dear Henry," for he had instructed her to note down and send to him the "little daily occurrences." The letters at first are affectionate, perhaps because of the basket of fruit Henry had sent as a good-bye present, beginning with the salutation "Dearest"

---

from the *Tribute* appendix. Letters from Gallaudet, June 19, 26, July 5, 8, 13, 1853. Among the letters is an ornately printed formal acknowledgment from the Trustees of the Brown University Library for the donation of the book, May 23, 1853.

62. Letter to Lord, July 3, 1852, RIC; to Mann from J. Barnard, June 19, 1852, MHS; from Mann, June 14, 1852, NYU; to Mann from Barnard, July 5, 1853, on letterhead Office of the State of Connecticut, Superintendent of the Common Schools, MHS; from Read, July 23, 1852, NYU.

63. Letter from Charles Baker of the Yorkshire Institution for the Deaf and Dumb, July 10; from David Buxton of the Liverpool School for the Deaf and Dumb, July 2; from James Martineau, August 7, sending names of other training schools; from Charles Baker, Doncaster, August 20, September 4, 21; from James More, Edinburgh, August 7; all 1852, NYU; from Archbishop of Dublin, August 14, 1852, CHS. Letters from Hermann Wimmer, July and August, indicate that he expected Barnard in Dresden. In a letter from Lewis Weld, July 9, 1852, CHS, to the headmasters of fourteen different institutions for the deaf and dumb, Barnard is introduced as the president-elect of both the universities of Michigan and Indiana.

or "My dearest" and, in one, "I am almost sorry *I did not go with you.*" But then she added an incomplete sentence which revealed her sense that her husband had preferred that she did not accompany him. She cheerfully recounted household news and sent clippings announcing his honorary degrees, but she grew increasingly despondent when she failed to hear from her husband. "You will come for my confinement, won't you?" she asked, and again, would he buy her "a plain cloak in Paris" if he had "the means." Finally in mid-August, she received a parcel of letters, but, she complained, they "were just as cold as if they had been addressed to the most indifferent person & wound up with 'Your friend,' Henry Barnard." Her husband had scolded her, perhaps for wishing him home, for she objected, writing it was "slanderous" to say that she had asked him to come home, "before he had enjoyed himself or even begun to feel better."[64] Barnard may have taken exception to her farewell plea to go "to some Catholic chapel occasionally," but it is hard to be too sympathetic with him. His wife was at home, with a teething and fretting child, pregnant with another, and he was off on a jaunt. This was not the first evidence of petulance and self-centeredness, and of the fact that Henry Barnard seemed to take his family very much for granted.

Barnard was equally unfeeling in his dealings with the faithful Baker, who for years trudged through the boondocks, employed and for the most part ignored by his employer. The letters from this unstable enthusiast range from triumphant, to factual, to pleading, to incoherent; he had a "glorious" session; he needed money; he had an infected leg; he was "ragged and in some way must have some clothes." But his letters were always lively, and none more so than the one he wrote from West Woodstock. He quoted a former assemblyman who had "heard that little whipper snapper of a Barnard had been out into their *deestrick* and *clumb inter the winder* to look at their schewl house." Most of all Baker begged for a response from the commissioner, to see him, to hear from him, to be paid. Barnard did send thirty dollars to his agent one November day, and probably more at other times, but he never seems to have heard or cared to hear the cries from the wilderness. It is hard to reconcile the picture of the benevolent reformer whom everyone found so sympathetic with the evidence of his coolness to Baker. But Barnard could be heartless, or at least thoughtless. Twice Wilkins Updike wrote in a pathetic tone and in an uncertain and elderly hand, "I hate to be forgotten by an old friend."[65]

64. Letters from Josephine Barnard, July 14, 21, 28, August 11 (fragment but with date), August 19, 1852, NYU.

65. The letters from Baker are too numerous to cite, beginning January 17, 1853, and continuing through March 1854. Mrs. Baker was even more long-suffering, for frequently she went a month with no news of her husband; on February 28 she turned in despair to

Barnard's chilliness surfaced in his unfeeling treatment of an unfortunate colleague a few years later. Linus Brockett had asked his more illustrious friend to write an introduction to his *History* early in 1859. Brockett somehow, and the evidence is sparse, had fallen on bad times and was arrested, for some "terrible crime which has blighted all my earthly future," as he wrote in a hasty penciled letter. His wife turned to Barnard asking if he could please hurry with the introduction, that she was desperate for money, that the book remained at the publishers who refused to print it without Barnard's endorsement while her husband lay in jail. She wrote again, and again, pleading that the $250 promised for the book would pay her husband's debts; Brockett himself implored Barnard, assuring him that "what was required would take only two or three hours." After a delay of more than two months, Barnard complied grudgingly, under, as he wrote to the poor Brocketts, "circumstances of bodily prostration and exhaustion." After this, one wonders why on earth Brockett was still willing to write for Barnard's *Journal*, and one speculates about the kind of man Henry Barnard really was.[66]

It is only fair to him to include contradictory evidence. Among the letters Barnard received in the fall of 1853 was one from a Normalite, Ebenezer Bassett, who wrote that he was soon to graduate, after a year and a half of study. Bassett "ached" to teach and wondered if a position in a "colored school" had come to Barnard's attention. One had, in New Haven, a school of 500 scholars, with forty "picked ones," all in one class. Although Barnard offered to pay for another year of study in New Britain (so wrote Bassett forty years later), the young black man, with gratitude, took the job, and, like any beginner, he was filled with self-doubt. "If I fail I bring disgrace not merely upon myself and the colored people of New Haven but upon my *Alma Mater.*" Apparently the acquaintance continued over the years, for when Barnard was the national commissioner of education, Bassett sought his support in obtaining the post of consul general in Haiti. In his old age, that former young man wrote a letter suffused with warmth, recalling his struggles with prejudice and the superintendent's "kindly, courteous, and generous attention." It may have been hyperbolic and in response to the proprieties of an anniversary celebration to write of "the silent, unspoken influence this mysterious

---

Barnard: "Is he a sample of the Common School men? Ask Mrs. B. How long must I endure such aggravations? Long as I live?" Letters from Updike, January 11, 1853, December 13, 1854, NYU.

66. Letters from Brockett, May 9, July 25, 1859, January 28, 1862; from Mrs. Brockett, June 3, August 3, 25, 1859; NYU. In the 1862 letter Brockett said he had completed an article on West Point but he doubted that Barnard would pay him enough for it.

power of high character," but it is a fact that Barnard displayed unusual sensitivity to Bassett, unusual for a man in his position, and for him.[67]

When Barnard returned from Europe, he was faced with just the type of administrative nightmare he abhorred. He had never been very much concerned with the diurnal details of his office and had consistently delegated responsibility to his loyal associates. But now affairs in New Britain demanded his attention. Over 300 teachers had attended the Normal School during the previous winter, yet the school was in shambles by the fall of 1852, primarily due to the hostility between Principal Stone (of the Normal School) and Principal Guion (of the high school). Both resigned before the start of the fall term, yet Barnard and the trustees insisted that the school be open to receive the students who were converging on New Britain. Poor David Camp stepped into the breach. He declined the principalship on the grounds of his youth, but during the winter term he was actually in charge, head teacher in both the Normal School and the high school; in frequent letters to his boss, safely isolated in Hartford, he worried about such matters as necessary alterations in the schools of practice and inadequate privies. In his free time he conducted over thirty institutes and, during the winter recess, he was dispatched by Barnard to recruit teachers. Baker successfully persuaded John Philbrick to come from Boston to head the Normal School, and Moses Brown to come to the high school. Barnard probably knew both men, Philbrick from the American Institute, and Brown from the Providence days, but he played no active role in their recruitment, nor in the School itself.[68]

The Normal School survived, with 67 students, mostly "ladies," enrolling in March and a total of nearly 200 for the year. The Trustees were able to report that eight would graduate in the fall, that a total of 519 had attended in the first three years of the school's existence, and that "in its quiet and thoughtful methods of scholastic exercise, in its firm control over the attention and mental habits of its members, and in their exemplary demeanor and scholarly performances," the Normal School had rendered a real service to the state. But, they pointed out, the sum allocated to the school by the legislature was grossly insufficient.[69] The Trustees

67. Letters from Bassett, September 19, December 23, 1853, October 3, 7, November 9, 28, 1867, NYU, January 21, 1897, TC. It is worth underlining the fact that a black attended the Normal School in 1853; there still is a Bassett School in New Haven.

68. Camp, *Recollections*, 341ff., letters January 12, 19, 31, 1852, February 10, 1853, NYU; letter from E. B. Huntington, trustee, January 1, 1853, NYU. It may have been Barnard, in a gesture of appreciation, who was instrumental in getting an honorary M.A. from Yale for Camp, the man who was never able to realize his ambition to attend college; *CC*, August 6, 1853.

69. *Fourth Annual Report of the Trustees of the State Normal School* (1853), 3–9, quota-

were not alone in their assessment. The governor, a Democrat, had visited the school in January, to observe the "ordinary exercises" and to inspect the model school. Apparently, in spite of the recent turmoil, he liked what he saw, for in his annual message he supported his superintendent and praised the school. Then, sounding like a Whig, he suggested that it might in the future be advisable to institute "a seminary of a higher grade" for the study of the practical sciences, agriculture, and the mechanical arts, even civil and military engineering, all of which would constitute "a whole, a complete education for the American citizen." The legislature listened and concurred in part; after the usual political skirmishes, a proposal for an annual appropriation of $4,000, for a period of five years, eventually passed.[70]

By the summer of 1853, then, Barnard's major goals had been achieved. The Normal School was established on a firm and almost permanent financial footing, and the principle of increased taxation for the provision of schooling had been established. He was still the superintendent, however, obliged to attend to the queries which continued to flow to his office. No wonder he was loosing interest, for the requests were so familiar—could he recommend a teacher, a principal, a text, and always, could he come to deliver a lecture. Then there were the letters from John Philbrick who needled Barnard about Normal School concerns and about assisting in the arrangements for the New Haven meeting of the American Institute. Barnard must have loathed being asked to guarantee "free entertainment" for the ladies although he certainly was willing to attempt to arrange free train travel for the normalites. He did attend the meeting, offering a "cordial welcome" to those gathered and lecturing on "Practical Lessons to be Drawn from an Educational Tour of Europe."[71]

Barnard's national prominence brought opportunities. Joseph Henry invited him to deliver a course of lectures at the Smithsonian Institute during the early winter; "I know you are so full of your subject and so ready a speaker that you cannot fail, without much preparation, to inter-

---

tion, 9. According to the Catalogue, 91–102, in 1853 women outnumbered men nearly two to one at the school whereas it was customary that more men than women attended institutes. Hartford County, where the school was situated, sent twice as many students as Litchfield County (137, 66); this supports the view that normal education was a form of higher education within the local context. It was common for several members of one family to enroll, the Camps, with five, being outstanding. See also *CCSJ*, n.s., II, 11 (November 1854): 339ff.

70. *CC*, February 5, 1853; an editorial urged others to visit the new school: trains made the trip easy. See also May 7, June 18, July 23, 1853; editorial supporting Barnard's report, July 9, 1853.

71. Letters from Philbrick, January 24, July 20, 1853, NYU.

est an audience." Unfortunately, the weather was so severe in Washington that on the evening of the first lecture Henry decided not to order the hall to be heated, being certain that no audience would appear. In the next year, Barnard was approached by the paternalistic owners of the Pacific Mill, in Lawrence, who were anxious "to promote the intellectual and moral welfare" of the young girls employed in the mill, and desired to open a library. According to the catalogue, Henry Barnard had provided "many useful hints in the arrangement of books and the classification of the Catalogue"—and that catalogue reads very much like those he had previously published in Rhode Island.[72] To assist in the establishment of a mill library was entirely consistent with Barnard's commitment to continuing education and to "self-culture."

Personal concerns preoccupied Barnard to a great extent during 1853. Some were apparently financial. He was able to lend some money to an impecunious German friend in June, but he felt shaky; in October William Fowle wrote to rejoice that his friend "could see daylight from his financial depths." Barnard, who was all too prone to cry wolf, may have exaggerated his fiscal problems, but he also must have made some ill-advised business transactions; he was both buying property and investing in mortgages during this time. Then there were family matters. A son was born in January, and from February through May, the father was deeply distressed by the serious illness of one of his daughters. It is unfortunate that we can only read the reflection of Barnard's distress in the responses of his friends, but they are many and ring with warmth.[73] Barnard was perhaps a distant, and thoughtless, and, we may surmise, demanding, father but he was remembered with affection; the daughter survived, and continued to live with her father until his death.

Perusal of the *Connecticut Common School Journal*, of which Barnard was still the editor, confirms the impression that Barnard was withdrawing himself from the Connecticut scene in order to devote himself to

72. Letters from Henry, January 8, February 7, November 8, 1853. *Catalogue of the Pacific Mills Library* (Boston, 1855); Barnard is erroneously identified as Commissioner of the Public Schools in Rhode Island. See *AJE* I,iv (May 1856): 649, "Educational Movements and Miscellany," for a notice of "Library for Factory Operatives." Barnard added the editorial comment that a "valuable library" was a suitable quid pro quo for wages, that the amount necessary for its support was "trifling" and well paid back in greater income. But then he did not have to work for mill wages.

73. Letters from Wimmer, February 21, June 14; from Fowle, October 9; a number of letters mention the daughter's illness. Of course, it is always possible that Barnard exaggerated, as an excuse, as he did in the case of his own health, but I accept the evidence at face value. It was in the summer of 1853 that Barnard received his "triplicate LL.D.," an additional honorary doctorate, from Harvard this time, as he wrote with thanks, due to the "jogging" of his old friend Potter, letter, July 28, 1853, NYU.

national activities and to scholarship.[74] The first two issues of the 1853 volume contain announcements and news about the Normal School as well as the customary inquiries for the school committees, but the December Circular to the school visitors was cursory at best—only thirteen queries. The first half of the volume is taken up with a reprinting of large sections of *Normal Schools*, and pages 17–256, which have no individual number identification, are devoted to education in Germany, with subsequent issues completing a report on public education in Europe. In the September issue came confirmation of Barnard's intent. E. B. Huntington, the president of the State Teachers' Association, in his annual address, urged the teachers to join and to be active in their association, and he announced that the group was assuming publication of the *Journal* at Barnard's request. The editor handed over the reins to a committee of teachers in December.

> With this committee I have been associated against my wishes; but at their urgent solicitation, I shall cooperate cordially in the work, so far as I can consistently with other arrangements.[75]

In the January 1854 number he added a self-serving note:

> I have devoted a portion of my time and salary, in the absence of all legislative aid, and of any cooperation of teachers, to sustain a monthly periodical devoted exclusively to the dissemination of educational documents, and articles of permanent value and interest.

It may have been a courteous gesture, or at his insistence, that Barnard was listed first among the ten editors of the revised journal; John Philbrick was named the resident editor. Poor Philbrick. Barnard purportedly had withdrawn, but he was unable to stop meddling, and he kept Philbrick on a very tight rein indeed, so much so that the latter considered resigning. Barnard even dickered with Josiah Giddings about taking Philbrick's place. The editor finally capitulated, vowing to try "to improve on the past." "I desire to consult your pleasure in all things, and to profit by your

74. It took me some time to unravel the mystery of the serialization of the *Journal*. Very few copies of volumes five through eight appear in library catalogues; only one university lists volume seven, and no wonder. Volume six ends with number 12 (December 1852); volume eight commences with 1 (January 1853). For some inexplicable reason, or from a careless printer's error, Barnard omitted volume seven!

75. *CCSJ* VIII, ix (September 1853), xii (December 1853); see letters from Huntington, September 6, October 1, 1853. The revised journal added the words *and Annals of Education* to the old title although the common citation remained *CCSJ*. Sheldon Emmor Davis, *Educational Periodicals During the Nineteenth Century* (1919, repr. Metuchen, N.J.: Scarecrow Reprint Co., 1970), 45, points out that the usual pattern for antebellum educational journals was first, publication as official organs of the state, usually under the editorship

counsel."[76] Gradually Barnard did relinquish control of the publication, and his name disappeared from the list of editors when he left the state in 1858, and his only contribution to his former journal was an account of his later trip to the London exhibition. The change in editorship perhaps had not been designed as a significant one, but it was a harbinger in the development of the identity of the professional teacher. He and she had an association, and now they had a house organ, with an expanded name, edited by the man who stood at the head of the teaching corps in his capacity as principal of the Normal School, and who was soon to succeed Barnard as commissioner.

In the April 1854 issue of the *Connecticut Common School Journal* an advertisement of a new work by Henry Barnard appeared, a volume of "almost 900 pages" covering the educational systems of Europe.[77] Barnard had been working on the topic for years, and his trip to England had provided him with opportunities to meet with the reformers whose work he knew as well as ready access to the sorts of documents he avidly sought. Originally, he had intended to write a second edition of the *Normal Schools*, with some eighty pages of new material, chapters on universities, libraries, and institutions for the blind and deaf. However, when the "new" edition was completed it comprised a hefty volume of 890 pages, more than twice the length of its predecessor. In the preface, the author noted his sources: an early trip to Europe (unidentified), documents collected during his period of public service, materials gathered on his recent trip, and the great reports of Stowe, Bache, Mann, and Joseph Kay. He claimed that he provided "more reliable statistics and fuller information respecting the whole subject of public education in Europe" than was available anywhere else, and in addition, he disclaimed any originality. His book did not

> consist in conveying the speculations and limited experience of the author, but the matured views and varied experience of wise statesmen, educators, and teachers, in perfecting the organization and administration of educational systems and institutions, through a succession of years, under the most diverse circumstances of government, society, and religion.[78]

---

of the state official, then assumption of the responsibility by the teachers' association.

76. Letters from Philbrick, November 30, 1853, January 24, 26, February 6, 8, 15, 20, quotation from 6, 1854; from Giddings, February 2, 11, 1854; all NYU.

77. *CCSJ*, n.s., I, 4 (April 1854): 144; noted in *CCSJ*, 5 (May): 176, and 8 (August): 272.

78. *National Education in Europe*, 2d edition (Hartford: Case, Tiffany & Burns, 1854; hereafter cited as *NE*), preface. Note that Barnard called this a second edition even though

In this statement is a key to an understanding of Barnard's contribution to scholarship and to the history of education. He was not an interpreter, nor did he ever seek to be one; he was, instead, a compiler. He sought to retrieve the full record of educational progress (and that word is crucial), over the centuries and more especially during the current era, in order to present wise views and worthy models; his was always an instrumental goal.

To a some extent *National Education* is a second edition of *Normal Schools*. The overall form is the same, a nation by nation examination of measures to provide education, beginning always with an historical survey. There is an enormous amount of repetition as a comparison of the sections on Prussia in the two works proves:

Normal Schools	National Education
17–48	17–48
49–56	81–88
57–60	165–168
63–98	191–226

In the earlier work Barnard gave a scant two pages to the historical background of English schools; in *National Education* there were forty, beginning with King Alfred's purported allocation of one-ninth of the royal revenue to the support of the monastic schools. Not surprisingly, he concentrated on the nineteenth century, introducing Raikes and his Sunday school and Lancaster to the monitorial system (of which he approved for its "very perfect state of organization"). He traced the origins of adult and evening schools, of the Mechanics Institutes, and of the Industrial, Ragged, and Reform schools, all vital elements in a national system of education. But then the repetition resumes:

Normal Schools	National Education
303–329	761–785
330–343	786–799
347–361	804–826
363–393	823–853
395–413	855–873
415–416	875–876

---

it was not; subsequently he called many of his books second editions because the material had previously been published in the *American Journal of Education*; in this case some of the material had appeared before, in *NS*. Letter to Lord, January 1, 1853, RIC.

Even the blank pages are identical, an indication that whenever possible, in the interest of economy and with an eye to future publication, Barnard had his publisher use the same plates for the two volumes.

Much of the new material is devoted to novel institutions, Sunday Schools, agricultural schools, reform schools, evening schools, and institutes. Such a broad view of the configurations of education is consistent Barnard; education should take place through out society and should be supported by that society. But at times this broad definition conflicted with Barnard's overall organizing principle. Near the close of the section on France he devoted some twenty pages to agricultural and farm schools; then, before turning to the schools of Belgium, he considered farm schools in Switzerland, Germany, Belgium, and England; next he included an account of an 1851 conference on reform schools, and accounts of several such schools, including two by Stowe and Mann. This section suggests that Barnard had assembled his materials by topic, and had he possessed a more analytical mind, he might have handled his subject in a more thoughtful, less encyclopedic mode.[79]

Evidence of Barnard's research in the years after 1850 constitutes the major difference between the two works. There are numerous Irish documents, a translation of an 1851 report of the Belgian Inspector General of Prisons and Charitable Institutions, an account of Russian education from the *Annuaire des deux Mondes* of 1851–52, a report, published after 1848, on the Agricultural School in Brittany. One reference is to an 1853 book by Sir James Kay-Shuttleworth, in which the author asserts "the moral advantage of a tax on the poor in the form of school pence" because "it establishes the parental authority, and vindicates personal freedom"—ideas bound to appeal to an American Whig reformer.[80] Barnard's far-flung correspondence was another source. I. P. Hazard and David Buxton wrote from England describing institutions for the deaf; Samuel Parsons dispatched a book on public instruction in Europe and promised more, specifically on Belgium; Vere Foster, who had visited Barnard and his wife in Hartford in the spring of 1853, acted as an agent for his friend in Ireland and forwarded an enormous batch of reports. Joseph Kay sent his book on education in Europe and said his brother's on education in England and Wales, then in press, would follow as soon as it was available. Although the only citation for the chapter on Russia is the *Annuaire*, Daniel Gilman was in St. Petersburg during the winter of 1853–54 and

79. *NE*, 487ff., concluding 578 with a five-page account of the Farm School at Red Hill in Surrey.

80. *NE*, 485, 557, 629, 700–12, 746. Sir James Kay-Shuttleworth was the brother of Joseph Kay, also a manufacturer and reformer, who had been knighted for his service to education.

gathered material; by 1854 Barnard had Gilman on retainer, advancing him a handsome amount to collect documents—in modern terms we would say that Barnard used him as a research assistant—and there were other paid assistants, such as Hermann Wimmer, in Germany.[81]

Barnard's book was well received in the circles he expected. The *Westminster Review* called it " a comprehensive treatise" which relied on "actual data" and concentrated on the "link between the ideal and the actual." However, it did not sell widely, especially among the groups Barnard hoped to enlighten. Charles Northend, while attempting to soften the blow by calling the book a tribute to its author, reported that he had only been able to sell fourteen copies at sessions of the autumn institutes.[82]

We should not allow hindsight and our contemporary critical standards to blur our judgment of Barnard's accomplishment. *National Education in Europe* was an important work, although not original in concept. It may be viewed as a parallel or companion to volumes such as Wimmer's on American education, and it was more inclusive than the monographic reports of Stowe and Bache. It made available primary documents from an enormous array of sources and from numerous countries. Before interpretation there needs be information, and it was information that Barnard strove to bring before the public throughout his career, and in this he succeeded admirably. He succeeded, too, in another way. The antebellum period in the United States was one of intense nationalism, of an inward preoccupation, often noted with scorn by European travelers. Barnard, and his colleagues, had a transoceanic perspective, and in making available to an American audience, admittedly a small one at the time, current practices in foreign lands, he helped to combat contemporary parochialism. There were, after all, some things schoolmen in the United States could learn from abroad.

There is ample evidence that Barnard was withdrawing from state affairs in addition to his relinquishing the *Journal*. He did not attend the semi-annual meeting of the State Teachers' Association in May, at which a subscription for his portrait was made and filled.[83] In the same month he

81. Letters from Hazard, April 12, 1852; Foster, May 29, 1852, July 24, 1853, March 7, 1854; Buxton, July 22, 30, 1852; MacLeod, February 15, 1853; Parsons, March 13, 1853; Joseph Kay, February 22, 1853; Gilman, June 30, 1854. Gilman's relationship with Barnard was very much that of mentor and student, and it is not generally realized that Gilman actually served as secretary of the Board of Education in Connecticut for two years, 1865–67, before he went on to greater renown.

82. *CCSJ*, n.s., II, 1 (January 1855): 98–99. Letters from Northend, October 8, November 7, 1855, NYU.

83. See *CCSJ*, n.s., I, 6, (June 1854): 194–98, for a report of the meeting. The fact that a portrait was commissioned is evidence of Barnard's iminent retirement. That portrait,

presented what was to be his final report to the legislature; it was made orally, as had been the last one in Rhode Island—I hazard a guess that it never was written. Apparently it was a valedictory, part history, part recommendation, part recrimination. Barnard stressed the necessity of increased taxation and of the consolidation of districts, and he suggested that the state should put some muscle into its requirements by tying continued funding to demonstrated local improvements. He concluded with his customary rhetorical flourish, that the schools should be cheap enough for the poorest to attend, and good enough so that the wealthiest "would deem it a privilege" to send their children. After considerable debate, most of the superintendent's recommendations were adopted; moneys were appropriated, to the Normal School, to the institutes, and to send the newly designed *Connecticut Common School Journal* to the school visitors. There was, however, a significant difference in the thrust of the legislation. *Towns* were authorized to tax up to 1 percent of their grand list, *towns* could consolidate districts, and *towns* were given the right of eminent domain for school purposes.[84]

Barnard was now hard at work on what he intended to be the European edition of *Normal Schools*, and what could have been a more attractive prospect than the possibility of another trip to Europe, for research and restoration? Such an opportunity presented itself with the announcement by the British Society for the Encouragement of Arts, Manufactures and Commerce of a centenary celebration—an Educational Exhibition to be held in London in July 1854. Only two states, Massachusetts and New Jersey, were designated on the official invitation, but Barnard proposed that he be delegated as an official national representative, and be compensated by the federal government for his expenses. He was politely, even deferentially, refused by the functionary to whom he wrote, who, while noting Barnard's "arduous efforts to the cause of education," emphasized that the government did not pay private citizens to attend conferences or to act as governmental couriers.[85] Thus rebuffed, Barnard turned to another possible source, his own legislature.

Shortly after submitting his report, and on the eve of his departure (he

---

reproduced here on page 208. A later portrait hangs in the center room of the Connecticut Historical Society in Hartford (see page 330); one of the aspects which strikes me is the size of Barnard's hands—they are those of a man who has labored with his hands, which Barnard certainly had not done.

84. *CC*, May 13, 1854. There is no notice of a legislative order for the printing of the report, although the one on the School Fund was so ordered. See *CCSJ*, n.s., I, 7 (July 1854): 228–30.

85. Letter from A. D. Mann, May 5, 1854. Barnard had suggested that he might carry some official documents to London.

intended to go even if he failed to get assistance), he requested a stipend of $500, to help defray his travel expenses and to assist him in the purchase of educational documents for the state. Although John Philbrick later reported that the request received "the harmonious action of all parties," the record indicates that this was not so. In the debate Barnard's supporters spoke eloquently of his fifteen years of faithful service to the schools of the state, but the Committee on Education, under Democratic control, reported unfavorably on the matter of the request and recommended an inquiry into the benefits to the school districts of the office of the superintendent; they queried whether the localities had flourished or declined during the current regime. Politics again, just as it had been politics in 1842; Barnard's request had given the Democrats had an opportunity to attack him, his policy, and his party. In this instance, however, never in any of his letters is there anything akin to the vitriolic reaction he had on the occasion of his earlier dismissal. He simply did not care any more. Ultimately he did receive, after the Democrats had vented their spleen, and refused to appoint him an official delegate (a fact he amended in his later version), $1,000 for travel and expenses as well as the confirmation of most of his policies.[86]

Barnard sailed in late May, for his invitation to the London festivities was directed to him in Liverpool. He had with him a letter of introduction from Henry Dutton, the governor of Connecticut addressed "To Friends of Education in England and Elsewhere," introducing Barnard as "a gentleman of distinct literary attainments, of untiring zeal in the cause of Education, and of high standing and character."[87] During his stay he visited a number of institutions, the Liverpool Institute for the Deaf and Dumb, the St. Mark's and the Battersea Training Schools, the Cheltenham Training College, the Borough Road Normal School of the British and Foreign School Society, all of which he had described in *National Education in Europe*; he even received, from Henry Dunn, the director of the British Society, a ticket for the annual examination of the student teachers, and from the Home Office, he procured a letter to the Governor of the Pentonville Prison allowing him, and three friends, to visit on any

86. *CC*, May 27, June 3, 10, July 1, 8, 1854; *CCSJ*, n.s., I, 6 (June 1854): 202.

87. Invitation, May 31, June 15, NYU; both were addressed to him as Commissioner of the Public School of Rhode Island. Letter from Dutton, May 26, 1854, CHS, which suggests that Barnard was going as the official representative of the state. In a footnote to a letter to Mary Peabody, *AJE* XXX (March 1880): 1, Barnard referred to a Report to the Governor of Connecticut on the International Exhibition of Educational Systems and Material at St. Martin's Hall, by Henry Barnard, "delegate from Connecticut by appointment of the General Assembly, 1854." I have not located it. There are many letters of introduction from one English reformer to another in the NYU archive.

day. He dined frequently with British liberals, including Richard Cob-
den, and the phrenologist George Combe. In short, he had a splendid
time in the reform environment of England.[88] The high point of his stay
was the exhibition's opening dinner on July 3. Barnard wrote a full report
of this splendid occasion for the *Connecticut Common School Journal*, pref-
acing it, of course, with a three-page history of the society.[89] The festivities took place "in a spacious banqueting hall" in the basement of the
Crystal Palace.

> The arrangement of this hall was such as to permit of a distribution
> of the company in somewhat of a classified order, with the view of
> showing that it was not an ordinary mixed assemblage.

Barnard made it very clear that his place in the "classified order" was
among the most honored guests, along with other foreign commissioners, British lords, and Society dignitaries. Lesser folk sat at thirteen parallel tables set out within the larger semi-circular one. The banquet must
have been very long, with toast upon toast in succession. Barnard was
called upon to be one of the two respondents (the other was M. Milne
Edwards, Membre de l'Institut de France, who "spoke English with
remarkable facility") to Lord Mahon's toast.

We can picture Henry Barnard, rather short, sturdy, smooth faced,
impeccably attired, rising with confidence and satisfaction. His speech
(punctuated, he reported, by "loud cheers" and cries of "hear, hear") was
diplomatic; he recalled the "many hospitalities" he had encountered over
the years in England; he addressed his "fellow-citizens"; he noted that he
was coupled with a representative of his nation's "ancient ally"; and he
declined to make a traditional oration on what was the eve of his nation's
birthday. Rather, he instanced Connecticut's debt to the grammar schools
and universities of the mother country whose graduates were responsible
for the colonial school legislation which required that a child learn "to
read the Holy Word of God and the good laws of his colony." He noted
with "peculiar pleasure . . . after an interval of twenty years . . . such
marks of educational progress" as he had seen in the previous three weeks,
and he closed saying that he would "carry away with me very important

88. Letters, May 31–July 24, NYU and a few TC. Emma Willard, by then 67, also
planned to attend the exhibition and to spend some time in London, for she urged
Barnard to share her lodgings, letters June 9, 16, 1854; see *AJE* VI, xvi (March 1859): 166,
where Fowler says that Barnard introduced Willard to the officers of the convention and
to other eminent visitors. Lutz, *Willard*, 122, repeats Fowler.

89. *CCSJ*, n.s., I, ii (November 1854): 363–65, and n.s., II, i (January 1855): 81–89;
while writing this article, Barnard certainly had at hand the published program with its
lists of tables and guests.

lessons, which I trust will be felt in the schools of my own state and my own country." Then he smiled benignly and sat down to "Much applause."

Barnard lingered in England after the opening of the exhibition and then crossed to the Continent to visit the network of scholars he had come to know. He was in Paris in mid-July, for on July 15 he drafted an open letter to the School Teachers of America. The occasion was his receipt of the news of the death of Josiah Holbrook, and he described, in self-consciously formal terms, his emotions upon visiting the "rooms" (public reading rooms) in Paris inspired by Holbrook.[90] He was invited to Liège where he met with Alphonse LeRoy, who had translated into French Hermann Wimmer's work on the American schools, and who paid handsome tribute to Barnard's "labors, studies and observations" in a review subsequently published in the Connecticut *Journal*.[91] Barnard also visited his long-time friend Wimmer in Uhyst, an extremely difficult little town to reach in Saxony, and he met with his frequent Swedish correspondent, P. A. Siljestrom, in Hamburg. The trip was something of a triumph, from its start in England until the end. Barnard, to some, was a prophet, if not always so honored in his own land, or so he made it seem in his reports of his trip.[92]

When Barnard returned from Europe, he must have felt that emptiness so common when one has completed a phase of one's life. He had achieved his goal in Connecticut, for the New Britain Normal School was now a going concern with 243 students in attendance during the previous winter and 15 graduating in September.[93] He had sought to implement certain centralizing reforms and had been, to a degree, successful. He had revived his journal and had passed on the torch of leadership to another. He had published a well-received history and had reaped the reward in a recognized national and international status. It is not

90. Handwritten draft, NYU; the letter does not seem to have been published. For the AII's resolution on Holbrook, see *CCSJ*, n.s., I, 9 (September 1854): 296; see also "Memoir of Josiah Holbrook," *AJE* VIII, xx (March 1860), subsequently published separately.

91. Letter from LeRoy, Liège, August 18; *CCSJ*, n.s., II, 12 (December 1855): 502–05. LeRoy emphasized Barnard's "direct action on the instructors themselves" and the unity "of his system."

92. Letters from Wimmer, June 26, August 15, 24; from Siljestrom, August 17, 18; from Julius Friedlanery, Berne, August 18; 1854, NYU. See *CCSJ*, n.s., II, i (January 1855): 91, for Wimmer. This, and the one on LeRoy certainly are from Barnard.

93. *Fifth Annual Report*. Barnard was still listed as principal, for he did not resign until January 1, 1855. The *Sixth Annual Report*, while noting his resignation, contained no formal tribute to him. In the *Seventh Annual Report*, 7, Emma Willard, a Normal School Visitor, did refer to the school's duty "to fulfill the high mission which BARNARD and its other founders designed."

surprising that David Camp's bulletins from the field and John Philbrick's missives about the journal failed to warrant the attention they deserved. Even requests to lecture in other states appeared onerous, although it probably gave Barnard pleasure to address the graduating class of the Normal School when Philbrick fell ill. Naturally he reported on the London congress, promising a fuller report for the *Journal*, and he spoke on recent educational developments in Europe, especially about the reform schools and the polytechnics—all scarcely what the graduates expected.[94] But this was a swan song of sorts. On October 23 he wrote to Huntington that, because of a severe illness, he would be unable to attend the State Teachers' Association and the regular meeting of the editors of the *Journal*. There is a note of farewell in the letter, almost of regret, when he mentioned that it would have been his last as superintendent; he paid tribute to the host of teachers, living and dead, who had served the state, beginning with those who had attended the first gathering in 1838, and he passed on the torch of leadership to John Philbrick, who "on my nomination, has been appointed by the unanimous vote of the Trustees" Principal and Superintendent. The words he employed to describe his successor, "his ability, common sense and devotion to his duties," seem lukewarm to those accustomed to Barnard's prose style, and he managed to denigrate the teachers by referring to them as the "indispensable auxiliaries" to his labors.

John Philbrick paid Barnard a handsome tribute upon his retirement in the Resident Editor's Department of the *Journal*.

> We should do injustice to the readers of this Journal, as well as to ourselves, to allow this important event to pass in silence, though we have neither the space nor the time to devote to it which we could desire.

In compiling the list of Barnard's "noble ambition to be useful to his native State" and to the "altar of public education," the editor first cited the invaluable books on *School Architecture*, *Normal Schools*, and *National Education in Europe*, and the numerous Reports, all of which "have aroused and incited thousands of leading minds to engage in this cause." He called attention to Barnard's prestige abroad, where "in the metropolis of Europe, he stood preeminent in the august congress of educators." Most of all he stressed Barnard's devotion to his native state; "for her he

---

94. Letters from Camp, October 8; from Philbrick, November 11; from Northend, August 10, October 2; from W. H. Wells, asking him to Chicago, October 27; 1854, NYU; *CCSJ*, n.s. I, 11 (November 1854): 345ff.,361–63; at the graduation ceremonies the Normal School choir sang a hymn written by Lydia Sigourney which contained memorable lines: "go forth, ye faithful bands / who till the mental field."

has chiefly labored, and his labors in her behalf will not cease with his retirement from office." Despite obstacles, "the jealousies of party, the prejudices of ignorance and the hostility of the blind though honest conservatism," the retiring superintendent had persevered, had seen the Normal School established, the concept of taxation of property for schools reasserted, increased appropriations for institutes passed, improvements in school houses and in the teachers themselves become realities. All of this, with the recently enacted laws of school organization, "seem to herald the approach of the day . . . when every school in the state shall be 'good enough for the best and cheap enough for the poorest,' or better, *free for all.*"[95] It is difficult not to suspect that the source for the tribute was Henry Barnard himself, for the style and the choice of words are characteristically his. Huntington had written to him in early November asking for a chronological sketch of the eras of his educational life and for a list of his published works; he had asked Barnard what had first drawn him to education, and he had even questioned "who could write this?"[96] Barnard, never hesitant to embellish his own image, must have complied, and another chapter in the myth was written.

A substantial section of that myth suggests that one of Barnard's great accomplishments was fostering the formation of a teaching profession, through his insistence on the proper preparation of teachers, his encouragement of teacher education, in the institutes and normal school, and of teacher organizations. Professionalism certainly was an issue in the 1850s. The American Institute considered the matter often, and in 1853 at New Haven, for example, tabled a resolution (perhaps drafted by Barnard) "That the highest interests of the community demand of the various legislatures the permanent establishment of the Teachers' profession."[97] Barnard was consistent in his support of measures to encourage teachers. Early in his career he had insisted on "the necessity and the means of giving a higher social position and intellectual power to those who are practically engaged in education." At the close of his farewell epistle to the state teachers, he commended the association for its role in promoting professional feeling:

> All the advantages felt by those who prepare in common for the same profession . . . —friendships, springing from congenial tasks, and the same difficulties encountered and triumphs achieved —mutual encouragement and assistance in studies, discussions, and

95. *CCSJ*, n.s., I, 12 (December 1854): 404–06. The final italicized phrase is without a doubt Philbrick's, but echoing Barnard.

96. Letter from Huntington, November 2, 1854, NYU.

97. *AII*, *Proceedings*, New Haven, 1853.

comparison of views,—the attainments of solitary reading and isolated experience quickened by the action of the living mind . . .
—the old defective methods held up, exposed and corrected,—the
tendency . . . to a dull monotony of character withstood, and obvi-
ated, the social position and influences which follow the combined
action of large numbers in the same pursuit, and the awakening of a
deep parental interest in the work of the teacher, and thus bringing
the home and the school into closer sympathy and cooperation
—all these results will be experienced in a still larger measure than
now.[98]

Barnard frequently had dwelt on the excellences of certain eminent teachers, on their knowledge, on their ability to explain facts in context, on
their liveliness, on their sympathetic understanding of their pupils, and
above all, on their moral nature. But to him "an admirable example of the
best type of American professional teacher" was Daniel Hager, a man
who began to teach in 1833 at the age of 13 and who graduated from
Union College ten years later, having attended off and on between stints
of teaching. Barnard stressed the methods and morals of another revered
teacher who, in addition to careful preparation and lively and appropriate
presentations, "studied . . . [his students'] moral natures and sought to
wake in their youthful hearts aspirations for goodness and purity."[99] Neither of these portraits resembles what we would call a professional; both
men were characteristic, if highly admirable, antebellum teachers.

Barnard did value teachers, even romanticized them, but he did not
considered himself one of them, nor they his equals. He encouraged them
to organize in Connecticut, and to his everlasting credit he created, with
assistance to be sure, a college for them. But he never really taught them,
for he preferred to inspire them. Significantly, he played only a minor
role, as an honored guest, in the national organization of normal schools
between 1856 and 1859.[100]

Another thrust of Barnard's second tenure in Connecticut was toward
centralization under the state, in a manner similar to his efforts in Rhode
Island. Here he was successful to a degree, yet, in an ironic twist, the
ultimate result of the Connecticut legislation of the mid-1850s was the

98. *CCSJ*, II, 9 (February 15, 1840): 133; ibid., n.s., I, 11 (November 1854): 361.

99. Draft of biography of Daniel B. Hager, TC; *Eminent Men*, 466–67 for portrait of
David Perkins Page which Richard Emmon Thursfield, Henry Barnard's *"American Journal of Education"* (Baltimore: The Johns Hopkins University Press, 1945), 323, identifies as
written by Barnard.

100. *Proceedings*, First Annual Convention of the American Normal School Association, New York, 1860.

return of the control of education to the local authorities. Granted, it was to the towns and not the districts, a move toward consolidation and efficiency Barnard favored, but at the expense of the supervisory function of the state, something he favored more and for which he had labored. Not for more than a century would the states again seize the initiative in educational policy.

It is very difficult to characterize Henry Barnard as a school reformer. Paul Mattingly argues for two generations of common school reformers, for a group of "schoolmen" who were succeeded by "a professional corps of educators." The first group, born between 1790 and 1800, was led to battle by the Carters, the Gallaudets, the Manns; the second, all born about 1820, was represented by men such as John Philbrick. Time and enormous social and intellectual differences separated the two. The trouble, as Mattingly admits, is that there "are several important figures" who do not fit his scheme, and Henry Barnard is preeminent among them. He belonged, in class, education, and sympathy, among the first generation. He shared their social biases, their preoccupation with moral goals, their desire for efficient and centralized administration of social agencies, their emphasis on scientific instruction, and, in a muted fashion, their evangelical style; and he belonged to their organization. Symbolically, however, he was one of the founders of the newer association to which the second generation of schoolmen flocked. He did not really fit with them either, for they were budding administrators which certainly he was not. Nor did he belong with the teachers. He considered himself superior to the poor boys and girls, with their rising ambitions, who struggled in the district schools and flocked to the institutes, and then joined the state associations. David Camp was one of them, and he always remained a lieutenant to Barnard.

V

COLLEGE

PRESIDENT

*I would recommend among other particulars, the admission of pupils to any department or study, and for any period of time, provided they are found qualified, on examination, to enter, and will conform to regulations—the classification of pupils by their individual studies, not by any grouping of studies, or by the period of residence; the conferring of all degrees and certificates of proficiency after public examination . . . ; the arrangements of the terms and vacations so as better to accommodate both students and instructors . . . ; and the appointment, hereafter, for specified periods of time, and with salaries to some extent dependent on the amount of time devoted to instruction and the number of pupils dependent on each. (*Twelfth Annual Report to the Regents of the University of Wisconsin, *1859)*

By mid-century Henry Barnard was at the height of his powers and prestige. In 1855 he was forty-four, married, a man of substance in his community and among the educational brotherhood. He had a growing family and, apparently, ample means.[1] He had completed his second period of service in his native state, with a large measure of success, and

---

1. A child was born sometime in the spring of 1856, for Frederick Perkins mentions an addition to the family in a letter of May 16, another in February 1857, for both Sanford, February 12, and Philbrick, February 24, mention the happy "domestic event."

he had resigned amid congratulations in order to follow his own dictates. His national status was such that his days were filled with educational matters. Letters winged their way to Hartford from colleagues throughout the country, from Mississippi, from Illinois, from Iowa, as well as from nearer to home, and even from Sweden. His advice was sought about textbooks, about school apparatus, about school law, and, as a recognized authority on school architecture, he was asked about schoolhouse construction. President Nott of Union College wanted him to come to consult about their proposed new building, and, naturally, asked him to deliver a lecture. Barnard, with his usual procrastination, did not respond to Nott's first letter, or the second, but he did go to Union in March. About this time, according to a New Orleans newspaper, he drew up a plan for the reorganization of that city's schools, but he declined an offer of the school superintendency there. Of course he was asked to recommend teachers, and he provided references for both Huntington and Philbrick as they sought new positions. Josiah Giddings peppered his mentor with letters about his future, and Barnard must have been very much relieved when Giddings finally secured a position in South Carolina.[2]

Barnard's increasing fame made his presence requested at various ceremonial occasions. He was asked to sit on the stage at the Trinity College graduation, and his old friend, Elias Loomis, now the head of New York University, wanted him to speak (for only fifteen minutes) at the opening of a new girls' school in New York. He received, and kept, a formal invitation for the elaborate ceremonies honoring George Peabody, in Danvers, Massachusetts, and he played an active role in the dedication of the Norwich Free Academy. For over a year, B. V. Blewell, of Bethel College in Russellville, Kentucky, implored him to come to deliver "a thrilling speech such as one we know you are capable of making, one that may awaken our people and move them to effort"—in other words to inspire the common school movement in the border state. Barnard dilly-dallied but finally promised to deliver not one, but a series of lectures.

His activities on the behalf of teachers made him much sought after in

2. Letters from Charles Schmidt, Pennsylvania, April 24, 1856; from Huntington, January 26, 1855; from Robert Peters, Lexington, March 10, 1855; from George Magoun, Iowa College, April 29, 1855; from John Phillips, May 7, 1855; from Siljestrom, May 11, 1855; from J. R. Hamilton, Mississippi, January 11, 1856; from Alex Cummins, Pennsylvania, January 22, 1856; from Newton Bateman, Jacksonville, January 30, September 23, November 4, 1856; from Judge Putnam, Boston, December 18, 1856; from Giddings, January 17, February 21, March 3, 22, April 4, 1855 (he hoped to get the position as head of the new Norwich Academy), April 23, May 3, 10, July 7, 18, November 9, 24, December 26, 1856, the last three from Charleston where he was very happy.

Engraved by H. W. Smith

Henry Barnard, 1854

the normal school circles. He did not accept an invitation to address the Springfield normalites, nor W. F. Phelph's request that he deliver "such an off-hand effort as you can readily give without special preparation" at the dedication of the New Jersey State Normal School, but he did lecture to the New Jersy State Institute the next year. Philbrick wanted him at the Normal School's closing exercises, as did William Wells at those at the Westfield, Massachusetts, Normal School—he probably went to both.[3]

3. Letters from Philbrick, July 23, 1855; from Wells, July 27, 1855; from Phelphs, March 14, June 12, 24, November 3, 8, 14, 1856 (Barnard did not go but promised to include an account of the dedication and the plans in the *AJE*); from Blewell, April 8, June 19, 1856,

No copy of any of his speeches exists, and we can assume that Barnard delivered them extemporaneously. It would have been easy—the themes of exhortation rolled from his tongue with the practice of twenty years.

The lectures that Barnard gave at the Smithsonian in the winter of 1855 must have been of a different character, for Joseph Henry was editing a series of "Contributions to Knowledge" of which the lectures probably were a part. After the lectures were delivered, Henry had as much trouble getting their text from Barnard as others had in similar circumstances before; the Smithsonian director refused to send an advance on the payment he had promised until he had the material, or at least not until July, but when he finally received the corrected proofs of Barnard's text, he promptly dispatched a check for $350. Subsequently he was to have even more difficulty extracting a report on education which he had commissioned the Connecticut editor to write. But relations between the two men, both of whom had been presidents of the American Association for the Advancement of Education (Henry in 1853, Barnard in 1855), were never easy. Barnard had hoped for the Smithsonian position which eventually went to Henry, and Barnard, when slighted or crossed, could be crotchety if not downright vindictive.[4]

During his presidency of the American Association, Barnard lavished considerable effort on the organization. His letters during the spring and early summer dealt with organizational problems and with plans for the annual convention; he also tried out on his correspondents some ideas he intended to present at the meeting. He discussed with Amos Perry an offer from the Smithsonian of $1,000 toward the salary of a national education agent; if an additional thousand could be raised he himself would undertake the task. Another colleague thought the proposal of a national journal was a splendid idea; one edited by Barnard would "sweep the horizon."[5]

February 7, 11, 1856; from Northend, August 11, 19, 21, 25, 1856; from Conant, August 6, 1856; all NYU; formal invitation to Peabody celebration, CHS; Barnard's notes on the Norwich dedication. Barnard described the last three events in his *Journal*.

4. Letters from Henry, March 14, August 4, 6, 1855, April 11, May 15, 1856, January 13, 1857; in the last Henry was curt: "*send* the report." It is difficult to untangle the relationship between the two men. Thursfield, *Barnard*, 24–25, takes at face value Barnard's vitriolic view, that Henry had reneged on a promise to republish any material on education which first appeared in the *Journal*. But in his April 11 letter, originally sent to Potter and forwarded to Barnard, Henry made it clear that the Smithsonian had a policy of never reprinting anything already published; Henry even tried to accommodate Barnard by suggesting he "remodel" his report. Barnard later referred to Henry's "malignity" and failure to keep his word, draft of letter to Senator Dixon, 1862, TC.

5. Letters from R. L. Cooke, July 21, 30, August 6, on program; from Perry, June 28,

At the Association convention in August considerable attention was given to national issues. Alexander Dallas Bache delivered an address advocating a national university, and Barnard submitted his "Plan for a Central Agency." It was an ambitious scheme, indeed, but one entirely consistent with the purposes of the organization. What Barnard envisioned was a permanent arm of the Association, with an officer and a publication, "to be entitled the American Journal and Library of Education."[6] Every facet of education, practical and theoretical, informal and formal, contemporary and historical, was to be included, a broad sweep indeed. A committee approved the project, but no funds were allocated, and the dream slumbered. The organization itself was languishing, although it continued to meet, and by 1857 one of its stalwarts questioned the very need for such a group. According to Charles Davis, its intent was too general, and it no longer enlisted "warm sympathy"; only Bishop Potter and Henry Barnard remained committed to it.[7] By mid-century forces which Barnard had helped to set in motion, the increasing sense of identity among the teachers and specialization in the academic profession, were conspiring to make such gentlemanly annual gatherings obsolete. The teachers, with their institute and normal school backgrounds, congregated in the state teacher organizations, and college professors, graduates of the colleges and newer universities, eventually founded their own associations, based on their academic disciplines. The American Association for the Advancement of Education was a transitional organization, and eventually it expired.

Barnard had a number of other interests. He showed that he was still a loyal son of Yale by managing a subscription drive for a portrait of his recently deceased friend, the former Professor Stanley, and most of his classmates contributed the $10 he requested. He himself proved to be not as responsive when Benjamin Silliman, Jr., approached him on behalf of the Linonian Society. Barnard pledged $100 but needed more than one reminder, and he may never have paid.[8] There was always travel to

from Parish, July 16, on journal; 1856, NYU.

6. See *AJE* I, 4 (May 1856), for Bache's address; I, i (August 1955), for the plan. In June, 1856, Emma Willard had written to her "dear friend" Barnard about the proj. 'd meeting: "I suppose there you will ever preserve your appropriate dignity, and not allow Susan Anthony, or any other 'female woman' a seat on the platform. It may be foolish —but I am unwilling to expose myself to such mortification for my sex, as such conduct on their part inflicts upon me."

7. Letters from Davis, November 12, 1855, January 7, 1857.

8. Letters from Andrews, April 21; Loomis, April 23; George Andersen (Tallahassee), June 9; Ray Palmer (with a very affectionate letter recalling a pleasure jaunt to Maine twenty years before), July 20; 1856; from Silliman, December 4, 1855, January 30, 1856.

occupy him, too. He made visits to Washington, Baltimore, Philadelphia, and New Jersey in 1855; in January 1856 he was in Cincinnati; and both summers he accompanied his wife to Detroit.[9]

In the autumn of 1856 he was planning another Western trip; Newton Bateman had heard that he was coming and took the opportunity to ask Barnard to speak to the December meeting of the Illinois State Teachers' Association, and Loren Andrews arranged to meet him in Columbus. The purpose of this trip apparently was to engage in discussions with individuals who had sounded Barnard out about the possibility of his accepting a position in Wisconsin. Evidence about the matter in the correspondence is sketchy, but Barnard, with his customary enthusiasm, designed elaborate schemes, and he must have invited Andrews, then the president of Kenyon College, to participate in them. Andrews was hesitant. "You have planned a noble work for a great & free state," but it would be extremely difficult to carry out, and Andrews was not certain that Wisconsin was the proper place for Barnard's exertions.

> Can you remove the direction of educational affairs from direct *political* control? Can you free your broad & liberal plans from the danger of sudden partisan revolutions? Will you be able to secure the *hearty* cooperation of the leading influences of the State? Will you find it possible to escape the virulent opposition of partisan or sectarian influences? Or is there danger of that more paralyzing obstacle, an indifference which will neither foster co-operation nor excite opposition?[10]

Andrews added that it had been just those concerns which had led him, although sorely tempted, to decline a similar position in Iowa. Past experience made Barnard pause, and nothing came of the matter at the time.

This was not the first time that Henry Barnard had toyed with the idea of a heading a university. He had hoped, vaguely, for Brown at the end of his tenure in Rhode Island. Then in 1852 such a position almost became a reality. During that winter letters had flown back and forth between Hartford and Detroit on the subject of the University of Michigan presidency. Apparently Barnard was not the first choice of the trustees, Henry Tappan was, but in June Barnard's booster wrote that he had been elected, and

9. In a letter, February 28, from Newark, David Cole wrote that Barnard had left his overshoes behind after a visit; letter from Russell, January 26, addressed to Cincinnati; letter from Cornelius Welles, to Mr. and Mrs. Barnard in Detroit, full of various business and family details, including that "Gracie" missed "little Henry."

10. Letters from Bateman, September 23, November 4, 1856; from Andrews, December 12, 28 (in which he said he had sent money for a journal two months previously yet none had come), December 31, 1856, NYU.

that the board wanted him to come out for consultation before they made any other faculty appointments. Barnard temporized, annoyed the Michigan folk, perhaps declined—the scenario is muddled. He may have used his health as an excuse, for in July he received another letter from his man on the spot who reported that although another had been elected, nothing was settled; would Barnard's health now allow him to accept if the other candidate declined? There is no resolution of the negotiations in the correspondence, and it is a matter of history that Henry Tappan, not Henry Barnard, became head of the University of Michigan.[11]

At the very same time, Barnard was approached by Daniel Read, a professor at Indiana University; would he accept the presidency of that institution if it were offered? Barnard next received a telegram informing him that he was "the President of Indiana University." There were those who advised against his accepting the post because of the shaky condition of the institution, but Barnard was attracted to it (or to Michigan) because of the challenge.

> [He] would like nothing better than to labor with teachers, and officers of schools of any grade, in one of these states & make the University felt in educational policy.

This comment is significant as Barnard's first articulation of his view of the role of higher education. He saw a chancellorship or presidency in terms of the overall structure of a centralized state school system, and he developed detailed plans for uniting the university with the common schools. Professor Read replied in a gratifying manner: "The State is ripe," and there was great satisfaction at Barnard's election—the legislature had passed a new school law and had appropriated a larger sum of money than had been anticipated. All that was required was for Barnard to be in Bloomington for the August graduation.[12]

Barnard never went to Indiana. He may have been frightened off by local politics, for there is ample evidence of political maneuvering in the appointment process.[13] The Michigan situation is equally cloudy. In 1854

11. Letters from Z. Pitcher, July 20, 23, 29, 1851; from George S. Hand. January 6; from T. S. Lambert, January 24, February 14; from Charles Palmer, April 28; 1852, NYU. Barnard harbored no resentment against Tappan; see *AJE* XIII, xxxii (September 1863): frontispiece, and Memoir, 451–54, of Tappan.

12. Letters from Read, May 12, 29, June 4, 21, 24; from Johnson, June 10; 1852, NYU. Barnard to Lord, July 3, 1852, RIC. In July 1867, James D. Maxwell of Bloomington recalled Barnard's election to the presidency, letter, NYU. Barnard's friends seemed to have thought he had accepted Michigan; Leonard Bacon recommended a friend for a faculty appointment there.

13. Later Read wrote to Barnard to inquire if he had received any anonymous letter or

Barnard's old friend and supporter, E. A. Lansing sent a clipping from one newspaper of a letter he had written to the editor in response to what he considered inaccuracies in an article in another paper, all having to do with the dealings with Barnard. The Detroit *Inquirer* had reported that overtures had been made to Henry Barnard, "a thorough, efficient and skilled business man, a shrewd and judicious financier, a thorough scholar, and a man second to none in practical experience," but ill health had kept him from responding favorably. Lansing insisted it was not ill health at all "but an anonymous letter, fairly supposed to have been written by some partizan of Dr. Tappan, filled with falsehoods and misrepresentations."[14] It is reasonable to surmise that politics surrounding new state universities were as Byzantine as any Barnard had encountered in Connecticut, and that he had been advanced by one group and competitors by others. He may have been promoted by cabals in each state, he may never have been offered the presidency by the trustees of either institution, he may have been appointed in Indiana; we will never know for certain. It served Barnard's purposes to spread the most favorable version of the matter in his later years.[15]

The mutual interest of the educational leaders of Wisconsin and Henry Barnard was not new. At the invitation of John H. Tweedy, Yale '36 and now a Whig lawyer in Milwaukee, Barnard had delivered two lectures to the state's constitutional convention in 1846, where he rehearsed his familiar maxims, emphasizing his favorite topics—gradation, proper schoolhouses, punctuality and attendance, qualified teachers—and outlining an entire system of public schooling which ranged from elementary schools through the projected university, including normal schools. School reform was an active issue in the state during the next decade, how much due to Barnard is, of course, not clear. The constitution created the position of the state superintendent of instruction; institutes were held as early as 1852; and a normal department at the university, under Barnard's friend Daniel Read, was created in 1855. The new university was a mere fledgling, if an ambitious one, and other institutions also claimed the role of pro-

---

any with a "feigned" signature during the previous year, letter, January 13; and Joseph McPheeters reported a rumor that Barnard had been give some information which had led him to refuse the position, letter, February 7; 1852, NYU.

14. Letter from Lansing, January 30, 1854, NYU. The description of Barnard is amusing in light of his business performance, but it does indicate his image as a man of property in Michigan and also serves to outline the requirements for an academic presidency.

15. *AJE* XXX, (March 1880), unpaged, but 198–200. Barnard added an editorial parenthesis (in the third person) to the account of his national career stating that he was offered, and declined, both positions.

vider of higher learning. The primacy of the state university was not assured, and strong competitors with the new department were the denominational colleges and academies whose normal departments were supported by the income from the sale of the federal swamp lands.[16]

Sometime, during the summer of 1855, Barnard had met John K. Lathrop, the chancellor of the young University of Wisconsin, when both were in Detroit, and Barnard's possible association with the university was most certainly broached.[17] Such an exploratory conversation was entirely understandable. Barnard had been considered for a position in higher education by midwestern schoolmen before, and he was at this time available; moreover, as president of the American Association for the Advancement of Education and a former official in the movement for educational reform in two New England states, he was highly visible —his name was on everybody's list. On his part, John Lathrop was anxious to find someone else to carry the burden, political and administrative, of furthering the cause of his university. The question was: was it an appropriate fit?

Scholars of higher education have traditionally focused on the antebellum New England colleges and their midwestern progeny, and the current canon dates the era of the modern university to the founding of Cornell and, later, Johns Hopkins.[18] This interpretation stems from the Eastern bias of scholarship, which of course is partly due to the work of Henry Barnard, as well as a natural desire on the part of historians to have eras tidy. The founders of the midwestern institutions, grandly labeled universities (when in fact most of them were mere high schools and had at best a handful of graduates) had vastly different dreams during the antebellum period than had their Eastern counterparts. Chancellor Lathrop in his inaugural address depicted the University as the apex of the educational *system*; he advocated a thorough reorganization of the struggling school, into four departments, of which the first was the

16. Lloyd P. Jorgenson, *The Founding of Public Education in Wisconsin* (Madison: University of Wisconsin Press, 1956), 53. Conrad E. Patzer, *Public Education in Wisconsin* (Madison: issued by State Superintendent John Callahan, 1924), 29, 87–88, 133–34. Albert Salisbury, *Historical Sketch of Normal Instruction in Wisconsin* (n.p., 1893), 7ff.

17. A. D. Mayo, *Report of the Commissioner of Education, 1896–1897* (Washington: Bureau of Publications, 1898), 800. Plan Submitted to Chancellor Lathrop, 1855, NYU. Lathrop, a graduate of Yale, class of 1799, came to Wisconsin in 1849 from the presidency of the University of Missouri; Madison at the time was a village of 1,500 souls. See Merle Curti and Vernon Carstensen, *The University of Wisconsin*, 2 vols. (Madison: University of Wisconsin Press, 1948), I:57ff.

18. See Frederick Rudolph, *The American College and University* (New York, 1962), esp. chap. 13; and Laurence R. Veysey, *The Emergence of the American University* (Chicago: University of Chicago Press, 1965).

Department of Science, Literature, and the Arts (science coming first), and the fourth was the Department of the Theory and Practice of Elementary Instruction. The university was never to stand aloof from the populace, he added, for it was always to rise to its utilitarian purpose, and it was to be the "school of the school master"—anyone vowing to teach in the schools of the state would pay no tuition.[19]

Such ideas were consistent with Barnard's, and he, perhaps at the suggestion of the chancellor, designed a scheme for the university; in it he sketched his vision of higher education as formerly he had drawn a blueprint for the common schools. His Plan was "to combine the advantages of college and (Continental) University Education" by the creation of eleven Departments of Instruction: Mental and Moral Science; English Literature; History; Ancient Languages and Literature; Modern Languages and Literature; Mathematics, including Civil Engineering; Natural Philosophy and Astronomy; Chemistry and its Applications to Manufacturing and Agriculture; Physical Geology; Botany, Zoology, and Physiology; and a Normal Department. (Barnard's bias was so strong that the normal department was the only one which did not fit into his scheme, the only one which was based on vocational training rather than on an area of study or a discipline.) This was to be no antebellum college. To Barnard, a college education was "of little value except for the professions," and he underlined the importance to the public at large of the "natural and applied sciences"—an orientation entirely consistent with the stance of the Whig antebellum entrepreneurs. Thus, it is clear that he accepted the traditional definition of the professions, one of which teaching did not seem to be, and at the same time, he broadened the definition and scope of higher education. The plan scarcely addressed the organization and curriculum of the university, with merely an undetailed entry titled "Facilities" and a cursory mention under "Modes of Instruction" that lectures should be both "directory and suggestive."[20]

Cause and effect are never easy to trace, and it is impossible to document that Lathrop received Barnard's plan. But in 1858 the Chancellor reorganized the University into twelve departments, rather than the four he had proposed, in a step which was highly unpopular with some faculty members. Then in the same year Henry Barnard was chosen to succeed Lathrop as Chancellor of the University of Wisconsin. The trustees who selected him must have had some idea what his views were.

The tender of the offer from Wisconsin reveals much about the net-

19. Curti and Carstensen, *Wisconsin*, 72–75.
20. Plan Submitted to Chancellor Lathrop (notes in Barnard's characteristic method of listing), NYU. At the 1855 AAAE several papers on scientific subjects were read, all of

work of educational reformers and about the rudimentary nature of institutional organization in mid-century. The idea may have originated with Daniel Read, now the Normal Professor at Wisconsin. "This is my second attempt to bring you where you ought to be," he wrote to Barnard. Another professor, seeking names for a replacement for Lathrop, had received Henry Barnard's from both Benjamin Silliman and Francis Wayland to whom he had written. Barnard's most persistent and aggressive supporter was Lyman C. Draper. Draper was almost a carbon copy of Barnard, the state superintendent of schools and, in addition, the secretary of the State Historical Society; in that capacity he had corresponded with Barnard, receiving from him, in 1854, "a box of documents." Upon the passage of the Normal School law in 1857, Draper became the secretary to the Board of Regents of the Normal Schools, thus sitting in the identical seats as had his Connecticut friend. Lyman Draper looked to Barnard as Barnard had looked to Mann, for in one letter he pledged that he felt "like deferring" to the more experienced man "in almost everything."[21]

Both Lathrop, the Chancellor, and Lyman, the schoolman, wooed Henry Barnard during the summer of 1858, although neither knew what the other was up to. In August Barnard received notice that he had been elected Chancellor, "with special institutional duties in the Normal Department," but at that time he was only in communications with "members of a Normal Board . . . and the Superintendent of Public Instruction . . . looking for a larger plan of operations for the professional instruction of teachers."[22] It is clear from the correspondence that the two positions were never considered as one, although Barnard initially may have intended to attempt to combine them, as he had the principalship and the superintendency in Connecticut. He was to be hired by two separate boards, was to report to each board independently, and he was to inherit two sets of problems.

In his usual cautious fashion, Barnard vacillated, although his former

which Barnard subsequently printed; see *AJE* I, ii (January 1856): 175–85, and iii (March 1856): 269–84, for F.A.P. Barnard's address "On Improvements Practical in American Colleges."

21. Letter to Draper, April 9, 1854, Wisconsin Historical Society (hereafter WHS); from Draper, August 3, 1859, NYU. Draper certainly was cut from the same cloth as Barnard. He introduced his *Tenth Annual Report* (1858) with references to Saxon and Norman education and the history of the passage of the Northwest Ordinance, and he referred to the social conditions of England and what Plato paid for books; see 33–97.

22. Letter to Gilman, August 4, 1858, the Johns Hopkins University Library (hereafter JHU). Curti and Carstensen, *Wisconsin*, III, say that Barnard received 8 votes, Mann 1 and Carr 1.

subordinate, John Philbrick, immediately sent congratulations on the new job. Lathrop wanted the new chancellor to be present at the meeting of the Board of Regents at the end of the month of August—a session scheduled to coincide with the state fair—and the chairman of the Regents of the Normal Schools urged Barnard to arrive for an interview at the September 1 meeting of that board. The news that he had been displaced as the main outdoor speaker at the fair by Cassius Clay may have miffed Barnard, or he may have been preoccupied with his *Journal*; in any case, it was not until late September that he wrote Draper that he planned to arrive in Madison on October 4 for "a tour of observation and inquiry." He attended the meeting of the Normal School Regents and was unanimously elected their agent the following day. Although he had not yet accepted the position, he did agree to prepare a plan of operations, one which has not survived if it existed. He also delivered an address at the city hall which, according to one who was present, revealed an "appreciation" of the importance of "teaching the industrial population in the practical sciences" (an odd message for rural Wisconsin) but "surprisingly denied to women just claim to an equal share in the educational patronage." Nonetheless, the *Wisconsin Journal of Education* exalted. If Mr. Barnard were to accept the responsibilities extended him, Wisconsin could look forward "with confidence to the day not distant, when she shall stand in the front rank in all that pertains to an enlarged, sound, thorough and universal system of education."[23]

Barnard returned East in November, leaving an uneasy Draper who sent "on behalf of the University, Normal and Common Schools of Wisconsin, the Macedonian cry—'Come over and help us.'" Others, including John T. Clark, the chairman of the University Regents, pressed for a response. Barnard wrote privately to Draper, "*My own mind is made up in the affirmative,*" but he claimed that some people in Connecticut still wanted to talk to him, about what he did not explain. Shortly afterwards he gave his answer, which was yes, and wrote again to Draper "I will do anything you say, for you and the cause, including the Historical Society." John Clark was relieved. He announced the appointment "to public delight," he reported, and he located a house for the Barnards that was "available cheap."[24]

23. *Wisconsin Journal of Education* (hereafter *WJE*) III, 5 (November 1858): 146. The editor, Craig, was not totally enamored with the appointment, perhaps because he saw Draper as his rival, and he refused to print a portrait of Henry Barnard in the *Journal* when Draper requested he do so.

24. Letters to Draper, September 6, October 12, November 5, December 3, 1858, WHS; letters from Philbrick, October 12, 13; from Draper, October 30, November 11; from Clark,

Henry Barnard had always abhorred controversy, personally and phil-osophically, yet he accepted the Wisconsin appointment despite clear dan-ger signals which were very similiar to the ones that may have deterred him earlier from agreeing to go to Indiana. The university was new and struggling, facing opposition from the smaller, denominational colleges, and from some of the populace who viewed it as an expensive luxury which did not properly serve the real needs of the state—all these feel-ings were exacerbated by financial insecurity stemming from the panic of 1857. Although Draper sensed that the newly elected legislature was favor-ably disposed to educational initiatives and to the university, it needed to be cultivated and coddled. The faculty was split, with two members attack-ing Lathrop for his insufficient support of science and failure to maintain high standards, and another protesting his own dismissal as professor of modern languages due to his inadequate command of German. All of the professors were terminated in the summer of 1858 in order to give the in-coming chancellor a free hand, and all peppered him with letters of advice, and spite.

Lathrop, weary from his ten years' labor on behalf of the fledgling university, wanted only to teach, but he promised his support and urged Barnard to hasten out to Wisconsin to meet the professors and the all-important legislature, and he warned of "disorganizing influences . . . likely to awaken into activity which might have been kept in quiet slum-ber by your presence." He recommended Daniel Read as a strong arm to lean upon, especially in those times when Barnard's other duties would require him to be absent from Madison.[25] (Wisconsin seemed to have accepted Barnard on his own terms.) To Lathrop one of the possibly disruptive influences was Ezra Carr, an advocate of scientific and technical education, and an ally of Draper's; but Carr claimed in a letter to Barnard that the "whole tenor of Lathrop's course is to give the impression that your connection with us would be nominal and temporary." In addition to the internal problems of the university, there was the matter of the sectarian colleges which looked to Barnard, in his capacity as the Normal

August 25, September 16, November 15, 27, December 3; from Read, September 3, 13, October 8 (a letter of introduction to the governor of Minnesota; Barnard was on a lecture swing); from Lathrop, September 1, 4; from Carr, December 22; of all of the letters the one from Alfred L. Castleman, a regent, November 22, was the most helpful—he summarized that Barnard's acceptance would "allay all ill feeling." *CCSJ* VI, i (January 1859): 30, noted Barnard's acceptance: "We hope his health and strength will prove sufficient for his large and comprehensive scheme of educational improvement in that state."

25. Read remained a friend of Barnard's after the Wisconsin days; there is a moving letter, November 21, 1867, NYU, in which he describes his losses from the Civil War—two brothers killed, one at sea, and a son lost at Appomattox.

agent, for support against the encroaching university, of which he was now the head. Their natural allies were the teachers, led by Albert Pickett of the State Teachers' Association who saw the University as "a circle of its own" and the Normal Department as dangerously independent. Against such formidable foes the current state superintendent of schools had little power, but Barnard, in Pickett's view, could change all that.[26]

Finally there was the matter of expectations. Wisconsin's welcome to Henry Barnard was orchestrated by Lyman Draper who proclaimed Barnard's "advent" as the "most important event that had ever occurred in our educational history."

> We shall best honor ourselves, and bless our State, by listening confidently to, and promptly carrying into effect, whatever suggestions and advice such a man as Henry Barnard, in his ripe experience, and noble devotion to the good of his race, may deem it his duty to offer upon matters pertaining to the great cause of popular education in Wisconsin.

The editor of the *Wisconsin Journal of Education* published a laudatory biography of Barnard, taken from the *Massachusetts Teacher* which included the effusive summary that Henry Barnard "had done more than any other man to shape the educational policy of the nation." The Wisconsin teachers, for their part, passed a resolution at their Seventh Annual meeting: "That we hail the advent of the Honorable Henry Barnard among us, and pledge him our hearty co-operation in his labors in behalf of our Common Schools."[27]

Barnard's advent may have been hailed, but few knew precisely what to expect, and many surmised. The new Chancellor responded quite sharply to Carr that no one was entitled to speak for him until he arrived except to address some general points, which he proceeded to outline. He was determined to make the University *"felt in the educational movements of the state,"* and he intended to develop its "external life" in an effort to meet the needs of the population, while at the same time maintaining collegiate education; he expected the high schools and academies to serve as preparatory institutions, rather than making the University the "State High School." Support for the university should come from the legislature, augmented by private donations, and the legislature should fund a

26. Letters from Lathrop, November 26, December 29, 1858, January 28, 1859; from Carr, December 22, 1858; from Pickett, November 22, 1858; NYU. Carr marked his letter confidential but said that Draper had read it.

27. *Tenth Annual Report* (1858), 115. The vocabulary and the images used by Draper are those of the earlier, eastern reformers. *WJE* III, 8 (February 1859): 225–30, IV, 2 (August 1859): 55. The phrase was surprising considering the source.

Polytechnic Department rather than creating another institution. And last, as the "great work toward which" he would at first "bend" all his energies, the University should provide good teachers for the schools of the state.[28] Barnard had no intention of replicating the Yale of his youth. As a life-long proponent of gradation in schools, he saw the university as the highest step in the system of public education, freed from the job which properly belonged to the high schools; as a fervent supporter of community-wide education, he could easily accept the University's role in what would become an extension service; and as a convert to the importance of science and technology, he was ready to redefine the traditional college to include technological as well as professional education. In short, as early as 1858, Henry Barnard anticipated the modern public university in all but its research capacity.[29]

Barnard also let Carr know that he was aware of the rumors about the strength of his commitment to his new position.

> I give no assurances as to my stay—once in harness I shall not voluntarily put it off, but as I have no motive at my time of life to fight a doubtful battle, I shall not stay an hour if I am satisfied that the work can be better done by any other.

He vowed to remain as long as he was useful, and he predicted that at least five years would be necessary to effect the changes he recommended. But he had never stayed anywhere for five years.

The new Chancellor wrote to Draper in a different, and more tentative, vein, and gave a hint of potential conflict between his two roles. On the one hand he opposed the granting of scholarships for future teachers to local and denominational colleges, preferring to reserve such assistance for the university, and particularly for the agriculture and normal schools; here the Chancellor spoke. But the Normal School agent insisted that his

> anxiety was to be made known to the people and the teachers of Wisconsin in my *public school* antecedents and with the estimation in which I am held for my lifelong labors in that department of the educational field.

There was consistency here, in Barnard's proposal that the University occupy an exclusive position at the apex of the state's system, but there was also a suggestion of obduracy and a lack of sensitivity to the political

---

28. Letter to Carr, December 27, 1858, NYU; draft TC.

29. At least one colleague recognized Barnard's innovative ideas; on December 4, 1866, Andrew D. White, recently elected to head the new Cornell, wrote, "I have believed and still believe" that "you are the man . . . You are master of the plan we need."

realities in Wisconsin. Still he worried to Draper. "I will try to deserve
your good opinion . . . but I fear you and other friends entertain too
favorable ideas if my power to be useful." He may even have heeded the
warning which his cousin, and fellow university president, F. A. P. Barnard sent along with his congratulations:

> I wish you all manner of success in Wisconsin. Indeed I predict for
> you there a splendid career, and results worthy of any man's ambi-
> tion. But you will have a heavy labor to go through before you
> reach them. Perhaps you are not much to be commiserated on that
> account; for I don't think you will be happy any where without a
> heavy labor on your hands.[30]

Unfortunately, Wisconsin had to wait for its salvation. "I am afraid my
health will break down under the pressure of this month" wrote the new
appointee, and later he complained that he had "too many irons in the
fire"—the March issue of his *Journal*, a volume promised for the Ohio
State Library on educational biography, a report on normal schools and
teachers' institutes, and as many as ten letters a day to answer.[31] Still the
bulk of the letters to him during the winter dealt with state and university
business, a number concerning plans for his inauguration as chancellor.
The date was set for February 8, and an elaborate ceremony was planned,
one which included an impressive procession of officials, including the
governor. But references to his health crept more and more into his letters
and on February 1, Josephine Barnard wrote Draper that Dr. Barnard was
very ill, in bed with pneumonia.

Barnard was without a doubt sick for most of the month, a fact which
caused concern among his friends in the East and his colleagues in the
West. Draper was disheartened, for the delay would put the common
school movement "a year behind" if Barnard could not arrive before the
legislature adjourned, and Lathrop concurred. Both urged some action
on Barnard's part, and he did dispatch George Emerson and William
Baker to act as agents on his behalf in normal school matters. He was well
enough on February 17 to write a detailed letter to Draper as proof of his
"good will, his returning strength." He admitted that his *Report* to the
Regents was not finished, but he projected that when it was it would be a
document of 350 pages, covering education in the states and other
countries—scarcely what the Board expected. As far as action was con-

30. Letter to Draper, January 14, 1859, WHS; from F. A. P. Barnard, January 15, 1859,
NYU.
31. Letters to Draper, December 3, 26, 1858, WHS; typically Barnard quantified his
obligations: 500 pages for the biographical work, 400 for the one on normal schools.

cerned, the only "essential" part of his plan was legislation, "absolutely necessary," to procure funds for agents who would examine teachers and instruct in institutes, and a Normal School. He also hoped for legislation limiting the number of officials responsible for schooling and for a library law which would include funds for itinerant lecturers. Still, for the most part, he brushed aside Draper's conscientious reports and his pleas for advice and assistance, and he ignored for over a month a request for a letter in support of the library bill. When he did respond, he was critical: "I notice one or two errors . . . in your Report which I will note."[32]

Despite his sickness, Barnard managed to correspond extensively during this time about his *Journal*, and the March issue appeared on time, or at least before mid-April. Then he took a trip South for recuperation, visiting in Georgia and Alabama, and stopping in Washington on the way back.[33] At last, in April Barnard was ready to take up his baton. His letters became businesslike, he looked for a suitable house, and by June he was in Madison ready for battle on all fronts. He composed an inquiry to the members of the faculty of the university:

> That I may act advisedly in my present office, and that we may co-operate efficiently with each other in our several allotments of administration and instruction, I respectfully ask a written communication from you in reply to the following queries which I shall address to each member of the Faculty.

His "queries" fell into four categories; he wanted a summary of the curriculum in each area, and of the "apparatus" employed in instruction, a list of the "desires and suggestions" of each member, and anything on the "physical training, social habits and moral culture" of the students. His clear intent was to survey the condition of the university as he had surveyed Connecticut and Rhode Island. All of the members of the faculty respectfully replied, and the response of Ezra Carr was representative: thoughtful, detailed, emphasizing the vital importance of the sciences (especially "practical and analytical chemistry"), and ambitious; he argued for a new curriculum, in which the Agricultural Department was "second only to the Normal Department in importance," against the older, "colle-

---

32. Letter from Josephine Barnard, February 1; from Barnard, February 17, March 22, 25; WHS; from Draper, January 27, 28, February 5, 14, March 1, 17, 18, 21, 27; from Lathrop, February 26; from Baker, who found Madison "ornate" with its "wide-spreading elms"; from Philbrick to J. Barnard, February 8; from Thayer, February 24; from Dixon, March 16; from Sears, April 13; all 1859, NYU. *WJE* III, 8 (March 1859), noted Barnard's illness and convalescence and regretted his absence during the legislative session.

33. Letters from Dixon, March 16; from Sears, noting the March issue, April 13; 1859, NYU.

giate" one, and for extensive, additional, support. In Carr's view most of the state's residents saw the University as too focused on the preparation of an elite for the professions, and the private colleges opposed the faculty as "fossil men." What was required was a "laboratory man" who would offer courses similar to those at Yale and who could also act as an agricultural agent.

On the surface it would appear that the Chancellor had a valuable ally in Carr, for he professed total agreement with Carr's advocacy of science and practical methods. Barnard had begun negotiations with David Boswell Reid, of New York (and the author of a book on ventilation), in January, and by June Reid had accepted a new position as Professor of Physics and Hygiene and Director of the Museum of Practical Science. Carr, who was urging an appointment in science, thought that Reid's appointment might be "problematic" with other members of the faculty, for he and Barnard had a different interpretation of the role of science in the university. Barnard saw Reid as a a popularizer, a teacher of teachers of science, almost in the Lyceum tradition, and the new museum much like the famous Barnum one, whereas Carr envisioned a department of applied science with responsibilities to the greater Wisconsin community.[34] Where the two men agreed was in the importance they gave to the Normal School within the University, and there, of course, Barnard had opponents in another quarter.

The Chancellor had been in the state for nearly a month before he was officially appointed in his second capacity. On June 22 the Board of Regents of the Normal School invested him as their agent, specifying his duties: he was directed to conduct Institutes, to deliver addresses in support of the public schools, and to hire such assistants as he deemed necessary. His overall responsibility was to supervise the normal departments in the colleges and academies and high schools, a duty which not only would compete with those of his other position, but which ran counter to his vision of a unified system of education.

The Regents of the University confirmed his appointment as Chancellor the same day at a session during which he delivered his plan for the institution's development. He recommended that the preparatory department be disbanded, and that the high schools in each large town be charged with that responsibility. The first two years of the university

34. Letters from Carr, June 13, July 5; from Reid, January 17, June 9, 12, 17, 18, 22, 23, 29, July 15, 22, August 3, 10, 1859, NYU. Reid wrote "You are the first chancellor of any university, so far as I am aware, who had combined the different object contemplated by this chair." Letter from L. P. Brockett, July 30, 1861, NYU, described Reid's accomplishments.

should constitute a general course in which modern languages would be considered equal to the ancient ones; the University would be divided into the Schools of Education, Law, Medicine, Agriculture, Mining, Engineering, and Commerce, where students would concentrate their study in their final years; and the Normal Department would stand "as the crowning feature of the state system of the professional training of teachers." A cohesive plan indeed, and one which combined liberal and professional education. The only disappointment for the Regents must have been the fact that it virtually replicated Lathrop's agenda of the preceding year. Barnard also stipulated that he would not be required to teach, an exception unique among contemporary presidents, and that he could act as the agent for the Normal Schools.[35]

A joint committee of the two boards set his salary at $1,750 for the chancellorship and $1,250 as agent, the total amount identical with what he had received in his previous positions. Barnard was probably content with the amount, which was not significantly less than the norm, for he made no complaint, but he was "sorely disappointed and troubled" at the paltry $250 allocated for the expenses of the institutes. "The sum is altogether inadequate for the accomplishment of any large or immediate results, which you or the friends of common school advancement . . . expect." As he had been authorized to employ subordinates, he wanted to hire Baker for at least a period of six months, a sum the money from the Regents would not cover, and which he could not pay.[36]

Apparently Barnard then made a quick trip back East, for Draper wrote to him in Hartford, and John Philbrick expected him to address an institute in Massachusetts. But he returned to Madison for his inauguration on July 27, an celebration which was not as spectacular as Lathrop and Draper had originally planned. The conjunction of the event with the annual meeting of the State Teachers' Association signaled who were Barnard's true allies.[37] The Chancellor's inaugural address, according to a reporter, "was characteristic of the man, giving in earnest, eloquent language, broad and comprehensive views of education . . . pervaded all through by strong common sense" and a very pragmatic approach "to the particular circumstances" in the state. Barnard's specific recommendations reiterated his conception of the University. He urged instruction in arts and sciences, and their application to health and industry, "as a cardinal object of the educational policy of the State," on an equal footing

35. *AJE* XVII, 1 (September 1867): 755–56.

36. *WJE* IV, i (July 1859): 20–21, 24–25; ii (August 1859): 61–62; letter to Draper, June 23 (marked private). See Curti and Carstensen, *Wisconsin*, 163–70.

37. Barnard also lectured to the teachers, explaining what he hoped to accomplish through a series of lectures and teachers' institutes; see *AJE* XIV, xxxv (June 1864): 387ff.

with instruction in languages and mathematics. Innovations in curricula, such as the introduction of the study of drawing and physiology, and in methodology, such as the use of observation and experimentation, should be implemented at every grade, and all public high schools, academies, colleges, and Normal classes should aim to prepare for "a thorough scientific course" at the University or at a special Polytechnical School. Coordinated with formal schools would be a Museum of Practical Science and local museums of Fine and Industrial Arts, all of which would provide lectures for youth and adults.[38] One regrets that the entire speech does not survive. Some of the recommendations, such as for the introduction of drawing, are mere repetitions of ones made for the common schools, and Barnard offered few specifics for the curriculum of the University other than his espousal of modern languages and a scientific thrust. Here his emphasis on the applicability of higher learning to "health and industry" reflected again the pragmatism of reformer-entrepreneurial contemporaries. What interested him most, as it always had, were matters of structure. By 1859 he had combined two of his constant visions; one was of the necessity of providing community-wide opportunities for life-long learning, and dated from his earliest Connecticut years; the other was of an articulated and centralized system of schools, such as he had advanced in Rhode Island, but here to be capped, by a state university. This horizontal and vertical model was a plausible one, a neat and efficient one, and one which would require tenacity and political sensitivity and skill to implement—traits not Henry Barnard's strong points.

By his own admission Barnard was "obliged" to be absent from Wisconsin for all of the month of August, but he did not shirk his duties. The day after his inauguration he issued a call for teachers' institutes, promising to conduct as many as he could attend or staff.[39] He laid down certain conditions: attendance of at least thirty had to be guaranteed, and local committees had to make all of the arrangements, procuring suitable accommodations for the participants as well as free halls for the daily sessions and evening addresses. In other words, the agent was to be held responsible only for scheduling and securing the instructors, and he worked hard on that task. John Philbrick said he was too pressured but suggested William Alcott who "would like to be an educational missionary in his declining years—can you use him?" Unfortunately Alcott died

---

38. Letter from Draper to Hartford, July 2; from Philbrick, June 21, 1859, NYU. *WJE* IV, i (July 1859): 31; ii (August 1859): 61–62; the account of the inaugural was in "Educational Miscellany," and no full version of the speech was printed.

39. *WJE* IV, ii (August 1859): 59; reminder in iii (September 1859): 89. Barnard did deliver the baccalaureate address in the fall of 1859; he urged the graduates: "Be men. Bear in mind that nothing worth having in this world was ever got without a struggle."

before Barnard could respond. Moses Brown (in Toledo) could not come, Asa Lord declined for unspecified political reasons, and Thomas Beecher and Lorin Andrews said no; Charles Hovey would come from Illinois for a week, and Charles Northend was anxious to help, if Barnard and he could agree on his duties and compensation, and if David Camp would release him from his teaching in New Britain.

In truth, the old order was passing, and Barnard found that he had to turn to a new generation of schoolmen such as Hovey and Northend. In August he wrote to James Wickersham (of Pennsylvania) to inquire about the Allen brothers, one of whom he had recently met at the annual meeting of the normal schools in Trenton. Wickersham recommended Fordyce Allen, who, although he "wants *thoroughness* and *system*," gave an inspiring talk and ran an institute efficiently. A second source saw Charles Allen as the better classroom teacher but urged Barnard to hire both brothers. The Allens were the proprietors of a Pennsylvania normal establishment and were available for "instituting" for six weeks in the fall, as was John Ogden, another normal teacher from the Quaker state.[40] Institutes were changing in a subtle way. Although still designed, in part, to arouse the general citizenry in the evening lectures, they were evolving more and more into professional gatherings. Francis Russell had been something of an itinerating instituter, and of course William Baker had originated the role, but Camp, Hovey, Northend and the Allens were well-established teachers who viewed instruction in institutes as a professional responsibility rather than a missionary endeavor. Barnard was forced by necessity to recognize this shift, but his role in the institutes remained that of the prophet.

The fall institutes were highly successful despite some administrative mishaps, such as last minute changes in dates, and John Rickard's insistence on charging admission for an institute at his academy. Henry Barnard provided "general direction" and managed to speak at thirteen of the fourteen gatherings. Two institutes were scheduled for the same week, yet he opened the one at Elkhorn with an address on Public Education and managed to be in Sheboygan two days later where his appearance caused "a rainbow of smiles" to "arch" the schoolroom; his remarks, on the dire lack of uniformity in texts, the cost to the community of irregular school attendance, and the lack of gradation, "fully sustained" his reputa-

40. Letters from Philbrick, March 29, 31, June 21; from Hovey, June 25, July 27, October 3; from Brown, June 27; from Lord, July 2; from Beecher, July 5; from Andrews, July 11; from Northend, June 30, September 4, October 1; all 1859, NYU. Barnard had written Philbrick in a naval metaphor, hinting at his administrative style; he liked "a well disciplined crew and a good captain"; Philbrick suggested that he might be a midshipman or a gunner—"I rather like shooting."

tion. At Waupan and at Mineral Point he delivered an "exceedingly practical" lecture, whereas at Beloit, "in one of his stirring and powerful appeals to the *educated* and *educating* public," he asked his listeners to "rescue the common schools, the foundation and feeders to the Colleges and the University." Here he was being both politic and polite; his host was his former classmate, the president of Beloit College. Fittingly, the final institute was held at Madison in the third week of November. In his address, the Agent and Chancellor summarized the fall accomplishments: 1,500 teachers and "future" teachers had attended the week-long sessions; 500 families and 10,000 individuals had heard the evening lectures; 12,000 schools would thus be improved—he did not specify how he arrived at this total. Each of the institutes had had a "two-fold" character, "reaching at once the teacher and the community, the school and the homes, thus making the work both broader and more permanent."[41]

Barnard seemed to relish his work, writing to Gilman "I wish you was here to share the excitement."[42] Gilman was not the only one he tried to entice to join him in Madison; F. A. P. Barnard got as far as to inquire, "What would be my position and pay?"[43] It is difficult, however, to discern just what Henry Barnard did for the university. He published an announcement that instruction "in the history and principles of education and classification, teaching and discipline of schools, will be given by the Chancellor" despite the agreement that he would not be required to teach, but there is no evidence that he ever delivered any instruction. He followed up his hiring of David Reid by proposing to build, by private subscription, a building "devoted to the promotion of science among the whole population," where exhibits would be housed and public lectures offered. In the public announcement he listed eighteen topics for the series, commencing with one on "The resources of science in ameliorating the moral, social, and physical condition of man. His imperfections . . . The new Institution: Public Objects to which it may be devoted." Surely these are more Barnard's notes for a lecture more than a title for

41. Letters from Pickett, August 4, September 14, 22, October 1, 2; from Craig, August 25, October 16, 19; *WJE* IV, v (November 1859): 155–56; vi (December 1859): 169ff.; vii (January 1860): 204ff. When Barnard spoke at Beloit he addressed an institute headed by A. S. Chapin, an old friend and now the president of Beloit college, hence his inclusion of the colleges in his remarks. Barnard's statistics came from a questionnaire which was distributed at each institute, a source of massive and fascinating information; see summary in *WJE* IV, vii (January 1860); 992 completed the forms, of the 1,425 registered, and 737 of the respondents were between the ages of 16 and 18.

42. Letter to Gilman, October 29, 1859, JHU.

43. Letters from F. A. P. Barnard, June 17 (in which he described rules for attendance and examinations at the University of Mississippi), 25, 28, July 16, October 10, 20, November 17, December 19, 1859, NYU.

one, and just as surely he expected to be the lecturer. Maybe he intended to deliver the entire series; topics 4–7 focused on ventilation—or perhaps Reid was to give those.[44]

Barnard had been appointed by the Regents in part because they wanted a strong hand on the helm, and there is some evidence that he did attempt to establish tighter control over the operations of the university. It was probably at his suggestion that the Regents decreed that no professor could order any supplies without an authorization from the Chancellor or the president of the faculty. Curti and Carstensen suggest, however, that he failed to stem the excessive building costs during his brief tenure as Chancellor. And then there was the odd affair of the stable—or cowshed according to some. During renovation of the boarding hall, and in an effort to beautify the grounds, workmen tore down a structure which either belonged to or was used by Ezra Carr; Carr, in a fury, telegraphed to Barnard, who was on the road; the foreman subsequently apologized to Barnard, assuring him that he had never had any intention of usurping his authority or harming Carr; he claimed that Carr was just being "Carrish and dishonest." Another vexing matter was what to do about J. L. Pickard who had been removed from his faculty chair of modern languages because of his inadequate German; in a number of letters Pickard insisted that his German had been perfectly comprehended when he employed it in a local shop.[45] Such petty annoyances are the only evidence that survives among Barnard's letters for his activities on behalf of the university.

He was far more active as the normal agent, both before and after he went back East in February 1860, due to the illness and death of his youngest daughter.[46] He attended the November meeting of the Board of Regents of the Normal School where he delivered his oral report and outlined his plans for future operations. He emphasized that he had attempted a great deal,

> much of it novel, all of it important, touching many interests, institutions, and individuals, spread over a large amount of territory, and in a period of time, not long, even if the whole of it could have

44. *WJE* IV, iii (September 1859): 88; Circular, NYU, and in *WJE* IV, v (November 1859): 158–59.

45. Resolution, Executive Committee of the Board of Regents, October 8, 1859; letter from Tenney, October 8; see Curti and Carstensen, *Wisconsin*, 114–15 on Pickard, and letters from Pickard, December 24, 1859, and July 2, 14, 1860, NYU.

46. The child was ill during February, for there are a number of letters expressing concern, and she died before the end of the month. The cause was probably whooping cough, for Barnard's cousin, M.L. Seymour reported in March that the "whoops were much feebler"; letter from Hartford, March 30, 1860, NYU.

been devoted to the work, but largely abridged by a period of severe illness.

He summarized the institutes and recommended the creation of a well-equipped normal school as "unquestionably the most direct and efficient instrumentality" for the training of teachers. The staff of such a school could serve in a dual capacity, conducting institutes and examining teachers when not occupied in their professorial duties—the Connecticut pattern.[47] (Barnard never admitted that such a school would immediately run into head-on collision with the private normal schools or departments in the colleges.) Oddly, this compulsive planner ignored other obligations. He had not yet drawn up the regulations for the selection and purchase of the books for the school libraries authorized by the preceding legislature nor had he developed recommendations for revisions in the school law as directed; both tasks were natural ones for Barnard, similar to ones he had already completed in other states, but he never set to work on either one.

Barnard did not attend either of the two county Teachers' Associations held in March, and he exercised only very "general direction" over the spring institutes, although he delivered an oral report at the Annual Meeting of the Normal School Regents. He detailed his activities in the previous year, the institutes, the results of the eighteen examinations of normal classes (one suspects he did not conduct many of these), and he outlined plans for future institutes. On his suggestion, the Board passed three resolutions: an applicant to any normal class was required to pass a written examination for entrance; no student could continue in a normal class for more than two or three years without passing another examination; and the Agent could employ an assistant for the examination of normal schools. The Agent was also requested "to draw out details of a system of Teachers' Certificates to be issued by the Board" for the next meeting.[48] The Board was slowly moving in the direction of standardization, under the guidance of the man who had instituted similar measures in Rhode Island.

Barnard had not been able to attend the January meeting of the University Regents, and he had no plan to present to them at their February meeting. Optimistically, it was announced in March that the Chancellor was "actively engaged in his duties," but this was a pious hope. His sup-

47. *AJE* VIII, xxi (June 1860): 673–78; *WJE* IV, vi (December 1860): 185; letters from Chapman, November 1, December 5 (Chapman had to nag Barnard to write up the report); from Allen, December 24 (he also refers to the Normal report); from Ogden, November 24 (he had been inspecting schools); from Baker, December 1, 5; 1859, NYU.

48. WJE, IV, 9 (March, 1860), ll, (May, 1860).

porters claimed that "he will endeavor, as far as circumstances will permit, to make the influence of the University felt, as a living, active agency
in our educational system," and for a time he did seem to be interested in
university affairs. From Andrew D. White he received a detailed account
of the improvements Henry Tappan had effected at the University of
Michigan, and one assumes he intended to replicate them; he also tried
again to entice Lorin Andrews and F. A. P. Barnard, to join the faculty in
Wisconsin, and he attempted to establish a chapter of Phi Beta Kappa.
But by May he had returned to Hartford. James Butler wrote him frequent, chatty letters about the state of things in Madison, as if Barnard
was merely away for a holiday, but the Chancellor was that in name only,
and in June he submitted his resignation. For some inexplicable reasons,
the Regents were unwilling to accept it. They dispatched an emissary,
Carl Schurz, who was campaigning for Lincoln in the East, to meet with
the recalcitrant Barnard, they besought him to write up a plan of reorganization, and they begged for him to "assume decisively the responsibility" of dealing with the faculty. Barnard toyed with the idea of going out
to Wisconsin in August, and in January some of his supporters were still
clinging to the hope that he would return to the state. He did not, and
the Regents finally bowed to fate, and accepted his departure.[49]

The story of Henry Barnard's service in Wisconsin is an odd one. He
came amid welcoming trumpets, and he left to muted farewells. His
ardent supporters would later speak of the "steady advance in education"
and the "gratifying success" of the institutes, and he did energize the
nascent teacher preparation movement. The representative of the teachers
was almost wistful:

> Much had been anticipated from the labors of a man so widely
> known and so deservedly respected as Dr. Barnard. Much has
> already been done. Sickness has checked, but, I trust, not entirely
> ended his work with us.[50]

The Regents and, one assumes, the faculty, on the other hand, felt
betrayed, and back precisely where they were two years before. One newspaper called him a "humbug," and as late as 1867 James Butler would

---

49. *WJE* IV, ix (March 1860): 297, "Educational Miscellany"; Resolution of the Board,
July 12, refusing to accept the resignation. Letters from White, February 2; from Andrews,
March 14; from Lathrop, April 24; from Butler, May 27, June 3, July 12, 20; from J. L.
Pickard, June 26, 29; from Hall, August 20; all 1860; from Sterling, January 2; from
Philbrick, February 12; 1861; NYU. Philbrick responded to Barnard's plea of ill health,
"You have already done a life's work & after a 'vacation' I trust you will come up as good
as new."

50. *Twelfth Annual Report*, 1860.

write to the former chancellor that "[m]en have not been wanting all over this state who have bitterly derided your career here."[51] Barnard, of course, took no blame upon himself. His plans, "much larger even than have yet been realized," had been severely crippled, he later said, by inadequate resources which were less than half what he had been promised; in the end he had had to relinquish his position "in consequences of a severe illness which was followed by a prolonged physical prostration." This was Barnard's own report, but written in the third person, eight years later. He was not easy with the denouement of his first presidency, and even in 1874 he was still striving to set the record straight. He wrote to Draper that before his health had again broken down three years before he had intended to publish his ideas on higher education "embracing what I aimed to do in Wisconsin." If he ever completed his version, he promised to send it to the Wisconsin Historical Society, "for I know that my projected work for Wisconsin is not appreciated or even known."[52]

Glimpses of creative ideas appeared in Barnard's letters, and from his acquaintance with national educational leaders, he had access to a variety of proposed innovations. He had every opportunity to implement them —the willing and enthusiastic cooperation of two governing boards, a receptive audience, and early success. But from the very commencement of his abbreviated career in Wisconsin, he and his employers had different conceptions of his role. He was hired first and primarily as Chancellor of the University, for which he had no relevant experience and little preference; he saw his responsibility as primarily for the "professional" preparation of teachers, as he had written Gilman, and he devoted most of his energies to that task.[53] That was what he knew how to do. Had he been more flexible, and had he remained longer on the job, he might have created a different model for the organization of education within the state, one in which all facets were integrated, from the primary to the tertiary level, the liberal and the professional, in a system in which the university stood at the head, but never divorced from other forms of further education. In his brief tenure, however, most of his innovations and suggestions about the University were derivative, and he lacked the skills, and energy, necessary to implement them. Certainly there were obvious contributing factors, family tragedy and his own health, but more significant were his personal failings. Once again, Barnard had wanted a job but had shrunk from the responsibility, had sketched in broad outline challenging suggestions which clearly resonated with those who

51. Jorgenson, *Public Education*, 176–77; letter from Butler, April 12, 1867, NYU.
52. Letters to Draper, June 27, 1874, May 9, 1876, WHS.
53. *AJE* XVII, i (September 1868): 755–56.

employed him but had failed to attend to the details of implementation.

Even the excuse of poor health is suspect, for during his time in Wisconsin Barnard published four of the five volumes of the second series of his *Journal* (six through nine), and his correspondence during those years was predominantly concerned with his publication. His colleagues did not seem to mind; rather they felt that the national periodical lent reflected glory to the state. The serial volumes were consistently of a high quality, and they appeared with regularity, twice a year during this period. From notations on Barnard's surviving letters, it is apparent that his editorial assistant, Frederick Perkins, handled much of the work of preparing the materials, but nonetheless the selection of the authors and of the topics was Barnard's; Perkins was little more than a secretary or a stand-in when his editor was away. And, unlike the Connecticut and Rhode Island predecessors, this journal was truly national in scope, although oddly, aside from one entry under Miscellany in the June 1869 number, there is no mention of Wisconsin or educational developments in that state.[54] Barnard kept his two careers entirely separate.

Whenever Barnard had served as an editor, he had always intended to parallel the publication of a journal with the creation of a Library of Education designed to create a literature for teachers. He realized this ambition in the Wisconsin years. The first two volumes of his *Papers for the Teacher* were published in 1859 and 1860. In his introduction to the first volume, which he signed as Agent of the Regents of the Normal School, Barnard proposed to issue an annual document which would summarize the proceedings of the year's Teachers' Institutes and any other papers "worthy of study and preservation by the Teachers of Wisconsin"; the length, choice of subjects, and the style would "depend on his discretion." In other words, the *Papers* were to serve as professional materials, similar to yearbooks.[55] Both of the first two volumes did contain selections bound to be of interest to the teacher, the first being more of a course in the foundations of education, with lofty-minded, almost paternalistic sermons from William Russell, Thomas Hill, and Gideon Thayer, and the second more methodological, although based entirely on material from Great Britain. Missing from each of these works is any reference

54. *AJE* VIII, xxi (June 1860): 673–79, "Extracts from Report to the Board of Regents of the Normal Schools in Wisconsin."

55. *Papers for the Teacher*, Number One, 1859 (New York, 1860); there was no subtitle although in later lists Barnard gave the title as *American Contributions to the Philosophy and Practice of Education. Papers for the Wisconsin Teacher*, Number Two (New York and Chicago, 1860); the subtitle was *Object Teaching and Oral Lessons on Social Science and Common Things*; note the innovative words *social science*, a term popularized by the American Association for the Advancement of Social Science.

to Wisconsin, to the institutes, or to the normal classes Barnard was alleged to have visited. The *Papers* were *not* designed for the Wisconsin teachers, despite the editor's protestations to the contrary, but with a larger audience in mind.

After his resignation, Henry Barnard returned to Hartford where he lived and worked for the next five years, years of solid accomplishment. Despite his apparent failure in Wisconsin his reputation was secure. It certainly must have tickled his vanity to have been elected a Corresponding Member of the United School Masters of Great Britain and an Honorary Member of the Vermont Historical Society, as well as an Honorary Member of the Athenaeum Society of Wisconsin. The few clouds on his personal horizon, even family tragedy, did not seemed to disturb his equanimity. He never mentioned, for instance, the fire that destroyed his barn and the animals within (the newspaper account said the cottage of his "faithful tenants" was saved).[56]

The mention of tenants in the account of the fire is tantalizing because it provides a smidgen of evidence about Barnard's financial situation. It is extremely difficult to untangle his business dealings, and, in fact, his cousin, M. L. Seymour was never able to do so. Barnard invested in real estate, in the West and South, and in Detroit and Hartford; he also seems to have speculated, profiting from the rather unscrupulous guidance of his old Yale friend, Ashbel Smith, now the Surgeon-General of the Texan army. But at the time of the Panic of 1857 Barnard was virtually strapped, and only the businesslike assistance of Seymour and another old friend, Rollin Sanford, kept him afloat. Barnard was forced to sign over a Detroit bond to Seymour, who in reply cheerfully said he was forwarding a case of "Edinburgh ale," and Sanford twice dispatched a note for $1,000, adding "Keep a stiff upper lip & go ahead"—presumably with the *Journal*. Barnard's money troubles persisted during the next few years, and his lack of common sense must have nearly driven Seymour to distraction. Barnard asked to borrow money for an institute when one of his buildings was unrented, Barnard lost a check ("I've a notion it's somewhere in your pockets," wrote Seymour), and once Barnard's note for $1,000 was protested, so Seymour had to cover it. Poor Seymour; he himself suffered severe reversals ("went bust") early in the war years, complicating Barnard's already shaky financial situation.[57] Barnard was spending a great

56. Letter from J. Tilleard, October 3; Certificate, October 7, 1859, NYU. Undated letter from Lydia Sigourney, addressed to Madison, enclosing a clipping of an editorial which described the fire and decried the fact that such an exemplary man should suffer a second loss so soon after the sorrowful death of his child.

57. The letters on Barnard's financial woes are numerous; see from Sanford, January 27, April 16, August n.d.; in October, 1859, Sanford wrote in desperation—he had to

deal of his own money on his *Journal*, but because of the coinciding of his gravest financial worries with troubles in the economy, one suspects that speculation played more of a role than publication.

For over twenty years lectures by Henry Barnard had been a familiar feature at educational gatherings; invitations were fewer now, despite his prominence.[58] The educational scene was changing, for a new national organization, the National Teachers' Association, a group of "practical teachers," had entered the fray so long dominated by the lay schoolmen. The group first met in 1857, called by the presidents of the state associations, under the initiative of William Russell; of the forty-three founding members, including two women, none was from Connecticut, and the delegate from Wisconsin was never Henry Barnard. The group met annually, except for 1861 and 1862, and Barnard addressed them only once although he was not totally forgotten. His stalwart friend and erstwhile associate, John Philbrick, introduced a resolution at the 1858 session that the *American Journal of Education* "is regarded by the members of this Association, as a work of great value, and one which deserves the support of all our teachers throughout the country." The following year, Zalmon Richards, the first president, who had frequently asked Barnard to lecture in Washington, urged the assembled teachers to subscribe to the *Journal*. Barnard, for his part, did not seem to resent his exclusion, and he determined to create a new role for himself, to become the historian of the nation's teachers. He volunteered to print full accounts of all state and national teachers' meeting, and he promised to write a complete history of such organizations before the next annual meeting. This, in fact, he began, and never completed.[59]

It was during this period that Barnard's scholarly and publishing inter-

---

have $500; Barnard must have answered graciously, for Sanford thanked him for his good wishes and regretted "they cannot pay debts"; two dozen letters from Seymour between March 8, 1857, and November 17, 1860, NYU; Seymour was a business associate, as well as a relative, the owner of mills which supplied the editor of the *Journal* with paper; throughout his dealings with Barnard he maintained a cheerful and breezy tone, a bantering one which more often than not mentioned spirits—he was sending some cognac, or wine, in May "when it was too cold for juleps or punches." See also Thursfield, *Barnard*, 43–44.

58. Barnard did address the American Normal School Association in 1859; see letters from W. H. Phelphs, April 20, 28; but his mention in *AJE* XV, xxxix (June 1865), and XVI, xlv (December 1866), of earlier speeches in 1846, 1850, and 1855, suggests his sense of fading glory.

59. Henry Barnard, *Proceedings of the National Teachers' Association from Its Foundation in 1857 to the Close of the Session of 1870* (Syracuse: C. W. Bardeen, 1907); see 28, 40–41 (1858, Philbrick), 152 (1859, Richards). See also National Education Association, *History of the National Education Association of the United States* (Washington, 1892); Richards in his "Historical Sketch," gave a lavish tribute to Mann and makes no mention of Barnard.

ests veered toward the entire field of scientific and technical education. The sources of this orientation were three. He had, from the very beginning of his career, displayed a general interest in matters technological, as became a gentleman reformer, and he had promised to include accounts of "Military and Naval Schools of different countries, with special reference to the extension and improvement, among ourselves, of similar institutions and agencies" in his *Journal*. He consistently advocated scientific and technical schools as part of an entire system, based always on the solid rock foundation of the common schools. Then, in 1862, a "current necessity" demanded more focused emphasis.

> The terrible realities of our present situation as a people—the fact that within a period of twelve months a million of able bodied men have been summoned to arms from the peaceful occupations of the office, the shop, and the field, and are now in hostile array, or in actual conflict, within the limits of the United States, and the no less alarming aspect of the future, arising not only from the delicate position of our own relations with foreign governments, but from the armed interference of the great Military Powers of Europe in the neighboring republic, have brought up the subject of **Military Schools, and Military Education**, for consideration and action with an urgency which admits of no delay. Something must and will be done at once.[60]

National peril, the Civil War and possible European intervention in Mexico, required a national response—augmented military strength through preparation. Finally, there was a more personal motivation.

Throughout his career, Barnard's ventures had always reflected the influence of his circle and his acquaintances, and his emphasis on technical education at this time was in part due to his association with Samuel Colt, the Hartford entrepreneur and manufacturer of arms. Colt was another of those wealthy benefactors Barnard so admired. He was an inventor and promoter, a brillliant and driven industrialist, a reformer in the mold of Robert Owen, who built model ("Swiss") dwellings for his employees, and included in the planned community Charter Oak Hall, a

---

60. Henry Barnard, *Military Schools and Courses of Instruction in the Science and Art of War* (New York, J. B. Lippincott, 1862; rev. ed. New York: E. Steiger, 1872), preface, 7, and 8. This was repeated in *AJE* XII, xxviii (September 1862): 3–4. A number of Barnard's letters in 1861 and 1862 deal with plans for the Military book; E. L. Molineux, an instructor at West Point, wrote a proposal for military education in the public schools, letters November 4, 1861, March 1, 21, 28, April 7, 1862; L.P. Brockett prepared an article on West Point but doubted that Barnard could pay him enough for it, letter January 28, 1862.

reading room with a place for lectures or debates or even parties. Colt
was a man who

> desired to elevate the whole laboring class to a higher plane of intel-
> ligence, enjoyment, and effort, and to make their homes healthy,
> happy and hopeful, for themselves and their children.[61]

Colt supported Barnard's research and publications, and he asked the
editor to assist him in expanding the Hall into a School of Mechanics and
Engineering, wedding an institution Barnard had long advocated to the
European Polytechnical School he so admired; after the outbreak of the
war, the design of the school shifted to include military drill and history.
Unfortunately, Colt battled continually with the city of Hartford over
taxes and withdrew his proposal; after his death in 1862, it was abandoned
entirely, thus depriving the city of a possible Colt Polytechnic Institute.

The widow Colt, however, wished to memorialize her husband, and
the next year she approached Barnard and asked him to undertake the
task. The result was a charming volume, part Hartford history, part biography. Much was not by Barnard's pen, and he admitted, in his preface,
that the volume was completed "only through the cooperation of Professor J. D. Butler" of the University of Wisconsin. In August Butler was
"deep in pistol-making," spending considerable time at the Armory,
according to Mrs. Barnard (for her husband was away), and by September, he and his manuscripts were "safe home" in Madison where he could
correct his "pistol-preachment." Poor Butler—he sent his manuscript (the
technical section of the book) off to Barnard, waited for acknowledgment, then was denied the use of his materials, even in teaching his own
students, and in May 1864 was still waiting to be paid for his efforts. Yet,
such was his devotion to Barnard, that he was willing to come to Hartford the following summer and again provide (unspecified) assistance.[62]
Mrs. Colt had responded to Barnard's request for personal recollections
with an extended memoir which Barnard published uncut. The bulk of
the book, with its historical thrust and romantic style, not to speak of its
peculiar organization, however is distinctly Barnard. No one but a Whig
reformer would have concluded as he did:

> Nor should it be forgotten—though it often is—that he who gives
> men employment, and hence feeds the labor-loving, is a more genuine
> benefactor than he who enables them to eat the bread of idleness.[63]

61. *Armsmear*, 48.
62. Letter from Josephine Barnard, August 7, 1863, from Butler, September 8, 17, October 24, November 2, 19, 21, December 14, 1863, March 22, May 24, 1864, all NYU.
63. *Armsmear*, 390.

Even if Colt's legacy was not to include an educational monument, Barnard could place Colt's achievements in the context of history.

It was logical and timely that next Barnard proposed to issue, ahead of the scheduled publication of the material in volumes twelve and thirteen of the *Journal*, a work entitled *Military Schools and Courses of Instruction in the Science and Art of War*. He wrote in the introduction that the book was a "most comprehensive survey of the Institutions and Courses of Instruction" of European military education, " . . . together with several communications and suggestions we have received in advocacy of Military Drill and Gymnastic exercises in Schools." He repeated his fundamental educational conviction, with some emendation: "Our old and abiding reliance for industrial progress, both social well being, internal peace, and security from foreign aggressions," rested on a better system of elementary education, a system of public high schools to which students are admitted by competitive examination, and a system of "Special Schools, either in connection with existing Colleges, or on an independent basis" for science, at the head of which reigned a National School of Science, similar to the Polytechnic School of France and "preparatory to Special Military and Naval Schools." Barnard had added a new justification and proposed new institutions for a system of public schooling, in an expanded but not altered vision.

The book is actually far from comprehensive and is less than original. The volume issued in 1862, which was announced as Part I, was devoted to Prussia and France; in fact, however, it was a republication of an 1857 "Report of the Commissioners appointed to consider the best mode of organizing the System of Training Officers for the Scientific Corps" of Great Britain—in other words, with a few additions, Barnard utilized a British state document as the basis of his book, and it is not until page 276 that he so indicated. He listed seven German sources, his own 1852 work on national education in Europe, and Alexander Bache's 1838 report, and he only included two other selections, one by Professor Helldorf of Berlin, and another by W. M. Gillespie, a professor of civil engineering at Union College. The book, in short, may have been topical, yet the topic was at best sketchily treated, with some out-of-date materials, and the volume had no unifying theme. It was instead a mere compilation of some existing materials, and one with a very limited sweep.

Publication occupied most of Barnard's time during this period, but his ambition remained. Like so many others he sought a position in the federal government, and he served a brief stint in the Census Bureau, a position well suited to his passion for statistics. He hoped for an appointment to succeed Cornelius Felton as a Regent of the Smithsonian Institute and carried on an active campaign with his old friend, Senator James

Dixon, acting on his behalf. Unhappily for Barnard, according to Dixon, Joseph Henry was still "hostile" to Henry Barnard, preferring President Woolsey of Yale. Barnard claimed his efforts to have education included in the writ of the Smithsonian was the cause of Henry's opposition—he could never admit that his previous performance might be at fault.[64]

On one of Barnard's trips to Washington to promote his career, he stopped in Maryland, for an interview with the Commissioner of Public Schools, probably to sell his *Journal*. The following year, in 1864, he was asked by some of the state's educational leaders to address the legislature, which, through some confusion, he never did.[65] The process may have been similar to that which had transpired in other states: reformers committed to reinvigorating the schools turned to the man most prominent in that crusade, Henry Barnard, for edification and then for leadership. In Maryland at this time the need for action was especially pressing due to the occupation and subsequent devastation of the state and deterioration of its institutions caused by the Civil War.

In 1865 the state legislature determined, as one step in reviving the state's schools, to reopen St. John's College. The college had originated in the Maryland legislation of 1784, which had created a University of the state to be composed of two colleges, one on the East and one on the West shore of the Chesapeake Bay; a pre-existing school, King William's, provided the foundation for St. John's, which was chartered in 1785 and opened its doors four years later. During the Civil War years, the college suffered along with the entire area; a railroad had been constructed through its grounds, and for four years its buildings served as a military hospital, although the preparatory school remained open.[66] In determining to reopen the dilapidated college, the legislature was taking a first step in restoring the structure of schools in the war-torn state.

The legislators appropriated money for the repair of the buildings, and they turned to Barnard, and probably others, to suggest names for the presidency. Of course it was impossible for him to submit a simple

64. Letter from Dexter A. Hamkins, March 10, 1862; from Dixon, March 14, 18 (no year but refers to Barnard's letter of March 9 as does Hamkins's); in another letter Dixon wrote that Barnard had almost got the appointment as Collector of Taxes, but Gideon Welles had defeated it, April 4, no year; Dixon promised "to make a personal appeal" to have his friend appointed as a Visitor to West Point, letter May 12, 1863. For a fuller discussion of Barnard's national activity see below, chapter VI.

65. Letter from the Commissioner, December 9, 1863; from I. R. Davenport, Annapolis, February 8, 1864, describing the mix-up.

66. Philip Randall Voorhees, *Address on the One Hundredth Anniversary of St. John's College* (Baltimore: W. K.Boyle & Co., 1889), 20–47; Thomas Fell, *Some Historical Accounts of the Founding of King William's School and its subsequent establishment as St.John's College* (Annapolis: Press of the Friedenwald Co., 1884), 15–20.

response. In his answer he expanded upon the necessary qualification for a president, and he suggested ways in which St. John's could become part of "an overall system" of public instruction. The reply must have impressed the legislators, for they appropriated $85,000 for the college, of which $15,000 was to be spent annually, and they elected Henry Barnard, whose "antecedents justify us in looking for a continuation and increase" in the college's "usefulness," Principal; the vote was nearly unanimous, another proof of Barnard's reputation and standing. He was granted a salary of $3,000, "to be quarterly," and the use of a dwelling "with a suitable garden for his residence."[67] In calling Barnard to the principalship the trustees were entrusting him with the leadership of another state university, a small one with a strong tradition but in a sorry condition, and once again great trust and high hopes were placed in him.

Barnard, as was habitual, and sensible in this instance, commenced his service to the college by presenting the trustees "a careful study of past conditions and present resources, and . . . of the educational needs of Maryland" with the "view of placing St. John's College in a position to meet those needs."[68] The Report was thorough and thoroughly business-like. Barnard first surveyed the physical plant. He recommended land-scaping and the construction of facilities for physical activity and the reconstruction of the existing buildings to include improved heating and ventilation, and the total revamping of the laboratories. Not all of this could be accomplished in one year, but rebuilding should proceed according to a "well-considered plan" which would place the college in a competitive position with any other college. Facilities were as deficient as the plant, and the library particularly so, lacking the standard works in the classics and philology and the newer scientific materials. As "a well selected consultative library is an indispensable help in the work of collegiate instruction," it was imperative that the professors have access to modern scholarship (and know modern languages) and that the reading room should be totally accessible, open every day.

From the plant Barnard moved to the curriculum. He sketched a broad view of a liberal education, as he had in Wisconsin, one which included new areas of study and extended from elementary school upward, with

67. Letter to Board of Trustees, November 11; Resolution appointing Barnard, November 30; letter from Thomas Karney, of the Naval Academy, describing the meeting; from N. Brewer, Treasurer and acting secretary, December 15; from Judge A. Randall, also confirming the appointment and inviting Mr. and Mrs. Barnard to come to visit in order to make the arrangements for their move; undated clipping announcing the appointment; all 1865, TC.

68. "Communication to the Executive Committee of the Visitors and Governors on the Re-Organization of St. John's College," *AJE* XVI, xliv (September 1866): 539–48.

the goal of preparing men (and only men) for all paths in life, rather than exclusively for the professions.

> My own conviction is, that the Public High School, and the next higher grade of school, known as the College, should give a liberal as well as a practical education (in its aims, subjects, and processes) to a much larger number of businessmen of the community than they have yet succeeded in doing.

What followed was the fullest description of an ideal curriculum that Barnard ever drew. It is an odd combination of the utterly expected and the utterly surprising, typical Barnard and a new Barnard. First and foremost in importance to him were the "Principles of Education and Religion with Application to Methods of Study, Formation of Character, and the Conduct of Life"—subjects suitable for formal study for teachers and for future policymakers. The orientation here was traditional, the moral goals those of the earlier Whig reformers. Of almost equal importance was the study of Physical Culture, and it was essential that there be a Professor of Education who could deliver "familiar, practical lectures" on health and personal habits; sports should also be encouraged. This new emphasis on physical training was something Barnard had recently and widely advocated in the *Journal* with the publication of articles by Dio Lewis.[69] He listed the obligatory study of English next in importance. His recommendations in the area of science were specific and expansive: he required three professors of mathematics, physics, and astronomy, a professor of chemistry and chemical technology, and one of the natural sciences who would work with the youngest students. Truly innovative was his suggestion that instruction be offered in the "Geography and History of the National Industries," and in law and "Public Economy" for all, not just for the future lawyers. Rounding out the curriculum "for all who come to study for at least a year" was a course in the Fine Arts. Languages were important for those pursuing a degree, and it was Barnard's "deep conviction of the desirableness of providing for a large and thorough course of instruction in the modern languages" that made him insist that proficiency in the modern tongues was equal in importance to that in the ancient ones, anticipating by more than twenty-five years a similar position in the famous Report of the Committee of Ten.

The course of study at St. John's, if implemented as recommended by its principal, would have been a far cry from the Yale of 1828, and had Barnard remained at the college, he might well have been remembered as

69. *AJE* XI, xxvii (June 1862): 531–62, and XII, xxix (December 1862): 665–700. Letters from Lewis, December 14, 1861, March 6, 1862, NYU.

one among those who helped to change the face of collegiate education in this country. He seemed to be aware of just how radical his proposals were, moreover, and he sounded cautious. Crucial, of course, was leadership. He was "ready to assume at once the responsibility of inaugurating such a system." Second in importance was the appointment of the staff to carry out the plan. Necessary was a "full corps of resident professors"—at least five—and a number of instructors and lecturers "as the exigencies of the institution may require . . . ," all, of course, dependent on the financial limitations imposed by the Board and the legislature.

Once installed, Barnard developed very specific details in his plan. He projected three terms for the academic year 1866–67, at the cost of $66 per term, and state scholarships should be provided. The enlarged five year appropriation from the legislature should be publicized to stimulate donations to the college; alumni should be put on the Board to increase participation in the affairs of the college. The State Teachers Association should be encouraged to meet at the college, and teachers should be entitled to enroll in courses free of tuition. Barnard was explicit on this:

> I hold it to be the duty and the privilege of every educated man, and especially of all institutions charged with any portion of the higher instruction of youth, to co-operate in the general education movements of the state.

Barnard's plan contained the seeds of a very modern institution, a college with a curriculum designed to reflect the needs of the state in both the public and the private sectors. It was one which integrated the common schools with the facilities for liberal education considered preparatory to all subsequent professional training. It introduced new subjects into the classical course of study and suggested that all of the subjects would be of equal value. And it implied a differentiation in the teaching staff which was to implement it. In sum, what was described was a transitional institution, something between the postcolonial college and the modern university. Henry Barnard thus proposed not only to reopen and revitalize St. John's but actually to revolutionize it, and such a proposal demanded a leader ready to devote the time and energy to the task.

Barnard stayed at the college less than a year, and he accomplished little, although there were those who credited him with restoring some of the place's former prestige. He reorganized some of the existing departments, he brought David Camp home from a trip to Europe in order to head the preparatory department (which exceded the college in size), he invited Zalmon Richards to deliver a series of lectures (probably to teachers), and he seems to have participated in various meetings of the states' teachers which were held at the college.[70] His closest associate at St John's, however, felt the "ludicriousness . . . of trying" to apply a "plan large enough to run a university" to a "second rate Grammar school"—much as he supported the vision and the plan.[71] Barnard may have been too ambitious in his design, but it was well conceived, an amalgam of ideas originated in Rhode Island, expanded in Connecticut, and formalized in Wisconsin. He might have succeeded in the smaller state where he did not encounter the competition of other colleges and he apparently enjoyed unified support of the local schoolmen—if he had persevered; unhappily, he tarried in Maryland less than two years.

The college did open in September 1866, but there was no graduating class until 1871, and by then others were in charge. When Barnard submitted his resignation in March of 1867, the Faculty, in a resolution, praised his "urbanity, his kindness of heart, his whole bearing towards" them and begged him to remain at least until the end of the term.[72] Whether he had come to realize that the position in Maryland demanded political skills that he did not possess, and the framework of politics in the border state certainly were a challenge for anyone, much less a Northerner, or whether he had accepted the job simply as an interim one, is unknown. But by the time of his resignation he had realized his long-standing ambition to hold national office, and he had been appointed to one which apparently was ideally suited to a man of his background.

70. Letters from Richards, November 10, 26; from John Harkness, November 12, 16, December 4; 1866, NYU; Camp, *Recollections*, 58–59.

71. Letters from G. W. Atherton, April 6, June 24 . Atherton hoped to go to Cornell where the resources and facilities were more promising, and he asked Barnard for help in securing an appointment as a visitor to West Point; like Camp, however, he was loyal to Barnard, frequently served as his secretary, and he spent September in the Midwest, acting as an agent for Barnard, letters, April 24, September 17, 18, 19, 26; all 1867, NYU.

72. Resolution, March 21, 1867, copy, TC.

VI

NATIONAL

EDUCATOR

*The peculiarities of our government require that the spirit of the people shall be educated in conformity to them. Unless the popular mind is trained in sympathy with republican ideas, or, if under the right of freedom of opinion, aristocratic notions of society are allowed, different castes of society will spring up, theories of a modified form of government will arise, popular faith in a republic will be weakened, and its surest basis of support—the attainment of the people—will gradually crumble. . . . Hence, not only the propriety but the necessity of government's exerting its influence to encourage a system of education which will harmonize with republican ideas and republican civilization. (*American Journal of Education *XV, xxxix [June 1868]: 183)*

Coupled with Barnard's varied official duties over the years was his prominence on the national scene. In the middle decades of the century, usually at the initiative of one of his circle of reformer friends, he was in demand as a speaker. It may have been one of his in-laws who invited him to address the Thursday Evening Club in Charleston in 1849, but it was William Wells who induced him to lecture to the Illinois State Teachers' Association in 1846 and again in 1856, and Zalmon Richards who repeatedly begged him to come to Washington to address the teachers there. Barnard spoke at the National Teachers' Association, at the meeting of the Officers of Colleges and Academies, and at the convocation of the New York State University, all in 1863. The high point of his career as a lecturer came the next year when he was invited to address the Lowell Institute, that elite Boston lyceum.[1] None of these addresses survives, but we can assume that many dealt with "The relations of free and universal education to the moral character and the temporal prosperity of the people," and that they became increasingly focused, as Barnard developed his conception of the national responsibility in education.

In his own official biography, written in 1880, Barnard slightly exaggerated that aspect of his career, dating his interest in national affairs to his earliest years as a state legislator. He claimed that in 1838 he had "submitted in rough outline" a plan for a national role in education along with a suggestion for the inclusion of educational statistics in the census of 1840, a myth which all subsequent scholars have perpetuated. That year's massive survey did include such data, but there is no evidence that this was due to the initiative of a young Connecticut lawyer or that his vision extended beyond his own state at that time. It is also doubtful that it was his efforts that led to the inclusion of an educational component in the original plans for the Smithsonian Institution—education was Smithson's concern.[2] It was the combination of political philosophy, governmental experiences, and participation in national voluntary organizations which led Barnard and other schoolmen along this path. He had noted the Smithsonian bequest, a bill introduced by Robert Dale Owen to establish a national institution for the advancement of knowledge, and a proposal for a national normal school in the *Journal of the Rhode Island of Instruction* in 1846—he "intended" to submit a comment on the related ideas but deferred them to another time. In Wisconsin he had proposed a unified, state-wide system of schooling. He was familiar with the suggestions made by the founding fathers concerning a national role, he was active in a variety of national groups, and his service as a state administrator had revealed him as a centralizer.[3] It was an easy, and natural step, for him to join in the growing agitation among the educational leadership for a federal office of education.

Barnard's schoolmen friends based their conception of a national responsibility for education on two sources, the benevolent optimism of

1. *AJE* XV, xl (September 1865): 502; xlii (March 1866): 152, 158; xliii (June 1866): 364, 380. Letters from Richards, October 2, 1858, August 22, 1859, November 19, 1863, for examples; letters from Woolworth, June 3, 4, 9, 1864; from Cruikshank, June 20, August 24; from Philbrick, June 11, August 11; from Cotting, January 18, 1864.

2. *AJE*, National Series, XVII, i (September 1867): Preface; XXX (March 1880): 193ff. Subsequent biographers, such as Steiner, *Barnard*, 103ff., have accepted Barnard's version.

3. *JRIII*, extra X (April 1, 1846): 134–35. *AJE*, National Series, XVII, 1 (September 1867): 41ff., "Education Recognized as a National Interest," includes a review of the historical development of the federal role.

the eighteenth century *philosophes* and the centralizing example of Prussia.[4] Education bore the heavy duty of developing responsible individuals, able to govern themselves and to contribute to the well-being of the nation, but not all individuals perceived their proper role, and patently, not all were capable of undertaking their own education. Hence government had to be efficiently organized, with worthy men in high positions prepared to labor for the benefit of all. Barnard put the matter succinctly: "It is indeed a law of educational progress that its impulse and stimulus come from without." The supreme example of enlightened leadership, was supplied by Prussia, for there the Minister of Instruction was held in high esteem, and his department was as well organized and had as much responsibility as any other one.[5]

A federal presence in education had never been totally absent, even from the earliest days of the Republic. A precedent was contained in the Ordinances of 1785 and 1787, and subsequent enabling acts for the admission of new states required that state constitutions include education among the responsibilities of the state — the impetus for reform efforts in the old northwest, a fact Barnard failed to comprehend. Such governmental initiative was entirely consistent with Whig ideology; aid to schools constituted a form of internal improvement and fostered Whig social goals. Thus grants of money, from the surplus of 1836 and from the revenues of the swamplands in 1849, were predecessors of the Morrill Act, first proposed in 1857, and therefore not strictly a war measure as some have suggested.[6] Little noticed, for a variety of motives, and following no consistent pattern or policy, the federal government supported education, that "schools and the means of education might forever be encouraged."[7]

4. This chapter on Barnard's national career depends heavily on the excellent book by Donald R. Warren, *To Enforce Education: A History of the Founding Years of the United States Office of Education* (Detroit: Wayne State University Press, 1974); see also the introductory chapters in Gordon C. Lee, *The Struggle for Federal Aid: A History of the Attempts to Obtain Federal Aid for the Common Schools, 1870–1890* (New York: Bureau of Publications, Teachers College, 1949); and David Tyack, Thomas James, and Aaron Benavot, *Law and the Shaping of Public Education, 1785–1954* (Madison: University of Wisconsin Press, 1987), Part I, esp. chap. 2.

5. *AJE* XXX (March 1880): 198–99, account of the 1862 National Convention of School Superintendents. Warren, *Enforce*, 30ff. Even as Barnard described the Prussian minister, he went on: "The energies of a single, well balanced mind should be employed in collecting and combining materials which shall give greater force and efficiency to the system."

6. Lee, *Struggle*, chap. II, 6–28.

7. See the collection, edited by Paul H. Mattingly and Edward W. Stevens, Jr., " . . . *Schools and the Means of Education Shall Forever Be Encouraged*" (Athens: University of Ohio Press, 1987).

Some members of Congress advocated more. As early as 1829 Joseph Richardson, congressman from Massachusetts, proposed that an education committee be established by the House, and William Cost Johnson of Maryland later moved, unsuccessfully, that a committee be appointed to appropriate a specific proportion of the surplus revenue for educational uses. In addition, lay schoolmen such as the persistent normal school lobbyist, Charles Brooks, and the national university advocate, Alexander Bache, pushed their proposals for a national presence, privately and at the annual meetings of the educational fraternity. In 1830, the Lyceum, the American Institute of Instruction, and the Western Literary Institute all began to agitate for a centralized governmental role as a means of strengthening the common school movement. By 1850, the goal of educating the nation for responsible citizenship was augmented by another imperative, the desire to fend off the threatened division of the union; throughout the decade the American Association for the Advancement of Education and the National Teachers' Association pressed for a permanent federal role.[8]

In his early years Barnard had displayed an active interest in politics, more as an observer than as a combatant. He had also traveled extensively in the South where he had close family and personal friends. Given these factors and his rather benign and cautious nature, it is scarcely surprising that he was never an abolitionist, unlike many of his fellow reformers. He abhorred passion in politics, and the lawyer in him saw the constitutional possibility of secession.[9] The educator in him, however, believed in the potential power of education to develop right-thinking men and women, so it was only to be expected that he would join those who sought in education the solution to the nation's impending trauma. It was in this context, in the tumultuous mid-fifties and to a national organization meeting in the nation's capital, that he advanced his plan for a federal role in education.

At the fourth session of the American Association for the Advancement of Education, in December 1854, Barnard introduced a Plan of a Central Agency for the Advancement of Education. He proposed that either the Association or the Smithsonian appoint an educational agent and sponsor a plan of publication "for the increase and diffusion of knowledge" of education, especially of public education.[10] He clung to his

8. Warren, *Enforce*, chap. 1.

9. Letter to Henry Watson in Detroit, February 4, 1851, in Lannie, *Barnard*, 29.

10. The plan first appeared in *AJE* I, i (January 1856); it is summarized in *AJE* XXX (March 1880): 194; it was printed in a number of Barnard's publications; see Henry Barnard, *Proceedings of the National Teachers' Association from its Foundation in 1857 to the Closing Session of 1870* (Syracuse, N.Y: C. W. Bardeen, 1909; hereafter *NEA*), Appendix

theme and as president of the Association the next year, titled his presidential address "The Magnitude of the Educational Interests of the United States." After citing the census of 1850 for evidence of the extent of schooling in the country, he suggested some of the services the central government could provide to enhance educational opportunity; he repeated his insistence on the necessity of increased appropriations for the education of teachers; he recommended the mandation of public schooling to meet the needs of the children and to "protect society from the neglect of parental duty"; and he advocated competitive examinations for candidates for military, naval, civilian, or diplomatic service.[11] When no action was taken on his proposals, other than the passage of supporting resolutions, Barnard embarked on his own publication, the *American Journal of Education*, whose very name emphasized his commitment to the creation of a national voice, as the voice of a national campaign. The parallels with his state activity are striking.

Barnard communicated his idea for a national agency to his colleagues often, for Richards wrote in 1859, "I wish you could carry out your great plan in this city, as I know you have long dreamed."[12] But after the election of 1860 he hatched another scheme. Despite his repeated pleas of poor health, he had abundant energy to lobby for an appointment under the new administration, one which seemed designed for his personal advantage rather than to advance his national proposal. The negotiations and their aim are a bit difficult to unravel, but in early 1861 Barnard wrote to William Wells, the superintendent of schools in Chicago, a long-time colleague, and someone who might have influence with the new administration, for assistance; Wells orchestrated a grand campaign, writing careful letters to Secretary Seward, among others, and urging his friends to do the same. Zalmon Richards served as Johnny-on-the-spot, for Barnard's interests and his own, and he assured his Connecticut friend that he had secured unanimous support for an appointment from the Wisconsin delegation. Apparently what Barnard sought was to be appointed ambassador to Berlin, a post which went almost immediately to another.[13]

H, 425–26, or *Recent English Pedagogy* (Hartford, 1884), following 554; *Circular* (May 1855), repeated in the Preface to the *Journal*.

11. *AJE* II, vi (September 1856): 452; *AJE* XXX, (March 1880): 195. Barnard delivered two other lectures at this meeting which lasted from August 12–15, and then he attended the American Institute of Instruction annual convention at Springfield from August 19–23 where he spoke "On the Home and Parental Element in Public Education."

12. Letter from Richards, August 22, 1859, NYU.

13. See letters from Wells, February 28, March 4, 9; from Richards, January 29, March 9 (in which he reviewed the steps in the failed campaign); from Burrowes (Barnard was in Washington at the time); from Davies, March 7; all 1861, NYU.

Here is a cross-roads, a failed opportunity which might have made a significant difference in Barnard's career. Germany, and especially Berlin, was the very center of developing modern scholarship, the Mecca to which new world academics flocked.[14] Had Barnard gone to Berlin he would have been thrust into a world very different from that of the gentlemen amateurs of the United States and the Benthamite reformers with whom he had constantly corresponded and frequently met in England. He would have encountered challenging intellectual and philosophical trends, and he might have grown in stature—he might have become a real historian. Instead he remained at home.

Henry Barnard was still ambitious for a federal position, as were so many others given the war-time expansion of the government. The evidence about the next episode is also sketchy, but in 1861 Zalmon Richards inquired if Barnard was coming to a clerkship in the Census Bureau. A year later J. P. Usher, the Assistant Secretary of the Interior, sent Barnard a peremptory letter: "You will please send me as early as convenient" an abstract of the census "as far as you have progressed with the same." F. A. P. Barnard (who held a position in the Department of the Interior) was even more direct and admonishing. The situation with the Secretary was embarrassing, for Henry, who "was nominally in charge of the office" was away from Washington so often and had produced so little there were charges of favoritism and hints of a possible Congressional inquiry. Henry must be in the city to direct the Bureau clerks even if he departed for Hartford occasionally. "It is evident that the matter will not mend itself if you stay away." Henry Barnard apparently had received an appointment, in charge of the Census Bureau, and he ostensibly worked there three years.[15] But during the same period he edited three volumes of his *Journal* and several other works. Barnard wanted a position for prestige, and pay, and he received an appointment because of his reputation and connections. But the familiar pattern repeated itself; he did not produce, other than the numbers of his publication.

It was not long before he had an opportunity to serve in a capacity somewhat more suited to his abilities. In 1863, the year after the publication of his work on *Military Schools*, Senator Dixon managed to secure him an appointment to the Board of Visitors at West Point. His fellow visitors included Ralph W. Emerson, Henry S. Randall, and William H.

14. See Carl Diehl, *American and German Scholarship, 1770–1870* (New Haven: Yale University Press, 1978).

15. Letters from Richards, June 17, December 2, 1861, July 4 (Barnard had just left Washington), November 8, 17, 1862; from Usher, May 12, 1862; from F. A. P. Barnard, March 17, November 14, 1863; NYU. Lannie, *Barnard*, 28, says Barnard spent three years at the Bureau.

Russell, with Oliver S. Munsell as chairman. Barnard probably wrote the final report, and he presided over several meetings of the Visitors in Hartford, called to discuss the draft, a fact which led Richards to refer to him as "chairman," an error Barnard did not hasten to correct. The document does sound like him, especially in the introduction: "This Academy belongs to the whole Nation. So as far as its purpose and numbers permit, it is the People's College." It had not been created for the benefit of any "section, sect, party or class" and neither exclusiveness nor dogma had a place at West Point.[16] A criticism leveled at the Academy by the Congress and the press, and one foremost in the minds of some of the committee members, especially the lone New Yorker, Randall, was the high rate of academic failure at the school. The rate averaged nearly 50 percent, scarcely admirable and totally unacceptable during a time of war. Barnard seized the opportunity in the report to trumpet a cause he had already espoused, that of competitive examination, as one method of raising standards.[17]

He also proved to be his usual dilatory and difficult self on this assignment, procrastinating on the writing of the report and refusing to send a copy to Henry Randall who was unable to attend the meetings (or he was notified too late), called to discuss it. Randall said he was "mortified and puzzled" and wondered if his "New England colleagues" failed to trust him. Barnard ran the risk of offending more than his friend in the report, due to his adherence to the principle of competitive examinations. The commandant of West Point was quick to point out that many thought the insistence on qualification "strikes at the root of Republican Insitutions." This echo of earlier Democratic objections to the agenda of the schoolmen reformers did not deter Barnard and his fellows, and the report, unamended, was finally delivered to the Secretary of War in late winter.[18]

According to Barnard, he was appointed to the Board of Visitors of

16. *AJE* XIII, xxxiii (December 1863): 19ff.

17. James L. Morrison, *"The Best School in the Union": West Point in the Pre-Civil War Years, 1833–1866* (Kent: Kent State University Press, 1986), 137. Barnard addressed the National Teachers' Association the next year, on August 12, on "Competitive Examinations applied to appointments to Public Service"; *AJE* XIV, xxxvi (September 1864). Thomas L. Haskell, *Emergence*, 63–64 and 116, asserts that merit examination and civil service reform were companion pieces in an effort to institutionalize "sound opinion" and create a "system of functional elites."

18. Letter from Richards, December 19; from Randall, August 29, October 31, November 9; from Hubbard, November 30; from B. G. Nothrop, who apparently was a War Department underling and said he would write Secretary Stanton that Barnard was forwarding the report, November 14; on December 26, Northrop sent Barnard $3.35 for his share of the expenses for the report; 1863; letter from Captain Boynton, January 13, 1864.

the United States Naval Academy the next year and between May and July spent almost every day at the Academy; this has led his biographers to say that he was a Visitor at Annapolis and to connect his service there with his subsequent appointment to St. Johns.[19] In fact, Barnard was appointed on May 17, "a member of the Board of Visitors of the Naval Academy at New Port, Rhode Island"; he was to be paid $100 for his service which was to begin May 20. The United States Naval Academy was located in Rhode Island at this time, rather than at Annapolis, so a part of Barnard's account is true. But, according to his own correspondence, he became ill and never went to Newport at all. His absence was apparently regretted, and the authorities at the Academy offered to bring the examinations to Barnard for his inspection in Hartford, an offer which he declined, and they then urged him to come to Newport to meet with any of the men he might want to interrogate. He does not appear to have accepted that offer although he was grateful when one officer sent a history of naval academies created prior to the founding of Annapolis.[20] He seemed to have been more anxious to establish himself as an authority than to act as one, and his interest in the Academy was more historical than current.

Still the report in the *Journal* sounds like Henry Barnard, with its strong emphasis on competitive examinations, its recommendation of a system of naval schools (evening, junior, and senior), its insistence on the necessity of credentialed teachers, and its repeated references to naval education in other countries, especially in Great Britain. To entertain the suspicion that Henry Barnard wrote the report without visiting Newport is to cast harsh judgment upon him, but there is no evidence to the contrary. By printing his conclusions in the form of a report he was able to publicize his own convictions; had he actually visited Newport they probably would not have differed.

A careful reading of the Barnard correspondence leaves one with the impression that the Civil War scarcely intruded on his orderly life. His friend John Philbrick wrote enthusiastically to him early in 1861 about the possibility of raising a teachers' regiment in Massachusetts but never sug-

---

The report had not reached Northrop by February although Gideon Thayer had received a copy on January 28; NYU. See *AJE* XV, xxxvii (March 1865): 51–60, for "Debate in the Senate on Competitive Examinations at West Point."

19. *AJE* XV, xxxviii (March 1865): 17–50, Report. See Steiner, *Barnard*, 95.

20. Letter of appointment from Northrop, May 17; from Foster, June 24; from Forde, August 4, 17, November 27; 1864, NYU. According to Senator Dixon, letter May 21, the appointment as a Naval Academy Visitor prohibited Barnard's second term as a West Point one. The material Forde sent probably was the account of "Naval and Navigation Schools in England" which appeared in the December 1864 number of the *Journal*.

gested that Barnard attempt to do the same. William S. Baker sent him wrenching letters about his fear for his soldier son and later about the son's death on the battlefield; he besought Barnard's aid in dealing with the frustration and the expense of trying to bring his child's remains back to his native soil.[21] But almost never, except for an occasional aside, do Barnard and his friends discuss the War. His concern was his *Journal*. It is true that only two numbers appeared in 1861, but Barnard inaugurated a New Series of the publication in March 1862, pledging again to "leave the work of controversy to those who have more taste for it than we have."[22] He suggested that better education might have forestalled the War, and he published articles on military exercises, repeated from the volume on military education. The thrust of the bulk of the articles, however, was toward a stronger national role in education, a cause he and his schoolmen colleagues advocated strenuously throughout the decade.

It is beyond the scope of this study to untangle the web of Reconstruction politics, but it must be recalled that Barnard had begun his life as a Whig, and that the Whig political role had, in the main, been assumed by the new Republican Party which stood for a strong federal government. Ideology, and the exigencies of fighting a war, led to greater centralization than the antebellum politicians could have dreamed of achieving. The draft and the blockade of the South and even Lincoln's suspension of civil rights were excused on the grounds of survival, and subsequent interventions during Reconstruction were accepted as necessary for the reunification of the nation. One of these was the effort to educate the freed Blacks in order to prepare them for their new civic and social responsibilities. What is often overlooked by contemporary historians is the attempt on the part of the government to expand its role in education throughout the entire nation.

The National Teachers' Association pressured for the same end. Its third meeting in Washington in 1859 was indeed a national gathering. Among the states reporting to the convention were, of course, Massachusetts and Connecticut, but also Missouri, Virginia, North Carolina, and Alabama. The assembled delegates considered a proposal to sponsor *The National Teacher*, a periodical to be published monthly by a board of unpaid editors, very much as the various state journals were; this plan

21. Letters from Baker, November 13, 16, 1863, February 9, 30, April 28, November 7, 30, 1864, February 16, April 28, May 1, 1865, NYU; Baker was living in a house owned by Barnard and also tried to arrange to have his remaining son purchase it. It may have been out of compassion for Baker that Barnard decided to have a portrait of Baker as the frontispiece of the September 1864 issue of the *Journal*, an overdue tribute to an odd, difficult, and loyal man.

22. *AJE* XI, xxvi (March 1862): Circular.

was tabled after considerable discussion. The group did agree to appoint a committee of three to confer with the Secretary of the Interior in respect to the statistical data to be included in the next census and "to memorialize Congress in relation to the establishment of a National Agency, to collect and disseminate the statistics of schools and education in the several States and Territories." Appointed to the committee were Read of Wisconsin, Tilton of Maryland, and Starke of Missouri, all regular Barnard correspondents.[23]

The Association did not meet during the early years of the War, and it was not until the 1864 annual meeting, held in Ogdensburg, New York, that the matter of a national agency was again discussed. Superintendent Sheldon H. White, of Ohio, read an essay on "A National Bureau of Education" in which he noted that there was no national system to parallel the existing state ones; a national agency would assure the "existence, prosperity and perpetuity of our institutions," would unify the states, and would make their efforts in education more efficient. The nationalization of education would serve to "harmonize republican ideas and republican civilization" and would lend power and influence to the role of education in national life. Finally, a national agency would, in furthering the cause of education for all, serve to unify the country.[24] White skillfully adopted the rationale of the earlier state reformers, as well as their vocabulary, and applied it to national necessities made more pressing by the division of the country. His words must have resonated with schoolmen such as Philbrick and Barnard, and they appealed to Republican politicians. The Association concurred, approving two resolutions, for a bureau such as White proposed, and for the appointment of a committee to lobby for it. White, Zalmon Richards, and Henry Barnard constituted that committee.

Precisely what the committee was to do was not clear, but Barnard saw what he could contribute, and he announced his intention in the September number.[25] His *Journal* could serve as the national organ of the teachers, publicizing their activities and bringing their leaders to national

23. *NEA*, 138–42, 146–47. Probably the failure to establish a journal helped Zalmon Richards have a resolution passed supporting Barnard's *American Journal of Education*. Barnard's job in the Census Bureau may have originated in this committee.

24. *AJE* XIV, xxxvi (September 1864): 593–98 account of the meeting; speech in *AJE* XV, xxxviii (March 1865): 180–89. Barnard attended the meeting and was granted Life Membership; letters from Philbrick, August 3, and S. S. Greene, September 5, 1864; NYU.

25. See *AJE* XIV, xxxvi (September 1864): 593–99, for summary of the annual meeting, including notice of motion, by Barnard, authorizing the publication of the proceedings. From letters to him it is clear that he nearly drove the Association leaders mad with his delays in publication, and there seems to have been continued disagreement about the form that the accounts were to take.

prominence; through this means a sense of unity and identity could be achieved by the profession on the national level as it had been within the individual states. Barnard was true to his intention. The frontispiece of the December number featured Samuel S. Greene, the president of the National Teachers' Association, whose biographical sketch had appeared in the preceding issue, along with an account of the organization's annual meeting.

A goodly proportion of Barnard's correspondence in 1864 was with the presidents of the state associations, as he sought material for publication. He had always favored biography, so a typical report commenced with an engraved portrait of the current state president (if the individual, his friends or family, would supply one); a history of the teachers' organizations within the state followed, with a biographical sketch of the president or at the very least a list of all of the preceding presidents.[26] Whenever possible, the editor noted significant contributions to educational history. He gave a summary of the development of Teachers' Institutes in the various states, and he printed a documentary history of Normal Schools. He described the Education Room in the headquarters of the Massachusetts Association as "worthy of imitation in all our large cities," and he included a bibliography of Horace Mann's "Educational Controversies." When he could he emphasized the role of Ladies Associations —Connecticut and Illinois had such groups. Some material appealed to the teachers' pride, such as an address read at the 1865 meeting of the American Institute of Instruction on the "Dignity and Pride of the Schoolmaster's Work" or a London prize essay on "The Expediency and Means of Elevating the Profession of Education in Society." A sense of continuity was fostered by educational reminiscences of former teachers, and a challenge was offered by Frederick Jewell of the New York State Normal School when he asked "Public School Teaching—Can it Become a Profession?"[27] In other words, the *American Journal of Education,*

26. *AJE* XV, xl (September 1865): 477–505, New York, 507–38, Massachusetts; xli (December 1865): 593–616, Connecticut, 617–32, Vermont, 633–46, Michigan, 647–87, Pennsylvania; xlii (March 1865): 149–70, Illinois. Barnard printed what he was sent, and he also, in most cases, insisted that the state association bear the cost of engraving and printing the portraits.

27. The final number of volume XIV and all of XV and XVI, until number xlv (December 1866), can be viewed as the publication of the National Teachers' Association. To call the *Journal* national was no exaggeration (except for the South). The California Education Society was noted in number xlv (December 1866): 785–90; John Swett was the president of the Society and acted as Barnard's agent although he found it terribly difficult to work with the editor and only managed to sell four copies of the *Journal*; letters, October 26, November 26, 1864, February 11, 1865. David Camp was responsible for the Connecticut State Teachers' Association; letter, February 16, 1864, NYU.

between 1864 and 1866, became the proposed *National Teacher* in all but name. Henry Barnard could have made a real contribution to the teaching profession through his *Journal* by becoming the voice of the nation's teachers, but unfortunately, he again became distracted.

Others contributed to the growing chorus praising federal intervention. Venerable and persistent Charles Brooks wrote a pamphlet on national education which advocated a cabinet-level Minister of Public Instruction, but he believed that the Constitution would have to be amended before any legislation would be possible, so he planned to go to Washington to discuss the matter with Lincoln.[28] Samuel P. Bates, claiming that he had "influence," telegraphed Barnard that he, too,was going to Washington on business of mutual interest. The conspiratorial tone of his report that "no action was taken" suggests, however, that Bates may have been acting as a personal envoy for Barnard who in all probability was hoping once again for a position in the government.[29]

The focus of the annual meeting of the National Teachers' Association in 1865 was on the nation.[30] Schoolmen everywhere looked to education to repair the shattered union, as they had looked to it to repair the fragmented society in an earlier era. James P. Wickersham spoke on "Education as an Element in the Reconstruction of the Union," and Andrew Jackson Rickoff directed his remarks to the necessity of a National Bureau of Education.[31] According to Rickoff, it was the duty of the Association to labor for the extension of the common schools in the occupied South. Education had played a role in the final vistory of the North:

> Thank God that through the energy and intelligence fostered in the free schools of the Union, the enemy has been routed on the battlefield, and his legions have been dispersed.

Now the slaves of the South as well as the free men of the West must be educated (shades of the zeal of Lyman Beecher here), and if anyone should object to national action on the basis of state or local privilege, he should consider what the South might do to the former slave; he might, in addi-

28. Letters from Brooks, November 23, 1864, February 8, 1865, NYU. Note that Brooks's projected title is the European one.

29. See Warren, *Enforce*, 62ff., for a discussion of the various proposals for a national agency. Telegram from Bates, February 11, letters February 15, 21, 1865, NYU. Barnard wanted to go to Washington for the Inaugural (and some business), but Richards wrote that his house was too full to put him up.

30. The meeting was held in Harrisburg, August 16–18. Barnard had planned to attend but did not go; he sent a letter that he "was too weak from a severe illness caught on a recent educational tour of the West."

31. *AJE* XV, xli (December 1865): 805–15, for Proceedings; Rickoff's speech is in XVI, xliii (June 1866): 299–310.

tion, consider the precedent for federal action in the history of federal land donation. The government was obligated to recognize its duty to provide education—a Department of Education was as essential as the new Department of Agriculture which others were strenuously supporting. Rickoff's argument was strong, and yet, when he came to delineate the duties of the Commissioner he proposed, they were few: the dissemination of information on educational matters at home and abroad, the publication of annual reports, the creation of an educational library—in short, Henry Barnard's 1854 Plan. Like the state reformers of the antebellum period, the national teacher reformers, with few exceptions, dared not match their rhetoric with action. They shied away from confronting troublesome administrative details or the discrepancies between their various plans. They sought a symbolic presence which would encourage educational activity while at the same time enhancing the emerging profession.

The Association responded to Rickoff by passing a resolution appointing a committee consisting of three members from each state who were charged with circulating a petition urging the creation of a Department of Education. Representative of their efforts was a speech of the Commissioner of Commmon Schools of Ohio, Emerson E. White to the National Association of School Superintendents in Washington on February 7, 1866. White argued that universal education was a matter of deep national concern and that the government should encourage, induce, or even force state efforts to provide schooling. The projected Bureau should encourage "uniformity" and "accuracy" in state educational policy, and it could, by trumpeting "correct" ideas of moral and economic value, become the "strength and shield of free institutions." The success of the Bureau would, of course, depend on "the manner in which it is officiated."

> The work of such a Bureau must be directed by a mind that comprehends the aim and scope of education, its philosophy, its history, its processes, its practical details.

What was needed, he proclaimed, was another Horace Mann. Barnard immediately objected to White's allusion, feeling slighted, and in his complacency, he did not realize that in fact, White, who had designs on the job, was alluding to himself.[32]

In his account of the campaign for a Department of Education Barnard emphasized the leadership role of the schoolmen and teachers of the

---

32. *AJE* XVI, xlii (March 1866): 177–86. Barnard had quoted White's support for the *Journal*, in the *Ohio Education Monthly*, in the circular he mailed out in February 1865, announcing the new volume of the serial. Letter from White, March 3, 1866, NYU.

nation, and he slighted the part played by some members of Congress, who admittedly had more political motives. To Radical Republicans, Congressional school legislation was a legitimate aspect of reconstruction. In 1865, Representative Ignatius Donnelly, a Radical Republican from Minnesota, who had earlier attempted to strengthen the Freedman's Act, introduced a resolution instructing the Joint Committee on Reconstruction to inquire into the advisability of a National Bureau "to enforce education without regard to color" in the South.[33] The following year James A. Garfield responded to the memorial drawn up by White and introduced the teachers' bill with its vaguer mandate on February 14, 1866.[34] The bill was referred to a committee of four Republicans (including Garfield and Donnelly) and three Democrats (including Samuel Randall, Barnard's former friend, who opposed the bill). The committee reported favorably, and the bill was approved comfortably on June 19, a fact which Barnard noted in the *Journal*.[35] The House bill contained a key amendment, undoubtably Donnelly's, which considerably strengthened the original reformers' proposal. Instead of a relatively obscure Bureau of Educational Statistics within the Department of the Interior, it provided for a Department of Education, with a commissioner appointed by and reporting to the President, and a suitable support staff of four.

The Senate failed to act on the House bill, but Garfield was a valuable ally and championed the cause with his Congressional colleagues. "So far as I have been able to see the prospects of the Bill are favorable," he wrote to Barnard. Pressure from the National Teachers' Association was orchestrated by Emerson White who asked each state superintendent to write to his senator urging passage of the bill—a very modern touch. White expressed gratitude that Barnard was "interesting" himself in the campaign, adding that in his view the problem really lay with the President. White had come to fear that there were, in fact, two hurdles to overcome: passage of the bill and appointment of a suitable commissioner. "Some fear that he [Johnson] will destroy the efficiency of the Bureau by an injudicious appointment."[36]

Henry Barnard, nearby in Annapolis, was a behind-the-scenes observer;

33. Letter from John Hubbard, September 21, 1867, NYU; Hubbard was responding to a letter from Barnard asking for background on the bill, and Hubbard insisted that Donnelly, who was "a promising man," get some credit—Barnard gave him none.

34. White asked Barnard to express 240 copies of Garfield's address to the representative who wanted ammunition to convince his colleagues; letter from White, March 24, 1866, NYU. Barnard often made material available in offprint form, usually the biographical sketches, for private circulation by the subjects.

35. *AJE* XVI, xliii (June 1866): 390; letter from Richards, June 20, 1866, NYU.

36. Letter from Garfield, January 30, from White, February 4, both 1867, NYU.

it is impossible to ascertain how important a role he played in the legislative process. He wrote Benjamin Silliman in January 1867, that he had been called to Washington "to look after the Bill in the Senate," but one suspects that he went more to look after his own interests, for he emphasized his own desire for the "post" of commissioner.

> It is the only office under the gift of the Gov't which I would turn on my heel to get—but thirty years study & action have fitted me for this work—& I should like to wind up my educational labors in inaugurating this office.

He must have been reassured when a colleague wrote "I do not see how any one can for a moment be thought of in competition with yourself" should a commissioner be established. But Barnard remained cautious. To Gilman, in a letter marked "strictly private," he reported that Senator Dixon had taken "an active interest" in the passage of the bill and had spoken to the President "in reference to my appointment as Commissioner," but nothing was certain.

> "Put not your faith in Princes of blood royal or plebian" is a caution to all of us who aspire to serve this country in official position.

He suggested that a letter from "Yale" might serve to persuade Connecticut's Senator Foster, who was "mysteriously obscure" as to his opinion of the bill, and who needed to be convinced of Barnard's "ability to inaugurate such a system as the Bill contemplates."[37]

Despite Barnard's worry that the proposal might be lost due to the "non-action" of the chairman of the Judiciary Committee, the Bill establishing the Department of Education was reported out of committee and debated by the Senate on February 26, 1867, with Dixon speaking in favor. The Act was approved the following day in an unrecorded vote. Garfield telegraphed the news to Barnard: "Education bill just passed senate without amendment. The schoolmaster is abroad."[38] The law as passed provided for a Department with very limited powers; it was to collect statis-

37. Letter from Barnard to Silliman, January 10, 1867, NYU; he employed nearly the same words in a letter to Gilman, February 10, 11; 1867, JHU. In a postscript to Silliman, Barnard turned to matters of his journal, and to Gilman, he discussed the possibility of the latter's accepting a position at Madison or Peabody Institute in Baltimore. Senator Dixon, a conservative Republican, was an able politician with a Whig background and great experience, and a consistent Barnard supporter; for Connecticut politics at this time see James C. Mohr, ed., *Radical Republicans in the North* (Baltimore: The Johns Hopkins University Press, 1976), chap. 2, by John Niven.

38. Letter from Garfield, December 23, 1866, CHS; telegram, February 28, 1867, NYU; the wire came collect, at a cost of 39 cents. For a summary of the legislative history see *AJE*, National Series, XVII, i (1867): 41–64. Barnard managed to stress his own contri-

tics and facts about education and to diffuse such information as would assist the states in establishing efficient school systems and promoting the cause of education. The Department was to be headed by a Commissioner of Education, at a salary of $4,000 annually, assisted by a chief clerk and two other clerks; the total amount specified in the bill was $85,000, with an annual appropriation of $15,000. The Commissioner was to submit an annual report to the Congress with recommendations "as would serve the purposes of the law," and the first such report was to be an accounting of the federal land grants in support of education.[39]

The only remaining hurdle to final enactment was the possible opposition of the President. Barnard feared a veto, but Johnson, despite hesitation based on a fear that the bill constituted an undue extension of federal powers, was persuaded by Senator Dixon that the Department would only do "the work every year which the census undertakes to do every 10 years." The President signed the bill on March 2.[40]

Henry Barnard was not the only man in the United States to dream of a prestigious position in Washington, and applicants for the head of the new Department of Education, whose salary was to exceed that of the president of Harvard or the director of the Freedmen's Bureau, were many.[41] Among the prominent contenders was Emerson White, whose efforts for the creation of the Department were well recognized, and who was the candidate of Garfield and of the new generation of professional teachers such as James Wickersham, now the president of the National Teachers' Association. Had White been appointed the Department might have become the voice of a new professionalism in the school policy of the nation, but the opinions of the older schoolmen still carried great weight. In any case, political tensions, those between Garfield and Johnson on other issues, prohibited White's appointment.

---

bution throughout, although he gracefully recognized Garfield's importance when he printed Garfield's likeness as the frontispiece of the first number of the new National Series of the *American Journal of Education*. In a letter, June 7, 1867, Garfield sent his "photograph" and his speech introducing the bill, and suggested that they be printed together; the speech was omitted by Barnard. During the following summer he skirmished with the engraver about who was to pay for the work—Garfield finally did.

39. Barnard must have had many circulars printed which replicated the bill, for numerous letters to him, from the office clerks, were written on the surplus ones. The amount appropriated was identical with the money appropriated by the Maryland legislature —why cannot be determined although it is possible to surmise that Barnard might have suggested the figure.

40. Letter to Potter, March 2, 1867, NYU; Warren, *Enforce*, 90–91.

41. Warren, *Enforce*, 91–97, analyzes the competing contenders in detail, emphasizing the political conflicts as well as the personal ones; he does not sufficiently discuss the contenders' roles within the education community.

A second candidate was Edward D. Neill, a man very much cut to the pattern of the mid-century schoolmen. He was a clergyman and, like his rival, Barnard, an avid amateur historian. He also had experience in education as the superintendent of instruction in Minnesota both when it was a territory and after statehood. The difference between the two men was their subsequent experience. Neill had served Presidents Lincoln and Johnson as secretary and had become a new breed, a bureaucrat, in Washington; he was "rather the promoter than the successful administrator, with more versatility than tenacity of purpose."[42] Neill was comfortable in an atmosphere with which Barnard was unfamiliar, and uncomfortable.

Henry Barnard, of course, had been a candidate all along, and he had the backing of a coalition of old-time schoolmen and moderate politicians. Senator Dixon, a man skilled in the machinations of Washington, convinced the President of Barnard's qualifications and wired Barnard on March 11 that he had been nominated to the post he sought. The new commissioner was confirmed unanimously by the Senate March 15, and on the March 20 he met with the President. Johnson made it very clear that it was his understanding that the purpose of the legislation was not to establish a national system of education but rather to assist the states in their local efforts. He expressed his confidence in Barnard's "ability, experience, integrity, and devotion to the whole country," and he insisted that Neill be appointed as Barnard's chief clerk. The new Commissioner replied with remarks which he felt were "good enough."[43] He took the oath of office on March 27 and began work.

As soon as Barnard's appointment was known, congratulations flooded in. Emma Willard closed her letter of good wishes "With a kind of maternal pride in your promotion, and confidence in your success . . . ," but Samuel Randall, now estranged from Barnard, was reserved and formal: "A new educational era has opened upon us: and upon you will devolve the great task of its organization." Charles Davies asked simply "Can I help?", and some, such as William Russell and H. L. Morton, the principal of a normal school in Arkansas, sent specific proposals; unlike the President, and like Donnelly, they saw the creation of the Department as providing an opportunity for a stronger role in educational matters for the federal, and northern, government. Russell emphasized the reconstructive aspect; Barnard's new office was "so much needed to give

42. Ibid., 94, quoting *Dictionary of American Biography*, XIII:408.

43. From copybook marked Private and titled "Memoranda and Agenda of Henry Barnard, Commissioner of Education," handwritten in pencil and pen, apparently based on a diary for 1866–67, with a detailed summary of the events of February–April, 1867; the remaining sixty pages are infuriatingly abbreviated, sometimes lists, sometimes merely headings; NYU.

efficiency to an appropriate system of measures for the intellectual regeneration of the South." Morton went so far as to propose that Congress should appoint a Commissioner of Schools for each state in the defeated south, as the existing Freedmen's Bureau was "inadequate and inefficient," and he suggested that Congress publish texts for the normal schools.[44]

Then there were the job seekers. John Tenney of Massachusetts penned a four page paean ("Your record is sure for history. Further times will do you justice") closing with a plea, "Do you have a place for me?" So did Alexander Sessions, a friend from Monson days who recalled "the boy Barnard that was wont to beat us in running round the Academy if he couldn't inside of it." Barnard responded to all such inquiries that "the appointments in my gift are already disposed of"—a reference to his deal with the President, and one made ruefully.[45] Although he had agreed to appoint Neill, he neglected to complete the formalities, a lapse which annoyed Neill and worried Dixon until Barnard, who had returned to Hartford a mere three weeks after his own appointment, finally signed the secretary's commission. This initial ruffling of the waters was a harbinger of times to come, and Zalmon Richards, now Barnard's loyal second clerk, warned:

> If he has the influence with higher powers, which he claims, you will need some wisdom, and prompt decision, to get along smoothly, in managing the affairs of the Department, with him as your chief subordinate officer.

What Richards saw as essential were precisely the qualities Barnard lacked, and from hindsight it is obvious that his tenure was doomed from the start.[46]

Unfortunately, the diary which Barnard referred to in his notebook account of his commissionership has not survived, nor is it possible to date the notebook itself. It reminds one of the abortive attempt to summarize his Rhode Island years, and I suspect is from the period of his retirement, along with his "Memories of Presidents"—perhaps from those years when Will S. Monroe took the milk train to Hartford early in

44. Letters from Davies, March 13; from Willard, April 12; from Randall, April 14; from Gideon Thayer, April 8; from Russell, April 8; from Morton April 16, May 4; all 1867, NYU. Davies was the only one to mention Josephine Barnard "that is hearafter to be a public functionary in Washington." There is no evidence that she ever accompanied her husband to the capital city.

45. Letters from Sessions, March 13; from Tenney, March 14; from H. R. Oliver, from H. S. Ripley, March 21; 1867, NYU.

46. Letter from Richards, April 6, 1867, NYU; see Lannie, *Barnard*, 35–37. Lannie is more sympathetic to his subject than the evidence warrants.

the morning in order to work with Barnard on his memoirs. The note-book does serve as a source for this period but must be balanced by the more contemporary letters, for Barnard had a tendency to re-write history, especially his own.

The new commissioner commenced work with enthusiasm. He placed an order for printing and arranged for franking—actions which suggest his approach to his new endeavor. The franking privilege would be of enormous value to one with such a far-flung correspondence, and now could be justified because such letters sought information—the statutory duty of the commissioner. On his agenda the continuation of his *Journal* was an integral part of the Commissioner's duties; while he was still in Annapolis, he had announced a new National Series. In the Preface he described the creation of the new department as "the realization, in a most unexpected way" of his original plan, and he promised that his future publications would be more thorough because of his "official position and much clerical help"; it was unfortunate, however, that the "clerical force was so utterly inadequate to inaugurate an efficient system of inquiry and dissemination" as he intended.

> If he had not great reliance on his material already collected, and on the means and methods of dissemination already tried, he should at once retire from the position and continue his labors in his old unofficial and unpaid way.[47]

Even as he commenced his new career, Barnard gave primacy to his *Journal* and planned that it would benefit from his new position. And once again he complained about the resources available to him.

With Richards's assistance, Barnard set up a temporary office, and he sketched a "General Plan of Operations as Comissioner of Education." He noted his need for a chief clerk, familiar with the governmental system, "genial and loyal" and "ready with pen & tongue to work for & in & with the Department" and "the proper complement of clerks." He would eventually require five, a messenger, and an assistant messenger, and for this he estimated his expenditures, including $1,000 for books and $1,600 for additional help in 1868, and $4,800 in 1869, far more than Congress had anticipated. Barnard lived in a dream world as he wrote these plans, as Congress had barely managed to pass the department's initial funding bill. Another part of the dream was his conception of "matters to address." He made one of his detailed outlines, which dribbled off into jottings on the second page; an appendix listed three topics: the Connecticut School Fund, Donations of Individuals for Educational Purposes, Grants by the

---

47. *AJE*, National Series, XVII, 1 (September 1867): Preface.

States, all which he had previously published. In his flush of excitement Barnard was both ambitious and reactionary; he intended to accomplish great things, but lacking vision of what they were, he fell back on habit.

Barnard was accustomed to delegating, so he assigned tasks to his assistants: the chief clerk was to research the land grants, the early history of education in Virginia and other Southern states, and the history of special institutions of education, to assist Richards in matters relating to Washington, and to handle the general correspondence; Richards was to be responsible for the survey of Washington's schools, a task assigned by Congress to the department as part of the compromise agreement on the annual appropriations. (One suspects that the department's supporters won over some of its opponents by adding to the duties of the new agency.)[48] After this initial burst of energy, the Commissioner departed for Hartford, where he remained throughout the spring and summer while Richards wrote him detailed and increasingly desparing letters from the make-shift office.

The problems Richards reported were in part administrative, in part personal. Barnard had failed to attend to countless necessary details before he left, such as issuing requisitions for the clerks' salaries, authorizing expenditures, selecting the location for a permanent office, and clarifing the conflicting responsibilities of the clerks. Neill stood on his primacy and objected to the fact that Richards opened Barnard's mail, but Richards was expected by Barnard to act as a private secretary. Richards insisted that Barnard should give Neill a specific outline of work to do and complained that the chief clerk came to the office only in the mornings; the former hinted that the latter, who had maintained his office with the President, spent the remainder of the day causing trouble. Neill, on his part, voiced his dissatisfaction repeatedly, and hinted that he might complain directly to the President and request that he be appointed acting commissioner in Barnard's continuing absence. Richards pleaded with Barnard to return to Washington, for without his presence and pressure, Congress had done nothing for the department, and political opposition was brewing.

> I believe, with you, that when Congress, and the public see what you can bring forth from this Department, there will be universal satisfaction, not withstanding the evil forbodings and gloomy prognostication, which greet my ears so often.

At one point during the summer Barnard did send directions to Neill: the Commissioner would be leaving Hartford for the Institute meeting

48. Notebook, 1–6, 36–37, NYU.

in Boston and would then go to Albany for a meeting of the New York State Regents; he intended to go to Iowa and Minnesota for further addresses. Nevertheless, all private and official letters should be forwarded to Hartford where the commissioner would be "engaged on the work of the Department from 5 o'clock am to 10 when not absent in the service of Education."[49] In point of fact, the majority of Barnard's letters during the summer dealt with the *Journal* rather than the Department, and it was on the former that Barnard labored. The dates may be somewhat inexact, but numbers of the periodical appeared in January, April, and September 1868.

Some work was accomplished by the two clerks. Barnard had created a schedule of monthly circulars, designed as vehicles of communication between the commissioner and the state superintendents of schools. The June and July ones seeking information were printed and mailed; unhappily, the returns were few. The August circular was intended, in Barnard's original scheme, to contain Garfield's speech supporting the establishment of the Department, and in September the topic was to be the "Constitutional Provisions for Education." He planned to publish in October, the proceedings of the American Institute and state associations, and in November and December accounts Schools of Science, then Normal Schools, and something on Drawing and Music.[50] In actual fact Circulars IV and V were both devoted to the state constitutional provisions on schooling, VI dealt with the national land grants, VII reported on European systems, and VIII discussed the education of females—the last two being reprints of material from the *Journal*. Thus these Circulars merged, in Barnard's mind, with the Educational Tracts he had published elsewhere and with his periodical. On page 22 of his notebook he itemized proposed subsequent topics; the list is totally familiar, including number 19, "Education in relation to Crime, Insanity, Pauperism"—a pamphlet he had printed twenty-five years previously. What he intended to do was to print any article for which he had the plates and control, hoping to distribute at least 1,000 copies. In other words, through the agency of his office, he would strive to reach those who failed to read the *Journal*.

49. Letters from Richards, April 26, May 10, 16, June 18, 22, July 10, 15, 17, August 13, 20, 26; from Neill, July 31, August 3, 13; from Barnard to Neill, July 27; all 1867, NYU. Poor Richards had to pay for office furniture from his own pocket; he also hoped to rent his house, where his wife had recently run a school, to the department for offices. Barnard addressed the AII in August, and Northend proposed a resolution of thanks "for his lucid statement of the character and aims of the new national Department of Education" and to Congress for supporting education as one of the agents "in the wise reconstruction of the States." Resolution, NYU.

50. Notebook, 15–16. Characteristically, Barnard designated the number of pages for each circular.

Richards went directly to work on his specific assignment, the survey of the schools of the city, and he enlisted the aid of his brother, the head of the city police; the idea, and a sensible one, was that members of the force could serve as the agents for the census. Barnard failed to attend any meetings of the police commissioners in order to secure official approval, as Richards repeatedly requested, and then he determined to give the task of supervising the survey to another, Franklin Hough, a statistician from New York. Richards was dismayed and disappointed at being thus displaced, and he beseeched Barnard to let him do the job. He listed his claims, his knowledge of the city, and the fact that it was he who had first suggested the survey, and while admitting that he might not be able to do the job "as expeditiously and easily as an expert," he claimed he could do it "as accurately and cheaply" as Hough, who wanted $2,000 for the job. Barnard preferred his expert, or did not trust Richards, for he would not relent even though Hough could not commence work until October. The matter remained a thorn in Richards's side, and the two men never got along. Hough complained to Barnard that neither Richards nor Neill conveyed messages from Barnard, and Richards objected to Hough's methods, even through Hough proclaimed that he had finished "the *most complete* census ever undertaken in this country."[51] Why Barnard slighted his old friend, who had loyally advanced the cause of education and of the commissioner, is not clear, but by November Barnard recorded in his notebook that Richards "did not work out."

Nor did anything else. Barnard's notebook, sketchy and confused as it is, gives evidence of two aspects of his term in office: his paranoia about his staff and his almost reckless administration. These might be the embittered recollections of an old man, but the letters of the time confirm the overall veracity of the source. Barnard had not hired the third clerk authorized by Congress, preferring to use the money to employ assistants to undertake specific assignments, Daniel Gilman to work on a report of agricultural colleges, Charles Hammond, who left his teaching job at Monson to do research for Barnard, and Henry Rockwell, as well as Hough. When he had exceeded the department's appropriations, Barnard paid all of them out of his own pocket, and subsequently complained. In December he fired Neill, an action which jeopardized the very existence of the Department, after declaring the report on Washington "hurried and imperfect" and casting the blame on the chief clerk. By the spring of 1868 he had six part-time clerks, rather than the three author-

51. Letters from Richards, September 27, October 3, November 15, 19, 22; from Hough, October 19, November 13, 14, 16, 18; all 1867, NYU. Draft of letter to Hough from Barnard, notebook, 15; Barnard wanted Hough to undertake other jobs, and in this letter mentioned work in New York as well as payment of $1,600.

ized, all of whom were acting really as researchers. Barnard was advised of the disloyalty of one, Augustus Angerer, whom he had appointed to succeed Neill, by Richards in March but took no action against Angerer for nearly a year. When he finally discharged the man, he made a list of seven reasons, including "his disgraceful conduct to me personally" and the abuse, unspecified, of his position. "He is the most insidious, hypocrite I have ever had to do with in public office."[52]

Barnard's shortcomings as an administrator were not unknown. In the opinion of Emerson White, the commissioner "scatters too badly—undertakes too many schemes." Barnard's supporters warned him that his weakness was a liability to the Department; as early as September of his first year, Donnelly reported growing criticism in Congress. Barnard replied that he could not defend himself against those determined to defeat the department and said he relied, instead, on the high opinion in which he was held by his fellow schoolmen. Then he ended his letter with a self-serving, and false, claim:

> Since I accepted this position, I have devoted the working hours of everyday—and many more morning and evening hours, to maturing plans for making it useful. I shall do the best I know, ready at all times to receive suggestions and criticisms.[53]

In reality, Barnard spent precious little time in Washington, and he resented deeply any suggestions that he alter his approach.

Only crises energized the Commissioner. The deterioration of the atmosphere in his office and the necessity of firing Neill brought him to Washington for a few weeks in December 1867. The introduction of a resolution to repeal the act establishing the department forced him to return early in the new year, and to turn to his friends to lobby for the beleaguered office. Supportive letters came from the stalwart oldtimers such as Philbrick and Brooks and the new professionals such as Northrop and John Swett.[54] Their enthusiasm was not sufficient, however, for the crux of the matter was beyond their ken, and Barnard's—mainly matters of fiscal and administrative incompetence, although deep constitutional and philosophical questions were also at issue. From the very beginning the department had rested on a bed of sand, and its future very much depended on the waves of Reconstruction politics.

52. Notebook, 48–60; letters from Hammond, August 26, September 5, 1867, NYU. At the same time David Camp was serving as Barnard's secretary in Hartford.

53. White to Garfield in Warren, *Enforce*, 96; letter to Donnelly, September 19, 1867, NYU.

54. Letters from Donnelly, January 8, 9, February 3; telegram from Richards, January 11; from Hart, February 20; from Bateman, February 25; from Northrop, March 6; from

Inconceivably, Barnard returned to Hartford in the midst of the Congressional session, with his department under attack, claiming ill health. He wrote to Gilman in April that he had been "literally helpless for a week," and with a hint that he sensed the gravity of his situation, he threatened to return to Washington to

> put my house in order to quit, if the Dept must go down, & to resign, if I can continue to save the Dept for a younger and abler soldier.

Later he moaned that Washington made him "uncomfortable," and he determined it was time "to pass out of public life . . . of [his] own Choice."[55] With the writing on the wall an almost certain epitaph, Barnard seemed ready not to fight a last battle but to surrender.

James Garfield was still determined to save the Department, and to Barnard he did not mince words; in the Congressman's opinion results were required in order to silence the critics:

> My great interest in the permanence and success of the Dept. of Education induces me to suggest to you my fear that nothing but an early presentation to Congress of the valuable Reports which you have so nearly ready, will enable the friends of education of the Dept. to save it from abolition, and to defend you from the charge that is constantly being reiterated, that no good to the Nation is being accomplished by the Dept. — and that you are using the office in the interest of your Journal.[56]

Garfield's deduction was reminiscent of Potter's back in the Rhode Island days; both were astute men and both valiantly attempted to galvanize Barnard to action in order to achieve their mutual goal. Again Barnard responded at the eleventh hour and submitted the introductory pages of his annual report to Congress in June. The final and complete report, both the brief summary and well over 800 pages (a familiar number) of documents, was ready a month later, although dated June 2.[57] It was the only official report the Commissioner submitted during his tenure, although after his resignation he published several documents compiled in those years.

Swett, March 21; Brooks, April 21; from Philbrick, May 4; all 1868, NYU.

55. Letters to Gilman, April 29, June 26, 1868, JHU.

56. Letter to Barnard from Garfield in Warren, *Enforce*, 129–30.

57. *Report of the Commissioner of Education with Circulars and Documents Accompanying the Same*, June 2, 1868; repr. in *AJE* XXX (March 1880): 201ff.; in this reprinting Barnard dated the report March 15. The actual *Report* is pages ix–xxxii, the circulars are pages xxxiii–xxxix, and the total, with documents equals 856 pages.

Barnard had been directed to survey the state of education in the nation, a task similiar to those he had been assigned in his state positions, and characteristically he commenced the *Report* with a complaint about the "magnitude and delicacy" of the task. The available means were totally inadequate to survey the operations and institutions of education in the forty-six states and territories, in Barnard's opinion, yet his comment reflected former solutions.

> It is only when a searching inquiry is instituted by the National Census, or under State or municipal authorities in some form, or by societies and individuals in restricted portions of large cities, for some ecclesiastical purpose, or the antecedents of the victims of vice, pauperism, and crime are investigated, that the amazing deficiencies in our system, means, and methods of universal education appear.[58]

To meet his statutory duty of ascertaining the condition of education in the country, Barnard had planned a massive survey and had itemized in Official Circular I the information he had sought: "a full understanding of the general condition of the society and education in any community." He meant what he said in full. It took more than six pages of the Report to spell out what he expected, ranging from the obvious, information on common schools, to details on the local press, summaries of state school legislation, accounts of "the noblest benefactors" of education, and even "how far a provision exists in any of the States" for open competitive examination for state office holding "or nomination for admission to our national military and naval schools." The Commissioner had to admit that he had not really attempted to ascertain the condition of education in any but the principal cities of the country, clear evidence of his preoccupation with the evils of cities and a tacit recognition that his network of allies, mainly the schoolmen reformers and the city superintendents, had been to date his principle source. He expressed the hope that he would be authorized to "continue the investigations already instituted . . . ," for then in a "subsequent Report" he would be able, as required, to "show the condition and progress of education" throughout the nation.[59] Admittedly, the techniques of information gathering were indeed limited at the time, but data were accumulating, gathered by the statistics-minded postwar generation. Had he put himself to the task, utilizing the existing

---

58. Note Barnard's frame of reference here. Surveys, whether under public or private auspices, were primarily designed to ascertain urban conditions, and for moral and social purposes.

59. *Report*, in *AJE* XXX (March 1880): 203–04, 207–15.

material rather than amassing new information, Barnard could have met his statutory duty.

A second duty incumbent on the commissioner was that of "diffusing such information" as he collected. In Circular II Barnard had listed the plan for publication which he had "adopted and inaugurated" but which would "depend for its full development on the sanction and aid of Congress." He projected monthly circulars, and he proposed "to begin" a quarterly publication, the National Series of the *American Journal of Education*—now the "private enterprise of its publisher." He neglected to mention that he had begun the new series in 1867.

> The Department will be in no way responsible for the matter or the expense, but will avail itself of this mode of printing documents prepared by, or at the request of the Commissioner, which it may be desirable to issue in advance or aside any other form of publication.

And then he inserted a bit of advertising, the address of the publisher! To supplement the *Journal*, he proposed to prepare or revise a series of educational tracts and documents, each of which "will be devoted to an exhaustive treatment of a particular subject . . . "; and he promised future annual reports.[60] All of these materials would be, if authorized by Congress, available to the public, to any school officer, any editor, or any library.

Almost apologetically Barnard moved from what he had planned to what he had done, and it was precious little. He had "labored diligently, with such force as he was authorized to employ" to accomplish the tasks assigned and to "inaugurate measures by which the larger and wider results contemplated should, in a reasonable time, be realized." He had directed his clerk to inquire, by sending a circular to the governors of each state, about the status of the land grants and trusts for education, but the necessary responses had not been procured during the year's time. The only information produced was the constitutional provision for educational institutions submitted by the states as part of the application for statehood, material which had already been printed in Circular VI and which he repeated in the *Report*.[61] The Commissioner promised a further study on the states, which would be accompanied by "a comprehensive survey of the whole field of realistic and special scientific education in the principal States of Europe."

By a resolution of March 2, 1867, Congress had directed the depart-

60. Ibid., 215–18; the list of planned educational documents included every possible topic, including "Public Gardens and Popular Recreation."

61. The circular is page 64 of the *Report*. See ibid., 65–76 for "United States Educational Land Policy," 81–82 (chart), and 83–124, "Constitutional Provisions." It is highly probably that all of this material was easily available in Washington.

ment to institute another survey, the one on the condition of schools in the capital city. Barnard reported that he had begun "an exhaustive inquiry" in order to "form an intelligent opinion of the relative efficiency of the school systems" in the district; he claimed that he had met with school officers and made comparisons with other major cities of the country. He made absolutely no mention of the projected police canvas nor of Hough's activity during the previous fall. The delay in presenting his conclusions was due, he said, not simply to the magnitude of the task, but also to "the condition of his own health" and the fact that his staff was insufficient to visit every family and school in the district. Oddly, as if it would blind the legislators to his failures in carrying out their mandates, Barnard then went on to list what he had done, which was to publish in his circulars information, useful, certainly, but outside of the scope of his charge, and in some instances, merely reprintings of his previous publications.[62]

In the concluding section to this report on the "preliminary operations" of his department, Barnard seemed blissfully, or purposely, ignorant of the mind of Congress. He requested that he have more assistance in order to continue his investigations, an expense account for himself and one additional clerk in each class (three more); the lack of sufficient help had delayed his work and was "inconsistent with his highest usefulness, besides seriously impairing his health." He emphasized that he had borne many of the expenses of the department, for the gathering of information from abroad and for additions to the departmental library, outlays for purposes that Congress had not anticipated, and he asked for appropriations for a messenger and custodial care for the offices. He somehow had never heard of retrenchment, a battle cry in 1868.[63]

Barnard's *Report* displayed all of the characteristics of his previous work. It was clearly thrown together; the ordering of the topics and the pagination were careless at best. The treatment was consistently incomplete, and repeatedly the commissioner, or editor, promised to treat the subject in more detail at a later time. The report also proved, once again, the rut in which Barnard's vision was stuck. The words he employed, "vice, pauperism, and crime," we have heard before; recognizable, too, was his methodology, the sources and categories of information he sought and the topics he promised to discuss. The tone, too, was identical—optimistic and ambitious. Barnard continued to dream vast dreams and to project great enterprises, to intend and to promise.

62. Ibid., 218–23.

63. Ibid., 223–24; on the debate over the funding of the department, and the drive for retrenchment, see Warren, *Enforce*, 128ff.

In summary then, the failure of his first year as commissioner, for it is not unjust to label it a failure, was not as much the muddle of the office, nor the sparseness of the data collected, nor the inability to realize the expectations of his supporters, nor even the political turmoil he generated. Rather it was Henry Barnard's own failure, and it was seated deep in his very being. Time seemed to have stood still, and the Secretary of the Board of Education of 1838 was reincarnated in the Commissioner of 1868.

Not that his contemporaries and opponents saw all this. Some of his traditional allies lavished praise on his work, but others disagreed. Emerson White questioned the *Report*'s utility; what was needed was "not so much the history of education as the practical lessons of that history." And not unexpectedly Edward Neill pounced on the commissioner's work with glee.

> By the papers today I notice that the Commissioner of Education has presented his first report to Congress. If you will take the American Journal of Education for the year 1867–8, I think you will find, that it is simply a presentation of papers *already published* in that journal, including an *index of forty pages* covering the contents of that private journal for *17 years*.

A comparison of the published *Report* with Volume XVII proves that Neill was absolutely correct, for Barnard had done what he had done so often before: he had reprinted previously published material, utilizing the very same plates. Nearly 400 pages of the two volumes are identical; the material not included in the government report was either historical or pedagogical or a continuation of articles or topics begun in preceding numbers of the *Journal*. The detailed index, titled "Index to Report and Documents of the Commissioner of Education, 1867–1868," with entries ranging from "Academy, meaning of," to "Zschokke on female education," in fact was an index to the *Journal*.

That Barnard misread the Congress is obvious; that he misled them is untrue. From the very beginning of his commissionership he had seen the publication of the *Journal* as integral to the duties of his office. In addition, it should be noted that subsequent commissioners, John Eaton and William Torrey Harris for two, also utilized their *Reports* as vehicles for the communication and distribution of educational materials; the reports of the various educational committees of the nineties were all published by Harris as were articles on the state of education in Europe and speeches by eminent educators. The difference in those later cases was that the commissioners were not promoting their private enterprise, but then Barnard did not view his *Journal* as a private undertaking. In addition, those succeeding commissioners were not embroiled in such a charged personal and political atmosphere.

It was difficult to discern if Congress was disappointed in the material it received from its commissioner. Warren implies that the decision of the Senate to approve the printing of 3,000 copies of the report and only half the number of the documents, and the House's order for the printing of the report alone, was a sign of displeasure.[64] Given the mood of the Congress, with its concentration on the impeachment trial of Johnson and the necessity for fiscal conservatism, such an order was totally reasonable. But Barnard had made multiple mistakes. He had procrastinated in attending to his duty, he had produced precious little, and what he had given Congress was a stale document, both more and less than what they had ordered. Given the political climate and signs of opposition to the department, obvious to all observers, he actedd unwisely, to say the least.

The Commissioner had been directed to report on the state of education in the District of Columbia, pursuant to the Congressional authority over the city at the time the department was created, and the survey had got off to an acrimonious start in 1867. Somehow the project slumbered, for on January 17, 1870, the House passed a resolution demanding that the Commissioner, soon to be replaced, submit whatever he had completed. Two days later he responded, in a letter to the Speaker, that the information and recommendations had been ready, "with the exception of a few pages," since the summer of 1868, and "would have been printed much sooner . . . but for causes which the Commissioner could not control."[65] The letter constituted the report and was followed in the spring by over 700 pages of supporting documents. This study was far superior to the previous, hurried job, and is evidence of the quality of work Barnard could produce. It was well organized, quite readable, and focused. The census information given was clear, and the descriptions full; naturally, there was a great deal: comparative information from major American cities and European countries, plans for schools and descriptions of curricula, and Digests of Rules and Regulations in the schools of forty-nine cities. Most notable among the accompaning documents were the two long articles on education of the blacks, one which concentrated on the city of Washington, and one, probably written by Barnard, which was a historical survey of the legal status of blacks in the city and in every state of the nation.

64. Warren, *Enforce*, 116.

65. *AJE* XIX (1870): "Education in the District of Columbia" for the report and the supporting documents; the report, titled *Special Report of the Commissioner of Education on Public Instruction in the District of Columbia, and in Large American Cities* and the Table of

Barnard had developed his idea of utilizing the school system of Washington as a model to inspire local efforts in a speech to the state superintendents on March 3, just before he submitted his report, almost as if he were trying out the ideas. In the address, he suggested that the national commissioner should have increased powers, that he should be authorized to establish a model system of schools in the District, with federal funds, which would serve to inspire local governments, and in addition that he should be empowered to appoint superintendents and supervise the sale of public lands for the support of schooling in the new territories.[66] Such a federal officer was a far cry from the information gathering functionary President Johnson had appointed, and one wonders if Barnard's auditors fully comprehended what he was advocating. There could have been no question, however, what Henry Barnard, school administrator and national policymaker, said in his final official statement, the *Special Report* on the school system of Washington.

His approach to his task was unchanged, as were his excuses. The original survey was intended to be "exhaustive," but the "incompleteness" of the first one (Hough's) had necessitated "another and a more searching investigation into the historical development of education generally." Then, in order to judge the "relative efficiency" of the system, a comparison, embracing statistics, rules, budgets, salaries, architecture, and curricula, with major cities of the United States and of Europe, was essential; that document, too, was incomplete. Here Barnard the researcher spoke. He had never been able to set limits to any investigation, and the precedents for any educational development reached back in time and out in space. Past history and current practice had to inform policy.

Crystal clear and concrete were his recommendations for the amelioration of the "fragmentary, dissociated, and to some extent antagonistic school organization within the district": consolidation under a central District Board of Control, partially appointed and partially elected, some delegates elected by the teachers and one or more by the parents. This Board should have policy and fiscal responsibility, subject to review by Congress, and it should be well funded. Barnard pointed out that the federal "liberality" towards the states for educational purposes (which he had reviewed for his previous report) omitted the District.

Contents of Barnard's survey of the legal history of the education of blacks are repeated in XXX:241–68.

66. "Memorandum of Paper read before the American Association of State Superintendents, Washington, March 3, 1870," TC. Barnard was not addressing the gentlemen reformers of the AII or even the AAAE, but a group of emerging professional administrators.

In this magnificent endowment, the District has had no share. A similar appropriation in land or money to this District, at this time, would greatly aid in providing the necessary school accommodations, and meeting the expenses of an enlarged course of public instruction worthy of the capital of the country.

Barnard was correct that the ambigious position of the District, not a state in a federal system, meant that federal moneys, in this case specifically for the support of schools, by law allocated to territories and states, were denied.

Next Barnard moved to concrete proposals for the reorganization of the district system of schools into five divisions: elementary, intermediate, secondary, superior and special (including schools preparatory to teaching, for the arts and for commerce, and "for admission to any national special school"), and "Supplementary Schools and Agencies" such as adult or continuing education, classes for delinquent children, and libraries, museums, and other agencies for public enlightenment. The "crowning feature" of the District system would be a "National Polytechnic School or University" which could be established by the money saved from a reorganization of the two military academies, reducing the course at such schools by two years. Candidates for any of these superior schools would be selected by competitive examination, and thus "a stimulus of the most powerful character would be imparted to the public schools of the country."[67]

Barnard did not include a liberal arts college or university in his scheme as he had previously, although he referred to the "cherished purpose of Washington" to establish such an institution "where youths from all parts of the United States might receive the polish of erudition in the arts, sciences, and belles-lettres." The blame lay with individuals who had failed to display in Washington the liberality which had fostered colleges in so many localities, and with Congress, which had failed to provide comparable grants to the District as it had to the states.[68] The fact that Barnard did not attempt to graft a college on to the public school system, preferring a technical school, may have been a reflection of the difficulties he had faced in Wisconsin where the goals of the professors at the university were at loggerheads with the teachers at the colleges and the academies; or his recent tenure at St. John's may have reaffirmed his loyalty to the private colleges. It also reflected the pragmatic orientation of his fellow reformers and his admiration of European technical schools. No longer

67. *Special Report of the Commissioner of Education*, 240–44, 247–48, 254, quotations 250 and 251.

68. Ibid., 248. Barnard's analysis was, of course, correct.

was higher education to be solely the traditional curriculum and preparation for the traditional professions.

For once in this report, Barnard made few references to the training of
teachers, and in repeating his preference for teachers qualified for a particular grade level, he was unambiguously sexist:

> Whatever may be the number of grades into which the children
> many be classified, the teachers must be classified in reference to
> each grade, and to secure a home supply, in part at least, a normal
> course should at once be opened, in connection with the girls' high
> school, for those who show the natural apptitude for instruction
> and discipline; and a similar course in the high school for boys. for
> young men who desire to become teachers.

The difference between showing an aptitude for instruction and desiring
to become a teacher indicated the level at which each candidate was to
instruct—women in the younger grades and men at the upper ones—the
gender bias is implicit but clear. But for the most part, system and structure
rather than teachers and teaching occupied the bulk of the *Report*, and
Barnard's concern was the relation of the teachers to the whole. Teachers
would be entitled to elect a delegate to the Board of Control, and certain
teachers would share in the management of the system by holding leadership positions within their schools. No teacher in the system could be
appointed without a suitable examination, and permanent employment
would depend "on the additional evidence of actual success in teaching
and discipline in the District." Even more startling than that implied evaluation, was the commissioner's recommendation on compensation:

> To secure permanence, and, at the same time, to provide against
> disability by sickness, a system of special compensation, increasing
> with every five years of continued service, and of life assurance,
> should be adopted.[69]

More than any other of his public pronouncements, this report displayed
evolution in Barnard's conception of the modern teacher, and it certainly
reflected the views of the new leaders of the profession. Preparation had
been the cry of the antebellum period; new were the concepts of evaluation and security in the profession.

In the entire document, Barnard advocated a measure of bureaucratic
centralization, with executive duties vested in a Board of Inspection, and
an agent, the Inspector General (note the European influence here) who
had duties similiar to those of a superintendent and was assisted by cer-

69. Ibid., 249, 253.

tain teachers with supervisory authority. Yet, oddly, Barnard's recommendation that each school have two visitors, elected by the parents, was reminiscent of the old district school system—or a harbinger of the twentieth-century idea of community control.

This *Report* completed a model broached more than thirty years earlier during Barnard's first secretaryship. Then he hinted at and now he called for an articulated system of schools, under responsible leadership, to provide uniform and excellent education for all—"those with ample as well as those with small or no means but their daily labor; the educated as well as those who are unfortunately without the advantages of culture." The schools themselves should be convenient and well equipped, and there should be a system of enforced attendance, for any schools were deficient which do not "provide, induce and secure the universal education of the entire juvenile population" of the given community; absence of children under twelve, "or even fourteen," should not be tolerated, even on the grounds of economic necessity; the period of the early teens are "the teachable period of life."

> This non-attendance at school, and irregular, intermittent attendance of children of the teachable age, is the fatal weakness of American popular education; the growing cancer of our social and political life.[70]

Governance of the system was to be centralized under an incipient hierarchy of professionals, yet authority was to be shared with representatives of the parties most concerned, the teachers and parents. The proposed system differed in balance from the antebellum structure, as if Barnard had come to realize that it was no longer possible for the few elite laymen to monopolize the direction of the schools. Of course, whatever sharing of authority he advocated would be vested in the new breed of schoolmen.

Barnard included among the appended documents a report by the German Teachers Society of New York and endeavored to explain why German parents would support their special schools despite the existence of free public ones. This perennial advocate of common schools was opposed to the segregation of "impressionable" children, but he recognized that when the problem was language, the public schools must introduce the study of a native one if the community so demanded, as well as the dominant one—a very early argument for bilingual education.[71] And

70. Ibid., 252. Note that Barnard anticipated later legislation on the school leaving age.

71. Ibid., 245. Barnard admired these German schools "founded on German models and taught by men trained in the Normal Schools of Germany"—it is doubtful that he would have been as tolerant of Italian or even Swedish schools.

the inclusion of two lengthy documents on the education of blacks, both of which emphasized the studied failure to serve that element of the population, made this a truly exceptional document for the times. Once again one cannot but regret Barnard's tendency to "scatter" because of the unfulfilled promise of his insights and his foresight.

The District of Columbia *Report*, then, stands with the first Connecticut one and the only Rhode Island one as landmarks in the history of Barnard's career as a policymaker, and it marks the culmination and *finis* of that career. In it he advocated a highly centralized system, and he revealed a degree of theoretical administrative sophistication which is surprising. He expanded the vertical thrust of his proposed public school system beyond the secondary level to include higher technical schools, while maintaining the emphasis on community-wide educational opportunities. He suggested the skeleton of an administration, with a strong head who worked under an elected board. He enlarged on the idea of merit in professional selection which he had advanced in the West Point report and applied it to teachers, and he insisted on the suitable preparation for those teachers. If these recommendations had been implemented, the schools of the capital city might have been vastly improved, and the system might have served as an early beacon for administrative reform elsewhere. Barnard had this in mind, for his national perspective broke through again and again; he used phrases such as "children of this class everywhere" and "all the states" and "every city and village of the land." For the next thirty years the challenge of administering the urban systems, where children clamored for admission and schools had to be constructed almost overnight, was to occupy Barnard's successors. In the Washington report he had suggested a possible model structure, long before the giants of the urban systems appeared on the scene. Here was another lost opportunity, or one that came too early. Congress lacked the will, and the resources, and Barnard lacked the skill and the desire to implement his vision.

Between the time that Barnard addressed the Superintendents and the time he delivered his report, he lost his job. The entire Department of Education had nearly been abolished in 1868, when Congress, disgusted with Barnard and anxious to retrench, barely passed the annual appropriation, cutting the commissioner's salary and agreeing to demote the Department to a Bureau at the end of the fiscal year. Barnard had been inexplicably elated at the time:

> We have beat "Old Thad" and the great "retrencher" and shall live
> for one year more as a Dept., & after that (the deluge) as a bureau

in the Dept. of the Interior, which is probably its appropriate place.[72]

Or perhaps he was beginning that internal process so habitual to him, of withdrawing from impending trouble and retreating home.

There were plenty of ominous signs. The new chief clerk, Augustus Angerer, proved as troublesome as Neill, and Barnard attempted to fire him but was deterred by Angerer's threats to expose the endemic sloppiness in the office. In October Barnard received a letter from the President's secretary demanding an administrative report, a request which infuriated the commissioner who never in the past had been called to task and had never countenanced any criticism of his performance. To Mary Mann he wrote that he was "exhausted" from his duties and suffering under the "anonymous and outrageously false attacks on my official character by the President," which had been instigated by his clerks. He insisted that he had done no "intentional wrong" except "in *working* so hard and *spending so much money*."[73] Barnard was smarting, even as he wrote, under the attack which had appeared in the press a mere three days earlier.

> Charges of gross mismanagement are made against Mr. Barnard, Commissioner of Education. It is alleged that for a period of nearly two years he has been absent from Washington about two-thirds of his time; that he has used the clerical force of the department to assist him in editing a private journal at Hartford; and that he has been very irregular in the mode of drawing money from the treasury.[74]

Of course all of this was absolutely true. The only discrepancy between the view of the paper and of the Commissioner was one of interpretation. Barnard could not deny that he had spent more time in Hartford than in Washington, and that he had employed his assistants indiscriminantly on departmental business and research. If he had been lax in the allocation of government money and in accounting, he justified his actions on the grounds that much of the money was his in any case. Fundamentally, however, he differed from his critics in that he saw all of his work as a unified

72. Letter to Potter, July 12, 1868, NYU. The references are to Senators Stevens and Washburne, the former who opposed the department because of its ineffectiveness, the latter because of its cost; see Warren, *Enforce*, 131–36 for the struggles over funding the department.

73. Letter to Mary Mann, November 21, 1868, from Washington, MHS. Barnard complained of the work of unpacking sixty boxes of materials, as he set up his new office—all of this in a letter of condolence which reveals a singular lack of sensitivity to the bereaved.

74. Warren, *Enforce*, 139; on Barnard's dismissal, see 136ff.

effort on behalf of national education; public and private held no distinction for him, and historically the line between the two had never been clear in matters of schooling. What is more he found it inconceivable that anyone should criticize him or impugn the purity of his motives or actions.

Barnard blamed his subordinates, Neill and Angerer, for his troubles, perhaps with some justification, and even the long-suffering Zalmon Richards, whom he also fired, with none. He continued to have some support in Congress, and during the winter session of 1869, he was exonerated in a report of the House Committee on Education and Labor, whose chairman managed to praise the Commissioner. For inexplicit, but entirely understandable reasons, neither Garfield nor Donnelly, the erstwhile promoters of the department, persisted in their struggle to salvage it, and the measly appropriations for the fiscal year 1869–70 amounted to a death warrant for Barnard's dream. What was salvaged was a small office, with a pig-headed but dedicated head, operating on a fraction of the budget he had enjoyed in previous years, resolutely amassing information about the condition of education. Ironically Barnard found himself precisely in the position he had proposed in 1855.

The appointment of John Eaton, who succeeded Barnard as head of the reduced agency on October 27, 1870, lends some substantiation to Barnard's almost paranoid view of the political motives behind the attacks on him. Eaton was a savvy political appointee with a modicum of experience in education, and he had the support of the President and of the national teachers who strove to maintain some federal presence in education. Eaton succeeded to an an office "so crowded with books, pamphlets, and desks as to be wholly unfit for successful clerical work"—a vivid description which summons up a picture of Barnard's habitual work spaces. In the main, however, in his administration, Eaton mimicked Barnard's activities, gathering statistics and distributing circulars, although on a reduced scale; his reports were, however, less prone to the historical. The new commissioner even suggested that the government purchase the former commissioner's extensive library, but the idea came to naught. Years later Eaton would be generous in his assessment of his predecessor. Barnard's intentions had been laudable: to "make the bureau enforce the universal relation of education to all the details of man's improvement," by seeking and disseminating information, both historical and comparative, all with the most laudable aim, and with a lasting effect.

> Indeed, it will be hardly possible for a national office of education to find anything appropriate to publish which is not included in the plans of Dr. Barnard as touching on education and its relation.[75]

75. *Report of the Commissioner of Education* (1870), 5, 8; *NEA*, 412–14.

The story of Henry Barnard's service as Commissioner of Education is a sad, even dismal one, a tale of what might have been. His department was born of parents with discordant aims and became a pawn to be played by contenders struggling in a larger game, which was often entirely political. Then, as had been the case in Wisconsin, expectations among the department's supporters were unrealistically high, and most of them failed to anticipate that the machinery to implement their goals was lacking. Of course, any derilection or perceived failure was bound to lead the opponents of the department to pounce with delight on its advocates or its head. Barnard cannot be blamed entirely for the department's lack of demonstrasted success, for he had to contend with disgruntled subordinates, a restricted budget, and the often recalcitrant cooperation of state and local colleagues. Bureaucracy, local and federal, was still in an embryonic stage, and the Department of Education was not alone in its inefficiency and ineffectiveness. Yet history *has* blamed Barnard, and for this he must answer. He assigned the bulk of the credit for the creation of the department to himself, and it was his version of its demise that was accepted. He saw himself rejected, unappreciated for his magnificent effort, and he could only summon up petty, personal reasons for the rejection. And so he retired, for a final time, to Hartford and to his cluttered and welcoming study.

VII

EDUCATIONAL

HISTORIAN

*The education of a people bears a constant
and most pre-eminently influential relation
to its attainments and excellencies—
physical, mental and moral. The national
education is at once the cause and an effect
of the national character; and, accordingly,
the history of education affords the only
ready and perfect key to the history of the
human race, and of each nation in it,—
an unfailing standard for estimating its
advance or retreat upon the line of human
progress.* (Philobiblius [Lucius Brockett],
History and Progress of Education,
introduction by Henry Barnard, 15)

On February 26, 1855, Barnard had printed a circular in Hartford, addressed to all the school officials, requesting information for a
history of education in Connecticut. The form of the questions was similar to those he had previously sent out as superintendent; he specified
that he wanted responses in two categories: institutions other than the
common schools, and supplementary agencies of education. He received
numerous replies from throughout the state, all of which revealed active
and differentiated educational activity—Nathaniel Foote even described
the Norwich Academy of Music, founded in that very year. Although
Barnard did publish in his *Journal* a comprehensive history of the common schools in Connecticut, he never utilized the material he collected
that spring—another example of his unfulfilled intention.[1] By summer,

1. The circular and the responses are in the Trinity College archive. Barnard introduced Brockett's book, in the quotation which starts this chapter, as a "pioneer American

he was preoccupied with another scheme. As he began to move from the state to the national scene, so he began to dream of a national journal. Like his fellow reformers, he had always seen publication as one weapon in the arsenal of the school activists, lectures being another. His predilection was entirely understandable, for the antebellum period was a talky time. Words, words, words flowed, from the pulpit, from the lyceum stage and, more than ever before, from the press. According to a contemporary, the Americans were "emphatically a reading people." In New England there had been only 65 newspapers in 1800, but by 1850 there were 371, 46 of them in Connecticut alone; in 1810 there had been a mere 26 monthlies, but by mid-century 175 circulated. Not all, of course, had intrinsic value; "some of them are very substantial, and worth preserving, while many of them are light and trashy, intended merely to amuse the volatile and gay."[2]

It was relatively easy for an energetic and intellectually ambitious man to inaugurate a publication; presses sought business, contributors were eager, pirating or copying from peer publications was common, and there was no postage charged for the exchange of copies between editors, a very common practice.[3] Senior among the many contemporary periodicals was the venerable *North American Review*, which had first seen the light of day in 1815. This organ of New England liberal theology and social responsibility was modeled on the great British journals; its subscribers were of the same class and commitment as the British readers, educated, moral, reformist, and Whig. Under the editorship of proper Bostonians such as Edward Channing, the *Review* combined a basic conservatism with a devotion to popular education and moral uplift. More specialized monthlies or quarterlies served particular interests, for example the farmers, or the emerging professions, and others were published by literary groups, historical societies, and reform associations. Authorship and readership overlapped, and Barnard seems to have read an inordinate number of these periodicals, American and English, on education and a host of other topics.

The first specifically educational periodical to appear in the United States was the *Academician*, published in New York in 1818 by Albert Pickett, with his son John. It was designed to be the organ of the Society

---

work in its department" while ruing the fact that educators in the United States were for the most part "deprived" of a proper history of education as well as "of any thing like a scientific training in their profession"; he aimed to fill the void through his own publications.

2. Davis, *Half-Century*, 93–94, 98–101, quotations 99 and 101.

3. Sidney L. Jackson, *America's Struggle for Free Schools* (Washington, D.C.: American Council on Public Affairs, 1941), 10–11, 177n21.

of Teachers of New York City and featured, for example, a twenty-page article on Pestalozzi; unfortunately it died within the year, a common fate of many periodicals which came and went with confusing frequency. The *Academician* was succeeded in 1826 by the first "really important American magazine in the field of education," the *American Journal of Education*, edited by William Russell until 1830 and then by William Woodbridge (who added the words *Annals of Education* to the title).[4] The aim of the new journal was broad, to diffuse "*enlarged and liberal views of education*," emphasizing both the moral and the physical, and "to advocate and aid female education," but it was chiefly "devoted to early or elementary education." Among the topics the *Journal* pledged to cover were infant schools, the proper education of female children (as preparation for motherhood and teaching alike), practical hints for instruction (including "mutual instruction"), the need for seminaries for teachers, for mechanics' institutes, and for the education of the agricultural classes, the desirability of associations for mutual improvement, and a survey of foreign innovations in education (such as Sunday schools and "institutions for the Deaf and Dumb")—all pursuant to its effort to be "selective."[5]

The list of the *Journal*'s publishers, editors, and contributors reads like a roll of honor of the early schoolmen: Samuel Goodrich, James G. Carter, and the Williams—Russell, Woodbridge, and Alcott. They constituted the elite, and their journal was read primarily by the elite, their friends in the American Institute of Instruction. They sought, too, to inspire and to uplift the simple, struggling teacher, but they failed; their periodical was too learned, too expensive, and too high-minded. It was of very high quality. It appeared with regularity and was well written; at the end of each issue were notes and news, and reviews of books on education. A typical issue contained: an article on education in France, translated by a Yale professor from the French *Journal of Education*; "Suggestions to Parents on Female Education," by "a Mother"; selections from an address on the "Effects of Education upon a Country Village," delivered to the Brighton (Massachusetts) Evangelical Church; more selections,

---

4. In *NS*, 194, Barnard summarized the antebellum educational publications, commencing with Russell's journal, but in a later work, *NE*, 518–19, he credits Albert Pickett's Juvenile Monitor, 1811, with being the first. See *CCSJ*, n.s., I, 5 (1855): 150–56, for lists of publications to 1854, and *AJE* I, iv (May 1856) and XV, xxxviii (March 1865) 383–84, for a list to 1864; in the latter instance he asked his readers, "Please assist in perfecting the Catalogue."

5. *AmJEd* (1826): Retrospect, 751ff. The editor pledged in the future to be more focused, and yet, in IV, i (January and February 1829): introduction, the new editor promised to disseminate more general, useful knowledge.

from the Boston *Advertiser*, on Monitorial instruction; a review of a recent work, *Infant Education*; and the First Annual Report of the Infant School Society of New York.[6] In combination with the early Lyceum, whose voice the *Journal* became, its successive issues served to create and circulate a cohesive platform for common school reform.

The *Journal's* very title proclaimed its lofty goal, of becoming a voice for the nation, just as its readers belonged to the American Institute and attended the American Lyceum. But at the same time, other, smaller, journals were spawned in the states as mouthpieces for the burgeoning common school reform movement. Little noticed is the fact that these appeared first, not in the cultivated East, but in the West, in Illinois (1837, the first), in Ohio, and in Michigan, before Mann and Barnard and Francis Dwight initiated their legislative-sponsored publications. By 1840 there were over forty of these struggling publications, and then, abruptly, they failed, and there remained only three, in Massachusetts, Connecticut, and New York. Even these were vulnerable, dependent on grudging state subsidies and devoted editors.[7]

The influence of the first *American Journal of Education* on Henry Barnard is obvious. When he came to edit his own journal, he gave full credit to the "arduous labors" of William Russell who, unassisted, with no "pecuniary benefit," did double duty, teaching by day and editing by night, all in a selfless service to the cause of education.[8] With Russell's blessing, Barnard adopted the title of the now defunct predecessor, as well as its goals, and he utilized many of the same contributors. Great as was Barnard's achievement, it must be seen as part of a noble tradition.

Once again, because Barnard served as his own historian, it is difficult to detect the entire truth in the account of the founding of the *American Journal of Education*. According to him, after much of the first number of the projected journal was in print, he decided to collaborate with Absalom Peters, a Presbyterian minister rather more concerned with college than common school education, who was also contemplating initiating a journal. The first issue purportedly "was published in the type, style and matter" of Barnard with Peters's Prospectus. But Barnard had written to

6. *AmJEd* III, v (May 1828). Jackson, *Struggle*, 80, 84, puts the circulation of the *Journal* at nearly 900, which is large. A comparison of Davis, *Periodicals*, chap. IV, "Contributors," with the concept of the generations of schoolmen in Mattingly, *Classless Profession*, is instructive; both identify two generations, the generalist up to 1840 and the professional after 1860; Davis also detects, 68–69, a far less moral tone after 1870.

7. Davis, *Periodicals*, 7ff. Davis noted the peripatetic nature of editorship; the *Western Academic* (1837) was begun by the Picketts who had emigrated West.

8. *AJE* III, viii (March 1857): 139–46, certainly Barnard although not listed as such in the index.

Mann in July that he proposed to start a "Journal and Library of Education," to cover the entire field, from colleges to common schools, which "might" be in connection with the *College Review* of Reverend Peters; he wrote in a like fashion to a number of his friends. Throughout the spring and summer he was in active correspondence with Peters, apparently attempting to work out a *modus operandi* for the joint enterprise. Barnard does seem to have been largely responsible for the contents of the first number, and he also wrote a circular, to be sent to the members of the American Association for the Advancement of Education, which described the new periodical.[9]

Peters, in turn, reported that he had put the prospectus into shape "as well as I can, without your advice," and he suggested that it be sent to 10,000 prospective subscribers. He negotiated with the publishers, he set up "our office" (in New York), he found clerical assistance, and by August he had signed up 108 subscribers. Most of all, he attempted to cope with the frustration of dealing with Barnard. Peters's was a tidy mind, and he sought to establish a proper sequence of articles as well as some economy in the first number; he also tried to stem Barnard's exuberant expenditure and verbosity. Their partnership, he wrote, would require "some balancing" but "with a spirit of mutual accommodation," could work.[10]

The first number of the *American Journal of Education and College Review* is dated August 1855, despite clear evidence that it did not actually see the light of day until late October.[11] The prospectus outlined the vital need for a national association in the support of education and for a voice, a publication,

> which should, on the one hand, embody the matured views and varied experiences of wise statesmen, educators and teachers in perfecting the organization, administration, instruction and discipline of schools of every grade, through a succession of years, under widely varying circumstances of government, society and religion, and on the other, should harmonize conflicting views, expose real deficiencies, excite to prudent and efficient action, and serve as a

9. That Barnard hoped his new journal would be the unofficial organ of the AAAE is certain. On July 24, 1855, John Whitehead of the Newark Normal School forwarded a list of the members to whom Barnard could send the circulars.

10. *AJE* II, i (May 1856): Preface; Letter to Mann, July 3, MHS, from Mann, July 12; from Peters, June 19, 21, July 3, August 17, September 12, 17, October 20, 25, 27, November 17, 23; from Potter, July 4; from Russell saying he had received the circular; from Collins, Co., publisher, July 23, August 14.

11. The imminent appearance of the journal was announced in CCSJ, II (ns), 10 (October 1855), and it was reviewed in 11 (November 1855), 480. Two friends, Lorin Andrews and Caleb Mills did not receive their first numbers until December.

THE

AMERICAN

𝔍ournal of 𝔈ducation.

EDITED BY

HENRY BARNARD, LL.D.

VOLUME II.

HARTFORD, F. C. BROWNELL.
LONDON: TRÜBNER & CO., 12 PATERNOSTER ROW.
1856.

*American Journal
of Education,*
volume II, 1856,
title page.

medium of free and frequent communication between the friends
of education in every portion of the great field.

This sounds suspiciously, and characteristically, like Barnard despite his
identification of Peters as the primary author. The words "matured views"
and "prudent and efficient action" and the whole tone are totally familiar.
The contents of the first number was definitely Barnard's, for the first 136
pages were the long-promised *Proceedings* of the fourth session of the
American Association, with Barnard's "Plan for a Central Agency of Education" given prominence. In addition there were two articles, each of
which might have been of use to teachers, one on "moral and mental"
discipline and one on school government.

If the inaugural number gave indications of some haste in preparation,
the second, dated January 1856, did not. In a sense it should be considered
the first volume of the *American Journal of Education*, as the periodical
came to be called. The editors intended that it serve as a "specimen" and

mailed it *gratis* to several thousand prospective subscribers. In a strong introduction, they pledged that the journal "was designed not to float merely, on the tide of public opinion, but to influence it . . . , by free discussion of the weighty educational issues of the day." They alleged that the lack of a truly national journal was felt by the editors of the imperманent, smaller journals and by "enterprising teachers"; yet, in a rueful and perhaps prophetic aside, they wondered if the varied people of the entire nation would indeed support a common publication.

> Will the North agree with the South, and the South with the North, the East with the West, and the West with the East?

Sectional animosities, looming so ominously in 1855, had no place in the discussion and promotion of education, and the efforts of all states, whichever and wherever, should be equally recognized. Thus the journal would strive to be a national voice. It would also consistently maintain the importance of a moral and a Christian culture, although avoiding any denominational stances, and it vowed to welcome discussion of any debatable issue "for the sake of the light and the instruction which may thus be rendered available in their common benefit."

> Patriotism and the love of learning, and every principle of good citizenship, to say nothing of the laws of Christian kindness, will dictate a friendly discussion between those who are the widest asunder in their views.

Knowledge and information, not controversy or polemic was the goal, for "all mankind are interested in the right education of every state and every nation."[12] The *Journal* was to be a record of the history of education and of the continuing efforts to ameliorate that education in the nineteenth century, particularly in the United States. It was to be enlightened, moral, nonsectarian, and impartial, and for the entire nation.

In any survey of Barnard's correspondence and the hundreds of articles in the *Journal*, the casual reader is struck by the apparent cocoon in which the schoolmen reformers lived. There was almost a serene ignorance, or indifference, or even escapism in their single-mindedness, their concentration on education almost to the exclusion of anything else. Abolitionist fervor, sectional animosity, the rancor of politics, swirled about while they attended their meetings and delivered their lectures. Yet in this intro-

12. *American Journal of Education and College Review* I, 2 (January 1856): introduction, 137–40, signed P. Peters, November 17, sent Barnard a draft of an "editorial," and the emphasis on formal religion probably was his; Barnard's voice is clear in the emphasis on the national role.

duction we see just a glimpse of a reflection of the increasing national tension and of the impending national tragedy. Henry Barnard was not blind, nor unintelligent, but he was limited. He had some knowledge of the disputing sections of the country, and he sensed their separate identities—recall his comments when as a youth he traveled south for the first time. But his very soul recoiled, as it always had, at the thought of controversy, and being a rather benign man, unless thwarted, he was unable to comprehend the depths of passion which would rend the nation asunder. The answer, to him, was simple: education. He was indeed moving beyond the more parochial Whiggism of his youth, where education was perceived to be for moral and for more narrow political purposes; in education now might be found the salvation of the country. As Noah Webster had striven to create a nation by means of a common language, so now Barnard hope to preserve that nation by a common education. He remained a good conservative and, as editor, he hoped that by making available the right ideas of the best men, the people of the nation would respond, forgetting the minor cleavages in order to restore the former, more harmonious, whole.

The publication of the *Journal*, and this specific statement, marks a significant alteration in Henry Barnard's orientation; his focus and his canvas had broadened. Through his friendships, his travels, and his national memberships, and even through his research, he had moved away from Connecticut. During the next fifteen years he became increasingly committed to national activity, a direction which culminated, as we saw, in his appointment as the first national school administrator. And all because he saw education as a powerful, binding force, an idea first articulated by the schoolmen reformers of the thirties. They strove to maintain the social unity of the town or state; he had transferred that goal to the nation.

In the interim, however, there were to be many volumes of the *Journal*. The second number was of high quality. The American Association for the Advancement of Education received continued prominence with the printing of a number of addresses from the 1855 convention, including ones by the venerable Denison Olmstead and the rising F. A. P. Barnard. A new feature, which would become a hallmark of the publication, was the "Memoirs of Benefactors of Education, Literature and Science." Barnard himself wrote the first sketch, of Abbott Lawrence, and followed it with a description of the new Lawrence Science School at Harvard, a reflection of his growing interest in technology. The number closed, as had those of its predecessor of the same name, with a brief section entitled Educational Intelligence, for the most part a listing of impending annual meetings, of the august American Institute of Instruction, the newer American Association, and of the Western College Society.

Even before the first issue of the new journal had seen the light of day, there were those who saw the joint venture fraught with problems. William Russell, for one, worried that Barnard's partnership with Peters would limit circulation, and Mann had urged his friend to "keep your Journal & Library independent of any one else's schemes." Any shared editorship is bound to be problematic, and, given the personalities of the men involved, this one was doomed. In letter after letter Absalom Peters besought Barnard's cooperation, even his response. Barnard, in turn, who had always preferred to operate alone, or as the boss, attempted to dictate, to have, for example twenty-two pages for his memoir of Lawrence rather than the agreed upon eighteen, thereby, given the constraints of nineteenth century pagination, forcing Peters to abbreviate his own material. The sources of the tension were dual. Peters, who was obviously the more businesslike of the two, chafed at Barnard's constant procrastination. "This business must be hastened, or it will not be possible for us to issue the number in November," he pressed. Barnard, on the other hand, resented the pressure; "I have been harassed to death about this Journal," he wrote to Gilman. Any suggestions which did not originate with him seemed harassment; he wanted to operate on his own schedule, relying on his own judgment, and he expected Peters to assume the role of the willing and cooperative subordinate whom he could dominate, a Baker, a Camp, a Richards.

By December, when the second number was not yet through the press, the partnership dissolved, as Barnard reported to Gilman.

> Dr. Peters and I have agreed to seperate [*sic*]. After the issue of our next number we shall each *continue* the publication of an Educational Journal on his own plan and hook—each claiming *Nos.* 1&2—each commencing with No3.[13]

A few of Barnard's friends regretted the break, but most were delighted that he was now independent. Elisha Potter felt that the turmoil and subsequent split had "waked" his friend up a bit. William Wells spoke for the inner circle of reformers:

> Most of us have some doubts about Dr.Peters ever having established his claim to be taken as a leader in the educational world. It was *your* paper that I subscribed for.

13. Letter from Russell, August 20, 1855; from Mann, July 12, 1855; from Peters, September 20, October 20, 25, November 17, 21, December 19, 1855; NYU; to Gilman, Decem-

Although a few subscribers canceled their subscriptions, remaining loyal to Peters, and others were under the mistaken impression that Barnard had retired from publishing, most of his associates reassured him that he need not fear the competition, that, in the words of one supporter, Peters's publication "will not create much sensation upon its own merits."[14]

The epilogue to this brief episode does neither editor much credit, although we have only Barnard's account of the matter. Each had agreed to continue, each claiming the first two numbers for his own. Peters did edit the *American Journal of Education and College Review* for a year and a half with, surprisingly, Barnard's old and dear friend Samuel S. Randall as his assistant, and in his March issue he failed to mention Barnard's intention to publish a rival journal. Barnard, for his part, deleted any mention of Peters in the reissuing of the first number of his journal. By then he was calling Peters a "Parson Sly-boots," an untrustworthy associate whose perfidious nature was proven by his attempts to pirate material from Barnard and to lure subscribers away by false implications.[15] Mild-mannered Henry Barnard could indeed be vicious when angered. There was no need, for his *Journal* would, if not prosper, remain a monument to his learning and industry while that of Peters would wither away.

Anyone confronting Barnard's quarterly, the thirty-two octavo volumes which averaged 800 pages each and which were issued spasmodically between 1856 and 1881, can only bless Richard Thursfield for his careful and comprehensive study, published in 1945. There is no need to duplicate it, nor do I intend to do so. But that work has serious limitations, which the author realized, and an over-riding weakness, which he did not. Thursfield understood "that the story of Barnard's *Journal* is a story of personal journalism" and that it was a nearly insurmountable obstacle to separate the man from the work. He concentrated on the latter; I am concentrating on the former. I shall analyze the contents of the *Journal* only in so far as so doing will contribute to my goal of portraying Henry Barnard, reformer, schoolman, administrator, historian. Thus the *Journal*, fascinating in itself, will appear to be slighted. And, because my

---

ber 6, 1855, JHU. Barnard seemed to want Gilman to serve as an assistant or associate; one wonders if that association would have endured.

14. Letter from Potter, in which he congratulated Barnard on the addition to his family, January 18, 1856; from Alpheus Crosby, who was starting his own educational periodical and said, "I shall be very happy with my gun-boat to cooperate with you in your newly launched 'seventy-four,'" January 31, 1856; from Dwight, canceling, March 15, 1856; from Wells, January 12, 1856; from McCaster, January 31, 1856; from Zalmon Richards, March 26, 1856; all NYU.

15. See Thursfield, *Barnard*, 29–30; the author makes no attempt to question Barnard's version of the dispute.

focus is on Barnard, the man, warts and all, and because I am attempting to place the *Journal* in the perspective of the entire life, I find that I am more critical than Thursfield. The *Journal* was, without a doubt, a magnificent accomplishment, but one which, when inspected closely, had patent weaknesses and limitations; these will be discussed below. The *Journal* became Barnard, under his sole control and direction; its reputation became his reputation, which he chose not to share, not with collaborators such as Daniel Gilman, who obtained materials, nor with agents such as Cornelius Wells, who struggled to secure subscriptions. Thursfield accepted uncritically all of Barnard's complaints, about his health and frustrations, never questioning the fact that it is Barnard himself we hear. In short, I fear that Thursfield failed to challenge the Barnard myth.

In his own bibliography, Barnard listed the *American Journal of Education* as a periodical commencing in 1856; it was designed to be a quarterly although it appeared with regular unpredictability. By 1881 thirty-one volumes, of sizes ranging from 622 pages (XI) to 941 pages (XXX), had been completed, a six-foot-long achievement.[16] It is important to underscore the fact that there was a periodicity to the publication, that the entire *Journal* is, in fact, a coordinated series of journals, in part because Barnard designed it that way, and in part because its appearance always reflected his life, activities, and preoccupations over the twenty-five-year period. Each of the eras of the mini-journals is punctuated by the publication of at least one volume of material culled from the *Journal*, a work which concentrated on a single topic and was advertised separately; recall that Barnard always linked any of his journals with a Library of Education. He sought two diverse audiences with his paired publications, the elite and intellectual reformers with the *Journal* and the practicing teachers with the Library; he made, however, no compromises in his efforts to attract the latter, for the content was identical.

Volumes I through X comprise the First Series of the *Journal* and were issued from March 1856 (iii) until June 1861 (xxv), but Barnard was not always confident that he would be able to complete even that ambitious a project. In number xi of volume IV (December 1857) he printed a circular summarizing his achievement to date; he had met his "engagements" for 1857 with the publication of 1,352 pages and 10 portraits, which was 350 pages and 6 woodcuts more than he had promised; he pledged to continue through 1858, with numbers xiii through xv constituting volume V. Those five volumes would be the First Series and "the first installment of

16. At times Barnard's numbering and renumbering of the volumes and issues can be confusing; for instance, volume XI is also I (New Series), and XVII is I (National Series); I employ the consecutive scheme.

the Encyclopedia of Education." The word Encyclopedia is important; Barnard was not claiming to write analytical history but aiming to make available the materials on education, with the widest possible definition, to the American public. He was painfully aware that he was dependent on his subscribers, however, and he added that if all of the current ones would renew, and if each would forward one new subscription, he, the editor, would no longer be burdened by a "large pecuniary loss." Barnard's appeal for an additional 1,000 subscribers came at a time when he was in straitened circumstances, but he persisted in his ambitious plan. In December 1858, he printed a "note" from the editor, announcing the completion of the first five volumes and his intention to continue the *Journal*.[17]

The first volume of the projected Library of Education was published during this initial period of the *Journal*. *Preventive, Correctional and Reformatory Institutes and Agencies in Different Countries* was identical to material in volume III of the *Journal*, particularly numbers eight and nine.[18] The topic, a common concern of antebellum reformers, was one which had commanded Barnard's attention from his earliest days as a legislator; his entire career in the field of education had, as he said in words almost identical to reports and addresses issued during his second administration in Connecticut, convinced him of the

> necessity of establishing and employing special institutions and agencies, of various kinds, to meet the educational deficiencies and counteract the causes and tendencies to vice and crime among a large and increasing class of the population in cities and manufacturing villages.[19]

Given Barnard's consistently broad definition of education, it was entirely appropriate that a system of public instruction should include the instruction of those dwelling outside the normal range of the schools—hence his emphasis on evening schools, libraries, lyceums, and now institutions designed for the deviant. All of these educational agents had the same goal, that the "moral jungles" of the cities should be "broken up" and that children who from birth had been trained "to an utter want of self-

17. *AJE* IV, xi (December 1857): 542; V, xv (December 1858): 848. In number xi he included an index for numbers x and xi—he loved making them.

18. *Preventive, Correctional and Reformatory Institutes and Agencies in Different Countries*, Part I, European States, Part II, United States (Hartford: F. C. Brownell, 1857; hereafter *RI*); even the index is identical.

19. *RI*, 5–6. See also *AJE*, III, ii, Supplement; in the section on "Publications on Reformatory Education," there is an entry in the index to "Papers on Preventive, Correctional and Reformatory Institutions and Agencies by Henry Barnard LL.D., Hartford, F. C. Brownell, 360pg."; this notation was a necessary form of advertising.

respect, and the decencies and proprieties of life" by "vicious and intemperate parents" in "tainted homes" should be reformed through "systematic plans of local benevolence"; schools, Sunday schools, tracts, books, "cheap, innocent and humanizing games, sports and festivities," and, if necessary, institutions for the basest, would preserve society and restore it to its pristine form. The class bias is unpleasant here, as is the evidence of Barnard's harsh nature; although he did not share the theological beliefs of his more doctrinaire peers, he equaled them in his moral absolutism.

Through his extensive reading, correspondence, and visits abroad, and with the active assistance of Gilman, who did most of the leg work in Europe, Barnard had become something of an expert on contemporary innovations in the correctional field—at least on the Continent.[20] Although he alleged that his book was in two parts, implying that something akin to equal time would be given to the reformatory movement in his native land, in fact Part II consists of one page! As he had so often asserted, reform schools and similar institutions were necessary for those beyond the pale, those mired in pauperism who, in England, are "an actual nation by itself, almost as distinct, permanent and self-propagating as a body politic." Such poverty was "the great fountain of vice, beggary and crime" and a constant threat to the social order. The solution was to create institutions which would rescue the young from conditions of degradation and place them in ones designed according to the just principles of a moral order.[21]

When Barnard came to describe the characteristics of European reformatories, they sounded suspiciously familiar. He stressed the "distinctly preventive character of the movement generally" which was another way of saying its conservative, in the true sense of the term, nature. All the schools he instanced, Fellenberg's in Switzerland, the Christian Brothers schools in Rome, Mettray in France, Red Hill (which he had visited) in England, were based on a family plan of organization "to afford the best possible substitute for the parental care of which the pupils are deprived." All were first established on a small scale, the effort of a single individual, assisted perhaps by a group of friends who willingly aided the valiant and visible efforts of the dedicated altruist; once the value of the new school or farm was proven, and the need for support obvious, the state would step in, trading financial support for supervisory powers. Trained teachers, who possessed "almost missionary spirit," were essential.

20. In a letter May 25, 1857, Oliver Strong wrote from New York that the Board of Managers of the Asylum in New York had donated $50 toward Barnard's work, and Strong hoped that his own board (of the New York House of Refuge and Reform Schools) would contribute $200 or even $250; see Thursfield, *Barnard*, 54 and 41.

21. *RI*, 342; *AJE* III, ix (June 1857): 800.

It is only a spirit of the most immediate, practical, home benevolence, looking to the benefit of the nearest and neediest, and influencing a class with whom, with us, such motives have too little weight, which calls out this class of laborers in the field of reform.

Each of the reformatory schools should have a normal department attached where those called to serve could act as assistants. The program, or curriculum, might include some industrial training, but for the most part it should attempt to counteract the creeping urbanization of the times and reinforce the dwindling rural skills. Parents of the recalcitrant should be expected to make some contribution to their child's welfare, and women should be active on behalf of the school—in raising funds, in teaching the girls, and in acting as patrons to those who left the schools; patronage, the continued supervision and support of those who left the enclosed community, was essential to insure that none slide back.

What Barnard outlined was an embryonic system of social welfare, designed to counteract the horrors of the nineteenth-century urban centers; like his peers, he relied on personal intervention and initiative.

It may be added that nearly all of the excellencies above enumerated are directly or indirectly traceable to the extensive existence of personal, practical, active and painstaking charity among the individuals of European communities.[22]

Barnard, in suggesting the advisability of augmenting private efforts with state assistance and supervision, echoed his fellow reformers and many statesmen, all of whom were perfectly comfortable with mixed and non-hierarchical governmental support for social service. He was also thinking in his accustomed frame of reference. The evolution of correctional and reformatory institutions should follow the pattern of the common schools, commencing usually with private efforts supplemented by a stronger governmental role, when necessity dictated, and including training or normal schools. Barnard, like his peers, never sensed any contradiction between his repeated recognition of the efforts of individuals and his advocacy of state action for social purposes; it was not until later in the century that a clear and complete differentiation between the public and private spheres was established.

In the years 1859–61 Barnard published five more volumes of the *Journal*; each volume contained two numbers and, until 1861, two volumes appeared in a single year. It was a continual struggle to keep the enterprise afloat, and in the March 1860 number, the publisher, F. B. Perkins inserted a note that the new volume would only be sent to those who had

22. *RI*, 351–52; *AJE* III, ix (June 1857): 809–10.

paid in advance.[23] Barnard may have been under some sort of a warning from Perkins, who probably tried to control his friend and editor; in an obvious attempt to summon support, Barnard inserted a new circular in January. He recalled that he had intended the *Journal* to be

> national and catholic in aim and spirit, of sufficient extent to admit, in each issue, of full discussions of the History, Biography, Art and Science of Education, and of the organization, administration, and statistics of its Institutions and Systems.

His efforts over the several years to procure the support of state or national educational bodies, such as the AAAE, and to attract the steady subscribers had failed. Nonetheless, he claimed that

> this period was five of the best years of my life; which I was from the first prepared to give to the work, without the slightest expectation of receiving any compensation for time or editorial services.

He was reluctant to relinquish his dream, despite the frustrations and disappointments, so he determined to make one additional appeal. He promised to complete at least three more volumes which would include: a history of normal schools, a survey of Polytechnic and other special schools, the history and curriculum of "flourishing colleges and universities" in Europe and America, a description of the "most recent as well as the oldest" methods of teaching the "elementary and higher branches," and the biographies of "Teachers and Promoters of Education."[24] Quite an ambitious plan for a mere three volumes, and much of it realized in the succeeding numbers.

With the appearance of number xxv in June, 1861, Barnard declared the completion of the First Series of his *Journal*. In a note at the end of the Table of Contents, he promised that the index to volumes VI through X, which was to have been included in the final volume, would be published as a general index in a succeeding volume. For once the inveterate list-maker failed, probably because he was occupied with other publishing ventures; the Classified Index to volumes I through XVI was published in volume XVII in 1867.[25] In a sense this underscores the continuity of the next six volumes with the First Series. Barnard himself, in his preface to volume XI, inaugurating the New Series in 1862, promised

23. Perkins was the publisher of the Journal from 1858 to 1861; he was also the secretary of the Connecticut Historical Society and translated much of the material from von Raumer which appeared in the publication.

24. *AJE* VII, xx (March 1860): 320.

25. Ibid., XVII, i (September 1867): 17–40. See Thursfield, *Barnard*, 8off., for a discussion of indices to Barnard's work.

"with a moderated encouragement from the thoughtful friends of educational improvement" to continue his journal with little alteration. His topics would be the standard ones, the history of pedagogy, a survey of systems of national education and of normal schools, a description of the origin and key features of polytechnic schools, the history and current status of the "oldest and best" colleges, and the biographies and services of "Teachers, Promoters and Benefactors" of education. Nor would he alter his editorial stance. "We leave the work of controversy to those who have more taste for it than we have."[26]

Thus, the first sixteen volumes of the *American Journal of Education*, published from 1856 to 1866, and completed by the index at the close of number xlv in December, should be viewed as a whole. Style and content are consistent, although there is a discernible difference in the final volumes of the series when he attempted to dedicate them to the service of the nation's teachers. This ten year period marks Barnard's greatest achievement as an educational editor, and it is in the main in these volumes that his reputation rests.

The period was indeed a productive one. Barnard published several companion volumes, including the *Papers for the Teacher* series, *Memoirs of Teachers, Educators, and Promoters and Benefactors of Education*, *Armsmear*, *Military Schools*, and *National Education*. Of course he advertised his growing list, in notices of publications at the close of many numbers of the *Journal*. Once he alerted his readers to his "Books for the Teachers' Library," thirteen treatises, all compiled from the *Journal*, and now "issued separately, and under the general title of Papers for Teachers and Parents."[27] The first five were the original *Papers*, all already available; numbers vi through xiii had not yet been published independently, and most of them never were. The list, once again, is proof of Henry Barnard's good and unfulfilled intentions.

In a note to his subscribers dated June 8, 1867, from Washington, Barnard penned an apology. The constant "pressure of engagements connected with his withdrawal from the presidency of St. John's College, and with the organization of the Department of Education" had forced him to omit the March and June numbers (volume XVI had ended with the December 1866 number). He was reluctant, however, "to announce the suspension or abandonment of the periodical," whose stated aim was consistent with his goals as Commissioner. Thus, he felt "obliged to transfer the labors of the compilation" to another hand, to "the special management of Professor D. N. Camp, as proprietor and publisher" under

---

26. *AJE* XI, xxvi (March 1862): 3–4.
27. Ibid., XIII, xxxi (June 1863): 447 and 862.

the "general direction" of the former editor. Camp lasted less than a year as editor, supervising the only two numbers—which was not astonishing given the possessive feeling Barnard had for his literary offspring. Barnard, then resumed the editorship and for the next three years attempted to fulfill what he saw as a joint responsibility, to his reading public and to his official position.[28] He pledged to endeavor "with unwearied pains," to meet the "increasing demand for information," never alluding to the fact that he was required by law to do just that.

The National Series consisted of volumes I through VIII or, continuing the serialization, XVII through XXIV; the final volume, of four numbers, appeared in 1873, and the projected comprehensive index of the entire corpus, volume XXV, was never completed.[29] Barnard, in 1870, claimed that he had planned the series to constitute "a comprehensive survey of National Education," the project on which he had been working his entire professional life and which he had first published in 1854. Parts I and II were designed to focus on elementary and secondary education (with volumes on the German states, the rest of Europe, and the United States), Part III on universities and "Other Superior Schools," Part IV on "Professional, Classical, and Special Instruction," Part V on supplementary agencies, and Part VI on educational societies, lecture series, museums, and the like.[30]

The projected series reflected Barnard's passion for planning and organizing his accumulating knowledge and the persistence of his particular perspective, as well as his ambitious intentions. His failure to realize the plan can, to some degree, be excused on the basis of the political and personal stress under which he labored from 1868 until 1870, but not entirely. The pattern of grandiose scheme and lesser achievement is by now all too familiar. Barnard originally intended that volume XVIII was to "furnish statistics on schools and charitable institutions," a logical introduction to his history, and he had taken "unwearied pains" to collect such information; what he provided for his readers was "The American Year-Book and National Register, 1869"—merely a compendium of various government documents (ranging from astronomical information to a

28. Ibid., XVIII, National Series, Volume II (1869): Prefatory Note. In a bracket, certainly a subsequent editorial comment, Barnard added that until he could make other arrangements, he would publish official government documents and dispatch the *American Yearbook* of 1869.

29. See Thursfield, *Barnard*, 319–20, for a discussion of the odd history of volume XXV if such a volume ever was published.

30. *AJE* XXXI (1870): Prefatory Note; it is confusing that this note is dated January 15, 1871, and a second is dated seven months earlier. Barnard habitually added editorial comments when reprinting his materials.

summary of elections from 1836–1868), bound like the *Journal* to placate the subscribers.[31] Volume XIX was the entire *Special Report* on the schools of the District of Columbia; volume XX reprinted data on "Public Instruction in Different Countries," which had, for the most part, been published in volume IV in 1857; and volume XXI was a report on technical education which the House of Representatives had demanded from the Commissioner, and he had not completed before he departed from office. All of this material was valuable, and all would provide future historians with vital sources for later interpretation, but Henry Barnard had not realized his ambition to write the history he neglected as far back as when he responded to Governor Fenner's call.

The first three volumes of the National Series, to a minor extent, did serve as the link between the workers in the field and the Commissioner. He was able to repeat requests for information, reprinting circulars already sent out, but even in doing that, he could not resist including historical or supplementary information.[32] Rather than attempting to mask his repetition of previously published material, as Neill had charged, Barnard openly admitted it; to him, the *Journal* provided an opportunity to treat in greater detail subjects only surveyed in official circulars and to supplement previous publications. In other words, to fulfill the statutory responsibility of disseminating information. In number iv, for example, he began an article on "Instruction for the Professional Training of Teachers" by noting that much of the material had been written by David Camp for Circular XII, and he stated his "intention" to amplify and bring up to date information first summarized in his *Normal Schools*. The nearly two hundred remaining pages summarized normal education from Massachusetts to California, including major city normal schools, and in so doing the Commissioner may have provided useful information for those lobbying for increased support of such schools.[33]

It must have been with considerable relief that Barnard sat down in the tranquillity of his disorderly Hartford office to resume the "regular publication" of his *Journal* after he finally left the turmoil of Washington. His aim, if he received sufficient encouragement, was to "continue

31. The *Yearbook* included a detailed account of Barnard's first year as Commissioner; see *AJE* XVIII (1869): 190ff.

32. Ibid., XVII, ii (January 1868): 380, and iii (April 1868): 561; in the latter, after asking for information on academies, he included an account of Monson and an article on "Massachusetts Policy on Incorporated Academies," 563–75.

33. Ibid., iv (September 1868): 651–821. Note the word intention. Most of the accounts began with a quick history and included architectural plans of the schools. In the final entry on the Normal and Training School of Boston, Barnard said that the course of study would follow on the next pages; it did not.

our articles, original and selected," until he had concluded a "complete survey" of national education, its past history and its present condition, accompanied by a discussion of "Education as a Science and as an Art."

> These volumes are part of a comprehensive survey of national education in different countries, which was a leading object in the original establishment of the *Journal*, and has not been lost sight of in any year of its continuance.[34]

The ensuing volumes, which appeared in 1871, 1872, and 1873, demonstrated no overall conceptual goal and were rather national educational almanacs than either professional periodicals or a comprehensive history of education. Somehow Henry Barnard seemed to have come off the rails although he still had plenty of steam. Nonetheless, with consummate optimism, despite his precarious financial situation, after a silence of three years, in 1876 he began another series of the *Journal*, the International Series; he promised three volumes, each to have at least 800 pages (once again), "three Portraits from steel plates, and one hundred wood-cuts." The series would

> to be devoted to the completion (as far as practicable) of subjects presented in the previous Series, and a Historical Survey of National Systems, Institutions, and Methods of Instruction in the light which the former volumes of the Journal may contribute, and the material brought together by the International Exposition of 1876 at Philadelphia is expected to furnish.[35]

At a time when the nation was reveling in nationalism and proclaiming its unique place in history, Henry Barnard wanted to expand the horizon of its denizens and to remind all that all history could inform, especially the history of education.

The International Series actually comprised five volumes which appeared sporadically until 1882. Number one (XXVI) was exclusively three elaborate indices to the preceding twenty-four volumes, and the remaining volumes consisted for the most part of special reports, replications of previously published materials, and an occasional monograph, a hodge-podge collection. For example, in volume V (XXX), Barnard indicated his "desire" to include "the usual variety of topics of permanent value" while at the same time treating "the Kindergarten and Child Cul-

---

34. Ibid., XXI, second Prefatory Note, dated June 29, 1870. Ibid., XIX, (1870), Preparatory Note.

35. Prospectus to volume XXVI.

ture with . . . fulness".[36] He began the first number of the volume with a brief survey of the kindergarten movement by Elizabeth Peabody but moved immediately to a much longer biography of Charles Hammond, the former headmaster of Monson Academy, and a statistical summary of academies in operation in 1876. Two articles on higher education came before the editor turned again to childhood education and an examination of "Froebel's Educational Views" taken from the work of Baroness Marenholtz-Bulow. Then Barnard had "intended" to introduce extracts from a recent "remarkable volume" by E. C. Wines on *Prisons and Child-Saving Institutions in the Civilized World*, but instead reprinted the index of the book, accompanied, some fourteen pages later, by a reprinting of the index to Barnard's own *Reformatory Education*. A glowing account of "Repeated Visits" to Wellesley College followed, complete with its history, a description of its facilities and ground (including a section on "Ventilation"), and its curriculum, with special emphasis on the scientific departments and the "wholly original" Teachers' Collegiate Department. The issue closed with over a hundred pages of documents from Barnard's Washington career, official circulars, in no particular order, and his two reports.

Such an odd mixture persisted in the second number; after continuing with the Baroness's article, Barnard printed the *New England Primer* of 1777 and Charles Hoole's account of The Petty School, first published in 1659. By number three, however, the reader is able to detect the major topics, the history of the kindergarten (including the American Kindergarten Papers), the history of the education of women (a biography of Zilpah Grant), milestones in the history of education in the United States. And, being now familiar with Barnard's methods, the reader becomes equally certain that he was plotting the printing of separate treatises on these subjects. In fact he did announce the pending publication of *Kindergarten and Child Culture*, listing the Contents with the disclaimer that "The subjects and folios are not definitely fixed."[37]

It was in this period that Barnard reprinted many of his previous works. The second edition of *Military Schools*, and a third (he counted publication in the *Journal* as the first) of *National Education in Europe, Part II*, came out in 1872; in the same year he reprinted volume XXI of the

36. Note to Subscribers, *AJE* XXX, i (March 1880). In two self-serving footnotes to his letter to Mary Peabody, printed as a preface to an announcement of a volume on kindergartens, he claimed that in every year of every one of his publications, he had included "elaborate Papers" on the importance of early childhood methods, a patent exaggeration. Thursfield, *Barnard*, 49–50, explains that the American Foebel Union promised to underwrite any loss incurred by the editor in publishing the kindergarten materials.

37. Ibid., 3 (September 1880): passim, 3, for announcement of the book.

National Series as *Science and Art*. The following year number two of
Papers for the Teachers was reissued as *Oral Training Lessons* and number
three saw the light of day as *True Student Life*. He projected an ambitious
work on *Superior Instruction*, to cover higher education in Europe and the
United States in a volume of 1,000 pages, including the index, all to be
culled from the *Journal*; unhappily, "engagements" and "a nervous prostration . . . compelled him to abridge the Contents of the volume." America was omitted altogether. *American Educational Biography*, really the
Memoirs of 1859, came the following year, in 1874, and *The School and the
Teacher in English Literature* reappeared in 1876. Henry Barnard was meta-
morphosing from an educational historian to an educational publisher.
In 1875 he issued a four-page price list of individual treatises, all previously articles in the *Journal* and now available for purchase individually
or at a discount for orders of $20 or more. He even offered the eight
tracts originally written during his first tenure in Connecticut, all of which
had been published as pamphlets before 1845.[38]

His motivation may have been partially monetary, for at this time Barnard was openly complaining about his financial woes, "the old chronic
one," the debts incurred by his stubborn adherence to his plan for publication. He wrote to Potter in 1865 that he had accrued a debt of $20,000
over the *Journal* and moaned that no one was willing to "try to extricate"
him. Unless someone did help him meet his debts, the plates of thirty to
forty "distinct treatises" would have to be melted up. Later he repeated
the same threat to his friend and admirer Robert H. Quick, professor of
education in England and editor of *Educational Reformers*. The publication *was* costly, consuming perhaps as much as $1,300 a year; some esti-
mates placed Barnard's total investment over the thirty-year period at
$40,000 to $50,000.[39] Nevertheless, a gnawing skepticism remains with
anyone becoming increasingly familiar with Henry Barnard. He was a
complainer, and he also was manipulative, and not always totally trust-
worthy. Somehow he was able, while bemoaning his financial state, to
travel to Europe occasionally, and almost constantly in this country, to
keep a large house, to entertain friends, and not to work other than at
what he loved. His repeated sense of grievance may have had more to do

38. See for example, *Educational Tracts Number 1, The Condition of Education in the
United States as Exhibited in the Census of 1840; with a Sketch of the System of Common
Schools in New York and Connecticut* (Hartford: F. C. Brownell, 1844), TC.

39. Letter to Potter, May 5, 1865, and many others which between 1865 and 1878 repeat
the theme of hardship; Will S. Monroe, *Educational Labors of Henry Barnard* (Syracuse:
C. W. Bardeen, 1893), 28, for letter to Quick; cf., *AJE* XXVIII (1868): 973–74. On Barnard's financial embarrassment, see Thursfield, *Barnard*, 31–54.

with the limited fame and circulation of the *Journal* than with its expense, at least until his very old age.

In any case, the publication of individual tracts, culled from the *Journal*, and the republication of his works were neither of them novel practices, but rather frequent and customary Barnard ones. Previously there had been a pattern; successive numbers of the *Journal* would include articles on a given topic which Barnard then extracted and issued as a volume for the Library of Education. On occasion he had published a volume on a single topic when circumstances inspired him. Now one suspects that he had simply nothing else to do in his retirement but to mull over his papers, to make lists and outlines and indices, and to dream of informing the public. The conventional wisdom has it that Henry Barnard labored for nearly thirty years on his historical and editorial enterprises; labor he did but not create, and I repeat the opinion that the *Journal*, as a work of originality, in so far as it was original at all, actually came to an end after 1866, a view certainly not consistent with the Barnard myth. In a poignant, if narcissistic, letter to Gilman, in 1875, he revealed his awareness of the state of things:

> If I was not poor I could hire younger & abler pens to help me, and as it is, I am using up my own health . . . to bring my work to a decent conclusion—far short of my original plan as it lay in my own mind.[40]

From that time on Barnard, the editor, continued to make available to his public important materials, and his compilation of educational materials was of lasting importance, but his sense of editorial vision had died.

Barnard as editor *was* the *Journal*; his was the choice of articles, his was the organization, his was the scheduling. A representative number, the fourth of the first volume, contained the following in a few selected pages: an 1856 report on education in Bavaria, which was organized according to all of Barnard's categories; a brief notice of "Professional Education for the Military in France"; a survey of the "State of Public Education in Turkey" (from the New York *Tribune*); an announcement of "prizes for teaching common things" established in England by Lord Asburton; the "Twenty-first Report of the English Commissioner of National Education"; a report on "Female Adult Education" from the Irish *Quarterly Review*; a memorial to the Board of Trade on the Normal Lace School of Dublin; and Lord John Russell's "Scheme of National Education."[41]

40. Letter from Gilman, December 4, 1875, in Thursfield, *Barnard*, 305.
41. *AJE* I, iv (May 1856): 625–40.

Selection was one thing, but authorship was another matter. Barnard, by his own admission, "did not relish 'the task of having to sit down and *write* a long yarn.'"[42] It is difficult to ascertain which articles he actually wrote. His indices are not always dependable, for at times Barnard credited himself with authorship of articles clearly not his, and at other times internal evidence suggests he was the author although his name is not in the index. Careful analysis indicates that he was responsible for at least 75 pages of original material in the 316 in number xvi, and this is a higher proportion than was customary. He wrote a number of the biographical sketches, the account of Williston Seminary (basing it on the school's fourteenth annual report which he had at hand), articles on "Family Training and Agricultural Labor," on the State School for Girls in Lancaster, Massachusetts, and on the New York State Idiot Asylum, according to the index, although in those cases for the most part he merely included lengthy excerpts from published reports. And, of course, most of the statistics came from his pen. Sometimes he reprinted his own previous works, a speech of 1839 on public high schools, a memoir of David Watkinson delivered to the Connecticut Historical Society, his address at the opening of the Norwich Free Academy, and his 1842 pamphlet.[43] At other times he simply copied material which had been sent to him, as he frequently said, "by a valued correspondent."[44]

Barnard as editor was responsible for introductions, the news items, the Educational Miscellany, the Obituaries, and the notices of national educational meetings. Often when commencing a topic, he would insert some editorial comment, "a few notes and annotations"; for example, in a description of Transylvania University and State Normal School he proclaimed that there was

> no doubt about the influence for good which incorporation of the Professional School for Teachers into the University will do for popular education when combined with Teachers' Institutes, State Teachers' Association, active county superintendents, and Normal Schools for Female Teachers.[45]

42. Letter from James Fraser, in Thursfield, *Barnard*, 69–70.

43. The program for the Norwich dedication, with Barnard's notes, is in the NYU archive. Barnard exchanged a number of angry letters with John Gulliver over the printing of the account, and it took the mediation of a third party to straighten matters out.

44. See *AJE* I, iv, (May 1856); IV, xi, (December 1857). Barnard's correspondence in the NYT archive is so full of letters from contributors, either of articles or information, that individual citation is redundant. Elihu Burrit (January 2, 1855), Josiah Quincy (September 28, 1866), Archbishop Bayley (January 18, 1876), Catharine Beecher(April 15, 1878), give some sense of the variety of his sources.

45. Ibid., III, viii (March 1857): 219n.

In the articles he did write, and in introductions or asides, Barnard's voice can be heard consistently. By including a number of his own speeches, he reiterated his goal of education:

> to train boys and girls to mild dispositions, graceful and respectful manners and unquestioning obedience, to cultivate the senses to habits of quick and accurate observation and discrimination, to teach the use of the voice and of simple, ready, and correct language, and by appropriate exercises in drawing, calculation, and lessons in the properties and classification of objects, to begin the cultivation of the intellectual faculties.[46]

Such an education should take place in schools "common because [they are] good enough for the best and cheap enough for the poorest," where all neighbors would become one. "The isolation and estrangement which now divide and subdivide the community into country and city clans . . . will give place to a frequent intercourse and esteem of individual and family friendships." Education had political as well as social goals.

> In a Democratic Republic like ours, where all political power resides in and springs from the people . . . no subject can be presented to the citizens for their consideration more important than the education of the youth.

The school and the community are inextricably bound together, and the character of the school and of the teacher in any period is often represented in popular literature and "is to a still greater extent perpetuated by such representation." The provision of schooling is the first responsibility of the community, one which in past eras was neglected. Speaking of colonial Massachusetts, and incidentally displaying his research method, he commented on the "amazing indifference of the great mass" of the early settlers to schooling. "We shall look—I, at least, have looked in vain, for any evidence of farsightedness or liberality on the part of Town authorities." Leadership in cultural and educational matters had always devolved, and should continue to do so, on the responsible men of the community, men like David Watkinson who left his fortune to endow a library for the Historical Society and the Young Men's Institute, and such leadership should remain pure of "considerations of party success and service." Finally, education was not just to be had in schools; libraries, museums, and institutions as novel as the New York State Geological Hall and Agricultural Rooms were elements in the evolving configurations of education.[47]

46. Ibid., XIII, xxx (March 1863): n.p., from speech, 1838.
47. Ibid., II, vi (September 1856): 335; III, viii (March 1857): 155ff.; IV, xii (March

Rarely did Barnard address pressing issues of curriculum. Once he displayed a keen understanding of the persistent tension between the theoretical and the pragmatic goals of education when he alluded to

> the long protracted struggle between Humanism and Realism, or between, on the one hand, the study of languages for the purposes of general culture and the only preparation for the professions in which language was the great instrument of study and influence, and, on the other, the claims of Science, and of the realities surrounding every one, and with which every one has to do every day.

Neither Thomas Jefferson nor Benjamin Franklin could have put it more felicitously. But he glossed over the question rapidly to dwell on the necessity of "the gradual extension and expansion of the grand idea of universal education—of the education of every human being, and of every faculty of every human being."[48] Too much should not be made of Barnard's uncritical acceptance of faculty psychology, which was not uncommon, and more should be made of the fact that he was far more concerned with the provision of education than with its content.

Barnard's life-long passion for history probably had begun in his college years. Among the papers in the Trinity College collection is a note in his elderly hand titled "Historical Studies" in which he referred to his "graduate reading in the Linonian Library" and recognized the influence of Macaulay.[49] His membership in the Connecticut Historical Society lasted until his death, and he was an honorary member of a number of state historical societies (such exchanging of privileges was a common practice); he corresponded as an equal with serious contemporary historians, among them George Bancroft and John G. Palfrey. It is no exaggeration to claim that Henry Barnard was one of the great *researchers* of his time. He had thoroughly investigated the origins of colonial schooling for his biography of Ezekiel Cheever, in a paper presented to the Historical Society.[50] He had read a work of 1678 on English schools and Felt's *History of Ipswich*; he had consulted "torn and almost illegible" colonial records in the Historical Society; and he had read Gould's 1828 *Account of*

1858): 785ff., 837; VIII, xx (March 1860): 320; XXX (September 1880): 752, 817.

48. Ibid., XI, xxvi (March 1862): introduction, 4.

49. The note drifts off into autobiographical musing, and there are two different chronological listings and several tentative chapter headings. Biographers have based some traditional accounts of Henry Barnard on sources such as these, not recognizing the extent to which he was recasting his life into a pattern.

50. Draft, TC, notes the paper. He used it as a vehicle for criticizing practices such as the "barbarism of boarding round . . . which is the doom of teachers and drives men with families" out of the profession.

the Free Schools of Boston. Notes constitute three-quarters of the first five pages of the memoir of Cheever. Barnard also verified his findings whenever possible; Edward Everett Hale was particularly helpful, undertaking research in the Antiquarian Society (he regretfully told his colleague that he could not take books from the Society library) and checking disputed facts such as who was Cheever's second wife. Barnard maintained his interest in Cheever for more than twenty years and eventually had at hand all the materials for a definitive biography, which he never wrote.[51] The almost mythical school teacher was the historical figure on whom Barnard lavished the most research, but the "Memoir of Josiah Holbrook" runs a close second—notes take up almost as much space as text. The choice of Holbrook, the founder of that illustrious companion to the common schools, the Lyceum, was understandable, but Barnard seemed a bit lukewarm in his praise of Holbrook in the cause of educational reform: "None can deny him the merit of having been a most faithful and efficient laborer in promoting many of the most important of them."[52]

Another topic of Barnard's research was institutional history, and here he again displayed his firm founding in the documentary sources. The "History of the Common School" in Connecticut is a most complete account, understandably, and appears, in chronological order in seven succeeding volumes of the *Journal*—with one exception: Barnard began the story with his own first administration and then retreated to examine the origins of schooling in the state.[53] He also presented the history of various types of educational institutions, high schools, academies, schools for girls, those for the preparation of teachers, other specialized schools, and colleges; often, however, these establishments were introduced through the medium of the biography of the founder or of some illustrious leader or patron. Nonetheless, the repetition of certain categories, and a comparison with the various indexes, leads to the conclusion that Barnard pursued his research along topical lines, projecting an enormous and all-inclusive tome on national education, one which would have successive chapters on academies, on libraries, on colleges, on all of the formal institutions of education; in short an encyclopedia. One can

51. The initial biography is in *AJE* I, ii (January 1856): 297–314, and parts are reprinted in XII, xxix (December 1862): 530–49, in an article on the Boston Latin School, and in another article on the school in XVII, i (September 1867): 65–90 (many of the pages are identical); final mention in XXVIII, (October 1878): 134, 286. Letters from Hale, November 7, 1854, October 31, November 15, 19, 1855, March 4, 1856, NYU.

52. *AJE* VIII, xx (March 1860): 229–47, quotation 239, notes 249–56. Barnard had acted as an agent for Holbrook's apparatus; see Thursfield, *Barnard*, 36n.

53. *AJE* I (1838–42); IV, to 1800; V (1800–38); XIII and XIV (1842–49); XV (1849–54); and XI for summary in 1860.

almost see the file boxes in the Hartford study, overflowing with undigested information.

It is Barnard's legacy, and much to his credit, that he never succumbed to rampant nineteenth century nationalism as an historian, for he always saw American educational history as an inheritor and reflection of European developments. In the *Connecticut Common School Journal* he had noted the work of the Swedish Dr. Siljestrom, who became a frequent correspondent, and the subsequent *Journal* became the vehicle for the transmission of *selected* European educational thinking. Barnard's bias was clear. He revered the Germans, and through the translations of Frederic Perkins, vast amounts of Karl von Raumer's three volume history of education were made available to the American readers. As Thursfield astutely observed, "the German Protestant leader's insistence upon the duties and obligations of parent in the training of children, and . . . his belief that the state should require compulsory attendance" became the cornerstones of Barnard's public policy. Copmpatible, too, was von Raumer's moral stance. Barnard did however, at times, edit the German's work where it was "more theological than educational, and as likely to provoke unpleasant and unprofitable controversy."[54]

The Connecticut editor learned more than policy from the Europeans. Barnard had been an early advocate of Pestalozzi, but his full publication of the works of von Raumer, and of Hermann Krusi, with whom he often corresponded, introduced Comenius and the methodological innovations of that great Hungarian and the equally great succeeding Swiss educators. To a surprising degree, Barnard, essentially a conservative, became a progressive on matters of instruction, and in articles, and in the monograph on *Object Teaching*, he publicized novel strategies of instruction.[55] He probably did not realize how revolutionary these suggestions were, for classroom instruction had never been his *forte*, and Pestalozzi's moral maxims certainly attracted him more than the former's pedagogical theories. Nonetheless, full credit must be given to Barnard for the fact that he made available to the students of educational philosophy advanced and innovative perspectives, ideas which were to become central in the writings and practices of later nineteenth century theorists. Both John Dewey and Francis Parker owed a partial debt to Henry Barnard.

Barnard had failed to get the Berlin consulship, and he spoke no Ger-

---

54. Thursfield, *Barnard*, 143. See *CCSJ*, I:12, 379; *AJE* IV, x–xii (September, December 1857; March 1858); *AJE* VI, xvii (June 1859): 615, Educational Miscellany—through Wimmer Barnard found that von Raumer had objected that the "omission diminished the value of the author's historical survey."

55. It is probable that more teachers learned object teaching second-hand, through the institutes, but those who conducted them had read the new material in the *Journal*.

man, but he had traveled extensively and often in England, and he was totally at home with English literature, especially with the liberal reformer tradition. According to the analysis of Sheldon Emerson Davis, English sources almost equal the German ones in the *Journal*.[56] There were distinct differences, however, in the nature of the English sources, and they interjected very different notions. Barnard concentrated, first, on the classics in English literature: he cited, among others, Thomas, Elyot, Milton, Ascham on education; for philosophy, Locke; Alexander Pope, George Crabbe, Thomas Hood, Thomas Gray for narrative and literary views. Milton, was to Barnard "the most resplendent name for genius and culture, in prose and poetry," a man who held education to be "one of the greatest and noblest designs" devised by man; selections from the *Tractate* appeared in three different volumes of the *Journal*. Thus, while Barnard imbibed progressive ideas of method from his German sources, he adhered to the familiar and comfortable, predominantly classical, inclination of his British authorities; articles on English universities underscored this somewhat conservative stance.[57] One suspects the first national commissioner of education would have had as little trouble in compiling his own list of what every schoolchild should read as his modern-day successor.

On the other hand, through innumerable speeches, pamphlets, official reports and documents, his own visits and correspondence, as well as historical work such as that of the Kay brothers, Barnard collected and printed enormous amounts of factual material from England, all with obvious instrumental intent. The bulk of this focused on voluntary and governmental efforts to confront social dislocation and to promote individual betterment, the sacred cause of the transatlantic reformers. In addition, his English sources introduced Barnard to an assortment of contemporary European reports. He neglected some important Continental authors, except for the German ones, and his pragmatic bias led him to ignore key French figures; he did favor Guizot, like Barnard a gentleman public servant, a centralizer, and an historian. "There is nothing in the history of modern civilization more truly sublime than the establishment of the present Law of Primary Instruction in France," he wrote of Guizot's work.[58]

56. Davis, *Periodicals*, 57.

57. *AJE* II, v (August 1856): 76–85, XXII (January 1871): 181–90, XXIII (1872): 151–60 (note all have nine pages); for other English material see, IV, XI, XIV, XVI, XXII, and XXIII; it was published as *English Pedagogy Education, the School, and the Teacher in English Literature*, 2d ed. (Philadelphia: J. B. Lippincott, 1862).

58. *AJE* IX, xiii (December 1860): 382; see II, IV, VII, X, XII, passim. See Thursfield, *Barnard*, 167ff.

Scattered throughout the *Journal* was information on public instruction gleaned from correspondence with peers in many of the countries of Europe and a few of the Latin American ones. Despite his repeatedly stated intentions, there was not a great deal on Canada, and there was only random and infrequent information from other areas of the globe; the crux of the matter was the availability of authorities. Sometimes Barnard employed agents, as in the case of Daniel Gilman, who was paid a retainer during his time in Europe, and Hermann Wimmer, who both researched and translated German materials. Then there were men like Hartvig Nissen who contributed an article on schools in Norway, and Vincenzo Botta, an expatriate Italian, who wrote on the schools of Sardinia. Faustino Sarimento, the consul for Chile and Argentina in the United States, described South American practices in comparison with those of the United States.[59] But this material constituted a small fraction of the entire twenty-five volumes.

Most of Henry Barnard's colleagues were men of affairs, dedicated to creating new agencies to meet new social needs, so it is not surprising that the *American Journal of Education* accentuated institutional history. Portrayals of common schools, normal schools, academies, colleges and universities predominate. The erstwhile reformer, Barnard, also included novel institutions designed to respond to new-felt social needs. In addition to the full history and report on the New York State Idiot Asylum, based on its *Sixth Annual Report*, he described in detail the plans for a Floating Public School in Baltimore. This was a cooperative effort of the Board of Trade and the Board of Public Education, designed to raise the condition of seamen and to increase the supply of well-trained ones—a vocational school with a moral goal. The school which aimed to accommodate 300 young men who otherwise "might loiter around the docks," already had 90 pupils; the students gave "promise of becoming intelligent and useful members of the profession," and their training "will ultimately elevate the character, both at home and abroad" of Baltimore sailors.[60] Thus Barnard was able to reiterate his fundamental belief: schools should be purposeful, schools should have a moral and social use.

Certain other themes received constant attention from Barnard in his *Journal*. The training of teachers was an obvious one, and so, as has been noted, was the challenge of creating a profession of teachers. His early

59. *AJE* III, ix (June 1857): 513–30, continued in x (Italy); VII, xx (March 1860): 295–304 (Norway); XVI, xliv (September 1866): (South America); see also, VIII, xxi (June 1860): 348ff. (elementary education in Prussia and Bavaria), 545–80 (agricultural education in France), 581–614 (Belgium and Holland).

60. Ibid., IV, xi (December 1859): 416 (New York), 520 (Woodward High School); V, xiii (June 1858): 201–04 (Floating Public School).

focus on school architecture was expanded to include articles on school apparatus and teaching aids, with illustrations and occasional advertisements. His emphasis on moral education was to be expected, although his avoidance of the issue of the use of the Bible in schools (for sectarian purposes) underlined his passionate determination to shun controversy and, perhaps, a tolerance which might be attributed to the influence of his wife.[61]

During the first ten years of the periodical, Barnard advocated a number of new proposals, among them the further education of girls, "for the charitable, sanitary and reformatory work of society"; their gentle and instinctive natures suited them to the tasks of teaching and nurturing. Surprisingly, however, he added in one place that much more needed to be done "for training girls in the duties of nurses and physicians." He reported with approval the founding of Vassar Female College, although he gave more emphasis to the benefactor, Matthew Vassar, than to the college curriculum—which was not at all surprising considering his biographical and great-man bias. At the close of his career, however, in an article on Wellesley College, he cited the movement for the higher education of women as one of the most important developments in the latter part of the century; the college itself, with its magnificent architecture, well-equipped classrooms and laboratories, and affluent libraries, exemplified, he claimed, "the great principles and natural methods in education" to which the *Journal* had always been dedicated. Here he envisaged a less limited, and still lofty role for women, and in this he agreed with the Trustees of the college. The "main result which they desire to accomplish is to educate teachers worthy of the highest positions," and the Teachers' Collegiate Department demonstrated "progressive spirit and practical aims," almost a "true Normal College."[62] The highest positions were still circumscribed by convention.

Barnard also featured scientific and technical education, primarily in Europe where, in his view, it surpassed that in the United States. He described the Lawrence Science School at Harvard and reported on like innovations at Yale and other private institutions. Volume XXI, number v,

61. In 1865, in the controversy over the issue of the reading of the Bible in the Hartford public schools, Barnard sided with the Roman Catholics who claimed that the use of the King James version was a violation of their religious liberty; both he and they lost. See Lloyd P. Jorgenson, *The State and the Non-Public School, 1825–1925* (Columbia: University of Missouri Press, 1987), 38.

62. *AJE* III, ix (June 1857): 484–85; XI, xxvi (March 1862): 153–56 and portrait of Vassar; XXX (March 1880): 161ff. and 185. Barnard and Vassar corresponded often; on February 2, 1864, Vassar wrote to ask Barnard his opinion on the desirability of having female professors at the college.

of the National Series, summarized information on technical education in the United States and Europe.[63] Such an emphasis was, as we have seen, entirely characteristic of men of Barnard's orientation—men of affairs and of literature alike were fascinated with the emerging sciences. Significantly, however, in his definition of science and a scientific education, agriculture was as important to Barnard as more modern industry; he supported the Morrill Act, and as late as 1879 he gave ample attention to agricultural education. The farm, after all, was linked with the family and the school as agents for the preservation of Barnard's America, and the education necessary for the rural areas differed significantly from that required in the cities. Much as Henry Barnard strove for common education, it was common only in the lower grades. He accepted without examination differentiation based on class, occupation, and future expectations.[64]

In every one of his reports as a school administrator Barnard had linked the quality of the schools and instruction with the quality of the texts employed.

It is an excellent indication of educational progress, when the textbooks in use in schools and academies, instead of being prepared as they generally are, at first by mere tyros in science, are the careful products of the most eminent minds in the respective sciences taught.[65]

Repeatedly, during his tours of duty, he had been sent textbooks by optimistic authors who hoped for approval and sponsorship of their products, and as a result he amassed an enormous collection of over 10,000 titles, "the most extensive" in the country according to Linus Pierpont Brockett, and Barnard himself.[66] As an editor, he determined that the publication of a complete catalogue of texts would render an incomparable service to the nation's teachers and to the history of American education, so he proposed to provide one in his *Journal*. It would embrace every book in use and its author, a subject list of the same, a list of pub-

63. Ibid., XXI (1870); in the introduction, Barnard emphasized his role in furthering the demands for technical education, itemizing speeches in 1831, 1838, and various documents in 1840, 1847, all of which he said stressed technical education; this is an overstatement to say the least.

64. See *AJE* VIII, xxi (June 1860), and XXI and XXII, passim; XXIX, Report of the Commissioner of Education, 34–272 on college of agriculture; also I, i (August 1855): 217–24, XXVIII, 337–52, on the Yale Scientific School.

65. Ibid., V, xiii (June 1858): 319. In XIV, xxxvii (December 1864): 751–52, he stated that it was difficult to overemphasize the importance of textbooks "in the magnitude of the pecuniary interests involved to publishers, authors, and parents."

66. Philobiblius, *History*, 7–8; letter to Dixon, March 14, 1862, TC.

lishers, a comparison of each text within a subject, and the "Odds and Ends" resulting from his study of the texts, their origins, illustrations, "and the religious and political tendencies and aims" of the authors. He appealed to his readers, and to his correspondents, to aid him by correcting and supplementing his list to make it more accurate, and he offered to exchange any of his duplicate texts with theirs. The enterprise brought an enthusiastic response from his colleagues, such as John Philbrick and William Wells, and Linus Brockett who called the catalogue "a noble work."[67] Barnard did provide an enormous list, and his invaluable collection of texts rests today in the Trinity College library, but he failed even to attempt the analytical study he had delineated.

During the war period, Barnard broadened his definition of education and supported demands for physical education, which should be begun "far back in the home, with parents and nurses" and extended "into the daily life of every man, woman and child," for physical education was an integral part of any education.

> Let us have good teaching, and enough of it,—hard study and more of it, with suitable alterations of subjects and frequent infusions of exhilerating play as well as of systematic exercises,—useful work in the field and shop, with less intensity in the pursuit of wealth and office, and more indulgence in outside and fireside recreation—let us have more and better knowledge of the laws of health, more of the heart culture, as well as of mental and bodily vigor, more exercise of the gentle and kindly sympathies, more of the refining enjoyments of the beautiful in nature and art, more of the ennobling perceptions of moral beauty and virtue, and the daily practice of obedience, veneration, temperance and patriotism, and we shall be a healthier and a happier people.[68]

Play and useful work, mental and bodily vigor, enjoyment of nature and art, perception of moral beauty and virtue, obedience and patriotism —not self-actualization, but the development of the self as a purposeful and pure member of a healthy and happy society. New insights and methods, whether those of Dio Lewis or Pestalozzi, were still to serve traditional ends.

67. *AJE* XII, xxix (December 1862): 593–604; XIII, xxx (March 1863): 209–22, xxxi (June 1863): 401–08; xxxii (September 1863): 626–40; also XIV, xxxvi (September 1864): 601–07, xxxvii (December 1864): 753–77, introduction 751–52. Letter from Wells, April 6, 1863; from Brockett, January 4, 1865; NYU

68. *AJE* XI, xxv (March 1862): 460 (article on physical exercises of Dio Lewis); see also, for examples, 531–36 (public high school of Chicago, with plates); XXI (scientific and technical education).

Barnard's methods as a scholar are transparent in the *Journal*. First and foremost was his omnivorous reading. In an early number he itemized the materials lying "on our table": a letter on collegiate government and a "Report on a Plan for Instruction" from F. A. P. Barnard, an 1853 lecture delivered by Samuel A. Eliot entitled "A Complete System of Education," a series of "Common Essays" from the University of London, a discourse on "National Education" from the head of the Kneller Hall Training School in England, a pamphlet, "Contributions to the Cause of Education," written by a Scottish reformer, some "Lectures on Education" given to the Royal Institute of Great Britain, and many, many more. Cited in the section on "Educational Movements and Statistics" in the third number were the *Report of the Minister of Public Instruction* of Russia (from the London *Times*), a description of Belgian education (from the Dublin *Journal of Progress*), the French *Revue de l'Instruction Publique*, and a work on New England colleges by I. N. Tarbox. In fact, Barnard had such an abundance of information that he was forced to defer mention of other articles in order to include publication of the plans for the new girls' high school in New York and Elias Loomis's history of public schools. For another number he had read Coleridge, Walter Savage Landor's "Imaginary Conversations of Literary Men and Statesmen," the *Life and Educational Systems of Pestalozzi* ("in a translation by J. Tillcard in the *Education Expositor* of 1850"), an article on Kaiserwerth taken from a "32 page pamphlet," and the *Third Annual Report* of the superintendent of schools of Chicago.[69] One pictures again a very cluttered room in the house on Main Street with clippings and books and journals slipping over the tables to the floor until they were noted in the *Journal*'s Miscellany and then catalogued by the meticulous editor.

Although Barnard's reading, and to some extent his publication, seems haphazard, it is possible to detect a consistent intellectual orientation; his bias was that of the English utilitarians and their American counterparts, the antebellum reformers. He was not at all drawn to the German philosophers, as was his later successor, William Torrey Harris, nor was he interested in esoteric German theology, as was his compatriot, Horace Bushnell. Barnard read men who proposed to *do* something or *were* doing something and who shared his belief in the possible amelioration of the threatened social order. A second limitation in his sources was due to his geographic, rather than intellectual bias. With few exceptions he concentrated on the older sections of the United States, despite his personal ties with the growing new Midwest, or on those sections which reflected the

69. *AJE* I, iii (March 1856) and III, viii (March 1857); the sources are often in editorial comments or notes.

spirit of New England. His sources were men like William Wells who, although he moved to Chicago, always maintained his sense of his Eastern roots. The prominence of the northern states in the traditional view of antebellum school reform certainly can in no small way be traced to Barnard's editorial selection; later students of the period relied on him, and his selections became theirs. Equally significant was the fact that Barnard's foreign sources exemplified the dominant axis among these contemporary Eastern intellectuals; Prussia and England, for the most part, constituted their Europe.

Barnard's correspondence was with the urban and state superintendents, who sent him their reports, with members of benevolent societies both at home and abroad, and with the vast numbers of reformers, especially his friends in Britain. Once, after an article on Lord Brougham was "in type," he read the *Proceedings of the National Association for the Promotion of Social Science* for 1858 at which Brougham had spoken on the "Service of the Popular Press and Literature"—this particular piece came to his hands from Bishop Potter, who had attended the sessions, but other materials came from agents. Often the inclusion of one article would inspire Barnard to alert his readers to other sources; at the end of a piece on "Moral Education," he cited five lectures on the same subject which had been delivered to the American Institute between 1831 and 1844. Because of his linguistic inadequacies he was forced to rely on translators such as Perkins; Mary Mann rendered selections from Diesterweg, and an article comparing Prussian educational expenditures with those of France was submitted by "Miss E. S. Gilman"—Daniel's sister.[70]

The *Journal* as a publication is flawed. Barnard's tampering with his sources to meet his own editorial stance has already been noted; Thursfield felt that there was "evidence of editing by Henry Barnard," in a sketch of F. A. P. Barnard and in other biographical articles and "of considerable efforts to make the accounts appear other than autobiographical." In another instance John Philbrick, usually an ardent admirer, accused Barnard of purposefully falsifying an account and of depending too exclusively on a hostile source.[71] More frequent are the instances of carelessness or haste. Page references are often erroneous, and entries in the Tables of Contents equally often do not match the titles of articles. In XIII, xxx, March 1863 the Contents are all generic categories, "National Instruction

70. *AJE* II, vii (December 1856): 737–38, for list of materials; see also I, iii (March 1856): 248, 344; II, vi (September 1856): 337; IV, xii (March 1858): 824 (the Proceedings of the First Convention of Managers and Superintendents of Houses of Refuge and Reformation—a source he was to use later); VI, xvii (June 1858): 385, xvii, 511; letter from M. Mann, November 2, 1880, NYU.

71. Thursfield, *Barnard*, 120. Letter from Philbrick, January 18, 1864, NYU.

for Military Education," or "Benefactors," or "Plays, Pastimes, and Holidays of Children," but the matching articles are, respectively, the "Military Academy at West Point," "Miss Caroline Plummer," and (perhaps) "Schools As They were Sixty Years Ago." "Notices of Books" is item XVI in the Contents but item XIV in the text, and item XIV (there is no XIII) in the Contents is "School Architecture," which is entirely omitted in the text. "National Education" is a topic listed as pages 205–14; in the text the "National Schools of Ireland" runs from pages 145 to page 154. Barnard must have sketched or listed what he hoped, or intended, to include in each issue and then forgot it when he came to the actual compilation of the pages.

Barnard always projected a Library of Education to be published as companion volumes to the *Journal*, and these works exemplify the range of topics which he dealt with in his periodical. Not surprisingly, considering Barnard's espousal of the great man theory of history and his repeated emphasis on the importance of individual contributions to societal advance, the first of these was titled *Memoirs of Teachers, Educators and Promoters and Benefactors of Education, Literature and Science*.[72] The bulk of the sketches had been included in the first five volumes of the *Journal* although three (of Samuel Johnson, Emma Willard, and Wilbur Fiske) appeared subsequently.[73] All are repeated word-for-word, and in cases the pagination is identical; sometimes it is ingenious. The sketch of Walter Johnson occupied pages 781–96 of volume V, and that of Wilbur Fiske pages 297–310 of volume VI; in the *Memoirs* they are printed sequentially, pages 281–310. The job of the compositor was made easier, and the printing was less expensive if the plates could be reused. Included in the book were the many excellent engravings which had been intended "to embellish" the pages of the *Journal*, and which made the book "a splendid and appropriate gift-book to Teachers and Promoters of Educational Improvement."[74] Omitted from the book but prominent in the *Journal* had been the biographies of some dozen benefactors of education, men

72. *Memoirs of Teachers, Educators, and Promoters and Benefactors of Education*, reprinted from the *American Journal of Education*, edited by Henry Barnard, LL.D., Chancellor of the University of Wisconsin, Part I, Volume I, United States (New York: F. C. Brownell, 1859). Barnard called this the second edition, as was his custom, when material had appeared in the periodical first. Note that he indicated that other volumes would follow this one.

73. Personal reasons may have dictated their inclusion: Johnson, college president and Episcopalian; Willard, mentor and friend; Fiske, president of the rather upstart and neighboring Wesleyan College.

74. *AJE* I, ii (January 1856): Editorial Introduction, 137–40. Notice of *Educational Biography* in *Memoirs of Eminent Teachers and Educators in Germany* (New York, 1863), after 586.

such as Edmund Dwight, George Peabody, and the two Phillipses; these, Barnard promised, would receive their credit in a projected second volume—it never appeared, yet another example of his good intentions gone astray.

According to Barnard, most of the memoirs had been prepared by the editor, "or at his request, and in some instances from material furnished by him," to accompany the account of an institution with whom the individual was connected. In the *Journal*, most of the accounts are anonymous, but Thursfield, through minute examination of Barnard's correspondence, identified the authorship of the majority of the sketches, and once again, Barnard exaggerated his role.[75] Of the 115 accounts, only thirteen can be identified as from his pen, two of these are of doubtful attribution and two are cases of shared authorship; of the thirty Memoirs Barnard extracted for inclusion in the separate volume, only three, those of Ezekiel Cheever, Thomas Gallaudet, and David Perkins Page, were written by Barnard himself. He assisted Denison Olmsted with his piece, and, because of his editorial corrections (some of which were erroneous), he was credited, in a subsequent publication, with the authorship of the sketch of Mann. The majority of the accounts were by members of Barnard's close circle of colleagues, some of whom wrote their own sketches, as did William Russell; some had others edit their drafts, as did F. A. P. Barnard; and others entrusted the task of writing their biographies to another, as did Samuel Hall.

The scope of the book is rather narrow, and the thrust differed significantly from that of the *Journal*. Although Barnard originated the series with his excellent and scholarly biography of Cheever, this was the exception, for he chose to focus on his circle of contemporary common school reformers.[76] New England dominates; Calvin Stowe is included, but none of those leading comparable efforts in the southern and western states was deemed worthy of inclusion. The men (the single woman in the collection is Emma Willard) he chose to honor were indeed the elite of the schoolmen (again except for Cheever), members of the American Institute, for the most part the publicists of reform, rather than theorists,

---

75. Thursfield, *Barnard*, Appendix II, 322–25.

76. The biographical sketch of Ezekiel Cheever was originally a paper read before the Connecticut Historical Society in November 1855; in it Barnard developed his pet themes: "It is to be regretted that the early practice of attaching a house for the occupancy of the master, with a few acres of land for garden, orchard, and the feeding of a cow, adopted with the school from the old world, was continued with the institution of the new schools, down to the present time. It would have given more of a professional permanence to the employment of teaching and prevented the growth of the 'barbarism of boarding around' which is the doom of teaching and drives men with families out."

or the benefactors, connected with the creation of educational institu-tions. Charles Brooks was omitted although that seems to have been at his choice; he demurred in his answer to Barnard, declining to write his own sketch and saying that he had "no right to be set among the gods"; he did send some "facts" and may have been disappointed not to have been pressed.[77] Finally, a few were included because of their pedagogical contributions: Lowell Mason, a "veteran" teacher of music, long the champion of vocal music in schools, and Warren Colburn "whose cele-brated arithmetics are strictly Pestalozzian."[78] Barnard had long advo-cated both the teaching of music (many did for health reasons—singing expanded the lungs) and Pestalozzian techniques.

It was only to be expected that the second book of this period was a work on Pestalozzi.[79] As early as 1839 Barnard, echoing Russell and oth-ers, had insisted on the supreme importance of the Swiss reformer, and he made a conscious effort to acquaint himself and then his readers with the Pestalozzian corpus. He turned to Bronson Alcott, among others, requesting copies of the available books, and, beginning with the seventh number of the *Journal*, he offered his readers vast chunks of Pestalozzi's work in order "to induce the educational world of this country to give more attention to this subject."[80] The ideas had long been available second-hand, through accounts such as Stowe's of the Prussian educa-tional innovations, but the publication of von Raumer's laudatory biog-raphy and the translation of key Pestalozzi texts provided Barnard with a renewed opportunity to spread the gospel he had long advocated. Pestalozzi's emphasis on the child, and on the role of the environment in the education of children, his insistence on the importance of the real and the immediate as sources for the teaching of children, and his elevation of the teacher as the moral as well as intellectual guide for children, were all ideas which had pervaded Barnard's previous publications. Now he col-lected them, as a "Tribute to the Character and Services" of the revered

77. Letter from Brooks, June 21, 1859, NYU.

78. *Life and Educational Principles of John Henry Pestalozzi*, 2d ed. (New York: F. C. Brownell, 1859), 150.

79. Ibid.

80. Letter from Herman Krusi, July 6, 1857; Krusi was a German refromer working on a life of Pestalozzi; Barnard devoted pages 161–86 to his "Views and Plan of Education." For early references to Pestalozzi, see *CCSJ* I, 8 (April–May, 1839): 121–41. Letters from Alcott, July 13, 22, August 17, 1857, CHS. Charles Leslie Glenn, *The Myth of the Common School* (Amherst: University of Massachusetts Press, 1988), 148, emphasizes the mystical, aspect of Pestalozzi: "A theology centered upon growth rather than conversion, upon the continuities between nature and grace, upon human potential for growing into the like-ness of God, was characteristic of the most influential school reformers of the early nine-teenth century."

educator and as a "valuable contribution" to the literature on education—
a kind of Bible of pedagogy.[81]

It could easily be anticipated that Barnard would begin his book with
a biographical sketch or memoir of Pestalozzi. Characteristically, he took
a few detours before he turned to his subject; in Part I he discussed
Pestalozzi and the schools of Germany and the influence of Pestalozzi on
the Infant School System of England. He provided a sketch of von
Raumer; authorship of that section was not credited to Barnard in the
index, nor is it attributed to him by Thursfield, but it is succinctly stated
in the text that the account was "by the American author."[82] Barnard's
editorial observations began Part II. He noted Pestalozzi's "remarkable
powers of observation . . . considerable insight into the operations of
mind and feelings . . . great appreciation of character," while criticizing
his often illogical and contradictory, although intuitive, style. Overall, the
words of Pestalozzi were "valuable as a specimen of a mode of combining
instruction . . . with sound lessons in morals."[83] Then he presented the
sources themselves, excerpts from Pestalozzi's major works and several
addresses, most printed verbatim, with few comments. The "Course of
Instruction" in the normal and model schools of the British Home and
Colonial Infant and Juvenile School Society was included in the book
although it had not appeared in the *Journal*; Barnard must have received
it after the periodical was in press. The final section of the book was
devoted to biographical sketches of the Continental followers of Pestalozzi, material which could scarcely have been stimulating to the American reader. But to Barnard thorough coverage of the subject, and fealty to
the accomplishments of the disciples, demanded that they not be
neglected; in any case, he had the material at hand, most of it supplied by
his faithful disciple Hermann Wimmer.

Henry Barnard's interest in German educational scholarship was sus-

81. Most of the material in the book appeared in volumes III and VII of the *Journal*,
but there are sections in every volume between. A diagram of the parallel pages is unnecessary although some examples may be convincing: Part I, 49–126, is the same as III, ix
(June 1857): 401–16, continued in IV, x (September 1857): 65–126; Part II, 155–65, "Evening Hour of a Hermit," is VI, xvi (March 1859): 169–179; the section on "Assistants and
Disciples" for the most part is the same material, but the order is different; the order in
the work also differs from the Table of Contents!

82. Barnard was very familiar with the work of von Raumer, translated by Frederic
Perkins. As was his wont, he had sent a copy of the Pestalozzi book to the German, for he
quoted with pride a letter received in April, 1860: "in your PESTALOZZI AND PESTA-
LOZZIANISM, you have collected with the greatest diligence all that relates to Pestalozzi
and his school. I can hardly understand how you could have made such a collection in
America, or out of it either, even by aid of well informed correspondents."

83. *Pestalozzi*, Part II, 2, the comment is addressed to the Paternal Instructors, 228ff.

tained, and he continued to publish and republish German materials. As part of the projected European Educational Biography, in 1863, he produced a volume entitled *Memoirs of Eminent Teachers and Educators in Germany; with Contributions to the History of Education from the Fourteenth Century to the Nineteenth Century*; this was "reproduced" in 1878

> with omissions and additions to make the treatment more special and comprehensive of the great teachers, educators, and organizers of school systems in Germany, from the sixth to the nineteenth century.[84]

What never appears in the often replicated Barnard bibliographies is that these two books were actually Karl von Raumer's massive *Geschichte der Pedagogik vom wiederaufblühen klassischer Studien bis unsere Zeit*, translated by Lucius W. Fitch and Frederick B. Perkins. Barnard gave the proper credit both to the author and to the translators, in his prefaces, although he had not done so in the *Journal*, but few later adulators or bibliographers read or noticed his comments.

In number 31 of the *Journal* (1863) Barnard had printed a list of books suitable for teachers:

> The following works, issued separately, and under the general title of Papers for Teachers and Parents, and devoted to a practical exposition of Methods of Teaching and School Management in different countries, are compiled from "The American Journal of Education", edited by Henry Barnard, LL.D.[85]

With this notice the editor implied several things. He promised that the series would be for all of the participants in the education of the young, and the works would have a utilitarian rather than a theoretical thrust, perhaps resembling the various practical guides so common in the period. If such was the expectation there was bound to be disappointment among the subscribers.

The first volume in the series, entitled *Papers for the Teacher*, Number One, had appeared earlier.[86] The *Papers* were intended to serve as professional materials—apparently Barnard had forgotten his promise to

---

84. *Memoirs of Eminent Teachers and Educators in Germany* (Philadelphia, 1863; rev. ed., Hartford, 1878). The volume in the Yale library is inscribed "Presented by Hon. H. Barnard, 1863."

85. *AJE* XIII, xxxi (June 1863): 447 and 862; the identical listing appears in *German Educators*, 587. Prices were quoted "for the series" as far as published, or I–VII; XIII was to be *Normal Schools*, a work already in print although Barnard did not include it in those offered in this advertisement.

86. *Papers for the Teacher*, Number One, 1859 (New York: F. C. Brownell, 1860); there

include the parents. The first volume did indeed contain selections chosen by the editor with the neophyte teacher in mind. William Russell's series "Intellectual Education," Thomas Hill's "The True Order of Studies," and Gideon Thayer's "Letters to a Young Teacher" dominated three-quarters of the book, and the view of the role of the teacher they projected was a traditional one. To Russell, intellectual education was aimed at the perceptive, the expressive, and the reflective faculties; to Thayer, considerations such as self-examination, self-discipline, manners, habits, punctuality, and moral instruction, all took precedence over the techniques of instructing in spelling, reading, penmanship, and geography. The only clearly pedagogical selections in the book were ten pages devoted to "Questions for Examination of a School" and the "Catechism on Methods of Teaching," from Diesterweg, scarcely an American source.[87] Henry Barnard was no Samuel Hall, and his first message to the teachers was in the form of a paternalistic sermon, much as he used to deliver an introductory, inspiring address at a teachers' institute. Still the book gave teachers, most of whom had no access to any higher education, a lofty-minded literature, which was bound to enhance their pride and sense of value—if they read it.

Papers for the Wisconsin Teacher, Number Two, constituted a second preparatory course for the teachers, and it was specifically pedagogical. Subtitled *Object Teaching and Oral Lessons on Social Science and Common Things*, it appeared in 1860 and was one of the few instances in which material was published as a monograph prior to its publication in the *Journal*.[88] In it Barnard surveyed Great Britain's model and training schools, institutions he had visited, and he quoted extensively from his colleagues across the sea. He could not resist beginning Part I with an introduction on "School Houses and their Equipment" before moving to sections on "Oral and Gallery Training Lessons"; the final selection was a Prize Essay, "Education, A Prevention of Misery and Vice." Three parts of the book examined elementary instruction in Ireland, Scotland, and England, commencing in each case with a survey of the "Progress of Elementary Education" and encompassing curricula and methods utilized by the principals of *training* schools in each country—precious little pertaining to actual elementary schools was included. Barnard was more concerned with teacher training and school organization than with

was no subtitle although in Barnard's later lists the title was given as *American Contributions to the Philosophy and Practice of Education*.

87. It is a simple but time-consuming task, to identify the sources in the *Journal*. The Russell articles, 1–156, are in II (May 1856): 112–44, 317–32, III (December 1856): 47–64, 321–45; the Thayer ones, 1–104, are in volumes II through VI; the Diesterweg in IV.

88. *Papers for the Wisconsin Teacher*, Number Two (New York: F. C. Brownell, 1860).

actual teaching, and the poor classroom instructor found few model lessons, one on color by D. R. Hay being the exception rather than the rule. Still the teacher could learn what those in another country were doing from this volume of the *Papers*, and from the subsequent one on Germany, although not about experimentation in his or her own country.

Example was one thing, exhortation was another, and Barnard, secular preacher that he was, believed firmly in exhortation. What better guidance for the young teacher than the noble thoughts of noble minds, a sort of educational Bartlett's? Hence *Educational Aphorisms and Suggestions, Ancient and Modern*, the fourth in the *Papers* series. In his introduction Barnard said his aim was to embody "the most remarkable sayings . . . of wise and good men" on education and the schools, and that he had found his work made easier by discovering "The Pedagogical Treasure-Casket," of Dr. J. F. T. Wohlfarth. Actually, this first volume was entirely Wohlfarth's, leaving for a projected second one Barnard's own collection "with the intention of ultimately completing such a comprehensive and valuable collection" that all teachers and friends of education would find "something to stimulate reflection, to suggest expedients, or to solve doubts."[89] (The planned second volume was never written.) Once again Barnard was not precisely plagiarizing, for he did give credit to Wohlfarth, as he had to von Raumer, but from the public he alone received the recognition of authorship. The copy of *German Educators* in the Yale library has a penciled notation of authorship whereas *Educational Aphorisms* does not; von Raumer was well known, but who has heard of Dr. Wohlfarth?

The text, if not the headings, of this fourth volume of the *Papers* is identical with material in volumes VIII and X of the *Journal*. But Barnard, more than was customary, had thought out the arrangement and sequencing of the material which he subdivided into topics for easy reference. The book begins with the very general, quotations on "Man—His Dignity and Destiny," moves to the "Value and Essence of A Good Education," and then to the "Duties of Parents and Teachers." Next came sections on "Early Training," "Physical Education" (which included five pages on the care of the body), and "Obedience to Parents." To his credit, Barnard devoted twenty pages to the "Education of the Female Sex," and the final chapters covered instruction, religious and moral training, and discipline. Reading the collection it is easy to picture some poor teacher preparing a weekly homily for his or her class, or perhaps setting a writing exercise on a chosen text.

89. *Papers for the Teacher*, Fourth Series, *Educational Aphorisms and Suggestions Ancient and Modern*, Part I (Philadelphia: J. B. Lippincott, 1861); Barnard included an index for the convenience of teachers who presumably might want to begin each day with some well-chosen words of enlightenment.

The final volume of the *Papers, English Pedagogy: Education, the School, and the Teacher in English Literature* had little to do with pedagogy; it contained "the thoughts of eminent writers" and "the popular view in prose and verse" on education, from English sources, ranging from Ascham to Spencer.[90] Barnard did not pretend that the book was "a connected or exhaustive view," and he hoped "to make another contribution" subsequently. He did not; the *Papers* were never completed. The idea of creating a teachers' library, comparable to the many family libraries, was a sound one, and the first volumes demonstrated Barnard's vague editorial concept, that of providing a comprehensive course of study for those who had had no opportunity for further education beyond the common school. If he had persisted in the project, fulfilling the promise of the initial volumes, he might have supplied the isolated teachers throughout the nation, many of whom attended only the occasional institute, with a material for "self-culture" and professional development.

What can we conclude about Barnard as an educational historian, editor, publisher, teacher? Barnard's contemporaries were lavish in their accolades, beginning with William Russell in 1856: "The appearance of your March No is remarkably neat and tasteful"; "The May No I find full of matter of great and permanent interest. It is worth its price tenfold." Words such as *invaluable, grand, magnificent* appear in letter after letter from friends and colleague reformers, and Henry Barnard himself was wont to quote, in his later editions, the admiring assessments of his English counterpart, Robert Hebert Quick. Among the notes preserved in his old age, Barnard copied from Quick's appeal for the Barnard fund: "Our contributions are shrubs when compared with the forest of the *American Journal of Education*." Indeed, Quick spoke of Barnard as "the greatest living authority" and dedicated his own work to Barnard:

To Henry Barnard
who in a long life of self-sacrificing labor has
given to the English language an educational literature
This volume is dedicated
with esteem and admiration of the Author[91]

A tribute in the same vein came many years later from the president of Clark University, Henry Davidson Sheldon. To Sheldon much of the writing on education in this country had been "slight, superficial, and catchy,"

90. *English Pedagogy; Education, the School, and the Teacher in English Literature* (Philadelphia: J. B. Lippincott, 1862). It was based on volumes II through VI and XI for the most part.

91. Robert Hebert Quick, *Essays on Educational Reformers* (1868; International Education Series, New York, 1890), 91 and dedication.

and the profession had suffered; in contrast, Barnard's "great work will always stand as an impressive rebuke."[92]

William Torrey Harris publicly acknowledged his debt, both personal and professional, to his predecessor, referring with admiration to the "one great purpose" of Barnard's life, "namely, to enlighten the teachers and directors of education" through the publication of works in the history of education. At the same memorial session of the National Education Association, Newton C. Dougherty lauded the *Journal* while admitting its limited range. "But it is one of the blessed results of the utterance of truth that it passes from mind to mind." It was sadly true that only a few actually read the words, but what they read, he hastened to add, they "reiterated in educational meetings, in teachers' institutes, in normal and other schools." Stanley Hall spoke of the *Journal* as a "most valuable periodical . . . a vast encyclopedia of information . . . but grouped and indexed in a very confusing way."[93]

An entire generation of educational historians, lead by Ellwood P. Cubberley and Paul Monroe depended almost exclusively on Barnard's work. Monroe alluded to its "magnitude, scope, and quality" and concluded:

> No other educational periodical so voluminous and exhaustive has issued from either private or public sources. It will ever constitute a mine of information concerning this and earlier periods in both Europe and America.[94]

More recently, Carl Kaestle has credited Amory D. Mayo as the one who "established the New England interpretation with great force and a wealth of detail" and provided "the classic statement of the view that later dominated twentieth century textbooks on the history of education," but Kaestle ignored one of Mayo's sources. Lawrence Cremin recognized rather the lineage of the "Barnard-Wickersham-Martin-Mayo-Herbert Baxter Adams tradition."[95] It is entirely correct to view Barnard as the progenitor of the family of historians of education who dominated the field until the present generation. Henry Barnard supplied the sources

92. Letter from Sheldon, January 23, 1899, TC; one may want to take this birthday greeting with some modicum of salt.

93. *NEA*, 1901, Harris, 408ff., Dougherty, 395ff.; Thursfield, *Barnard*, 268.

94. *The Cambridge History of American Literature*, vol. III, *Later National Literature*, Part II (New York, 1921), chap. XXIII, 404.

95. Carl E. Kaestle, "The Development of Common School Systems in the States of the Old Northwest," in Mattingly and Stevens, ". . . *Schools*", 31; Lawrence A. Cremin, *The Wonderful World of Ellwood Patterson Cubberley* (New York: Bureau of Publications, Teachers College, 1965), 37.

and defined the interpretive framework on which subsequent historians perpetuated his perceptions, until the work of the revisionists in the past decade.

The constituent parts of his interpretation should by now be familiar. Barnard proclaimed the "homely, practical virtues of integrity, industry, courage, promptitude, public spirit, philanthropy, and perseverance" and "those habits of mutual help and courtesy" and "good practical home culture." He stressed the vital importance of the individual, the right thinking one, in public affairs and was incensed when an unthinking public frustrated the actions of the good; once he expressed "our amazement and indignation at the outrage done to the cause of good letters, and at the exhibition of ingratitude for large public service" when Henry Tappan was dismissed—was he perhaps internalizing his anger?[96] Barnard had faith in progress, a word he often employed, and he told a tale of the steady, onward march of the educational agencies of the nation. He believed that the state, and its agents, had a responsibility for that progress, and that the creation of institutions, public or private, under the guidance of the better class of men, would solve society's ills. Hence he wrote of great men and of institutions. He also wrote of European and New England men, ignoring simultaneous developments in other parts of the United States, to such an extent that it has been only recently that students of our educational history realized that New England did not lead the way alone, or even first.

Barnard's *Journal* was a failure on many counts. It failed as a business, for Henry Barnard was an appalling businessman. Though no subscriber lists or account books survive, we do have hints in the anguished letters from assistants and friends, and even his wife.

> Now there must be, as I have often remarked to you before, a great mismanagement, or there could not be so many complaints about the Journal not being sent. If "they have been sent," there is no reason why they should not have been received in Brooklyn. I have received three subscription moneys but have sent no numbers, knowing nothing about them as you left no instructions.—The weather continues cold & disagreeable, & I am lonesome & cross at being left so much alone, the evenings are too dismal to live through. Love to all but the Journal to whom [sic] I have sworn eternal enmity.[97]

Barnard constantly failed to fill orders, so that willing purchasers looked in vain in bookstores for new issues, and he neglected to send bills, or he

96. *AJE* I, 2 (January 1856): 205; 4 (May 1856): 609; XIII, xxxii (September 1865): 641.
97. Letter from Josephine Barnard, June 8, 1856, NYU.

PREFACE

This volume is composed of chapters on Superior Instruction in different countries, which have appeared as articles, original and selected, in successive numbers of the *American Journal of Education*, in prosecution of a plan announced in the original prospectus of that periodical, to give a comprehensive survey of the whole field of systems and institutions of education in different ages, under different conditions of government and religion. They are issued in this form as contributions only to the material for a historical development of this department of public instruction.

HENRY BARNARD

Hartford, Conn., July, 1873.

SUPERIOR INSTRUCTION.

In the first Number of the American Journal of Education for 1873, the editor announced his intention to close his studies for the present in the field of Superior Instruction, and indicated in the Title and Contents which followed, the Contributions which he proposed to embody in a separate volume, and which had been already printed in the Journal. Unexpected engagements and hindrances—engagements which made any further use of the material already gathered impossible, and a nervous prostration which for several months precluded all efforts at composition or revision—have compelled hinm to abridge the Contents of the volume, as shown in the following page, and to make the historical development and present condition of Colleges and Universities in different countries, embodied in this volume, less comprehensive than he at first announced. It will, however, be found, on examination, to contain valuable information both in reference to the historical development of superior instruction, the organization of studies and statistics of prominent institutions of higher learning, and the views of eminent statesmen, scholars and teachers, on the subjects treated—more than can be found in any one volume in any language.

HENRY BARNARD

Hartford, October 15, 1873.

Preface and Supplementary Preface to *Superior Instruction*, by Henry Barnard, 1873.

sent them when no copies had been ordered. He was frequently away from Hartford, dependent on his faithful assistants, yet he hated to delegate and procrastinated when pressured. And his repeated embarking on other ventures exacerbated the weaknesses of his editorial activity. Although eventually he always came home to his *Journal*, he never concentrated solely on it until after 1870, and by then he was weary from his labors and even less organized.

In the final decade of his life there was an abortive attempt to have the National Education Association assume financial responsibility for the existing plates of Barnard's *Journal*—an effort which has a sad irony to it, for his first proposal was that a national organization of educators sponsor his publication. All along the *Journal* had been a financial burden. As it is impossible to distinguish Barnard's personal finances from those of the *Journal*, it is impossible to ascertain precisely how much he had invested and how much he lost. The myth perpetuates his insistence that he had expended a total of $40,000–$50,000 of his own money, which Thursfield doubts; he does accept Barnard's stated average loss of $1,300 for each volume—which amounts to $40,000![98] That Barnard lost money is no doubt true, but that he acquired financial support which he did not acknowledge is also true. On many an occasion he turned to individual friends, and especially to Elisha Potter, and he also secured aid from organized groups. Just as *Reformatory Education* had the (unacknowledged) support of New York benefactors, so in 1879 Barnard received support from the American Foebel Union through the good offices of Elizabeth Peabody.[99] In neither case did he give any public recognition of the assistance.

Had Barnard been more responsible and responsive, in publishing the *Proceedings* of the National Teachers Association more promptly, for example, it is possible that he might have found a permanent source of funding for his periodical. Had he been able and willing to work with someone more businesslike, he might have achieved something like solvency. But the *Journal* was *his* journal, and he suffered no interference, only agents. His complaints always had a plaintive, personal, almost paranoic tone. "The Journal has never received any help—and for the last ten volumes I have not had a single order for a set or a copy from all the *Colleges* in the country . . . ," he once wrote to Gilman.[100]

The *Journal* failed, too, in circulation. Despite the constant promo-

---

98. See Thursfield, *Barnard*, 42–43.

99. Preface, volume XXX, not paged.

100. Letter to Gilman, December 4, 1875, JHU. But, as Thursfield, *Barnard*, 304n, points out this statement is untrue from the evidence.

tional forays of salesmen such as William Baker and Corneilius M. Welles, and the publicity endeavors of supporters such as William Wells, and the editor's own efforts, paid circulation may never have exceeded 500 copies. Of course, Barnard distributed *gratis* a far greater number, and the readership of a given number may have been significantly larger than the subscription list. Editors of other journals, James Cruikshank of the *New York Teacher* and Emerson White of the *Ohio Educational Monthly* for two, ordered volumes for themselves and culled material from them for their publications. Subscriptions to individual volumes or complete sets came from libraries, especially in normal schools, and from educational leaders, city superintendents such as Nathan Bishop and state ones; John Swett was an especially enthusiastic promoter who managed to sell five sets in California and various individual numbers despite the extreme unpredictability of delivery due to his distance from the editor's office —not to speak of Barnard's laxity in responding to Swett's letters.

As Thursfield points out, "the distinction of those who subscribed indicates a close association between subscriptions to the *Journal* and educational leadership."[101] Subscribers were, for the most part, men of Barnard's circle, reformers such as Samuel Gridley Howe and common school advocates such as Mann and Russell; the expanding group of the new, second generation, professional schoolmen, the city and state superintendents and pedagogical professors such as Philbrick, James P. Wickersham and Francis W. Parker read the *Journal* as well. From its pages they became familiar with some innovative pedagogy, with novel institutions, with classical educational theory, and with the deeds of the giants of educational history; and they had access to an enormous amount of original material. Henry Barnard nearly succeeded in creating an encyclopedia of education, but what he did not meet were the needs and interests of the next generation of educators who would increasingly define education in more narrow, more concrete, and more specialized terms.

In a sense, one can conclude that through his publications Henry Barnard did contribute to the raising of the status of the broad field of education in this country and of its leaders. He brought high standards to their discourse, he promulgated a consistent philosophy of public education, and he created a literature; he publicized the professions' organizations and the triumphs of the leaders. Two caveats are necessary, however. Bar-

101. Ibid., 288. For a detailed discussion of the circulation of the *Journal*, see 37ff.; for "The range of the *Journal*'s Influence," 270ff. Letters from the agents, especially Baker and Welles, and from all the friends who attempted to promote the periodical are too numerous to cite; see, for example, from Bishop, December 19, 1855, May 31, 1856, December 22, 1860; from Swett, November 26, 1864, March 20, 26, November 6, 1865; NYU.

nard's audience was limited not just in number; it was a small group of male, Protestant, predominantly Eastern, schoolmen, the ministerial and lay first reformers and the new professionals who followed them. Barnard's colleagues, mostly older than he, would pass from the scene long before he would, and the newer men would soon turn to newer concerns. By the turn of the century they could not learn from him.

Finally, Henry Barnard never reached those he professed he wanted most to reach, the teachers of the nation. One of his stated goals was the development of informed and cultivated teachers, and he selected material that was designed to inspire them and to guide them toward self-improvement, as he defined it. He had little intention of providing them with the specificity they needed, and thus he did *not* anticipate the day when professionalization would imply a set of skills as well as a body of inspirational literature. When he called for a profession, he had in mind an antebellum conception of a profession; his model remained that of the ministry. Moreover, neither his *Journal*, nor the companion volumes, ever appealed to the every day teacher. The entire corpus was too expensive, too scholarly, too theoretical and historical, perhaps even too bulky. And even when Barnard attempted to serve the teacher, as he did when he published the accounts of the state teachers' associations, he was writing for the male leadership rather than for the increasingly female corps of teachers in the schoolhouses across the land. When he attempted to write for teachers, as he did in the *Papers*, he aimed too high, and he soon lost interest in his task. The fact of the matter was that Henry Barnard, despite his professed intentions, really was not interested in and did not understand the new American teacher who refused to be what he wanted her to be.

VIII

NESTOR OF

AMERICAN

EDUCATION

*As a native-born citizen of Connecticut—
as one whose roots are in the soil—I am
ambitious of being remembered among
those of her sons whose name the state will
not willingly let die, because of some service,
however small, done to the cause of human-
ity in my day and generation; but I am
more desirous to deserve, at the end of life,
the nameless epitaph of one in whom mankind lost a friend, and no man got rid of
an enemy.* (Letter to the editor of the Norwich Aurora, *April 26, 1850, in* Connecticut Common School Journal, *n.s., V, iv
[December 185]: 136–38)*

After he left Washington Henry Barnard never again held public office, nor was he ever again active in any national organization. He
passed the time in Hartford, in the house where he had been born, growing old slowly. By 1890 he looked the part of the venerable patriarch—a
sturdy frame, not as yet bent, a furrowed brow, a flowing white beard
which reached nearly to his waist. As an eminent citizen of Hartford he
had been invited to deliver the July 4 oration in 1876, and he continued to
lecture to groups of educators, usually reminiscing about past achievements rather than proposing new initiatives. He took occasional trips, to
Europe once, to professional meetings, to visit his many friends. But
mostly he remained close to home, where he had always been the happiest. Sporadically, he issued volumes of his *Journal*, and he supervised the

republication of previously published works, and all the while, forever, intending to turn, at last, to the long-deferred massive history of education.

It is frustrating that we have only glimpses of Henry Barnard, the husband and father, for in his retirement he was a private rather than a public figure. His daughter Emily, when interviewed by a later biographer, cried "Oh, just tell them what a perfectly lovely, kindly man he was."[1] One wonders. Age may have softened her view, or, by then, she may have readily and happily accepted her role as her father's helpmate in his old age. He, on his part, scarcely ever mentioned his children. A few cautionary letters written to his son remain, along with a charming little autobiographical booklet written by young Henry, then in his boyhood, and dedicated to his father.[2] In 1872, Henry, senior, took the entire family to Germany, to Heidelberg, where the son attended lectures (and began to smoke, his father was sorry to say) while his two sisters went to German schools, and his mother tried to like German cooking. The girls of the family remain dim figures, but young Henry was seen as a "son of so much promise," perchance destined to emulate and surpass his father. The younger man became a lawyer, married, and, sad to say, died before he reached thirty, leaving an only daughter, Mary.[3] There is no evidence of Barnard's relationship with his daughter-in-law or his granddaughter.

Josephine Barnard remains an equally shadowy presence. Her few surviving letters reveal her as an affectionate and dutiful wife, who bore children and loneliness, her husband's absences and frequent guests, and who even agreed to open her house to her husband's cousin's daughter (so the girl could attend school in Hartford) as a paying guest. Occasionally she objected to her lot, and apparently she suffered a final, lingering illness with dignity. After her death in 1891, her closest friend wrote to her bereaved husband of Josephine's piety, of her refusal to learn to dance because "it would be an occasion to sin." "You will remember the modesty and simplicity with which she met your poetic courtship," she

1. Ralph C. Jenkins and Gertrude Chandler Warner, *Henry Barnard: An Introduction* (Hartford: Connecticut State Teachers Association, 1937), 96.

2. *Travels by Land and Water*, an account dedicated to "My Dear Papa." "This little book, which though small, has taken me many hours sitting on a hard stool by a dirty window to compose, is now finished—I hope to the satisfaction of my readers who are not numerous but select. Any body wanting a copy please apply to the author-son." How a boy copies the father.

3. Fragment of letter to Porter, January 14, 1872; from R. H. Dana, December 4, 1873; both TC. This trip was the only one on which the family accompanied Barnard; the fact that it was to Germany reflects his admiration of German scholarship. The granddaughter is mentioned in the probate records, October 23, 1900, as one of Barnard's three heirs.

Portrait of Henry Barnard by F. Tuttle, 1886

reminded Barnard.[4] Among his papers, Josephine's husband did keep a copy of her obituary, written by his friend William Andrews for the *Courant*, and he sent copies to his few surviving close friends.[5] Yet his phrases, "so good a wife" and "so many years of happiness" lack something in sincerity, and he may have harbored a resentment against her to his dying day, a vestige of his anti-Catholicism. In one of his fruitless and

4. Letter from Emily Mason, May 29, 1891; it is to her credit, and Barnard's, that the friendship was kept up; Miss Mason wrote annual birthday greetings to her friend's widower.

5. Letter from Archer, sending "Poem In Memoriam Mrs. Josephine Desnoyers Barnard, July 6," July 29, 1891, TC; by 1897 Archer and Barnard were the sole survivors of their class of 130 members, and the former died in January 1899.

endless lists, drawn up as an index to a book he never wrote, is an entry: "Roman Catholic. The Terror of Consternation & Catastrophe of Marrying One."

In his final years, Barnard's was an orderly and occupied life, his every need watched over by his daughters. His study was the room in which he had been born, and there he worked in a Windsor chair with a writing arm; his extensive library, the one James Fraser so envied, must have been scattered about the house.[6] The elderly man rose at four most mornings, never later than five, he claimed, having gone to bed by ten. First he would make himself a cup of "Bakers cocoa" and take a "Bozton cracker" which "warms the blood and prevents a 'sense of dizziness.'" Then to work.

> I have found that by securing three or four hours of solid work before 8 a.m. a large amount of fair editorial work can be done in the course of fifty years.—[added in hand] witness the 41 volumes of educational information.[7]

When the weather was fine he liked to toil a while in his garden, tending to his fruit trees with special care, until the unhappy day came when his daughters would no longer allow him to venture out alone, even with his favorite stick—a snow shovel handle he had fashioned into a cane.[8]

He attended to his correspondence—drafts of letters were meticulously dated and the time noted, for example "4:45 a.m." He was still a loyal son of Eli, and he corresponded with his former classmates until, one by one, they died; at last, in 1890, he took over the task of class secretary.[9] There were still matters of business demanding his attention, especially while he continued to publish the *Journal*. He had to write to the Secretary of Public Instruction in South Carolina that, although the state had received the *Journal*, no payment had yet been received; he also, certainly to his joy, enrolled a new subscriber who ordered a complete set of the publication. Horace Bushnell refused to submit an article, saying

6. Letter from Fraser, April 13, 1866; see also June 19, September 7, 1865. James Fraser was an English reformer, the Bishop of Manchester, a member of the Schools Inquiry Commission and the author of a part of its lengthy report; he visited Barnard and his "well-stocked library" in 1865.

7. Letter to Archer, January 1, 1894; see also another letter, in two copies, one typed, January 24, 1893, unaddressed; also collective letter to classmates, January 24, 1892; TC. A birthday letter from Barnard Horton (a grandnephew), of New York to "Grandpa Barnard," January 25, 1900, refers to Barnard's early rising and to the cocoa and gardening. Note Barnard's prideful count of his publications.

8. The photographs are reproduced in Hughes, *Barnard*, 5 and 7; Barnard described the stick, and drew a picture, in a letter to Archer, January, 1899, draft, TC.

9. Letter from T. G. Brainard, Grinnell, Iowa, June 12, 1890.

Barnard did not pay sufficiently, but Theodore Woolsey forwarded information on Hartford schools, and Andrew White sent a report of the annual expenditures of Cornell. As editor and an old friend, Barnard exchanged many letters with Elizabeth Peabody concerning the publication of kindergarten material, and his correspondence with his Swedish colleague, J. A. Siljestrom, was warm and affectionate. One ambitious author forwarded a copy of his new text, the *Patriotic Reader*, in the hope that Barnard would intervene on its behalf with the Hartford Board of Education, and another had a query about textbooks; Barnard sent information on editions of the *New England Primer* to another.[10] Thus, even in retirement his interests remained constant, and his circle of colleagues loyal.

Loyalty was indeed displayed in the matter of Barnard's financial situation. There is no way of deciphering his income at the end of his life, but he was, or felt, strapped.[11] Attempts were made by both the New England Superintendents' Association (in 1881) and the National Education Association (in 1890) to aid Barnard by taking over his existing stock and the publication of the moribund *Journal*. The newspapers seemed to have cooperated in this effort, for Edward Gallaudet, the son of Barnard's old mentor, wrote from Washington of "the great pain" he had felt when he read in the *Courant* of Barnard's "embarrassment" and sent a check for $100 "with gratitude for what you were to my father." The Henry Barnard Publishing Company was incorporated in New Jersey in 1891, with William Harris as president and Andrew Rickoff as treasurer; both Nicholas Murray Butler and Henry Barnard were directors. The company planned to continue the publication of Barnard's works and "other treatises on Psychology, Pedagogy, and Schools," and the directors hoped to enlist "the teachers and school men of the country" in the companion Henry Barnard Society. The goal was thus to support Henry Barnard and to continue the general publication of his work. The incorporated publishing effort met with little success although on at least one occasion the

10. Letter from Bushnell, June 8, 1870; from White, May 3, 1873; from Woolsey, April 4, 1878; from Sheffield, September 10, 1878; from Siljestrom, September 2, 1879, August 30, 1883; from Brace, June 18, 1881; from Winthrop, January 30, 1884; from Carrington, November 27, 1888; from Scarborough, June 21, 1894; all TC; from Peabody, January 4, 1880, March, 1881, May 24 (no year), March 25 (no year), NYU.

11. When Barnard died, the inventory of his estate listed $14,525 in total assets, $13,200 of which was the house on Main Street and its furnishings; the remainder was 30 shares in the Connecticut River Boat Company (valued at $1,200) and real estate in West Hartford (which his daughter sold soon to raise cash to meet the outstanding bills); from Probate Record, October 23, 1900, State of Connecticut. What happened to his investments is not recorded, and the probate record supports the view of Barnard's meager resources at the end of his life.

beneficiary wrote to thank Commissioner Harris for checks amounting to $311.96 for the fund.[12]

All the while Barnard continued to toil away at his historical research. In 1886 when he proposed to write a "History of Education in Connecticut," he turned to the legislature for support; wisely the Committee on Education approved the proposal in principle but declined to fund it until the work was completed. As late as 1897 he was still optimistic that his work was timely; George Plimpton, of Ginn and Company, responding to an outline sent him by Barnard, promised he would "do what he could to get a market" for some articles.[13] Barnard inserted corrections to his book on the Hartford Grammar School and his article on Monson Academy, and he began an outline of an account of the founding of the Historical Society with a list of the corresponding secretaries—he was the first. Once, when preparing a paper for the State Teachers' Association meeting in New Haven, he unearthed a discrepancy between their records and his memory as to the date of the organization's founding; after a search of documents, he "succeeded in compelling a correction" of an error nearly half a century old.

He made fragmentary jottings for a history of Hartford which display both his careful scrutiny of available sources and his random reminiscences. He noted the November 1827 fire in which the Gin Distillery burned down although ninety-one cows survived, the burning of Jackson in effigy on January 13, 1829, the erection of a log cabin on the corner of Trumbull and Asylum streets—evidence of the partisan politics he abhorred—and a fair in aid of the Greeks in June 1832; certainly for this material he had consulted old issues of the *Courant*. But elsewhere, in notes for a chapter on Hartford, he wrote of Dr. Todd and Thomas Gallaudet and David Watkinson, the Hartford Hospital and the Green, and swimming, and vacations "their infrequency and shortness"—these can only be his private musings. There was a shorter entry in his old hand, "Walks, Talks, and Papers about Hartford" with a prefatory note, as if these were being prepared for publication. And he began another outline, "Glance—Life and Works" with poignant headings which men-

12. See Thursfield, *Barnard*, 52–54; Leaflet, March 1891, and announcement of incorporation of the Society, December 1, 1891; letters to Gilman from A. S. Murray, secretary, November 25, and from Harris, November 27, 1891, JHU; letter from Edward M. Gallaudet, April 26, 1890, TC; letter from Harris, May 29, 1890, TC. There may have been another attempt to provide support for Barnard; an editorial in the Willimantic *Journal*, February 5, 1897, endorsed the idea of a pension for him, clipping, NYU.

13. Typed copy of news item in Hartford *Evening Post*, April 6, 1886, TC. Letter from Plimpton, February 13, 1897, NYU. There is an "Outline for G. E. Plimpton" in the Watkinson collection.

tioned being put to bed in a trundle bed and, under 1831–32, "Escape from School Teaching" and, "1841–2, *Bitter Disappointment.*"

Although he had written Harris that he "had reached that stage in his life that he could do no more as editor and publisher," Barnard was very active for a man of his age and his history of infirmities. He declined to attend the June reunion at Monson Academy in 1890, because he had to be in New Haven, presumably at a Yale commencement, on the same day. He did attend the Monson alumni dinner in 1894 and responded at length to a toast; he credited the academy as the place where his mind was first trained. At the Academy the students, "all earnest boys and girls, eager to learn," had profited from the "condensed and deliberate curriculum, the beneficial influences socially" which were superior to "the ordinary high school where so much is attempted but little comparative growth of individual thought and ideas can be accomplished." In old age, memories of his year at Monson glowed more brightly than ever, and his faith in the common high school, so optimistically expressed in his Norwich Academy address, had dimmed.

Barnard did not attend the meeting of the national superintendents in 1891, but he spent ten days at the Chicago Exhibition in 1893. There he was filled with "vigor and enthusiasm" and his days there were ones of "interest and fatigue," well worth the time and money expended. After the trip, he wrote to Thomas Cushing that the exhibition had been a "real object lesson"; it was to be regretted, however, that the superb buildings were to be used for such a brief time—they should be made permanent and put to some worthwhile community use. He also felt that more of the young people of the nation could derive educational benefit from the exhibition; perhaps outstanding ones could be awarded a trip to Chicago, aware always that they were charged with the responsibility of reporting back to their classmates on its wonders.[14]

In June of the next year, Barnard spent five days in Boston visiting friends and, while there, he awarded the diplomas to the graduates of the Chauncey Hall Kindergarten Training School. He had been quite absorbed in the kindergarten movement during the previous decade and had corresponded with several women who were spearheading the development. Yet his language to one, a teacher in Memphis, proved again that Henry Barnard had changed his view of teachers little over the passing years. He thanked Miss Wheatley for her letter "asking his benediction

14. Drafts of letters to Mr. and Mrs. Flint; typed, and corrected by hand, response to toast, June 19, 1894; fragment of letter to superintendents; draft of letter to Cushing and Vail, assorted notes; all TC. In the letter describing the fair, he went on to recollect an agricultural show held in Hartford in 1818 or 1820—somewhere in his house he knew he had a placard advertising the show.

on her work among the children and women" in the community in which she lived, a letter which had "touched" him deeply. Then, referring to one of the pioneers of the movement, Miss Lucy Wheelock, he concluded: "Go on, then, in your work, under the inspiration of such leading and teaching."[15] Teaching was still a mission to Barnard, and, presumably, to Miss Wheatley and her colleagues.

History more and more merged with autobiography. Episodic and still vivid recollections predominate among the papers in the Watkinson collection. Again and again Barnard sifted, organized, outlined, and began, all preparatory to writing, or to assisting Will Monroe to write the definitive account of his labors in the cause of education and also in response to queries directed to him. He made a chronological Outline of Educational Activity—Author, Editor, Publisher, marked in bold letters Tentative; in the margins he estimated the number of pages he expected to devote to each era of his public life, up to 1870. The organization in his memo for Plimpton is unexceptional: Home, Education, Professional Reading, Travel; incomplete is the section called "Unexpected and Unintended Introduction Into Public Life." The thrust of that final entry indicates that in his old age he was ever anxious that his be the final interpretation of his life story.

The longest and most complete document among the papers is a collection of more than twenty-six ledger sheets, at least one for each letter of the alphabet, headed "Topics in Autobiography."[16] Henry Barnard, true to form, had made the index for his as yet unwritten story. The first entry is "ABCs—how and when mastered." Oddly, although "Cattleshows and Agricultural Fairs," "Circus in 1824 and 1894," and "Chemistry in Monson in 1824" appear on the C page, there is no entry "Common Schools"; yet, under F he listed "Free School—erroneous idea." Some successive entries are inexplicable for a Barnard biography: "Illiteracy, Indians, Infidelity." Some are peculiar, such as, under N, "Now I Lay Me Down to Sleep." Two items under V, "Ventilation" and "Vice and Vicious Children," repeat his life-long preoccupations, and "Diploma—should have recognition in public service" reflects his advocacy of qualifications for civil service. Under O, along with "Oaks & other historic & symbolic trees" and "Obedience, the Holy Habit," Barnard listed three Olds: "Old and New," "Old and Young in Sparta," and "Old—Applied to Good Things."[17] Other entries reveal the old man, perhaps more than he

15. Draft of letter to Wheatley, October 26, 1893.

16. The sheets are all headed Hartford Insurance Company; how Barnard came by them I do not know, but, ever the Yankee, he could not waste such a fine workbook.

17. On the edge of another sheet Barnard jotted "old House . . . old tree . . . old man . . . all dilapidated, but all standing."

intended. In addition to the Roman Catholic entry mentioned above, he added "Rate Bill, paid in advance help to punctuality" which sounds like a reminder or a reproach; "Sanford, Rollin, Class of 1831—life long intimacy—laugh & talk" recalls Barnard's capacity for friendship, and "Self-Activity—work alone accurately" describes his preferred style. Most pathetic of all is an entry under *P*: "Prefatory Note—How this book came to be written." Because of course it never was.

That Henry Barnard was retreating more and more into the mists of his own memories is clear. He subscribed to a clipping service—wonders of wonders in 1890—and treasured scraps of articles from papers in New York, Georgia, Ohio, Pennsylvania, Minnesota, Kansas, Wisconsin, Utah, and most of the New England states.[18] He typed, or had typed, a long excerpt from the *Connecticut Common School Journal* describing the "Barnard and Gallaudet Festival," the "gala-day" in 1856 on which the portraits of the two Connecticut educators were hung, along with that of Major North.[19] He made copious notes on the ceremony marking his eighty-fourth birthday and kept all the congratulatory letters he had received, as well as clippings which described the dinner honoring him.[20]

Barnard's eighty-sixth birthday was a gala occasion, organized, as was only suitable, by Charles Hine, the secretary of the Connecticut Board of Education. There were three sessions at the Connecticut State House, and eighteen addresses in all. The speakers represented every phase of Barnard's life and included the governor and the mayor, Commissioner of Education Harris, Francis W. Parker of the Cook County Normal School, James L. Hughes, the Inspector of Schools in Ontario, David Camp, the faithful old lieutenant, and Will Monroe, the new disciple. At the final commemorative banquet, William G. Sumner was the main speaker, and a double quartet from the Yale Glee Club sang. Messages praising the elderly man were read from the presidents of Yale, Cornell, and Colby; tributes came from teachers' groups throughout the nation and from the General Secretary of the Teachers Guild of Great Britain and Ireland. The warmest remarks were those of Frank Hill, of the Massachusetts Board of Education, who proposed that Connecticut memorialize Henry Barnard as Massachusetts had Horace Mann:

18. Various envelopes with the name Henry Romeike Clipping Service.

19. On that great day Miss Frances Cheseboro read an "original poem," of forty-eight lines, addressed to Barnard, which began "Thy honored name we love" and included the lines "The heart / That wakes not, thrills not, to thy lofty deeds / Is less than human!" The words "lofty mission" and "weary struggle," and "holy trust" indicate the conception of teaching in 1856 was still that of a mission.

20. Clipping from *Christian Register* (identified in Barnard's hand), October 15, 1895; from the *Journal of Education*, October 29, 1895.

I want Henry Barnard, in his sweet-tempered, wholesome and beautiful old age to know how much his noble educational spirit and his
great educational work have been and still are prized in Massachusetts. . . . May there be nothing to postpone the memorial but the
years of continued health, vigor, and joy we wish with all our hearts.

The honoree made a speech in reply, one which must have rambled. He
recalled the bells which rang to celebrate the treaty of peace in 1815 and
alluded to the recent arbitration treaty negotiated by the government,
and he reflected on the children who were "the adults of tomorrow."[21]
Barnard collected all of the remarks and letters and telegrams and, characteristically, had them set in type—if they were printed no copy remains.
    Some of the adulatory messages which came to the house on Main
Street were from unknowns such as the woman who was a superintendent in Maine: "I never saw your face—never heard your voice, but your
personality is as real to me as that of most of the people I know well."
Others came from devoted followers. Will S. Monroe sent annual greetings to his "beloved educational hero" in 1899, and in 1900 the telegram
from him was fulsome:

> Hail author: Educator: Lecturer: Editor: Gardener: Warmest greet-
> ings from an ardent admirer. May God be good to us and spare for
> us the inspiration of your loving example for many years to comes.

James L. Hughes also never forgot Barnard: "If I should write to you as
often as I think reverently of you, you would be kept busy reading my
letters." That warm and personal note was echoed in a birthday letter
from Frank Hill:

> I think I see your garden this coming spring, climbing over your
> boundary fences, your early peas "sassing" your neighbors' peas
> earlier in June than ever before, and your strawberries both the
> envy and the despair of those who would beat the venerable gar-
> dener, but cannot.

Mrs. Hill joined "lovingly" in the sentiments in a separate letter.[22]
    Thus, by the end of his long life Henry Barnard had become almost an

21. Clipping from *Journal of Education*, February 4, 1897, article describing the affair,
by Will S. Monroe; from the *Yale Alumni Weekly*, January 28, 1897; NYU.
    22. Letters and telegrams on birthdays are too numerous to cite; see specifically remarks
of Hill; letters and telegrams from Monroe, January 24, 1893, 1894, 1899, 1900; from
Hughes, January 8 and 24, 1894, January 23, 1896, January 26, 1899, January 23, 1900;
letter from Mary E. Snow, Bangor, Maine, January 23, 1899; letter from Hill, January 24,

Olympian, a hero and a figure of myth. Schools dedicated trees to him and honored his birthday with exercises (perhaps their teachers had read James Hughes's suggestion in his biographical sketch that they do just that); dutiful pupils in schools throughout New England wrote stiff letters of congratulations in elegant chirography.[23] The Center Union School of East Hampton, Massachusetts, inscribed a scroll:

> It gives us the greatest pleasure to be among the many in sending a word of greeting to the one who has made the largest contribution to the literature of education; to the organizer of the first teachers' institute ever held in America; the founder of the school systems of Connecticut and Rhode Island; and the first United States commissioner of education.

Barnard drafted a reply which may never have been sent.[24]

In addition to the private tributes, there were repeated public ones. Samuel Goodrich had attested to Henry Barnard's "immense" contributions as early as 1857, John Philbrick was constantly faithful to his friend at meetings and in print, and Robert Quick alluded to Barnard's work frequently, beginning in 1875. Barnard's publications were submitted to all of the great international exhibitions by the commissioner of education, and he was awarded a bronze Medal of Merit at the International Exhibition at Vienna in 1873, silver and gold ones at Paris in 1878, a diploma at Melbourne in 1880, another at New Orleans in 1884, and an additional bronze medal at the great Chicago Exhibition in 1893. Various educational journals reported the awards:

> In the field of school organization he was a pioneer. . . . In the department of state and national supervision he has done a good life work; enough to have established for him a permanent reputation as an educational reformer. To these claims on the gratitude of the nation we must add the greater work of author, editor, and publisher, in which he has given the world the results of educational

---

1900. There are many, many other greetings, including an 1897 telegram from the Monson trustees and from various superintendents and educators such as Francis W. Parker.

23. Hughes, *Barnard*, 16: "Let the boys and girls learn that one of the noblest and greatest of American educators still lives, and let the 24th of January, when it comes around again, be celebrated in all public schools with ceremonies befitting the birthday of an epoch-making man, 'whose fame is the property of all nations.'"

24. Letter from James Savin on Arbor Day ceremonies, January 6, 1891; from the Center School, January 23, 1900; also from faculty of Hillhouse High School, January 24, 1899; from Faculty of Pedagogy, New York University, January 24, 1900; from Ninth Grade, Fall River, and class #18, South School, Hartford, January 24, 1900; and so many others; draft, Barnard; all TC.

research, both general and special, unequaled in value in any other language.[25]

Two of Barnard's contemporaries summarized his achievements in print shortly before his death, and thereby made permanent an interpretation. James Hughes, when ruminating on the debt owed to those who had "won the glorious victories of sixty-five years ago," wrote an uncritical paean; still, there was insight in his assessment of Henry Barnard as

the man whom the United States should recognize as the golden link between the present and the past, as the living man who did most to make the present better than the past.

The gentlemanly clergyman-historian, Amory D. Mayo, recognized that Barnard was "deficient" in "administrative powers" and not a politician but rather "a splendid scholar and an earnest advocate of the best theories of education" whose "greatest influence was through the wide circulation of his written documents."[26]

The accolades delivered at the annual meeting of the National Education Association in 1900, the year of Barnard's death, provided both his obituary and a summary of his achievements. The Commissioner of Schools in Hartford spoke of Henry Barnard's "personal devotion to the ministry of education, and his self-surrender to the work which made his naturally eloquent appeals irresistible." Francis Parker linked Barnard with Horace Mann as the "two imposing figures" in education who believed "that we are marching along the endless pathway of unrealized possibilities of human growth," and portrayed the former "in a broad and deep sense an all-around educator." The principal of the Millersville (Pennsylvania) Normal School emphasized Barnard's realization that "the teacher is the center of the school, and that all real progress in school work must finally be made thru the teacher." Newton Dougherty admitted that Henry Barnard had "by outward personal contact little influence in the West," but his publications had "informed" and "stirred" the citizens there "to a resistless and successful activity." All of the speakers agreed that the *American Journal of Education* would be Henry Barnard's enduring monument.[27]

25. Goodrich, *Recollections*, II:380–87, discussion of educational publications; Norton, *Sketch*, 128–29; Barnard, *AJE* XXX (1880): frontispiece and 913ff., notes all of the awards; thus he was the source for Norton and subsequent authorities. Congratulatory letter from Andrews, February 22, 1879; letter from Lincoln Smith, for Commissioner Eaton, describes the display at New Orleans: the books were in a black walnut case accompanied by Barnard's picture, March 19, 1885; letter from Charles Hine congratulating Barnard on a "well-deserved" award, June 8, 1896; all TC.

26. Mayo, *Report*, 782 and 804, and Hughes, *Barnard*, 5.

27. *NEA*, 1901, 395–408.

Barnard's American Journal of Education.

Extract from Letter of Hon. John D. Philbrick, LL. D., U. S. Commissioner to Paris Exposition of 1878.

" It was my great pleasure as one of the U. S. Commissioners to the International Exposition at Vienna in 1873, to announce to you the award of the Medal of Merit; and it is now my still higher pleasure to congratulate you on receiving both a Gold Medal and a Silver Medal for your exhibit in the Departments of Superior and Secondary Instruction in the Paris International Exposition of 1878."

The New England Journal of Education thus notices the award :

" The great work of Hon. Henry Barnard, the *American Journal of Education*, consisting of twenty-eight volumes, receives a Gold Medal at Paris. In this we most heartily rejoice, and our readers will agree with us that the honor is richly merited. Mr. Barnard has spent his life in the most industrious educational work. In the field of school organization he was a pioneer, and there is scarcely a city or State in America that is not directly indebted to him, either for the plan of its school-system, or some valuable and practical suggestions relating to its details. In the department of State and national supervision he has done a good life work ; enough to have established for him a permanent reputation as an educational reformer. To these claims on the gratitude of the nation we must add the greater work of author, editor, and publisher, in which he has given to the world the results of educational research, both general and special, unequaled in value in any other language. No educator's private library is complete without this vast collection, for it brings together the educational experience and suggestions of all civilized countries ; and on the topics of elementary, secondary, superior, normal, military, and technical schools it is almost exhaustive."

" In respect to European systems, old and new, Mr. Barnard has spent time and money to get possession of a vast range of experience and discussion ; and in Great Britain, Germany, and France his work is quite complete. It is most fitting that the World's Exposition at Paris should recognize his services, not only in behalf of the French Government, but also of all other European States. Mr. Barnard had received at Vienna in 1873 the highest recognition which the Austrian Government could give, and on our library shelves, just before us as we write, is the identical set, beautifully bound, which was sent to our Centennial Exhibition at Philadelphia. Mr. Barnard is still at work in adding to his collection of national and international discussion and statistics of schools ; and no better monument can be established for his industry, ability, and enthusiasm in behalf of education than his own *Journal*. He has our hearty congratulations on this latest well-merited recognition."

American Journal of Education, volume XXX, 1880. Page showing excerpt of letter from John D. Philbrick citing three awards made to Henry Barnard and reproductions of two of the medals Barnard received.

What should be the revised judgment nearly one hundred years later? Henry Barnard has not maintained a permanent reputation as a educational reformer. Should he be restored to some unbuilt pedestal by the side of his more famous colleague or should he rest in deserved limbo, a footnote in educational history and a possible source for scholars? The answer is not simple.

That Henry Barnard was an important figure in the phenomenon known as the Common School Reform is indisputable; what demands examination, before we can assess Barnard's contribution, is the nature of that movement as well as the role of the leaders. The Cubberley view of antebellum common school reform was of a sudden resurgence of commitment to schooling in the mid-thirties, led by a selfless band of schoolmen, among whom Horace Mann and Henry Barnard were outstanding; children flocked to schools, to well-constructed buildings, staffed by teachers increasingly well trained, all supported, perhaps unwillingly, by the tax payer. This interpretation has been successfully challenged, and laid to rest, by contemporary scholars. All aspects of the reform of the thirties, the demand for better teachers and school houses, the use of publicity and publication, even teachers' institutes, appeared in New England and the Midwest prior to the appointment of Horace Mann or Henry Barnard, and the pressure continued, slowly and at an uneven pace, throughout the antebellum period. By 1850 there was general acquiescence with the reformers' agenda and a tacit consensus about educational policy. The majority of the citizens and legislators believed, as Carl Kaestle has said, that the goals of education could only be achieved by "increased schooling, professionalism, standardization, and cultural assimilation."[28] Most states in the Union had some sort of a state educational official and a rudimentary apparatus for supervision, and teachers' organizations, which supported struggling journals, were common. Yet, as Albert Fishlow pointed out, there is little evidence of an increase in the number of children attending any school as a result of the reformers' activities, only in the number enrolled in *public* schools who remained in schools longer. It was in the antebellum period that the principle of mandatory public support of schooling became a national faith. By the turn of the century, when there was another period of intense agitation about the state of the schools, the focus was on the high schools, and the stage was the cities which had always concerned the antebellum schoolmen; the actors were new, academics and professional men. But the continuity of educational history cannot be ignored.

28. Kaestle, *Pillars*, chap. 9, esp. 218ff.; see also: Fishlow, *Revival*, 56–57, 64; Cremin, *Common School*, 176–78.

A band of idealistic, pragmatic, and gentlemanly reformers were instrumental as standard bearers for the antebellum movement. They published the essays and delivered the lectures; they attended the annual conventions and they pressured the legislatures; they served as school officials and instructors in institutes. But common school development never depended solely on the heroic actions of a few exemplary individuals. Rather they were nourished by the nameless and fameless contemporaries whom they represented and who frequently did the bulk of the work. The John Nortons of the various states, who proposed and debated and sat on countless committees, and the even less known visitors and teachers, sustained the campaign for improved schooling for decades. Henry Barnard ignored them entirely.

Nor did the common school movement originate and radiate out from New England alone. Henry Barnard knew this, for he corresponded with reform advocates throughout the Southeast and West. School reform was an issue in Ohio as early as it had been in Massachusetts—although of course many of the proponents did hail from the East—and the nature of the reform proposals there was significantly different from the pattern in the Eastern states, a factor Barnard missed. An institution for teacher education and an educational journal saw the light of day in Ohio before either of the two appeared in Massachusetts; the leadership was with laymen more than with the ministerial class; and boosterism was a vital factor in the establishment of educational institutions.[29] The provision of schooling was a matter for constitutional attention, due to federal directive, in every state admitted to the Union before 1860. The Midwest might look to the East, and its leaders, for guidance and assistance, and the traditional forms were transplanted by the immigrants to the West; but Horace Mann and Henry Barnard were not the fathers of schooling in that region. It is true that for a variety of social and cultural reasons, reform lagged in the South, but a revival similar to that in the New England states a decade earlier surfaced even there in the 1850s only to be halted by the Civil War.[30]

Henry Barnard may be credited, or blamed, for the acceptance of a Whig or a Great-Man or an Eastern interpretation of antebellum school reform, an interpretation, based on his publications, especially the *Journal*, which persisted until the revisionism of the past decade. He selected

29. See William J. Reese, *Power and the Promise of School Reform* (Boston: Routledge and Kegan Paul, 1986), chap. 1, who emphasizes the role of "the most progressive element in a local ruling elite" in the reform movement in western New York and Ohio; see also Donald Tewksbury, *The Founding of American Colleges and Universities Before the Civil War* (New York: Teachers College Press, 1932).

30. Fishlow, *Revival*, 49–50.

the materials, and his was the voice that defined the issues and identified the actors. He concentrated on the eminent schoolmen and benefactors, he focused on establishment institutions, he promulgated an Anglo-American platform, with its large planks of Prussianism. He depicted an era of revolutionary advance by his constant contrasting of schools as they were with schools as they are becoming and his highlighting of the contributions of his allies. And, with subtle skill, as I have attempted to prove, he emphasized his own preeminent role in the movement; he wrote its history, and he made it his.[31]

But Henry Barnard was ultimately forgotten, despite his self-advertisement. Part of the reason stems from the fact that new concerns occupied the postbellum schoolmen, and they were men of vastly different background and training. Francis Parker and Henry Barnard would have understood each other; Commissioner Harris and former Commissioner Barnard did not speak the same language. Amateurs had no place in a modern school system, and their moral message was considered old-fashioned and unscientific.

The growth of enormous city school systems, that dominant challenge of the nineties, brought to prominence the new schoolman, the professional superintendent. This entices us to consider a second aspect of Barnard's career, that of an administrator. He served in that capacity in several states, and in Rhode Island particularly he sketched an innovative and pro-active role for the state superintendent. He, like his entrepreneur colleagues, was an avid advocate of efficient standardization and systematization. Pressing matters demanded solutions; the magnitude of the challenge, or of the evil, to employ his term, revealed the inadequacy of former solutions and agents, and only through efficient organization, under competent and wise leaders, could progress be achieved. Whether the sponsorship was private or public, or a mixture of the two, was unimportant; what was important was that the moral order of the nation be preserved.

This was the thrust of Barnard's policy in Rhode Island and in Connecticut, and likewise it was the implication of his national proposals. But he was ill equipped to carry out his projected pattern to the stage of real implementation, as his countless retreats from the field of battle proved. It should not be overlooked, however, that in the antebellum period there was absolutely no state bureaucracy able to implement even the most modest ideal of a centralized system; Barnard invoked old solutions because new ones had not been devised—that was to be the task for the

31. See, for example, *NE*, 455 where Barnard credits Mann and Barnard, "particularly the latter" with publicizing the value of a graded school system.

Harris generation. After the Civil War, when new actors appeared on the stage, it was the college presidents, the leaders of the teachers' organizations, and the *city* superintendents who dominated the educational scene; significantly, the famous Committee of Ten did not include a single state superintendent.[32] Innovation in educational administration was to take place, for the most part, in the urban centers, where the antebellum reformers had known well that the pressing problems lay, and it was not until the reform movement of the 1980s that the states once again came to play a leading role. The new generation of schoolmen not only had very different backgrounds from men such as Barnard; they faced new challenges, and they sought allies with new training and new skills. They did not need, nor heed, Henry Barnard, even when they offered him homage. And all too soon, those who recalled him at all, mid-century men like Philbrick and Rickoff, were replaced by a later generation trained as professionals in the new schools and departments of education at Columbia, Stanford, and the great mid-Western universities. The annual meeting of the National Education Association of 1900 praised Henry Barnard, but the members effectively buried him.

New professionals dominated, but had not Barnard advocated the creation of a profession? Certainly, and not he alone; the entire educational establishment consistently insisted, as the American Institute of Instruction's 1853 annual meeting resolved, "That the highest interests of the community demand of the various legislatures the permanent establishment of the Teachers' profession." Fourteen years later, at another annual gathering, C. O. Thompson would still assert that an "organized profession is needed to harmonize and unify existing educational agencies."[33] The words are key. Although Thompson did suggest that a profession "demands accumulated learning on the subject of education, and a collection of books," neither he or his peers envisioned a profession as it came to be defined. A profession was seen by them to have a moral purpose, "to harmonize and unify" the teachers, and a profession could, even should, be created by legislative mandate. In the antebellum period the conception of a teaching profession was still in an embryonic stage, that of an amateur fellowship of the dedicated; recall the evangelical nature of the institutes and Barnard's sermons. To him "the law of affinity, which finally governs all associations" could be seen in the development of educational groups: first generation activists focused on the main, or general, object, then came special associations devoted to a particular aspect, and finally

32. See Edward A. Krug, *The Shaping of the American High School* (Madison: University of Wisconsin Press, 1964), vol. I, chap. 3.

33. *Proceedings*, 1853 (New Haven), 1867 (Boston).

all teachers and educators would meet on a common ground. Thus, first the gentlemen schoolmen in their American Institute of Instruction, then the second generation teachers in their various state groups, and finally, a unified profession, with common goals and dreams, was Barnard's model.[34] He preached mission and common identity, certainly aspects of professional orientation, but what he never suspected was that the teaching profession would become increasingly specialized and fragmented, if a profession at all, and that, for the most part, men of his ilk, the liberally educated men of quality, would abandon the field to a new breed of educators, based ironically only partially on the very institutions he promoted.

Barnard was temperamentally unwilling to predict that in the later decades of the century the emphasis would shift from an emphasis on education as mission to the view that teaching "was a theoretical discipline with empirical as well as philosophical aspects."[35] Specialization became the hallmark of late nineteenth-century economic and social organization, and the field of education was not exempt. The locus for the professionalization of teaching was, to some extent, in the normal schools, which Barnard had been instrumental in starting, and stronger in the new departments of pedagogy in the public universities, where he might have served. The leaders were new; men and women who made teaching a career not a calling and who looked for expertise rather than inspiration. The teaching semi-profession, to employ Etzioni's incisive term, evolved into something Barnard would not have recognized.

Except for the few years when the *Journal* served as the organ of the state teachers' organization, Barnard's educational publications did little for the emerging profession. The vast corpus of his work was too ambitious, too lofty, too impractical for the individual turn-of-the-century teacher to read, as it had been for her predecessor. Moreover, Barnard had never been a specialist, in his own work or in his outlook, and increasingly specialization became the hallmark of academic scholarship. The well-read amateur historians and philosophers were replaced by men with earned doctorates, and Henry Barnard did not belong among them.

Still, from the warm letters written to Henry Barnard in his old age, it was clear that there were countless teachers out in the small schools of the country who continued to revere him. For the most part these were

34. Barnard, *NE*, 517.

35. Henry C. Johnson, Jr., and Erwin V. Johanningmeier, *Teachers for the Prairie* (Urbana, Ill.: University of Illinois Press, 1972), 40. See also, Merle L. Borrowman, *The Liberal and the Technical in Teacher Education* (New York: Teachers College Press, 1956), 60–63; Daniel Calhoun, *Professional Lives in America: Structure and Aspiration, 1750–1858* (Cambridge: Harvard University Press, 1965), chap. 1, esp. 50; Mattingly, *Classless Profession*, 117–18.

women, "normalites," trained for a specific role in education, that of nurturing the very young, in institutions which were not empowered to grant degrees and which increasingly were the havens of women. They had not attended the universities nor had they studied under the professors of education; men had, the men who would staff the high schools and superintend the emerging systems. The development of the normal schools did not contribute to the creation of a unified profession but rather to its stratification, and to the perpetuation of the inferior role of women in teaching. Barnard had recognized the importance of women in teaching, but he agreed with his colleagues (including Willard and Beecher) that women had a unique responsibility as the conservators of society and the nurturers of the children. Unfortunately, in a graded system (one of Barnard's pet themes), women were segregated in an inferior, although purportedly highly admired, position. Like Cyrus Peirce in Massachusetts, whose students called him Father, Henry Barnard looked on "his" teachers as children to be led.

In the last analysis, it seems inaccurate to say that Barnard contributed to the development of *teaching*. He had failed as a teacher, and he failed to understand teaching. His recommendations, oral and written, inspired others to work for better conditions for teachers, for more comfortable schools and appropriate materials, but he had little to offer in the area of skills other than his advocacy of Pestalozzian methods. He sought to encourage and to enlighten teachers, and he labored mightily to provide them with instruction, but he left their actual training to others. Henry Barnard felt above the humdrum life of the everyday laborers in the common schools even though he was perpetually and paternalistically convinced he knew what was best for them.

For a brief moment in Rhode Island Barnard had an opportunity to develop an administrative structure for school systems; so, too, in Wisconsin, he had a chance to create a unified rather than a dual system of higher education. Had he been able to integrate his two roles, of chancellor and normal school agent, into one position of leadership within the educational system of the state, the developing split between the "liberal and the technical" in higher education, of teachers and other professions, might have been avoided. Similarly, at St. Johns, he sketched in outline a plan which integrated the common schools with the liberal arts college in a sequential curriculum designed to be preparatory to professional education—but he departed when the ink on his recommendations was scarcely dry. In both instances he had a dream, and one which surfaced again in his Washington report; the elements are entirely familiar—unity, commonality, standardization—consistent with his vision for the common schools of Connecticut, first enunciated in 1838.

Like most of the Whigs, and their partisan successors, Barnard was committed to systems and measures and to efficient and effective governmental intervention. He sensed the potential offered by state inspection and supervision of schools, and he realized that through certification the state could control and improve the teacher corps. The difficulty was that there was no machinery available to implement these ideas. The office of the secretary of the Board of Education of Connecticut was, after all, a small room up under the leaky roof in the old State House, and even as the national commissioner, Barnard had merely a staff of three. However, just as Horace Mann and Henry Barnard played out their parts in the ongoing drama of the evolution of schooling in the United States, so did their successors. The administrators of the next generation no more made a revolution than had Barnard and company; it was Barnard who first drafted rudimentary designs on which the superintendents would build.

Barnard's favorite role was that of a publicist. He began to lecture to Connecticut in 1838, and he was still lecturing to the nation fifty years later. He often relied on exhortation when more concrete measures were required, and when he faced the clear frustration of his ambitious designs, he retreated to the welcoming security of his home and his *Journal*. Henry Barnard's contemporaries and future apologists all agreed that the *American Journal of Education* and the companion publications were his greatest achievement. "In fact one might say that Barnard was the creator of American educational literature."[36] There can be no dispute on this point. Through successive reports and enormous volumes Barnard served as the nation's educator, a preeminent contributor to the antebellum "great awakening" in American education.[37] He laid out before the perhaps unreceptive public masses of information—statistical records, theoretical treatises, inspirational biographies, and descriptions of model and novel institutions—designed to enlighten and inspire. Through constant repetition of particular themes he reinforced the agenda and the biases of his fellow reformers. In the *Journal* and the companion volumes of the library of education he provided an invaluable, if biased, sourcebook for historians. Barnard's definition of education had always been an all-inclusive one, and he wrote from twin convictions, that history instructed, and that the future, when based on the best of the past, would be lustrous. By his selection of material to publish, he created an interpretation and a prediction which dominated the historiography of American education for nearly a century.

36. John S. Brubacher, *Henry Barnard on Education* (New York: Russell and Russell, 1965), 4.

37. The phrase, highly felicitous I think, is from Richard Knowles, "The Barnard Legacy," *School and Society* 89 (November 1961): 396.

The composite work is flawed, of course. As noted in the preceding chapter, Barnard's canvas was a limited one, and his sources painted a restricted picture. More important is the fact that the portrait is an incomplete one; not only did he omit much by choice; often he planned but did not deliver. Henry Barnard always intended more than he achieved. In his biography of Cheever he noted his intention to write a paper on early school texts; in an early number of the *Journal* he promised a long article on the "Condition and Prospect of Public Instruction" and several different indexes; he repeatedly pledged to write a "History of Schooling the United States" and several times a "History of the American Association for the Advancement of Education." In the very last volume of his periodical he proposed to write a volume on Kindergartens and Child Culture and a memoir of Dexter Hawkins.[38] The vibrant enthusiasm of Barnard's interests and intentions lends liveliness to his work, but one is left at the end with the impression of a man who had an uncritical and ill-disciplined, if overactive, mind, and yet was entirely secure in his judgments.

Intention drove Henry Barnard. Tradition, and an essentially passive temperament, throttled him. And his long life rendered him obsolete; the ironic tragedy is that he outlived his drama. His period of public service lasted from 1837 to 1870, or thirty-three years; the period of his retirement lasted from 1870 to 1900, or thirty years. In all that sixty-three year span, there is a curiously static quality to his work. In his lifetime he touched nearly every ramification of the nineteenth century educational experience—legislative initiative, rudimentary administration, community-wide education, formal teacher training, alternatives in higher education, embryonic professional organization, and articulated centralized policy. He had ideas, many derivative but not a few original, which he proposed to implement, with great zest at the start of each segment of his career. But he tired easily, and became "ill," and he never grew. The suggestions of the eager young legislator are repeated almost word for word by the elderly editor, and to the end he had no prescription for curing the sickness of the schools other than gathering and disseminating information. Flashes of insight and ambitious schemes appear from time to time, inspired by the challenge of a new opportunity, but soon to be muted and to fade into the shadows. What remained was the smile of a benevolent man and the memory of his good intentions.

38. See *Eminent Men*, 28n; *AJE* II, 5 (August 1856): 227 and 240; XV, xli (December 1865): 578; XVI, xliii (June 1866): 322; XXX (July 1880): 491, and (September 1880): 817; the word intentions is repeated again, too often to quote.

BIBLIOGRAPHY

CHRONOLOGICAL LIST OF WORKS BY HENRY BARNARD

Récit d'une visite à la fenêtre: fragment du récit d'une visite faite au comte de Sellon. Geneva: Impr. Bonnant, 1837.

Connecticut Common School Journal, 1838–42, 1850–54. Hartford: Case, Tiffany & Burnham.

Hints and Methods for the Use of Teachers. Hartford: Case, Tiffany & Burnham, 1842.

Legal Provisions respecting the Education and Employment of Children in Factories and Manufacturing Establishments. Hartford: Case, Tiffany & Burnham, 1842.

School-house Architecture. 2d ed. Hartford: Case, Tiffany & Burnham, 1842.

Educational Tracts, 1845–46. Hartford, 1846.

Journal of the Rhode Island Institute of Instruction, 1845–48. Providence, 1846–49.

Report on the Public Schools of Rhode Island. Providence, 1846–49.

School Architecture. 2d ed. New York: A. S.Barnes & Co., 1848.

Normal Schools and other Institutions, Agencies, and Means designed for the Professional Education of Teachers. Hartford: Case, Tiffany & Burnham, 1851.

Tribute to Gallaudet: A Discourse in Commemoration of the Life, Character and Service of Thomas W. Gallaudet. Hartford: Brockett & Hutchinson, 1852.

National Education in Europe. 2d ed. Hartford: Case, Tiffany & Burnham, 1854.

American Journal of Education, 1855–80. Hartford: F. C. Brownell.

Reformatory Education: Preventive, Correctional and Reformatory Institutions and Agencies in Different Countries. Hartford: F. C. Brownell, 1857.

Memoirs of Teachers, Educators and Promoters and Benefactors of Education, Literature and Science. Part I. New York: F. C. Brownell, 1859; 2d ed., 1861.

Pestalozzi and Pestalozzianism: Life, Educational Principles and Methods of John Henry Pestalozzi. 2d ed. New York: F. C. Brownell, 1859.

Papers for the Teacher. Vols. I–V. New York: F. C. Brownell, 1859–62.

English Pedagogy: Education, the School, and the Teacher in English

Literature. 2d ed. Philadelphia: J. B. Lippincott, 1862.

Military Schools and Courses of Instruction in the Science and Art of War. Part I.
    Hartford: J. B. Lippincott & Co., 1862; 2d ed., New York: E. Steiger, 1872.

Armsmear: The Home, the Arm, and the Armory of Samuel Colt. New York:
    Alvord, 1866.

"Educational Development." Repr. from Stebbins, *First Century of National
    Experience*, n.p., n.d. (data end 1870).

Report on School Architecture and Plan for Graded Schools. Washington, D. C.:
    Government Printing Office, 1871.

*National Education: Systems, Institutions and Statistics of Public Instruction in
    Different Countries*. 2 vols. [Part I, German States, Part II, Europe]. New
    York: E. Steiger, 1872.

Science and Art: Systems, Institutions & Statistics of Scientific Instruction. New
    York: E. Steiger, 1872.

Oral Training Lessons [Papers for the Teacher Number Two]. New York: A. S.
    Barnes, 1873.

True Student Life: Letters, Essays and Thoughts on Studies and Conduct [Papers
    for the Teacher Number Three]. Hartford: Office of Barnard's *American
    Journal of Education*, 1873.

*Superior Instruction: An Account of Universities and Other Institutions of Superior
    Instruction in Different Countries*. Hartford: Office of *American Journal of
    Education*, 1873.

American Educational Biography. Syracuse: C. W. Bardeen, 1874.

German Educational Reformers. Hartford: Brown and Gross, 1878.

The Old Hartford Grammar School. Hartford: Brown and Gross, 1878.

Kindergarten and Child Culture Papers. Rev.ed. Hartford: Office of Barnard's
    American Journal of Education, 1884.

*Proceedings of the National Teachers Association from Its Foundation in 1857 to the
    Close of the Session of 1870*. Syracuse: C. W. Bardeen, 1909.

HENRY BARNARD PAPERS

Barnard Papers, The Connecticut Historical Society, Hartford, Connecticut

Daniel Coit Gilman Papers, MS 1, Special Collections, Milton S. Eisenhower
    Library, The Johns Hopkins University, Baltimore, Maryland

Henry Barnard Papers, Trinity College and Watkinson Library, Hartford,
    Connecticut

Henry Barnard Papers, Fales Library, Elmer Holmes Bobst Library, New York
    University, New York, New York

Henry Barnard Papers and Elias Loomis Papers, Beinecke Rare Book and
    Manuscript Library, Yale University, New Haven, Connecticut

Horace Mann Papers, Massachusetts Historical Society, Boston, Massachusetts

Letters of Henry Barnard, Special Collections, James P. Adams Library, "Small
    Collection #1," Rhode Island College, Providence, Rhode Island

Lyman Draper Collection, The State Historical Society of Wisconsin, Madi-
    son, Wisconsin

Manuscript Collection, Rhode Island Historical Society, Providence, Rhode
   Island

OTHER PRIMARY SOURCES

Alcott, William A. *A Historical Description of the First Public School in Hartford,
   Connecticut.* Hartford: D. F. Robinson & Co., 1832.
American Institute of Instruction. *Lectures and Proceedings,* 1830–47. Boston:
   Board of Directors.
American Journal of Education. Vols. I–IV, 1826–30. Hartford: F. C. Brownell.
Annual Report of the Trustees of the State Normal School, 1850–1859. Hartford,
   1850–59.
*Annual Report of the Executive Committee of the Rhode Island Institutute of
   Instruction.* Providence, 1848.
Bache, Alexander Dallas. *Report on Education in Europe.* Philadelphia: Lydia R.
   Bailey, 1839.
Baldwin, Ebenezer. *Annals of Yale College in New Haven, Connecticut, from its
   Foundation to 1831.* New Haven: H. Howe, 1838.
Barnard, Daniel D. *Annual Address Delivered Before the Albany Institute.* Albany:
   Albany Institute, 1836.
———. *A Discourse on the Life, Services and Character of Stephen van Rensselaer.*
   Albany: Hoffman and White, 1839.
Beecher, Catharine E. *An Essay on the Education of Female Teachers.* New York:
   van Nostrand & Dwight, 1835.
———. *Educational Reminiscences and Suggestions.* New York: J. B. Ford, 1874.
———. *Suggestions Respecting Improvements in Education.* Hartford: Packard &
   Butler, 1829.
Beecher, Lyman. *A Plea for the West.* Cincinnati: Truman, 1835.
Boyden, Albert G. *History and Alumni Record of the State Normal School, Bridge-
   water, Massachusetts, to July, 1876.* Boston: Noyes & Snow, 1876.
Burton, Warren. *The District School As It Was.* Boston: Carter, Hendee & Co.,
   1833; repr. New York, 1969.
Bushnell, Horace. *Christian Nurture.* Ed. and intro. by Luther Weigle. New
   Haven: Yale University Press, 1967.
———. *Common Schools.* Hartford: Case, Tiffany, & Burnham, 1853.
Camp, David. "The Relation of Teachers to Advancing Civilization." *A Lecture
   Delivered Before the American Institute of Instruction, in Hartford, 1862.*
   Boston: Tichnor and Fields, 1863.
Carter, James G. *Essays Upon Popular Education.* Boston: Bowles & Dearborn,
   1826.
Catalogue of the Books in the Brothers and Linonian Libraries. 1801.
Catalogue of the Books in the Library of Yale College. 1808, 1823, 1831.
Catalogue of the Books in the Linonian Library. 1831.
Cunningham, Robert. *Thoughts on the Question Whether Normal Seminaries
   Ought to be Distinct Establishments or Ingrafted on Colleges.* Philadelphia:
   W. S. Martien, 1838.

Davis, Emerson. *The Half-Century*. Boston: Tappan & Whittemore, 1851.

Draper, Lyman C. *Tenth Annual Report on the Condition and Improvement of the Common Schools and the Educational Interests of the State of Wisconsin*. Madison, 1858.

———. *Eleventh Annual Report*. Madison, 1859.

Durfee, Job. "A Discourse delivered before the Rhode Island Historical Society." Providence: C. Burnett, Jr., 1847.

Dwight, Theodore. *History of Connecticut*. Hartford, 1846.

Emerson, George B. *History and Design of the American Institute of Instruction*. Boston: Tichnor, Reed & Field, 1849.

Fell, Thomas. *Some Historical Accounts of the Founding of King William's School and its Subsequent Establishment as St. John's College*. Annapolis: Press of the Friedenwald Co., 1894.

Gallaudet, Thomas H. *Plan of A Seminary for the Education of the Instructors of Youth*. Boston: Cummings, Hilliard & Co., 1825.

Goodrich, Samuel G. *Recollections of A Lifetime*. 2 vols. New York: Miller, Orton & Nulligan, 1857.

Grund, Francis J. *The Americans and their Moral, Social, and Political Relations*. New York: Longman, Rees, Orme, Brown, Green, & Longman, 1837; ed. and intro. by Robert F. Berkhofer, Jr., New York, 1968.

Hawes, Joel. *An Address delivered at the request of the Citizens of Hartford*. Hartford: Belknap & Hamersley, November, 1835.

Hills, Chester. *The Builder's Guide*. Hartford: Daniel Appleton & Co., 1846.

Johnson, Walter R. *Remarks on the Duty of the Several States in Regard to Public Education*. Philadelphia: W. Sharpless, 1830.

———. *Observations on the Improvement of Seminaries of Learning in the United States with Suggestions for Its Improvement*. Philadelphia: E. Littell, 1825.

Key, Francis S. *A Discourse on Education*. Annapolis: J. Green, 1827.

[Lamson, Mrs. Mary Swift]. *Records of the First Class of the First Normal School in America*. Boston: Published for the Class, 1903.

Mayo, Amory D. "Henry Barnard." *Report of the Commissioner of Education*, 1896–1897, chap. XVI. Washington, D.C.: Government Printing Office, 1898.

North American Review. 1830–46.

National Education Association. *History of the National Education Association*. New York, 1896.

———. *Journal of Proceedings and Addresses*. Fortieth Annual Meeting, Detroit, 1901.

Northend, Charles. *Obstacles to the Greater Success of the Common Schools, An Address Delivered before the American Institute of Instruction*. Boston: W. D. Tichnor & Co., 1844.

Packard, Alpheus S. *Characteristics of a Good District School, An Address Delivered before the Teachers Association of Bowdoin College*. Brunswick, Maine: J. Griggin, 1838.

Peers, Benjamin O. *American Education*. New York: J. S. Taylor, 1838.

Phelps, Almira. *The Female Student or Lectures to Young Ladies on Female Edu-*

cation. New York: Leavitt, Lord & Co., 1836.

Philbrick, John D. "Henry Barnard—The American Educator." *New England Magazine,* n.s., 1, 5 (May 1886): 445–51.

Philobiblius (Linus Pierpont Brockett). *History and Progress of Education from the Earliest Times to the Present Intended as a Manual for Teachers and Students.* New York: A. S. Barnes, 1859.

Pickard, J. L. *Twelfth Annual Report of the Superintendent of the Common Schools of the State of Wisconsin.* Madison, 1860.

Porter, Noah. "Henry Barnard." *Connecticut Common School Journal* II, 1 (January 1855).

Potter, Elisha R. *An Address Delivered Before the Rhode Island Historical Society.* Providence: G. H. Whitney, 1851.

Proceedings of the First Annual Convention of the American Normal School Association, August, 1859. New York, 1860.

Proceedings of the Western Literary Institute. Cincinnati, 1834–37.

Public Acts Relating to Common Schools. Hartford, May 1848.

Quick, Robert Hebert. *Essays on Educational Reformers.* New York: Longmans, Green & Co., 1868; D. Appleton & Co., 1890.

Quint, Alonzo H. "The Normal Schools of Massachusetts." *Congregational Quarterly* III (January 1861): 33–51.

"Remarks upon Mr. Carter's Outline of an Institution for the Education of Teachers." *United States Review.* Boston, 1827.

Report of the Committee of the House of Assembly Relative to the Establishment of a Normal School in the State of New Jersey. Trenton, 1848.

Report of the Committee on the Normal School to the General Assembly. May Session. Hartford, 1848.

Report on the Course of Instruction in Yale College by the Committee of the Corporation and the Academical Faculty. New Haven, 1830.

Russell, Gurdon W. "An Address Delivered at the Request of the Citizens of Hartford on November 9, 1835." Hartford, 1835.

———. *"Up Neck" in 1825.* Hartford, 1890.

Sigourney, Lydia H. *Sketch of Connecticut Forty Years Since.* Hartford: O. S. Cooke, 1824.

Spaulding, Bishop Martin John. *Common Schools in the United States Compared with Those in Europe.* Louisville, 1858.

Stone, Edwin Martin. *Manual of Education: A Brief History of the Rhode Island Institute of Instruction.* Providence: Providence Press Co., 1874.

Stowe, Calvin E. *Common Schools and Teachers' Seminaries.* Boston: Marsh, Capen, Lyon & Webb, 1839.

Transactions of the Fourth Annual Meeting of the Western Literary Institute. Cincinnati, 1835.

Voorhees, Philip Randall. *Address on the One Hundredth Anniversary of St. John's College.* Baltimore: W. K. Boyle & Son, 1889.

Willard, Emma. *A Plan for Improving Female Education.* Albany, 1819.

Wines, E. C. *Hints on a System of Popular Education.* Philadelphia: Hogan &

Thompson, 1838.

Wisconsin Journal of Education, 1857–60.

Woodbury, Levi. *An Address on the Remedies for Certain Defects in American Education, Delivered before Lyceums or Institutes for Education at Portsmouth and Exeter, New Hampshire, Baltimore and Annapolis, Maryland, and Washington, D.C.* Washington: W. Greer, 1842.

———. *How Shall I Govern My School*. Philadelphia, 1839.

SECONDARY SOURCES

Albree, John. *Charles Brooks and His Work for Normal Schools*. Medford, Mass.: Press of J. C. Miller, 1907.

Allmendinger, David F. "Mount Holyoke Students Encounter the Need for Life-Planning, 1837–1850." *History of Education Quarterly* 19, no. 1 (Spring 1979): 27–46.

———. "New England Students and the Revolution in Higher Education, 1800–1900." *History of Education Quarterly* 11, no. 4 (Winter 1971): 381–89.

———. *Paupers and Scholars: The Transformation of Student Life in Nineteenth Century New England*. New York: St. Martin's Press, 1975.

———. "The Strangeness of the American Education Society: Indigent Students and the New Charity, 1815–1840." *History of Education Quarterly* 11, no. 1 (Spring 1971): 3–22.

Anderson, Ruth O. M. *From Yankee to American: Connecticut 1865 to 1914*. Chester, Conn.: Pequot Press, 1975.

Antczak, Frederick J. *Thought and Character: The Rhetoric of Democratic Education*. Ames: University of Iowa Press, 1985.

Bailyn, Bernard. *Education in the Forming of American Society*, Chapel Hill: University North Carolina Press, 1960.

Bender, Thomas. *Toward an Urban Vision: Ideas and Institutions in Nineteenth Century America*. Lexington: University of Kentucky Press, 1975.

Benedict, Michael Les. *A Compromise of Principle: Congressional Republicans and Reconstruction, 1865–1869*. New York: Norton, 1974.

Bernard, Richard M., and Maris M. Vinovskis. "The Female School Teacher in Ante-Bellum Massachusetts." *Journal of Social History* X, no. 3 (March 1977): 332–45.

Bickford, Christopher P. *The Connecticut Historical Society, 1825–1975*. Hartford: Connecticut Historical Society, 1975.

Bidwell, Charles E. "The Moral Significance of the Common School." *History of Education Quarterly* 6, no. 3 (Fall 1966): 50–91.

Billington, Ray Allen. *The Protestant Crusade 1800–1860: A Study of the Origins of American Nativism*. Gloucester, Mass.: P. Smith, 1963.

Binder, Frederick M. *The Age of the Common School, 1830–1865*. New York: Wiley, 1974.

Blair, Anna Lou. *Henry Barnard: School Administrator*. Minneapolis: Educational Publishers, Inc., 1938.

Bledstein, Burton J. *The Culture of Professionalism: The Middle Class and the*

Development of Higher Education in America. New York: Norton, 1976.

Bode, Carl. *The American Lyceum*. New York: Oxford University Press, 1956.

Boorstin, Daniel J. *The Americans: The National Experience*. New York: Vintage Books, 1965.

Borrowman, Merle L. *The Liberal and the Technical in Teacher Education*. New York: Teachers College Press, 1956.

———. "The Legacy of Horace Mann." *Teachers College Record* 74, no. 3 (February 1973): 423–35.

Bowen, James. *A History of Western Education*. New York: St. Martin's Press, 1981.

Boyer, Paul. *Urban Masses and Moral Order in America, 1820–1920*. Cambridge: Harvard University Press, 1978.

Brown, Richard D. "Modernization: A Victorian Climax." *American Quarterly* XXVII, no. 5 (December 1975): 533–48.

———. *Modernization: The Transformation of American Life 1600–1865*. New York: Hill and Wang, 1976.

Brubacher, John S., ed. *Henry Barnard on Education*. New York: Russell and Russell, 1931.

Buckley, William E., and Richard K. Morris. "Connecticut Develops a Public School System." *Foundations for Educational Leadership*. Charles E. Perry, ed. Connecticut Association of Retired Teachers, 1976.

Buckley, William E., and Charles E. Perry. *Connecticut, the State and Its Government*. New York: Oxford Book Co., 1943.

Bunkle, Phillida. "Sentimental Womanhood and Domestic Education, 1830–1870." *History of Education Quarterly* 14, no. 1 (Spring 1974): 13–30.

Burpee, Charles W. *History of Hartford County, 1633–1928*. 2 vols. Chicago: S. J. Clarke Publishing Co., 1928.

Bushman, Richard. *From Puritan to Yankee*. Cambridge: Harvard University Press, 1967.

Butler, Vera M. *Education as Revealed by New England Newspapers Prior to 1850*. Philadelphia: Majestic Press, Inc., 1935.

Calhoun, Daniel. *The Intelligence of a People*. Princeton: Princeton University Press, 1973.

———. *Professional Lives in America: Structure and Aspiration, 1750–1858*. Cambridge: Harvard University Press, 1965.

———, ed. *The Educating of Americans*. Boston: Houghton Mifflin, 1969.

Cambridge History of American Literature. New York: G. P. Putnam's Sons, 1917–27.

Camp, David. *History of New Britain*. New Britain, Conn.: W. B. Thompson, 1889.

———. *Recollections of a Long and Active Life*. New Britain, Conn.: W. B. Thompson, 1917.

Carlton, Frank Tracy. *Economic Influences upon Educational Progress in the United States, 1820–1850. Classics in Education* 27. New York: Teachers College Press, 1965, reset from the *Bullentin of the University of Wisconsin*, no. 221 (Madison, 1908).

Carroll, Charles. *Public Education in Rhode Island*. Providence: E. L. Freeman, 1918.

Caskey, Marie. *Chariots of Fire: Religion and the Beecher Family*. New Haven: Yale University Press, 1978.

Chambers-Schiller, Lee Virginia. *Liberty: A Better Husband*. New Haven: Yale University Press, 1984.

Clifford, Geraldine Jonçich. "Home and School in 19th-Century: Some Personal-History Reports from the United States." *History of Education Quarterly* 17, no. 1 (Spring 1978): 3–34.

Clive, John. *Macaulay: The Shaping of the Historian*. New York: Knopf, 1973.

Cohen, David K. "The American Common School: A Divided Vision." *Education and Urban Society* 16, no. 3 (May 1984): 253–61.

Cohen, Patricia Cline. *A Calculating People: The Spread of Numeracy in Early America*. Chicago: University of Chicago Press, 1982.

Cohen, Sol. "The History of Education in the United States: Historians of Education and their Discontents." *Urban Education in the Nineteenth Century*, D. A. Reeder, ed. New York: St. Martin's Press, 1978.

Coit, Margaret L. *John C. Calhoun: The Fight for Union*. Boston: Houghton Mifflin, 1961.

Coleman, Peter J. *The Transformation of Rhode Island, 1790–1860*. Providence: Brown University Press, 1963.

Collins, Randall. *The Credential Society: An Historical Sociology of Education and Stratification*. New York: Academic Press, 1979.

Conway, Jill K. "Perspectives on the History of Women's Education in the United States." *History of Education Quarterly* 14, no. 1 (Spring 1974): 1–12.

Cordasco, Francesco. *Daniel Coit Gilman and the Protean Ph.D*. Leiden: E. J. Brill, 1960.

Cott, Nancy F. *The Bonds of Womanhood: "Women's Sphere" in New England, 1780–1833*. New Haven: Yale University Press, 1977.

Cowden, Joanna D. "Stability and Crisis in Connecticut Towns, 1858–1868." Paper read before the Annual Meeting of the Organization of American Historians, 1983.

Cremin, Lawrence A. *The American Common School: An Historic Conception*. New York: Teachers College Press, 1951.

———. *American Education: The National Experience, 1783–1876*. New York: Harper and Row, 1980.

———. *The Wonderful World of Ellwood Patterson Cubberley*. New York: Teachers College Press, 1965.

———, ed. *The Republic and the School: Horace Mann on the Education of Free Men*. New York: Teachers College Press, 1957.

Cremin, Lawrence A., David A. Shannon, and Mary Evelyn Townsend. *A History of Teachers College*. New York: Teachers College Press, 1954.

Cross, Barbara. *Horace Bushnell: Minister to a Changing America*. Chicago: University of Chicago Press, 1958.

————, ed. *The Educated Woman in America*. New York: Teachers College Press, 1965.

Cross, Whitney. *The Burned-Over District*. Ithaca: Cornell University Press, 1950.

Cubberley, Elwood Patterson. *Public Education in the United States*. Boston: Houghton Mifflin Co., 1919, 1934.

Current, Richard N. *Daniel Webster and the Rise of National Conservatism*. Boston: Little, Brown, 1955.

Curti, Merle. *The Growth of American Thought*. 3d ed. New York: Harper and Row, 1964.

————. *The Making of an American Community*. Stanford: Stanford University Press, 1959.

————. *The Social Ideas of American Educators*. Totawa, N.J., 1935; Patterson, N.J.: Pageant Books, 1959.

Curti, Merle, and Vernon Carstensen. *The University of Wisconsin*. 2 vols. Madison: University of Wisconsin Press, 1949.

Dahl, Robert. *Who Governs*. New Haven: Yale University Press, 1961.

Davis, David Brian. *Antebellum American Culture*. Lexington, Mass.: D. C. Heath, 1979.

Davis, Sheldon Emmor. *Educational Periodicals During the Nineteenth Century*. 1919; repr. Metuchen, N.J.: Scarecrow Reprint Co., 1970.

Dexter, Franklin Bowditch. *Sketch of the History of Yale University*. New York: Henry Holt, 1887.

Diehl, Carl. *American and German Scholarship, 1770–1870*. New Haven: Yale University Press, 1978.

————. "Innocents Abroad: American Students in German Universities, 1810–1870." *History of Education Quarterly* 17, no. 3 (Fall 1976): 321–41.

Douglas, Ann. *The Feminization of American Culture*. New York: Alfred A. Knopf, 1977.

Elsbree, Willard S. *The American Teacher: Evolution of a Profession in a Democracy*. New York: American Book Company, 1939.

Elson, Ruth Miller. *Guardians of Tradition*. Lincoln: University of Nebraska Press, 1964.

Etzioni, Amitai. *The Semi-Professions and Their Organization*. New York: Free Press, 1969.

Feller, Daniel. *The Public Lands in Jacksonian Politics*. Madison: University of Wisconsin Press, 1984.

Fleming, Donald. *William Welch and the Rise of Modern Medicine*. Boston: Little, Brown, 1954.

Flexner, Abraham. *Daniel Coit Gilman: Creator of the American Type of Universities*. New York: Harcourt, Brace, and Co., 1946.

Fishlow, Albert. "The American Common School Revival: Fact or Fancy." *Industrialization in Two Systems: Essays in Honor of Alexander Gershenknon*, Henry Rosovsky, ed. New York: Wiley, 1966, 40–67.

————. "The Level of Nineteenth Century American Investment in Education." *Journal of Economic History* 26, no. 4 (December 1966): 418–36.

Florer, John H. "Major Issues in the Congressional Debate of the Morrill Act of 1862." *History of Education Quarterly* 8, no. 4 (Winter 1968): 459–78.

Foner, Eric. *Politics and Ideology in the Age of the Civil War*. New York: Oxford University Press, 1980.

———. *Reconstruction: America's Unfinished Revolution, 1863–1877*. New York: Harper and Row, 1988.

Fowler, Herbert E. *A Century of Teacher Education in Connecticut, 1849–1949*. New Britain, Conn., 1949.

Fuller, Wayne E. *The Old Country School: The Story of Rural Education in the Middle West*. Chicago: University of Chicago Press, 1982.

Garrison, Dee. *Apostles of Culture: The Public Librarian and American Society*. New York: Macmillan, 1979.

Gettleman, Marvin E. *The Dorr Rebellion: A Study in American Radicalism, 1833–1849*. New York: Random House, 1973.

Gideonse, Hendrik. "Common School Reform: Connecticut 1838–1854." Ph.D. diss., Harvard University, 1963.

Gilman, Daniel Coit. *The Launching of a University and Other Papers*. New York: Dodd, Mead, and Co., 1906.

Glenn, Charles Leslie, Jr. *The Myth of the Common School*. Amherst: University of Massachusetts Press, 1988.

Goodenow, Ronald K., and Diane Ravitch. *Schools in Cities: Consensus and Conflict in American Educational History*. New York: Teachers College Press, 1983.

Goodsell, Willystine. *Pioneers of Women's Education in the United States: Emma Willard, Catherine Beecher, Mary Lyon*. New York: McGraw-Hill, 1931.

Grant, Philip A. "The Bank Controversy and Connecticut Politics, 1834." *Connecticut Historical Society* 33 (July 1968).

———. "Jacksonian Democracy Triumphs in Connecticut." *Connecticut Historical Society* 33 (October 1968).

Green, Elizabeth Alden. *Mary Lyon and Mount Holyoke College: Opening the Gates*. Hanover, N. H.: University Press of New England, 1979.

Green, Nancy, "Female Education and School Competition, 1820–1850." *History of Education Quarterly* 18, no. 2 (Summer 1978): 129–42.

Greene, Maxine. *The Public School and the Private Vision*. New York: Random House, 1965.

Griffin, Orwin Bradford. *The Evolution of the Connecticut School System*. New York: Teachers College Press, 1928.

Grimsted, David, ed. *Notions of American*. New York: G. Braziller, 1970.

Grizzell, Emit Duncan. *Origin and Development of the High School in New England Before 1865*. New York: Macmillan, 1923.

Hall, David D. "The Victorian Connection." *American Quarterly* 27, no.5 (December 1975): 561–74.

Halttunen, Karen. *Confidence Men and Painted Women: A Study in Middle-Class Culture in America, 1830–1870*. New Haven: Yale University Press, 1982.

Hansen, Allen Oscar. *Early Educational Leadership in the Ohio Valley*. Journal of Educational Research Monograph, 5. Bloomington, Ill.: Public School Publishing Co., 1923.

Harper, Charles A. *A Century of Public Teacher Education*. Washington, D. C.: Hugh Birch-Horace Mann Fund for the American Association of Teachers Colleges, 1939.

———. *The Development of the Teachers' College in the United States*. Blooming-ton, Ill.: McKnight & McKnight, 1935.

Hareven, Tamara K., ed. *Anonymous Americans: Exploration in Nineteenth Cen-tury Social History*. Englewood Cliffs, N.J.: Prentice Hall, 1971.

Harris, Neil. *Humbug: The Art of P. T. Barnum*. Boston: Little, Brown, 1973.

Harveson, Mae Elizabeth. *Catharine Esther Becher: Pioneer Educator*. Philadel-phia, 1932.

Haskell, Thomas L. *The Emergence of Professional Social Science*. Urbana: Uni-versity of Illinois Press, 1977.

Herbst, Jurgen. *And Sadly Teach*. Madison: University of Wisconsin Press, 1989.

———. "Beyond the Debate over Revisionism: Three Educational Pasts Writ Large." *History of Education Quarterly* 20, no. 2 (Summer 1980): 131–45.

Herdman, Donald L. "The Barnard Collection." *Trinity Library Gazette*, no. 2 (February 1955).

Higginson, Thomas Wentworth. *A History of the Public School System of Rhode Island*. Providence: Providence Press Co., 1876.

Hinsdale, B. A. "The Western Literary Institute and College of Professional Teachers." *Report of the Commissioner of Education for 1899*. Washington, D.C.: Government Printing Office, 1900.

Hoffman, Nancy. *Woman's "True" Profession: Voices from the History of Teaching*. New York: The Feminist Press, 1981.

Howard, Leon. *The Connecticut Wits*. Chicago: University of Chicago Press, 1943.

Howe, Daniel Walker. "American Victorianism as a Culture." *American Quarterly* 27, no. 5 (December 1975): 507–32.

———. *The Political Culture of the American Whigs*. Chicago: University of Chicago Press, 1979.

Hughes, James L. "Henry Barnard, The Nestor of American Education." *New England Magazine* 14, no. 5 (July 1896): 560–71.

Jackson, Sidney L. *America's Struggle for Free Schools*. Washington, D.C.: Amer-ican Council on Public Affairs, 1941.

Jenkins, Ralph C. "Henry Barnard—Educator of Teachers." *The Educational Forum* (November 1939).

Jenkins, Ralph C., and Gertrude Chandler Warner. *Henry Barnard: An Intro-duction*. Hartford: Connecticut State Teachers Association, 1937.

Johnson, Clifton. *The Country School*. New York: Thomas Crowell, 1907.

———. *Old-Time Schools and School-Books*. New York: Macmillan, 1904.

Johnson, Henry C., and Erwin V. Johanningmeier. *Teachers for the Prairie*. Urbana: University of Illinois Press, 1972.

Johnston, Alexander. *Connecticut A Study of A Commonwealth-Democracy*. Bos-ton: Houghton Mifflin & Co., 1887.

Jorgenson, Lloyd P. *The Founding of Public Education in Wisconsin*. Madison: University of Wisconsin Press, 1956.

———. *The State and the Non-Public School, 1825–1925*. Columbia: University of Missouri Press, 1987.

Kaestle, Carl F. "Common Schools Before the 'Common School Revival': New York Schooling in the 1790s." *History of Education Quarterly* 12, no.4 (Winter 1972): 465–500.

———. "Between the Scylla of Brutal Ignorance and the Charybdis of a Literary Education: Elite Attitudes Toward Mass Schooling in Early Industrial England and America." In Lawrence Stone, ed., *Schooling and Society: Studies in the History of Education*, 177–91. Baltimore: The Johns Hopkins University Press, 1976.

———. *Pillars of the Republic: Common Schools and American Society, 1780–1860*. New York: Hill and Wang, 1983.

———. "Presidential Address: Ideology and American Educational History." *History of Education Quarterly* 22, no. 2 (Summer 1982): 123–37.

Kaestle, Carl F., and Maris Vinovskis. *Education and Social Change in Nineteenth Century Massachusetts*. Cambridge: Harvard University Press, 1980.

Katz, Michael B. "The Emergence of Bureaucracy in Urban Education: The Boston Case." *History of Education Quarterly* 7, no. 2 (Summer 1968): 155–88, and no. 3 (Fall 1968): 319–57.

———. *The Irony of Early School Reform*. Cambridge: Harvard University Press, 1968.

———. "The Origins of Public Education: A Reassessment." *History of Education Quarterly* 16, no. 4 (Winter 1976): 381–407.

———. *Reconstructing American Education*. Cambridge: Harvard University Press, 1987.

———, ed. *Education in American History*. New York: Praeger, 1973.

Kaufman, Polly Welts. *Woman Teachers on the Frontier*. New Haven: Yale University Press, 1984.

Keller, Charles Roy. *The Second Great Awakening in Connecticut*. New Haven: Yale University Press, 1942.

Kelley, Brooks Mather. *Yale: A History*. New Haven: Yale University Press, 1974.

Kerber, Linda K. *Women of the Republic*. Chapel Hill: University of North Carolina Press, 1980.

Kersey, Harry A. "Michigan's Teachers' Institutes in the Mid-Nineteenth Century: A Representative Document." *History of Education Quarterly* 5, no. 1 (March 1965): 405–22.

Kett, Joseph. "Adolescence and Youth in Nineteenth Century America." *Journal of Interdisciplinary History* 2, no.2 (Autumn 1971): 283–98.

Klyberg, Albert T. "Toward a Rhode Island History." *Rhode Island History* 34, no. 1 (February 1975): 23–32.

Krug, Edward A. *The Shaping of the American High School, 1880–1920*. Madison: University of Wisconsin Press, 1964.

Labaree, David. *The Making of An American High School*. New Haven: Yale

University Press, 1988.

Lane, Jack C. "The Yale Report of 1828 and Liberal Eduation: A Neorepublican Manifesto." *History of Education Quarterly* 27, no. 3 (Fall 1987): 325–38.

Lannie, Vincent Peter. "William Seward and the New York School Controversy." *History of Education Quarterly* 6, no. 1 (Spring 1966): 52–71.

———, ed. *Henry Barnard: American Educator*, New York: Teachers College Press, 1974.

Lannie, Vincent Peter, and Bernard C. Diethorn. "For the Honor and Glory of God: The Philadelphia Bible Riots of 1840 [44]." *History of Education Quarterly* 8, no. 1 (Spring 1968): 44–106.

Lazerson, Marvin. "F. A. P. Barnard and Columbia College: Prologue to a University." *History of Education Quarterly* 6, no. 4 (Winter 1966): 49–64.

Learned, William S., and William C. Bagley, et al. *The Professional Preparation of Teachers for American Public Schools*. New York: The Carnegie Foundation for the Advancement of Teaching, 1920.

Lee, Gordon. *The Struggle for Federal Aid: A History of the Attempts to Obtain Federal Aid for the Common Schools, 1870–1890*. New York: Bureau of Publications, Teachers College, 1949.

Lerner, Gerda. *The Grimke Sisters from South Carolina: Rebels Against Slavery*. Boston: Houghton Mifflin, 1967.

Lockridge, Kenneth A. *Literacy in Colonial New England*. New York: Norton, 1974.

Luckey, George W. A. *The Professional Training of Secondary Teachers in the United States*. New York: Macmillan, 1903.

Lutz, Alma. *Emma Willard: Pioneer Educator of American Women*. Boston: Beacon Press, 1964.

Magrath, C. Peter. "Optimistic Democrat: Thomas Dorr and the Case of *Luther vs. Borden*." *Rhode Island History* 29, nos. 3 and 4 (August and November 1970): 94–112.

Maizlish, Stephen E., and John J. Kushma. *Essays on American Antebellum Politics, 1840–1860*. Arlington: University of Texas Press, 1982.

Mangun, Vernon Lamar. *The American Normal School*. Baltimore: Warwick and York, 1928.

Marsis, James, L. "Agrarian Politics in Rhode Island, 1800–1860." *Rhode Island History* 34, no. 1 (February 1975): 13–22.

Mattingly, Paul H. *The Classless Profession: American Schoolmen in the Nineteenth Century*. New York: New York University Press, 1975.

———. "Educational Revivals in Ante-Bellum New England." *History of Education Quarterly* 11, no. 1 (Spring 1971): 39–71.

———. "Professional Strategies and New England Educators, 1825–1860." Ph.D. diss., University of Wisconsin, 1968.

———, chair. "Institutionalization and Education in the Nineteenth and Twentieth Centuries." Panel at AERA, April 8, 1980. *History of Education Quarterly* 20, no. 4 (Winter 1980).

Mattingly, Paul H., and Edward W. Stevens, Jr., eds. " . . . *Schools and the Means of Education Shall Forever be Encouraged.*" Athens: University of Ohio Press, 1987.

McClellan, B. Edward, and Willard J. Reese. *The Social History of American Education*. Urbana and Chicago: University of Illinois Press, 1988.

McDonald, Adrian Francis. *The History of Tobacco Production in Connecticut*. New Haven: Yale University Press, 1936.

McLachlan, James. "The Choice of Hercules: Student Societies in the Early Nineteenth Century." In Lawrence Stone, ed., *The University in Society*. Princeton: Princeton University Press, 1974.

McLoughlin, William G. *Rhode Island: A Bicentennial History*. New York: Norton, 1978.

Mead, Sidney. *The Lively Experiment*. New York: Harper and Row, 1963.

Meader, James Laurence. *Normal School Education in Connecticut*. New York: Teachers College Press, 1928.

Merryman, John E. *The Indiana Story*. Clearfield, Pa.: Kurtz Bros., 1976.

Messerli, Jonathan C. *Horace Mann: A Biography*. New York: Knopf, 1972.

———. "James Carter's Liabilities as a Common School Reformer." *History of Education Quarterly* 5, no. 1 (March 1965): 14–25.

Meyer, D. H. "American Intellectuals and the Victorian Crisis of Faith." *American Quarterly* 27, no. 5 (December 1975): 585–603.

Meyers, Marvin. *The Jacksonian Persuasion*. Stanford: Stanford University Press, 1957.

Middlekauff, Robert. *Ancients and Axioms*. New Haven: Yale University Press, 1963.

Miller, Douglas T. *The Birth of Modern America, 1820–1850*. New York: Pegasus, 1970.

Miller, Zane L. *The Urbanization of Modern America: A Brief History*. New York: Harcourt Brace Jovanovich, 1973.

Mohr, James C. *Radical Republicans in the North*. Baltimore: The Johns Hopkins University Press, 1976.

Monroe, Will S. *Bibliography of Henry Barnard*. Boston: New England Publishing Co., 1897.

———. "Dr. Barnard and Educational Literature." *Connecticut School Document*, 10. Hartford, 1898.

———. *The Educational Labors of Henry Barnard*. Syracuse: C. W. Bardeen, 1893.

Morris, Richard K. "The Barnard Legacy." *School and Society* 89 (November 1961): 393–96.

———. "Parnassus on Wheels." *Trinity College Library Gazette*, no. 2 (February 1955).

———. "Barnard Sesquicentennial Address." Connecticut State Board of Education, January 24, 1961.

Morrison, James L. *"The Best School in the World": West Point in the Pre-Civil War Years, 1833–1866*. Kent: Ohio State University Press, 1986.

Morse, Jarvis Means. *A Neglected Period in Connecticut's History, 1818–1850*. New

Haven: Yale University Press, 1933; repr. 1979.

————. *The Rise of Liberalism in Connecticut*. New Haven: Yale University Press, 1933.

————. *Under the Constitution of 1818: The First Decade*. New Haven: Yale University Press, 1933.

Mosier, Richard D. *Making the American Mind: Social and Moral Ideas in the McGuffey Readers*. New York: King's Crown Press, 1947.

Mott, Frank Luther. *A History of American Magazines*, vol. I, *1741–1850*. New York: D. Appleton & Co., 1930; vol. II, *1850–1865*, 1938.

Mowry, Arthur May. *The Dorr War*. Providence: Preston & Rounds Co., 1901.

Mowry, William A. *Recollections of a New England Educator*. New York: Silver, Burdett & Co., 1908.

Nasaw, David. *Schooled to Order: A Social History of Public Schooling in the United States*. Oxford: Oxford University Press, 1979.

Nathans, Sidney. *Daniel Webster and Jacksonian Democracy*. Baltimore: The Johns Hopkins University Press, 1973.

National Society for the Study of Education., *Sixty-First Yearbook, Education for the Professions*. Chicago, 1961.

Naylor, Natalie A. "Holding High the Standard: The Influence of the American Education Society in Ante-Bellum America." *History of Education Quarterly* 24, no. 4 (Winter 1984): 479–97.

————. "The Theological Seminary in the Configuration of American Higher Education: the Antebellum Years." *History of Education Quarterly* 17, no. 1 (Spring 1977): 17–30.

Newmeyer, R. Kent. *Supreme Court Justice Joseph Story: Statesman of the Old Republic*. Chapel Hill: University of North Carolina Press, 1985.

Niven, John. *Connecticut for the Union*. New Haven: Yale University Press, 1965.

Norton, Arthur O. *The First State Normal School in America: The Journals of Cyrus Peirce and Mary Swift*. Cambridge: Harvard University Press, 1926.

Norton, Frederick C. "Sketch of the Life of Henry Barnard." *Connecticut Quarterly* IV, 2 (April–June 1898).

Nye, Russell B. *William Lloyd Garrison and the Humanitarian Reformers*. Boston: Little, Brown & Co., 1955.

Obituary Record of the Graduates of Yale University, 1900–1910. New Haven: Tuttle, Morehouse, and Taylor, 1910.

Pangburn, Jessie M. *The Evolution of the American Teachers' College*. New York: Teachers College Press, 1932.

Patzer, Conrad E. *Public Education in Wisconsin*. Madison: Issued by State Superintendent John Callahan, 1924.

Pawa, Jay M. "Workingmen and Free Schools in the Nineteenth Century: A Comment on the Labor-Education Thesis." *History of Education Quarterly* II, no. 3 (Fall 1971): 287–302.

Perkinson, Henry J. *The Imperfect Panacea: American Faith in Education, 1865–1976*. New York: Random House, 1968.

Pessen, Edward. "Did Fortunes Rise and Fall Mercurially in Antebellum America? The Tale of Two Cities." *Journal of Social History* 4, no. 4 (Summer 1971): 339–58.

———. *Jacksonian America: Society, Personality, and Politics*. Homewood, Ill.: The Dorsey Press, 1969.

———. *Riches, Class, and Power Before the Civil War*. Lexington, Mass.: D. C. Heath, 1973.

Peterson, Merrill P., ed. *Democracy, Liberty, and Property: The State Constitutional Conventions of the 1830s*. Indianapolis: Bobbs-Merrill, 1966.

Pierson, George W. *Yale: A Short History*. New Haven: Office of the Secretary, 1976.

Pitkin, Royce Stanley. *Public School Support in the United States During Periods of Economic Depression*. Brattleboro, Vt.: Stephen Daye Press, 1933.

Pulliam, John. "Changing Attitudes Towqard Free Public Schools in Illinois, 1825–1860." *History of Education Quarterly* 7, no. 2 (Summer 1967): 191–208.

Purcell, Richard J. *Connecticut in Transition, 1775–1818*. 1918; republished Middletown, Conn.: Wesleyan University Press, 1965.

Reese, William J. *Power and the Promise of School Reform*. Boston: Routledge and Kegan Paul, 1986.

Remini, Robert V. *Andrew Jackson and the Course of American Freedom, 1822–1832*. New York: Twayne, 1981.

Richards, Leonard L. *"Gentlemen of Property and Standing": Anti-Abolitionist Mobs in Jacksonian America*. New York: Oxford University Press, 1970.

Richardson, John G. "The American States and the Age of School Systems." *American Journal of Education* 92, no. 4 (August 1984): 473–502.

———. "Settlement Patterns and the Governing Structures of Nineteenth-Century School Systems." *American Journal of Education* 92, no. 2 (February 1984): 178–206.

Ricketts, Palmer C. *History of the Rensselaer Polytechnic Institute*. New York: Wiley, 1895.

Roth, David M. *Connecticut*. New York: Norton, 1979.

Rozwenc, Edwin C., ed. *The Meaning of Jacksonian Democracy*. Lexington, Mass.: D. C. Heath, 1963.

Rudolph, Frederick. *The American College and the University*, New York: Vintage Books, 1962.

———, ed. *Essays on Education in the Early Republic*. Cambridge: Harvard University Press, 1965.

Ryan, Mary P. *Cradle of the Middle Class*. Cambridge: Harvard University Press, 1981.

Salisbury, Albert. *Historical Sketch of Normal Instruction in Wisconsin*. N.p., 1893.

Sanders, William J. *The Spaulding Lecture*. Yale University, March 8, 1961.

Scott, Anne Firor. "The Ever Widening Circle: The Diffusion of Feminist Values from the Troy Seminary, 1822–1872." *History of Education Quarterly* 19, no. 1 (Spring 1979): 3–26.

———. *Making the Invisible Woman Visible*. Urbana and Chicago: University of Illinois Press, 1984.

Sheller, Tina A. "The Origins of Public Education in Baltimore." *History of Education Quarterly* 22, no. 1 (Spring 1982): 23–42.

Singleton, Gregory H. "Protestant Voluntary Organizations and the Shaping of Victorian America." *American Quarterly* 27, no. 5 (December 1975): 561–74.

Sizer, Theodore. *The Age of the Academy*. New York: Teachers College Press, 1964.

Sklar, Katharine Kish. *Catharine Beecher: A Study in American Domesticity*. New Haven: Yale University Press, 1973.

Sloan, Douglas. "Harmony, Chaos, and Consensus: The American College Curriculum." *Teachers College Record* 73, no. 2 (December 1971): 221–25.

Smith, Page. *The Nation Comes of Age*. Vol. 4, *A People's History of the Ante-Bellum Years*. New York: McGraw-Hill, 1981.

Smith, Timothy L. *Revivalism and Social Reform in Mid-Nineteenth Century America*. New York: Abingdon Press, 1957.

Spring, Joel. *The American School, 1642–1985*. New York: Longman, 1985.

Steiner, Bernard C. *The History of Education in Connecticut*. Washington, D.C.: Bureau of Education, 1893.

———. *Life of Henry Barnard*. Washington, D.C.: Bureau of Education, 1918.

———, ed. "The South Atlantic States in 1833 as Seen by a New Englander, Henry Barnard." *Maryland Historical Magazine* 13, no. 3 (September) and 4 (December 1918).

Stevenson, Louise L. *Scholarly Means to Evangelical Ends: New Haven Scholars and the Transformation of Higher Learning in America, 1830–1890*. Baltimore: The Johns Hopkins University Press, 1986.

Stokes, Anson Phelps. *Memorials of Eminent Yale Men*, vol. I. New Haven: Yale University Press, 1914.

Stone, Lawrence, ed. *The University in Society*. Princeton: Princeton University Press, 1974.

Story, Ronald. *The Forging of an Aristocracy*. Middletown, Conn.: Wesleyan University Press, 1980.

Swift, Fletcher H. *A History of Public Permanent Common School Funds in the United States, 1795–1905*. New York: H. Holt & Co., 1911.

Tewksbury, Donald George. *The Founding of American Colleges and Universities Before the Civil War*. New York: Teachers College Press, 1932.

Thursfield, Richard Emmon. *Henry Barnard's "American Journal of Education."* Baltimore: The Johns Hopkins University Press, 1945.

Travers, Paul D. "John Orville Taylor: A Forgotten Educator." *History of Education Quarterly* 9, no. 1 (Spring 1969): 57–63.

Trecker, Janice Law. *Preachers, Rebels, and Traders: Connecticut 1818–1865*. Chester, Conn.: Pequot Press, 1975.

Trumbull, James H. *A Memorial History of Hartford County, Connecticut, 1633–1884*. 2 vols. Boston: E. L. Osgood, 1886.

Tyack, David B. *George Tichnor and the Boston Brahmins*. Cambridge: Harvard University Press, 1967.

———. *The One Best System*. Cambridge: Harvard University Press, 1974.

———. "Pilgrim's Progress: Toward a History of the School Superintendency, 1860–1960." *History of Education Quarterly* 16, no. 3 (Fall 1976): 257–94.

Tyack, David B., and Elizabeth Hansot. *Managers of Virtue*. New York: Basic Books, 1982.

Tyack, David B., and Thomas James. "State Government and American Public Education: Exploring the Primeval Forest," *History of Education Quarterly* 26, no. 1 (Spring 1986): 39–70.

Tyack, David B., Thomas James, and Aaron Benavot. *Law and the Shaping of Public Schools, 1885–1954*. Madison: University of Wisconsin Press, 1987.

Tyler, Alice Felt. *Freedom's Ferment*. Minneapolis: University of Minnesota Press, 1944.

Ulich, Robert. *A Sequence of Educational Influences Traced Through Unpublished Writings of Pestalozzi, Froebel, Diesterweg, Horace Mann and Henry Barnard*. Cambridge: Harvard University Press, 1935.

Urofsky, Melvin. "Reforms and Response: The Yale Report of 1828." *History of Education Quarterly* 5, no. 1 (March 1965): 53–67.

Van Dusen, Albert E. *Connecticut*. New York: Random House, 1961.

Veysey, Laurence R. *The Emergence of the American University*. Chicago: University of Chicago Press, 1965.

Vinovskis, Maris A. *The Origins of Public High Schools: A Re-examination of the Beverly High School Controversy*. Madison: University of Wisconsin Press, 1985.

———. "Trends in Massachusetts Education, 1826–1860." *History of Education Quarterly* 12, no. 4 (Winter 1972): 501–30.

Vinovskis, Maris A., and Richard M. Bernard. "Beyond Catharine Beecher: Female Education in the Antebellum Period." *Signs* III, no. 4 (1978): 856–69.

Wagoner, Jennings, L., Jr. "Honor and Dishonor at Mr. Jefferson's University: The Antebellum Years." *History of Education Quarterly* 26, no. 2 (Summer 1986): 155–79.

Walters, Ronald, *American Reformers*. New York: Hill and Wang, 1978.

Warfel, Harry R. *Noah Webster: Schoolmaster to America*. New York: Macmillan, 1936.

Warren, Donald. *To Enforce Education: A History of the Founding Years of the United States Office of Education*. Detroit: Wayne State University Press, 1974.

Welch, Archibald Wesley. *A History of Insurance in Connecticut*. New Haven: Yale University Press, 1935.

Welter, Barbara. "The Cult of True Womanhood: 1820–1860." In Michael Gordon, ed., *The American Family in Social-Historical Perspective*. New York: St. Martin's Press, 1978.

———. *Dimity Convictions: The American Woman in the Nineteenth Century*. Athens: Ohio University Press, 1976.

Welter, Rush. *The Mind of America*. New York: Columbia University Press, 1975.

———. *Popular Education and Democratic Thought in America*. New York:

Columbia University Press, 1962.

Wesley, Edgar B. *NEA: The First Hundred Years*. New York: Harper, 1957.

Wieck, William M. "Popular Sovereignity in the Dorr Warr—Conservative Counterblast." *Rhode Island History* 32, no. 2 (May 1973): 34–52

Williams, Stanley Thomas. *The Literature of Connecticut*, New Haven: Yale University Press, 1936.

Winship, A. E. *Great American Educators*. New York: Werner School Book Co., 1900.

Wishy, Bernard. *The Child and the Republic: The Dawn of Modern American Child Nuture*. Philadelphia: University of Pennsylvania Press, 1968.

Wright, Louis B. *Culture on the Moving Frontier*. Bloomington: University of Indiana Press, 1955.

Woody, Thomas. *A History of Women's Education in the United States*. 2 vols. New York: The Science Press, 1929.

Wyatt-Brown, Bertram. *Lewis Tappan and the Evangelical War Against Slavery*. Cleveland: Press of Case Western Reserve University, 1969.

INDEX